The Burden of Sports

THE BURDEN OF SPORTS

How and Why Athletes Struggle with Mental Health

JOHN WESTON PARRY

ROWMAN & LITTLEFIELD

Lanham • Boulder • New York • London

Published by Rowman & Littlefield
An imprint of The Rowman & Littlefield Publishing Group, Inc.
4501 Forbes Boulevard, Suite 200, Lanham, Maryland 20706
www.rowman.com

86-90 Paul Street, London EC2A 4NE

British Library Cataloguing in Publication Information Available

Library of Congress Cataloging-in-Publication Data
Names: Parry, John, author.
   Title: The burden of sports : how and why athletes struggle with mental
      health / John Weston Parry.
   Description: Lanham, Maryland : Rowman & Littlefield, [2024] | Includes
      bibliographical references and index.
   Identifiers: LCCN 2023027672 (print) | LCCN 2023027673 (ebook) | ISBN
      9781538175538 (cloth) | ISBN 9781538175545 (ebook)
   Subjects: LCSH: Sports--Psychological aspects. | Athletes--Mental health. |
      Athletes--Health and hygiene. | Mass media and sports. | Sports
      spectators--Psychology.
   Classification: LCC GV706.4 .P364 2024 (print) | LCC GV706.4 (ebook) |
      DDC 796.01/9--dc23/eng/20230717
   LC record available at https://lccn.loc.gov/2023027672LC ebook record available at https://
   lccn.loc.gov/2023027673

For my three deceased parents, Hugh, Betty, and Helen, who helped to make this book almost inevitable. To my wife Elissa and daughter Jennifer, both lawyers who mostly hate sports but really know how to write well, better than me. And to my brother Brian, my sister-in-law Weezie, my nephew Dylan, and my nieces Brooke and Charlotte, who have all shown me, time and time again, how sports are healthy and rewarding parts of their very busy lives.

CONTENTS

CONTENTS

PREFACE

The mental health and emotional well-being of elite athletes, in the con-text of American spectator sports propaganda and our legal system, is an expansive topic whose basic elements have been concerns of mine since I was a child. My biological mother, Helen, was hospitalized for a variety of mental disorders, including alcohol abuse, in my pre- and early teens. My father, Hugh, was a widely published expert in propaganda and pub-lic opinion research, as well as a mystery and suspense novelist under the pseudonym James Cross. My mother Betty, an accomplished poet and promoter of the literary arts and Black intelligentsia in the Washington, DC, area, was the one most responsible for rescuing me from my own early adolescent mental and emotional troubles.

At Lake Forest College, my honors thesis was on sports, society, government, and the law. Before graduation, I was torn between pursuing a PhD in clinical psychology and going to law school. I chose to attend Washington University Law School in St. Louis but kept a secondary focus on mental health by taking two courses in psychiatry and law, as well as a graduate-level psychology class, outside the law school. I knew then that I wanted, if I could, to pursue a legal career focusing on mental disability law and the rights of people with mental disabilities.

Before I began that journey, however, I served as a VISTA attorney in New York working at the White Plains Office of Westchester Legal Aid, focusing on a variety of civil poverty issues, including many involv-ing people with mental disabilities. A couple of years later, I became a legal intern at the Mental Health Law Project at the ACLU in Man-hattan under the mentorship of Bruce Ennis, in the same office where

Ruth Bader Ginsburg was serving as the director of the Women's Rights Project.

Afterward, I was awarded a fellowship to Columbia University's School of Public Health, where I took classes in biostatistics, epidemiology, and public health law, among others. I reluctantly left Columbia after one semester, though, when I was offered the opportunity to direct the first protection and advocacy program for people with developmental disabilities in my home state of Maryland, a position I had applied for before I was accepted at Columbia.

Eighteen months later, I accepted a position as editor of the *Mental Disability Law Reporter* for the American Bar Association's (ABA) Commission on the Mentally Disabled. Two years after that, I became the director of that commission as well as the editor-in-chief of the *Law Reporter*. I stayed in that dual position, with certain changes, for about thirty years.

In 1987, I was a recipient of the Manfred Guttmacher Award, given jointly by the American Psychiatric Association and the American Academy of Psychiatry and Law, for my work coauthoring and coediting *The Mentally Disabled and the Law* (3rd ed., 1985) with Samuel Jan Brakel and Barbara A Weiner. I have written numerous other books and articles focusing on mental health law and the rights of people with mental disabilities. The most recent was *Mental Disability, Violence, and Future Dangerousness: Myths Behind the Presumption of Guilt* (2013).

Throughout my ABA career, I knew that someday I wanted to focus on topics related to sports and society. For years, I kept files of interesting articles in newspapers, magazines, and journals on sports-related topics, which I had read, cut out, and stored in various categories, that I thought might be useful later. After retiring from the ABA at end of 2012, I returned to my second academic love—sports—part time.

I began by creating and becoming the primary contributor to a website/blog, Sportpathologies.com. I have written dozens of essays over the past ten years on sports topics related to health, mental health, bad behavior, diversity, and major sports enterprises. I also wrote my first sports book, titled *The Athlete's Dilemma: Sacrificing Health for Wealth and Fame* (2017).

Thus, in certain respects, it can be said that my upbringing, education, career, and postretirement career made this current book, which melds my lifelong interests in sports, law, and mental health, almost inevitable. I just needed a willing publisher (Rowman and Littlefield) and a very insightful and patient editor (Deni Remsberg) and editorial staff to make it a fait accompli.

Introduction

In recent times, there have been two especially important spectator sports developments related to health. The first is a growing awareness that for far too long, the mental health and emotional well-being of athletes have been kept in the shadows, ignored, legally compromised, and sportswashed by the organizations that are supposed to protect them. *Sportswashing* is a relatively new term that broadly describes propaganda in which sports, and the goodwill sports generate, are used to enhance individual, organizational, and national reputations and/or to obscure or cover up corruption, criminality, negligence, or other transgressions and misdeeds.

The second health-related development has been the unexpected emergence, and continued presence, of COVID and its variants. This easily transmissible disease has affected, and is likely to continue to affect, athletes' mental health and emotional well-being in several unfortunate ways.

Mental health experts estimate that more than 20 percent, and arguably 25 percent, of all Americans will have a diagnosed mental disorder, which includes substance abuse, in any given year; more than 50 percent will have such a disorder during their lifetimes. Unfortunately, recent studies also suggest that those figures likely will have to be revised upward due to the longer-term risks of COVID, many of which are still uncertain or unknown. What is known, though, is that the virus not only can worsen preexisting mental conditions, but, according to a study published in the December 2022 issue of *Nature*, can infect people's brains.[1]

At the same time, mental health–related risks appear to be somewhat greater for elite athletes and those trying to become elite, due to several pre- or coexisting factors: the stress and anxiety of competition; chronic traumatic encephalopathy (CTE) and related brain damage, especially in boxing, mixed martial arts (MMA), football, hockey, soccer, and other contact sports; and substance abuse and drug dependency related to managing sports-related pain and injuries, competitive stress and anxiety, and performance-enhancing substances.

As a result of stigma, stereotyping, secrecy, and discrimination, only some people experiencing mental disorders openly disclose their symptoms or conditions to family and friends, and fewer still reveal them to their employers. A significant percentage of those affected are reluctant to even disclose symptoms to healthcare providers.

Recently, however, US Senator John Fetterman of Pennsylvania took the brave step of publicly checking himself into a hospital to treat his depression, which seems to have been triggered by a stroke that left him physically impaired in several different ways. For many in the media, Fetterman's openness about his mental condition was viewed as a risky political move that might hurt his election chances down the road. For others, like *Washington Post* columnist Dr. Leana Wen, it represented a paradigm shift for mental health.

Whatever Fetterman's response represented, it was no more than the possible beginning of a paradigm shift. Reluctance to be open about one's mental health challenges is well ingrained in the American experience. It also has been an established part of our spectator sports culture for decades. In many ways, that culture has made that reluctance more pronounced and an even greater liability to athletes' mental health.

While mental health awareness is somewhat better than it once was in American spectator sports, both domestically and globally—which includes professional, major college, and Olympic athletes—the inclination to hide the existence of mental disorders and other mental health and emotional challenges continues to be at least as strong in spectator sports as in the rest of American society. Elite athletes, and those trying to become elite, face an array of mental health challenges peculiar to them. They include:

- individual and team pressures to win and attain sports perfection, which affects not only their mental health but, for some, like Novak Djokovic (tennis) or Kyrie Irving (NBA), their willingness to take indicated medications such as the COVID vaccine
- prejudice and ignorance of fans, management, and corporate sponsors about mental health and emotional well-being concerns, not to mention the potential added mental health risks to athletes posed by the long-term effects of COVID, including risks that presently are uncertain or unknown
- an unwillingness or reluctance of sports enterprises, teams, players' unions, and management to adequately cover longer-term mental health and COVID care and treatment, especially for many former male athletes and most female athletes, whose compensation and benefit packages tend to be much less than those of their male counterparts
- the fact that training for and participating in spectator sports causes or contributes to a variety of sports-related mental conditions, including brain damage, substance abuse, depression, anxiety disorders, and/or extreme stress

Evidence continues to mount that contracting COVID probably increases the already elevated mental health risks of elite athletes and those trying to become elite. In addition, certain marginalized groups of athletes are subjected to discrimination and other forms of abuse, which negatively impact their emotional well-being and mental health.

While a few more sport stars, including Michael Phelps, Johnny Manziel, Simone Biles, Naomi Osaka, Aly Raisman, and Serena Williams, have been willing to talk about their mental health and emotional challenges—usually after their careers are over or following a painful public display that needs to be explained—it appears that the overwhelming majority of elite athletes are still unwilling to do so. This is especially true of male athletes in major American team sports during their active athletic careers. Typically, those athletes who have spoken up, like Royce White in the NBA and Jonathan Martin in the NFL, have seen their careers cut short, extinguished, or otherwise impeded.

Extreme secrecy, self-serving behind-the-scenes organizational manipulation, and even bullying remain predominant responses toward athletes with mental health and emotional well-being concerns in American spectator sports. Athletes who violate the rules of a sport because of a mental disorder or emotional challenge—especially males in major team sports—are likely to be penalized, harassed, released, or fired, without much acknowledgment of the distress and other difficulties those athletes are dealing with.

In too many instances, how these sports organizations respond to athletes with serious mental health concerns would seem to violate the intent and certainly the spirit of the federal Americans with Disabilities Act (ADA) and various state disability discrimination laws. The idea of reasonable accommodations/modifications is foreign to almost all spectator sports. Moreover, few, if any, people in the spectator sports world are taking meaningful steps to try to anticipate and deal with the longer-term effects of COVID on athletes' mental health and emotional well-being.

If the past is any guide, sports enterprises will continue to mostly ignore, marginalize, and cover up the mental health and emotional well-being concerns of their athletes, unless those concerns become public; then it is likely those organizations will try to deflect from their responsibility and any blame, using sports-generated goodwill as their shield.

This book examines the mental health and emotional well-being concerns of elite athletes and aspiring elite athletes from three vantage points. Part I introduces key factors that, over many years, have established a framework by which America's most popular spectator sports operate, both domestically and globally, and how this has jeopardized the health, mental health, and emotional well-being of these athletes. Those factors include:

- a single-minded, sometimes obsessive pursuit of spectator sports rewards, especially money, wealth, fame, and athletic perfection

- a legal system that favors major spectator sports, and the individuals connected to them, by providing them with special privileges and protections without obligating those entities to better care for and protect their athletes' and former athletes' mental health

- the use of sportswashing and other forms of propaganda to promote spectator sports enterprises and obscure and marginalize their misdeeds and wrongdoings

Part II focuses on mental health and related concerns that negatively affect elite athletes and those trying to become elite. These include:

- mental disorders that anyone might experience, such as depression or bipolar disorder

- mental conditions that are caused or aggravated by training and competing in a sport or trying to perform better, such as sports-related depression, stress, anxiety, or what is called "the yips"

- little-known, suspected, and unknown health and mental health risks of long-term COVID

- CTE and other forms of brain damage associated with contact sports, especially football, boxing, and hockey

- drug and alcohol abuse and dependency, especially substance abuse associated with participating in sports, such as pain and injury management, stress relief, and use of performance-enhancing substances

Part III delves into mental health and emotional well-being issues in sports that affect marginalized groups of elite athletes. Female athletes are confronted with a host of emotionally charged issues, including pregnancy, abortion, postpartum depression, menstruation, and motherhood, that their male counterparts do not experience or experience in different ways. In addition, too many young female (and certain male) athletes have had to deal with trauma after they have been sexually or emotionally abused, mostly by male coaches, team physicians, trainers, and other men responsible for their athletic welfare.

Homophobia continues to be endemic to American spectator sports, causing substantial emotional damage to LGBTQ+ athletes and their communities. Furthermore, discrimination and other forms of abuse targeting intersex and transgender athletes specifically have become widespread and appear to be growing.

The conclusion highlights major findings in the book, then presents lessons learned, which, along with specific recommendations contained in chapters throughout, are intended to provide guidance on ways to help fix America's broken spectator sports and better protect the mental health and emotional well-being of elite athletes and athletes aspiring to be elite.

PART I

THREE UNDERLYING FACTORS THAT JEOPARDIZE ATHLETES' HEALTH AND MENTAL HEALTH: AN OVERVIEW

THE MENTAL HEALTH AND EMOTIONAL WELL-BEING OF ATHLETES HAVE improved in incremental ways as a significant number, yet still relatively few, sports stars have been willing to disclose details about their struggles, usually late in their careers or when it has been in their self-interest to do so. This has prompted spectator sports organizations to provide incremental, but less than adequate, improvements to their athletes' and former athletes' mental health care and emotional well-being.

In other ways, though, mental health–related problems athletes face have become worse. Certain underlying factors have been responsible for creating this broken spectator sports environment. Three of them have been arounds for decades; the fourth—the unexpected emergence of COVID—is much more recent but likely to intensify and complicate almost all the other mental health concerns athletes face. The COVID pandemic and its effects on the health and mental health of athletes are discussed specifically in chapter 6, but the impact of COVID also is discussed throughout the book.

Chapter 1 focuses broadly on how a single-minded, often obsessive pursuit of the rewards that spectator sports offer—not only for successful athletes but also their coaches, teams, families, friends, and fans—can jeopardize athletes, especially once they are no longer able to perform up to expectations.

Chapter 2 describes how spectator sports enterprises have been able to use the American legal system and lawyers to insulate themselves, and those individuals closely associated with them, from scrutiny and accountability for their bad behaviors, including transgressions that jeopardize athletes' mental health and well-being.

Chapter 3 explains how major American sports organizations use propaganda, most notably sportswashing, to obscure, cover up, and justify bad behaviors and other transgressions associated with their sports. This includes actions and omissions that work to undermine their athletes' mental health and emotional well-being.

CHAPTER I

A Single-Minded Pursuit of Spectator Sports Rewards

ELITE AND ASPIRING ELITE ATHLETES ARE DIFFERENT FROM OTHER people. Those differences include extreme pressures on them to pursue and achieve some form of athletic perfection; the magnitude of the rewards bestowed on them when they are successful; and the stress, pain, and anxiety they experience should they fail to meet their own expectations or those imposed on them by so many others. No wonder sports psychology has become such a thriving business.

Heightened levels of stress, pain, and anxiety, which would be abnormal for most people, are too often accepted as integral and necessary parts of being a gifted and dedicated athlete. Such mental pathologies are typically viewed as challenges that good athletes are supposed to suppress or overcome, as opposed to warning signs that something may be very wrong that should be addressed and treated immediately.

Openly acknowledging, much less taking the steps to constructively deal with, mental disturbances and the destructive feelings they may produce continues to be viewed as athletic taboos rather than a rational or productive response to these all-too-human mental health traumas. This is especially true for male athletes, who must negotiate macho locker rooms and other cultural manifestations of sports manliness.

Real men, according to sports culture, suck it up and plow through their pain and mental impairments. Great athletes like Novak Djokovic, for example, are supposed to manage their difficult moods and

9

uncomfortable or disturbing feelings and pain, as if they are mastering a drop shot, a three-point basket, or a double play. Failing to do this too often becomes a sign of personal and athletic weakness. It is commonly believed that those athletes who sustain repeated injuries are not just victims of unfortunate circumstances; they are "injury prone," which is viewed as a negative character trait. Athletes who cannot perform due to mental or emotional issues become known as "head cases," which is about the worst label any athlete can be saddled with, short of being a sissy or, in male locker room parlance, a "pussy."

Female athletes must deal with additional pressures and bodily concerns their male counterparts do not experience, or experience less frequently or differently, that may negatively affect their mental health and emotional well-being. These life-altering circumstances include pregnancy, postpartum depression, maternity, and sexual and domestic violence and abuse (see chapter 9).

Elite and aspiring elite athletes experience a variety of mental and emotional pressures, especially from their dogged pursuit of wealth, fame, and perfection, differently than the rest of us. A sports-first mindset—which their coaches, trainers, families, friends, media, and fans typically help to inculcate or even insist upon—can compel, or at least encourage, elite and aspiring elite athletes to ignore, downplay, or mistreat mental and physical health impairments to their detriment, especially over the long term.

To quote and also paraphrase British sports scholar P. David Howe, the acceptance of risks—including mental impairment, emotional trauma, and pain—is an "inevitable consequence of professional, Olympic, and collegiate participation in sport."[1] Stated another way, elite athletes "tend to view health from a narrow prism of attaining fitness and pain endurance that are necessary to perform at or near peak levels for as long as possible."[2] That type of risk-taking appears to be inseparable from being viewed as a good or great athlete.

Unfortunately, the negative consequences that flow from such risk-taking on themselves, their teammates, and their sports are often difficult for athletes to manage in the context of the sports environment and culture that surround them. Health care for elite athletes provided by the sports organizations that benefit from their talents, particularly related to their mental health, tends to be inadequate or nonexistent once their athletic careers are over. Even at its best, "[s]ports medicine is . . . a tool used by sports administrators and club officials to fast-track elite sporting performers back to competition."[3] Too often mental or emotional health takes too much time to address or is viewed as the athlete's problem or weakness.

As a result of this spectator sports bias, two things are likely to happen. In the short term, athletes' lingering injuries, especially those related to pain or mental or emotional well-being concerns and their behavioral manifestations, tend to be ignored, misinterpreted, or minimized by devaluing or blaming the affected athletes. "Head case" is a stigmatizing label no athlete wants to receive or deal with, so too often athletes hide or self-medicate their mental impairments with alcohol or nonprescription drugs. In addition, if management or teammates buy into these negative stereotypes, the affected athlete's sports career can be jeopardized or ended and their mental health and well-being further compromised.

When it comes to pain management, the sports mantra is largely the same everywhere: Real men play with pain, as do women who want to compete like the men, or they are not allowed to compete at all. To participate in their sports, elite and aspiring elite athletes are often faced with a threshold dilemma: endure the pain, take too many prescribed medications, or self-medicate by misusing drugs or alcohol. Those solutions risk further, long-lasting or permanent injuries and may lead to life-long addictive behaviors (see chapter 8).

One type of addictive behavior is the use of substances, especially drugs, to enhance athletic performance. This is a quintessential sports-related pathology, which may or may not necessarily be rooted in mental health and emotional well-being concerns but, like those other substance abuse concerns, is associated with obsessively striving to obtain athletic rewards and perfection.

Whole nations have been implicated, directly or indirectly, in state-sponsored doping, notably Russia and China. Entire sports, including baseball, cycling, and football, have been involved in doping as well. For individual elite athletes, though, widespread doping poses another type of moral dilemma: (1) act ethically and be at an athletic disadvantage or (2) cheat, risk getting caught—which apparently is not that great a risk—and accept the potential adverse side effects that may comprise their health and mental stability now or sometime in the future (see chapter 8).

Almost all elite and aspiring elite athletes are actively encouraged to engage in various performance-enhancing measures, including overtraining and losing body fat. These are neither illegal nor illicit but may involve emotional abuse and have their own risks and adverse health effects. Making matters worse, many athletes are actively encouraged to do overly aggressive, violent, or otherwise dangerous things to help their teams and themselves reap various athletic rewards.

This is especially true in contact sports for men, such as football, hockey, and boxing. Deliberate or recklessly aggressive and even violent strategies and tactics are passed down in many other sports as well, but in football, hockey, and boxing the danger is much more pronounced and universal. All sorts of bodily injuries may result from this overaggressiveness, including most notably concussions, subconcussive impacts, brain damage, and CTE (see chapter 7).

Many of these dangerous strategies and tactics are taught and even symbolically rewarded by coaches and trainers. Perhaps the most blatant, and certainly the most publicized, example was the NFL scandal known as "Bountygate," where coaches provided cash rewards to players for incapacitating their opponents. The implied justification for allowing or encouraging what otherwise would be viewed as criminal assault, or at least clear evidence for civil liability, are the benefits that spectator sports provide to the fans who pay to see these competitions.

Overaggression and even deliberate violence in certain sports can produce a whole host of lingering physical and mental injuries for athletes, some of which may be life altering. Football and hockey players at all levels tend to be injured repeatedly. Pitchers in baseball are subject to chronic arm problems. One favored option for pitchers these days is having invasive Tommy John surgery early in their careers in hopes of restoring their arm strength, making more money, and preventing or delaying more precipitous arm deterioration during their playing careers.

In these elite athletic environments, there are relatively few words of caution, certainly as compared to the many prescriptions to go for broke, which is what the best athletes are supposed to do. Lindsey Vonn and Tiger Woods, for example, were known worldwide not only as a power couple but also as two superstar athletes who eventually wore out their bodies and may have compromised their minds and mental health due to the intensity of their training and performance protocols. Spectator sports are filled with stories of athletes who have pushed themselves too far, with unfortunate and sometimes tragic results.

Potential scholarships to private high schools and colleges, endorsement deals, and too often unrealistic dreams of lucrative professional and Olympic sports careers are more than enough incentive for many elite and aspiring elite athletes to risk their physical and mental health and emotional well-being. This is in addition to the pride, glory, and social status of being recognized as elite.

Unfortunately, these positive reinforcement mechanisms tend to distort reality, especially for the vast majority of athletes who never achieve elite status or do so for only very brief periods of time. When combined with the aspirations of those individuals and sports entities that surround them, the opportunity to reap these rewards can easily overwhelm the common sense that could be applied by someone in authority who prioritizes the holistic welfare and emotional well-being of these athletes.

Too often elite athletics seem to brush aside or minimize common sense. Dealing with mental health and emotional well-being concerns beyond the bare minimum to get the athlete back onto the field as soon as possible tends to be viewed as unnecessary and counterproductive baggage. There are very few incentives in place in major American spectator sports to push athletes toward the healthiest solutions, in contrast to the much stronger push for victories, athletic perfection, and the other rewards sports can bring to these athletes and those invested in their success.

The quick fix, including drugs or alcohol, and no fix at all continue to be the paths of least resistance. Even healthcare providers who specialize in treating athletes, including team physicians and athletic trainers, too often have interests that clash with their professional and ethical obligations. All of this tends to compromise athletes' health.

Within these skewed spectator sports environments and cultures, too many elite and aspiring elite athletes minimize or ignore their long-term health, not only physically, but also mentally and emotionally. Many athletes have bought into the overly competitive, and too often self-destructive, Kool-Aid that is being offered by sports entities—and the coaches, trainers, and other individuals associated with those entities—that surround these talented athletes, beginning early in their careers.

Making matters worse, too many elite and aspiring elite athletes are extremely vulnerable if they are severely or catastrophically injured early in their careers, before they receive substantial financial rewards, or if, like many female athletes, they participate in sports in which there are only relatively small rewards for most of them. Those athletes, including athletes who are severely or catastrophically injured in high school or college, are responsible for their own health care and livelihood going forward.

In addition, many sports-related impairments, like CTE, other forms of brain damage, and arthritis, become more severe over time, especially later in life. Most spectator sports associations do not provide health and mental health care for their former athletes, and even those that do have serious limitations.

Even in America's four major sports leagues, players who no longer can perform, whether due to injury or because they have been released, cannot fully participate in their league's pension and disability plans unless they played long enough to become vested. This is a big obstacle. In the NFL and NBA, vesting takes three full years; in the MLB it requires ten years of service; and in the NHL it is an incremental process, which begins after the first twenty games, but players are not fully vested until they have played the equivalent of ten full seasons.

Overall, the medical and disability provisions for elite athletes are either nonexistent or have serious gaps in their coverages. Often those pension plans are very stingy in how they allot benefits for health care and disabilities. As Domonique Foxworth, former president of the NFL Players Association (NFLPA), explained, even in major American spectator sports, current players are reluctant to reduce their salaries in order to benefit former players: "A roomful of 20-somenthings who are playing football [or any other major spectator sport] are not looking to have their earnings depressed because of lifetime health care."[4] These health care inadequacies apply even more so to mental health and substance abuse.

CHAPTER 2

The American Legal System Unreasonably and Unfairly Favors Spectator Sports Organizations and Enterprises

FOR NEARLY 150 YEARS, MAJOR SPECTATOR SPORTS ORGANIZATIONS AND enterprises in the United States have received favored treatment from the legal system. This began in the second half of the nineteenth century, when professional baseball formed the National and American leagues in order to operate as a cartel. Each baseball player became bound to one team unless he was traded or released by that team's owner.

Baseball's monopolistic business practices were well entrenched before the Sherman Antitrust Act was enacted in 1890. Teams dictated "the players' place of employment, salaries, working conditions, off-field conduct, and freedom of movement." Major League Baseball (MLB) has been mostly untouched by that historic antitrust law. Owners continued to "impose a system of labor control unequaled in American industry."[1]

In 1922, the US Supreme Court gave its approval to this labor-stultifying organizational structure by specifically exempting MLB from American antitrust laws in a head-scratching decision.[2] Justice Oliver Wendell Holmes created legal fiction by pretending that the two professional baseball leagues and their sixteen teams, located throughout the East and Midwest, did not engage in interstate commerce. That fiction remains in place today, even though MLB franchises are now located in western states and Canada as well.

Since 1922, various other legal fictions, lax law enforcement, and special privileges have produced an American legal system in which major spectator sports are treated much more like public charters than businesses whose primary mission is to generate profits and build wealth for themselves and their commercial partners. The United States Olympic and Paralympic Committee (USOPC) is the only major American sports enterprise that is the beneficiary of a specific congressional charter, but all the rest have been allowed to govern themselves with minimal judicial interference.

This laissez-faire approach has been allowed to exist even when those sports organizations, and the people associated with them, have skirted or violated civil and criminal statutes. These legal privileges have encompassed laws related to labor relations, higher education, drug use, gambling, civil rights, and criminal behaviors.

When the impact of these privileges for spectator sports is combined with the stigma, stereotypes, secrecy, and discrimination surrounding mental health in this country, it creates special problems for elite American athletes and athletes aspiring to be elite who face mental health and related challenges. Unfortunately, these talented and not-so-talented athletes have pressure on them from many directions to win, be the best they can be, and attract lucrative salaries, endorsement deals, self-promotion opportunities, and/or scholarships. This pressure makes them particularly susceptible to a variety of mental health problems.

Mental health stigma and stereotypes are centuries old and so ingrained in our culture that it is difficult, if not impossible, to overcome their effects, even today. For every public service message or other sentiment that expresses a belief that it is not unusual for people to experience a mental disorder or other emotional disturbance, there are even more expressions that such disturbances of the mind are shameful, often self-imposed, and presumably dangerous. The legal system contributes to this shame and distress in many ways.

Not so long ago, Americans were locked away like criminals in large, isolated, prison-like civil institutions if they were deemed mentally or emotionally disturbed or even just viewed as being different or difficult. Today, many of these vulnerable individuals tend to be dumped into jails and prisons or left out on the streets to fend for themselves. In most police or detective dramas, it is commonplace for a person with a mental disorder or disturbance to become a prime suspect. Whenever there is a mass shooting, those responsible are usually characterized as "mentally disturbed." The conversation soon turns away from gun control generally to specifically ensuring that people labeled as dangerous because they have or are suspected of having a mental disorder cannot possess firearms and are forced to undergo intrusive surveillance or treatment.[3]

The stigma and stereotypes associated with people who have mental and emotional issues are often magnified and intensified when they are applied to athletes: "Many of the worst stereotypes and prejudices in America's most popular sports involve mental impairments."[4]

Some of the most damning stereotypes in sports are reserved for athletes who are unable to compete due to a mental health or emotional issue. Too many athletes in mental distress are disparaged and/or discriminated against by their teammates, the sports media, fans, and the sports organizations to which they belong. Too often the pain, despair, anxiety, and/or anguish many athletes experience are attributed to their lack of character or athletic fitness.

Proposed solutions to such troubles of the mind, assuming these problems are even acknowledged, tend to serve the agendas of the sports involved, the corporate sponsors, and the fans, rather than the athletes needing help. Common prescriptions for athletes in distress—focus on athletics, train harder, pop a pill, or suck it up—all but ignore the underlying mental health issues responsible.

Given the stigma and often vicious stereotypes faced by athletes with mental conditions, it can be no surprise that secrecy and lack of transparency usually characterize the ways in which athletes deal with their mental health and emotional difficulties. Secrecy and lack of transparency also characterize how sports organizations, the media, teammates, coaches, team physicians, and trainers tend to deal with athletes who are experiencing substantial mental disturbances.

It is common for these types of personal problems in athletes to remain secret from the public or to emerge only after an athlete's career is over or when it is in decline. Rarely do athletes in their prime disclose mental or emotional tribulations unless they have had a meltdown in public that needs to be framed more sympathetically than what media and fan speculation would reflexively produce.

Perceived mental or emotional weakness is still kryptonite to most elite athletes. Yet the American College of Sports Medicine estimates that "approximately 35% of elite athletes suffer from disordered thinking, burnout, depression and/or anxiety,"[5] which is significantly higher than for the general population.

Many counterproductive attitudes and policies involving the mental health and emotional well-being of athletes could be addressed more humanely if major spectator sports organizations followed federal and state laws and regulations that are supposed to prohibit discrimination against people with mental disabilities and require mental health services to be delivered equally with other types of health care. As a practical matter, though, those statutes and regulations banning discrimination based on mental disabilities and guaranteeing mental health parity have fallen well short of their intent and purpose, especially in America's spectator sports.

In the sports world, legal implementation problems and enforcement deficits and inadequacies have been especially egregious. The organizations that are supposed to represent athletes' interests typically put their own economic, administrative, and organizational interests first. Furthermore, politicians and governmental agencies continue to look the other way when sports organizations appear to be violating disability discrimination and mental health parity laws. There rarely is an investigation, much less litigation, when the mental health–related rights of athletes are violated by teams, players' unions, and/or other sports organizations purporting to represent the interests of the athletes under their protection.

This is because it is difficult to prove disability discrimination by spectator sports organizations and enterprises, and these sports entities are given considerable deference in the law, including, where applicable, through discretion bestowed on their commissioners and the collective bargaining agreements between leagues and players' unions. The most important of these antidiscrimination laws for people with mental disabilities are federal: the Americans with Disabilities Act, Section 504 of the Rehabilitation Act of 1973, and the Mental Health Parity Act. States that have similar laws often try to mimic, with certain exceptions and exemptions, these federal statutes.

Despite the many instances in which athletes or former athletes with mental health and emotional difficulties in major American spectator sports seem to have been discriminated against or denied adequate care and treatment, there appear to be no publicized court cases that have been filed on these athletes' behalf, much less any that have gone to court and proved to be successful. Yet, as Sharon Masling, a disability rights lawyer writing in the *Sports Business Journal*, concludes, sports organizations and enterprises have an obligation under the ADA and Section 504 to provide reasonable modifications that "include changes in how things are customarily done or [by providing] adaptive equipment that will allow the athlete to . . . fully participate."[6]

In golfer Casey Martin's case, in 2001 the US Supreme Court said that meant allowing him to use a golf cart because he had a disability that made it difficult for him to walk. The problem, though, is that such modifications are rarely insisted upon because sports authorities can refuse to provide them if, in their judgment, doing so would fundamentally alter the nature of the sport involved. In Martin's situation, a golf cart did not, but sports organizations are generally given deference in determining which modifications present an undue burden. Moreover, no professional golfer since has asked for such an accommodation, not even Tiger Woods when he severely injured his leg.

Two notable, relatively recent examples of discrimination against professional athletes based on a mental disorder involved former NBA player Royce White and NFL offensive lineman Jonathan Martin. Both athletes were openly discriminated against, but nothing happened to the individuals and teams that participated in or aided in such discrimination. Instead, both players were drummed out of their leagues: in White's case, because his team would not fully accommodate his extreme anxiety about flying; in Martin's, because of extreme bullying. (See chapter 4 for more detailed accounts of what happened.)

A noteworthy exception in which athletes eventually received some measure of justice for their mental disorders was the 2017 concussion settlement between the NFL and its former players, which was based on personal injury, not discrimination or mental health parity. There, the former football players were collectively awarded a total of about $1 billion.[7]

Recently, however, a number of those former players successfully argued that they had been denied adequate care and benefits under that settlement, but their claims were based on racial, not mental disability, discrimination. A class of Black former football players was either denied eligibility for those benefits or had their awards substantially reduced because the criteria used to determine eligibility and benefit amounts were more restrictive for Black former players than those who were white, based on misleading and offensive racial stereotyping.[8]

In 2023 just before the Super Bowl, ten former NFL players sued the league's benefits plan for deliberately trying to do everything possible to prevent them from receiving the disability benefits the former players say they deserve. The plaintiffs also alleged that when their disability claims were denied and they appealed, the plan's lawyers and administrators violated federal law by failing to review the evidence fairly. The plan relied instead on the biased opinion of the doctors it hired to review these claims, who have a financial incentive to rule for the league (see chapter 7).[9]

Disability-based prejudice and discrimination are even worse for athletes with mental impairments. There have been countless instances, many of which are recounted in this book, in which athletes or former athletes with mental health and emotional well-being challenges have not received the same level of attention, care, and/or treatment as athletes and former athletes with physical impairments. As Masling has observed, "Historically, athletes have been given greater support for their physical health."[10]

One reason for this disparity, in addition to stigma and stereotyping, is sportswashing and other sports-related propaganda (see chapter 3). Another is the American legal system. Teams, leagues, other sports organizations, and players' unions embrace the importance of sports to so many fans, businesses, politicians, and government agencies as justification for the leeway they are given by the legal system to make self-serving legal determinations, even if in doing so these organizations skirt certain federal and state laws.

To a large extent, major spectator sports are allowed to govern themselves without much oversight from local, state, and federal officials. As a result, these sports organizations typically are in positions to manufacture more favorable legal outcomes for themselves. This happened most prominently, for example, in the national scandals involving brain damage to athletes (see chapter 7) and the sexual abuse of female gymnasts (see chapter 9).

Today, American sports organizations reflexively retain law firms to do so-called independent investigations when their scandalous actions or omissions become public. Those law firms understand that in order to enjoy these lucrative contracts in the future, their lawyers need to do what they can, within the flexible bounds of legal ethics, to keep their clients satisfied.

Usually, it is the client sports organization, and not the law firm, that determines what portions of the investigative reports, if any, will be revealed, and how and to whom the results of those investigations will be disseminated. One of the most pernicious examples of this legal slight of hand involved widespread sexual abuse of female students at Baylor by the university's football players.

As Vikram David Amar, dean of the Illinois College of Law, opined in the context of an independent investigation of Urban Meyer, the head coach at Ohio State who was accused of helping to cover up domestic violence committed by one of his assistant coaches, these inquiries are anything "but [independent]." The law firm involved was "paid hundreds of thousands if not millions of dollars by their clients . . . for this project and (hopefully) for future projects for this and similar clients."[11]

Ultimately, it was Ohio State University, as the client, rather than the coach's wife, who alleged the abuse, that was protected the most. Similarly, in the Olympic and college scandals involving sexual abuse of female gymnasts, the so-called independent investigations protected USA Gymnastics, the USOPC, and Michigan State University much more than it did the female gymnasts who were abused then or will be in the future. (See chapter 9 for a more detailed account of what happened.)

In the Baylor scandal, which was arguably the worst in college sports history, the university largely escaped accountability after it chose not to release the so-called independent investigative report to the public. Baylor's football coach and president were forced to resign, but with large paydays that together totaled nearly $20 million. The NCAA, for its part, did not issue any sanctions to anyone involved in that scandal.

Major sports organizations depend on lawyers to maximize the advantages the legal system already provides them with. Sometimes they are lawyers in the firms that are doing these so-called independent investigations. Most of the time, though, the lawyers are in-house or on retainer. By and large, these lawyers and law firms do an excellent job of shielding the sports organizations that hire them from civil and criminal liability and other legal entanglements. Lawyers in today's sports world are as essential as the public relations experts who help sportswash away bad publicity, including legal improprieties (see chapter 3).

CHAPTER 3

Sportswashing as Part of an Expanding Spectator Sports Propaganda Arsenal

PROPAGANDA HAS BEEN A PROMINENT PART OF SPECTATOR SPORTS going as far back as the ancient Olympics. Many, many years later, myths behind the Olympic ideal of building a better world through sports were propagated at the end of the nineteenth century in order to justify expenditures of large amounts of public funds and resources to establish and perpetuate the modern Olympic movement. It also was used more than a century ago to convince Americans that Abner Doubleday invented baseball in order "to distance the national pastime from its foreign antecedents, cricket and rounders."[1]

Throughout American history, propaganda has been used to promote spectator sports, stifle opposition to the uglier aspects of these sports, and cover up transgressions and misdeeds committed by major spectator sports organizations or individuals and entities associated with them. In addition, it has been used by American politicians, most notably presidents, who conspicuously show up at major sporting events to garner votes and generate higher approval ratings. Traditionally, though, American sports propaganda was mostly tethered to myths about the virtues of the Olympic ideal and star athletes as exemplary role models.

Over the years, however, sports propaganda has been employed for a variety of other purposes as well, including to:

- prepare boys and young men for war and celebrate the virtues of military service
- proselytize Christianity and Christian values
- promote the illusion that big-time college athletics are amateur competitions between student-athletes
- create the impression that sports entities embrace racial justice, even though not so long ago they presented obstacles to racial progress
- justify misogyny, homophobia, and ableism
- persuade parents that playing tackle football is a reasonably safe and healthy activity for children and adolescents
- obscure and cover up widespread doping by athletes in professional, Olympic, and college sports
- persuade large metropolitan areas to spend limited public funds on extravagant stadiums and arenas for extremely wealthy corporations and sports entrepreneurs

Throughout the twentieth century, promoting the ideals of sports globally became a favored propaganda tool to help rogue nations justify their totalitarian regimes and abhorrent policies. Offending nations began hiding their plots and transgressions behind the Olympic ideal and related sports aspirations. That propaganda facade was fully utilized by Nazi Germany at the 1936 Berlin Summer Olympics. Afterward, during the Cold War, nationalistic propaganda became a regular staple of the Summer and Winter Olympic Games.

In recent years, this type of global sports propaganda has often been labeled "sportswashing." The definition of sportswashing that launched the term into the popular English vernacular was narrower than what has evolved since then. Originally, the definition focused on nation-states using international sports competitions, especially the Olympics, to draw attention away from, and thus to try to conceal, human rights violations, government corruption, or warlike intentions. This is the definition of the term, as first coined by international human rights organizations, which fit the Berlin Olympics to a tee.

That definition also fits Saudi Arabia's attempt to sportswash its human rights violations, discrimination against women, and apparent dismemberment of a Saudi American journalist by sponsoring LIV Golf as an alternative to the PGA and European tours. Even Phil Mickelson, the most recognized golfer to join that "Saudi-funded effort," acknowledged these people are "scary motherf—ers to get involved with."[2]

Sportswashing has also been used to promote nations' global identity, including most recently at the 2022 Beijing Winter Olympics when American skier Eileen Gu was allowed to represent China without renouncing her US citizenship. In her version of the Olympic ideal, she said it was "to bridge the gap [between the United States and China] and to be a force for unity."[3] Many Americans, though, thought she was being used as a political pawn.

Sportswashing, however, is not something that only rogue nations employ. The definition should be broadened to include attempts by businesses, organizations, the media, and individuals to use sporting ideals and sports popularity to minimize or cover up their own bad behaviors or their associations with individuals or organizations that act badly. In that sense, the concept of sportswashing is becoming increasingly interchangeable with sports propaganda more generally, especially efforts by spectator sports organizations to promote and protect themselves and the individuals and entities that most benefit from those sports.

Major sports enterprises doing business in the United States routinely use sports propaganda to promote themselves and sportswash their misdeeds and transgressions. Such propaganda often emanates from, or is enhanced by, sports media, which too often are closely aligned with and economically dependent upon the spectator sports they cover. Where such conflicts of interest exist, which is frequently, the sports media tend to repeat, embellish, or even create their own versions of sports propaganda and sportswashing in order to attract a larger audience or protect the spectator sports interests that help feed them.

SPORTS MEDIA AND CONFLICTS OF INTEREST

Spectator sports propaganda has been greatly enhanced by sports media. In recent years, the impact of sports media has skyrocketed. Coverage of spectator sports, including a dazzling array of entertaining athlete- and coach-based narratives, conflicts, and scandals, are presented 24/7. Television and talk radio shows devoted to popular sports generally or professional, college, or Olympic sports more specifically—including football, baseball, basketball, hockey, soccer, tennis, golf, and NASCAR—help ensure that America's spectator sports businesses remain profitable, which in turn generates revenues and greater access for the media covering those sports. In their coverage, these broadcasters rarely, if ever, criticize the nations, organizations, or enterprises that are sponsoring the competitions, even when such criticism is well deserved.

When scandals and potential scandals erupt in the professional, college, or Olympic ranks, the local and national sports media are quick to provide forums for the perpetrators of bad behaviors to broadcast insincere explanations and excuses to the public. This type of sportswashing competes with or displaces truth and candor. Too often it is members of the media who concoct or are responsible for promoting dubious rationalizations, which appear to be credible only because they cannot be readily disproved and are popular among fans.

Sports coverage free of conflicts of interest has become the praiseworthy exception rather than the standard of practice. Conflicts of interest among the sports media and the major sports organizations have become commonplace, and highly ethical journalism more difficult to find. The standards of practice have been compromised by the never-ending pursuit of more revenue.

Nowhere are these compromises more evident than in the sports broadcasting business. Teams today often hire their own announcers rather than just influencing which announcers are retained by their broadcast partners. Few, if any, local broadcasters are called "homers" anymore, because being a homer has become a requirement of the job. Increasingly, broadcast "partners" are owned by the teams themselves, and when they are not, those partners have other vested interests in promoting the teams and leagues they cover. Making the coverage even more conflicted, sports enterprises buy or already own media outlets and use other mechanisms that allow them to bypass independent, or less dependent, media entirely, communicating with their fans as they see fit.

The damage to journalism from these conflicts of interest was illustrated well by a 2013 incident involving ESPN, the NFL, and the Public Broadcasting Service (PBS) that became a minor public scandal. Without any convincing explanation, ESPN—a major broadcast partner of the NFL—suddenly withdrew from a joint project with PBS to produce a documentary on concussions and brain damage among NFL players. ESPN had been on the project for well over a year before deciding to walk out, seemingly trying to remove all visible traces that its employees had ever worked on the project.

Numerous reports surfaced that the NFL had actively pressured ESPN to withdraw from the documentary as part of the league's concerted effort to sportswash any negative publicity arising from the concussion problem that it had gone to great lengths to cover up. Adding to that anecdotal evidence was the fact that members of the committee of paid medical experts studying players' head, neck, and spine injuries for the NFL suddenly canceled the on-camera interviews they had agreed to do for the critically acclaimed PBS show *Frontline*, which was producing the documentary.

This type of influence and pressure on sports networks from the professional leagues, college conferences, and teams they broadcast or otherwise cover is not unusual. Frequently, though, such sportswashing is aimed at individual members of the media. As an article in the *Columbia Journalism Review* concluded in 2007, it is not unusual for "leagues, franchises, and athletes . . . to attack sports writers who write things they don't like."[4]

Members of the media who are too critical tend to be marginalized and denied access to the teams they are covering. Furthermore, teams typically favor their broadcast partners in providing access to their teams and players, limiting access to almost everyone else. Thus, beat writers and other local media, who need such access to do their jobs well, have strong incentives to avoid stories that may reflect poorly on local teams and the athletes on those teams. Instead, sports reporters spout cliches that tend to avoid these uncomfortable realities.

SPORTSWASHING EXPLAINED AND DISCUSSED

The linguistic distinction between sports propaganda generally and sportswashing more specifically continues to narrow over time. Sportswashing, as it is used in this book, encompasses a broad array of sports-related propaganda tools and practices employed by nations, organizations, individuals, and/or the media to (1) boost their reputations or (2) protect themselves from being blamed for human rights violations, scandals, crimes, corruption, or other transgressions that they are either responsible for or closely associated with.

Sportswashing has become a standard practice for major sports organizations as well as rogue nations. An overriding purpose of sportswashing in the United States has been to convince national, state, and local governments to view spectator sports, and by association the individuals and organizations they partner with, as being particularly worthy of a special public status and trust. In these sportswashed narratives, spectator sports are supposed to be viewed as something all people need and enjoy, much like art, music, and Fourth of July celebrations. The single most celebrated and expensive publicly supported sporting event in the United States is the Super Bowl.

The downside of these seemingly noble sportswashed sentiments becomes apparent when the organizations that control—and benefit, either economically or politically, from—spectator sports misuse their privileged status to serve their own needs over the welfare of the public and/or the athletes they are supposed to represent and serve. Many of the worst abuses in the NFL are marginalized or ignored because of that sport's huge popularity. This type of self-interest can too easily morph into corruption when those sports organizations, or individuals closely associated with them, skirt or openly breach rules of law or commonly agreed-upon human rights and other moral principles in order to serve their own interests or agendas.

There is a fundamental difference between the ideals of sports competition upon which the Olympics were supposedly founded, for example, and the values and behaviors of the individuals and entities that benefit economically or politically from holding or supporting these profitable sports competitions. Sportswashing, in this broad sense, includes the use of propaganda to make it appear that there is little significant difference between what these sports organizations do in the name of profiting from their sports and the ideals of sports competition themselves.

Once that misimpression is firmly established, the illusion becomes difficult to penetrate. This facade provides cover for many transgressions and offenses these sports organizations and the athletes they are supposed to represent commit in the name of the sport. The legal system too often adds to this problem by giving these sportswashed organizations the benefit of the doubt, allowing them to govern and control their sports with minimal government or judicial intervention (see chapter 2).

Too many athletes, coaches, trainers, team physicians, and other people closely associated with these popular spectator sports try to hide behind or benefit from these sportswashed illusions when they transgress or offend. For the most part, the sports organizations they are associated with try to minimize or cover up their misdeeds in order to protect their investments and their sports' reputations.

Sportswashing Health Risks to Athletes

The broader definition of sportswashing encompasses an array of spectator sports pathologies that major spectator sports organization have facilitated, encouraged, or covered up using various propaganda techniques. Among those pathologies are the negative effects spectator sports have on the health, mental health, and emotional well-being of elite and aspiring elite athletes. The litany of health-related inequities, neglect, and abuse that negatively affect these athletes should be viewed as a disturbing social problem that needs to be addressed. Instead, such transgressions tend to be accepted as the cost of doing business in these sports rather than things that must be substantially changed, and soon.

Mental health challenges and related inequities typically originate with the inadequate care, treatment, and support these elite and aspiring elite athletes receive. The impact of that deficit in mental health care and treatment is magnified because training for and competing in these sports can contribute to or even cause any number of mental disorders, including severe stress, anxiety, depression, and brain damage. In addition, if athletes have preexisting mental disorders, those conditions can easily become worse.

Abuse and neglect affecting marginalized athletes or athletes in specific spectator sports, which is not uncommon, can also jeopardize their mental health and/or emotional well-being. Three of the most prominent examples have been:

- sexual abuse, especially of young female athletes, by coaches, physicians, and other men closely associated with their sports (see chapter 9)
- cover-ups and deception related to the known or suspected effects of concussions, concussive impacts, and other brain trauma on athletes who participate in contact sports, especially boxing, football, and hockey (see chapter 7)
- discrimination against and harassment and bullying of LGBTQ+ athletes (see chapters 10 and 11)

By inflating and distorting their commitment to traditional sporting ideals, spectator sports organizations frequently try to sportswash away discrimination against and abuse and neglect of marginalized athletes in their sports. Such propaganda often begins with the notion that spectator sports should be viewed as sacrosanct entities in American society, which, like Christian religions, should not have to obey laws and moral principles prohibiting discrimination and unequal treatment or be constrained by the civil and criminal laws that are supposed to apply to everyone else.

In professional and college football, especially, openly embracing Christianity has been an effective way to sportswash away the violence of that frequently brutal sport. Prayer circles involving Christian athletes are a common phenomenon after games. Their faith helps those athletes believe a Christian God will protect them or help them recover from their injuries. As the *New York Times* explained in a headline, "Players rely on an unseen teammate: their faith."[5]

Such Christian faith and prayer were on full display early in January 2023 a week after Buffalo Bills safety Damar Hamlin suffered a near-fatal heart stoppage while playing in Cincinnati. Many orchestrated moments of silence to pray for Hamlin's full recovery became the NFL's, and thus the sports media's, focus. The question of what needs to be done to change the game in order to substantially reduce the risk of severe and often permanent injuries to the players, most notably to their brains, became a secondary concern (see chapter 7). Based on its sportswashed responses to this near tragedy, the NFL's answer to this question was: Very little or nothing needs to be done.

PART II

ATHLETES' SPECTATOR SPORTS MENTAL HEALTH CONCERNS

PART I PROVIDED AN OVERVIEW OF THREE KEY FACTORS THAT HAVE negatively affected athletes in American spectator sports, which also directly impact their health, mental health, and emotional well-being. Part II focuses on five types of mental health concerns in these sports that affect elite and aspiring elite athletes. Each chapter includes narratives about the relatively few athletes whose mental health challenges have come to light.

Chapter 4 deals with mental health conditions that everyone, including athletes, are susceptible to, such as depression and bipolar disorder, but in the context of how different sports and athletes in those sports have dealt with those conditions. Chapter 5 addresses mental disorders, including the "yips," competitive stress, anxiety, and depression that specifically affect elite and aspiring elite athletes due to their participation in their sports.

Chapter 6 discusses the health challenges of COVID for elite athletes, especially known, suspected, and potential mental health–related COVID risks, both short and long term. Chapter 7 looks at mental health and related behavioral issues of elite athletes, athletes aspiring to be elite, and former elite athletes who have had concussions, brain trauma, and/or repeated subconcussive impacts. Chapter 8 examines the causes and health and behavioral effects of substance abuse and dependency on elite and aspiring elite athletes.

CHAPTER 4

Mental Conditions That Athletes, Like Everyone Else, May Experience

LOCKER ROOM BANTER, TEAM CAMARADERIE, AND OTHER BONDING influences and experiences are where much of the mental health–related stigmas, stereotypes, secrecy, and discrimination in American spectator sports have been incubated. This is not surprising, given the way the rest of America still generally seems to view serious mental illnesses with apathy and neglect, if not outright prejudice.[1]

Inculcation of these dysfunctional attitudes begins at a relatively young age, when immature and impressionable athletes with talent are often plucked away for special leagues and competitions reserved for those perceived to be the best—or whose families can pay to try to make it appear so. From that point on, at every step of their journey to become an elite athlete, these dysfunctional mental health attitudes are likely to be reinforced.

The disconnect between athletic fitness and mental health widens, and may even accelerate, as the rewards and benefits of sports increase. This skewed reality applies not only to the athletes themselves but, perhaps more so, to the individuals supposedly there to nurture and train them, too many of whom are balancing their own paydays or egos against the athletes' mental health and emotional well-being. Sports cultures, particularly those involving male athletes, have traditionally been kryptonite to mental health and emotional well-being.

That dysfunctional mental health culture appears to be slowly changing, but opposition to meaningful progress remains strong. Certain athletes, especially a growing number of women and girls, have become more open about discussing their mental health and emotional challenges. In addition, some sports organizations, especially those with substantial financial resources, have responded by making modest efforts to provide their current athletes with counseling and treatment options. Long-term mental health care for elite athletes and former elite athletes, however, remains a serious problem. Moreover, even today relatively few current athletes are coming forward with their stories.

On the positive side, as Louisa Thomas wrote in the *New Yorker*, "[t]he psychological challenges of sports have been talked about for ages. In 2021, athletes in a number of disciplines took action." Thomas observed that in "recent years stars in a range of sports have publicly discussed dealing with depression, anxiety, and suicidal thoughts. The NBA, the NCAA, and even the NFL . . . now have fairly robust counselling and mental health services."[2] The *Harvard Business Review* even called on "company leaders [to] learn from the sports world's mental health momentum,"[3] implying, unconvincingly given the facts, that the "sports industry" had suddenly transformed into a mental health role model.

Despite these incremental mental health improvements and perceptions about progress, American spectator sports remain resistant to change. Like the #MeToo and Black Lives Matter movements, after an initial flurry of publicity, the hard work that remains to be done to improve athletes' mental health and emotional well-being is more than just challenging; it is too often opposed by what appear to be even stronger social, economic, and political forces.

The National Basketball Players Association, for instance, has tried with limited success to get the NBA to provide care, treatment, and support to players with mental health needs without breaching confidentiality, especially between affected players and their teams. As Michele Roberts, the union's former executive director, who retired in January 2022, acknowledged, "the devil is in the details. . . . [I]f a player is unable to perform because of his issues, that opens up a different discussion."[4]

Indeed, it does—not only for NBA players, but perhaps more so for other elite athletes in major American team sports. Unlike most well-paid employees in America, athletes are on a very short leash when it comes to not performing because of legitimate mental health concerns.

It seems fair to wonder, given the recent and more distant histories of most major American sports organizations, whether this initial investment by sports organizations in the mental health of their athletes is more about public relations than genuine concern. The gestures to date are certainly better than the profound ignorance of the past; however, that progress still seems inadequate to make a substantial difference in the cultures of their sports when it comes to addressing the mental health and emotional well-being of most of their athletes and former athletes.

Athletes speaking out about mental health in sports tend to do so when their careers are either nearly over or in such jeopardy, due to on- or off-the-field behavior issues, that a certain amount of carefully managed transparency becomes a better career and business option than keeping silent. Based on the percentages of athletes with mental disorders of any kind, which is estimated to be "approximately 35%", a large percentage of elite athletes and athletes aspiring to be elite with mental health challenges,[5] must be still keeping their conditions quiet, and the sports organizations and unions to which they belong are protecting, if not encouraging, their silence.

One superstar athlete, Aaron Rodgers, who has famously avoided getting the COVID vaccine, apparently used his "mental health" as an excuse for not letting his former NFL football team, the Green Bay Packers, and the media know what his plans were for playing in the upcoming season.[6] To him, his mental health seemed more like a joke, or at least a clumsy justification for acting as selfishly as he did.

AN INVENTORY OF MENTAL HEALTH AND PSYCHOLOGICAL ISSUES INVOLVING ATHLETES

A research team for the American Medical Society for Sports Medicine (AMSSM) conducted what appears to be the most comprehensive inventory of "mental health issues and psychological factors in athletes" to date. The study, completed in July 2022, was based on "an in-depth literature review" of all the leading medical databases.[7]

The AMSSM identified and examined mental health challenges to athletes in three broad areas: "personality and athletic culture," "the psychological response to injury and illness," and "select mental health and psychological issues." Its list was remarkably comprehensive, including many, but not all, of the issues covered in this book. It identified concerns related to:

- "personality"
- "sexuality and gender"
- "hazing" and "bullying"
- "sexual misconduct"
- "the relationship between injury performance, and mental health," "response to injury," and "self-medication in response to injury/illness"
- "eating disorders/disordered eating"
- "depression and suicide"
- "anxiety and stress," "overtraining," and "sleep disorders"

While the AMSSM used its "taxonomy" mainly to form the basis for clinical recommendations to its members, it also should have been a wake-up call to the sports world. Despite recent incremental gains, so much more needs to be done to adequately address the many and varied mental health and emotional well-being challenges athletes face. The greatest concerns appear to be the dangers and pathologies that lie below the surface, mostly outside of public perception.

STIGMA AND DISCRIMINATION JEOPARDIZE ATHLETES' CAREERS AND WELL-BEING

In all major American spectator sports, there are systemic failures regarding stigma and discrimination, which can harm and even be devastating to athletes who have mental health or other emotionally based issues.

Some of the worst stereotypes and prejudices in these sports pertain specifically to mental conditions. For athletes, serious mental health issues can too often unnecessarily disrupt and destroy their careers.

For leagues, teams, other sports organizations, and the athletes themselves, mental health concerns are significantly outweighted by money—and the wins that produce revenues and fame. As the late Wayne Huizinga, who owned professional baseball, football, and hockey franchises in Florida, once explained, "Money is how [teams] keep score."[8] That conviction applies, to a disproportionate degree, to most spectator sports as well.

In such a skewed environment, mental health care and treatment in professional, Olympic, and major college sports continue to be viewed, and responded to, as a taboo, deliberately veiled in secrecy and rife with deception. Affected athletes, their teams, and leagues or sports organizations still often build walls of silence or even concoct elaborate ruses or deceptions to hide these conditions. In the process, necessary mental health treatments and supports too often are unavailable or left to the affected athletes to find—or to choose to avoid and ignore.

Many of the worst stereotypes and prejudices in America's most popular spectator sports involve athletes' mental conditions. What happens to those affected athletes, from the point of view of the sports organizations to which they belong, often depends upon an economic analysis rather than what is best for those athletes' mental health.

Team and organization officials, coaches, and trainers compound this bias with a heavy dose of mental health ignorance and shortsightedness. The threshold question tends to be whether athletes' mental conditions will prevent them from competing up to their normal standards. Those who cannot perform adequately are commonly labeled "malingerers" or "malcontents," especially if their mental health issues do not resolve quickly or are obscured and allowed to fester behind a veil of secrecy and silence.

Athletes who have multiple incidents or episodes of this nature that keep them from competing for relatively long periods of time are likely to be disparaged and devalued by teammates, sports management, the sports media, fans, and corporate sponsors. The common derisive term is "head case," a label that is very difficult for any athlete to come back from. Once that label is assigned, an athlete's mental health problems become character flaws rather than socially acceptable illnesses that deserve to be treated and cared for with adequate resources and compassion.

As a result, most athletes with serious mental health issues feel so stigmatized and afraid of being discriminated against and harassed that they try to hide or disguise their conditions and treatment needs; often they simply self-medicate with drugs and alcohol, making their situations even worse (see chapter 8). There is a double standard in sports when the mental health needs of athletes are being considered. With most physically based health problems, a concerted effort is made to treat or encourage the affected athletes to be treated promptly in order to get them ready to compete as soon as possible. That makes economic sense.

Athletes with serious mental health problems, however, face an additional agonizing dilemma, even if they are willing to acknowledge, for the purpose of treatment and support, that they have such a condition: Who, if anyone, can they trust with such information? Typically, these elite athletes confide in only a small circle of close relatives and friends, or no one at all, or pretend to themselves and others that their mental distress is physical or something else. This silence and secrecy tends to advance the progression of mental distress at the expense of the athletes' careers and even their lives.

Once these athletes reach a point where their athletic careers appear to be over or greatly diminished, even most of those relatively few sports organizations that might pay for athletes' mental health care and treatment during their careers mostly disappear, leaving the athletes to fend for themselves. Other sports organizations just leave it up the athletes to deal with. This is especially true in spectator sports for female athletes, which tend to have smaller financial rewards and benefits. In most American spectator sports for women, many of the athletes have second jobs or earn a disproportionate share of their income internationally, as Brittney Griner and a number of other WNBA players have done playing professional basketball in Russia.

The limited exceptions are lucrative team sports for men, which provide income and health benefits to some of their former players who have become vested in those plans. Nonetheless, when it comes to long-term mental health care and treatment, the players' unions in those sports too often fail to adequately provide for their former athletes. A significant proportion of athletes in America's most popular team sports must leave their sports due to injuries before they even qualify to receive a pension and disability-related benefits (see chapter 1).

There is a paradox that is closely tied to how players want to share the general revenues they bargain for from the teams and leagues that control those revenues. The percentage of revenues former players are entitled to, including their health care, must be subtracted from the share of revenues current players receive. Mental health care down the road has been a low priority.

Much like the rest of America, for current players, immediate gratification is valued much more than future benefits they will receive once they retire. Many current players still believe—or adamantly insist—that the mental health care and treatment of former players should be the responsibility of those former players—this is until they retire and have to pay for those expenses themselves—or that their alleged disabilities are a scam or exaggeration. In this environment, which is critical of and even hostile to mental health–related claims, it is difficult, and sometimes impossible, for players with legitimate mental health needs to receive adequate care and treatment, especially for long-term impairments.

Stigma surrounding mental health conditions in our favorite spectator sports appears to be even greater than it is in American society generally. American spectator sports still have a long way to go in protecting the mental health of their athletes. Leagues, athletic departments, and other sports enterprises continue to foster environments that unnecessarily jeopardize the mental health of their athletes. Narratives provided by elite athletes who have faced these serious mental health challenges remain relatively few, given the scientific estimates of how many athletes are affected.

Nevertheless, the stories of those who have been willing or forced to speak out illustrate how stigma and discrimination occur even with elite athletes and the negative effects of this prejudice on those athletes' mental health. For some of those athletes, their stories did not become public until years after their competitive careers ended. Others spoke out at the end of their careers or when avoiding the issue of their mental health was no longer a viable option because it was obvious something was wrong. In those cases, the athletes and/or their representatives tried to get in front of public or soon-to-become-public exposés, which often included episodes of bad or self-destructive behaviors.

The list of athletes whose mental health challenges have become known in recent years is growing, but it still is relatively small, given the number of athletes who apparently have had significant mental conditions. Those athletes who have gone public have experienced a variety of disorders. Issues with failure to perform, apparently due to depression or the stress and anxiety caused by being an elite athlete or an aspiring elite athlete are discussed in chapter 5, while problems seemingly related to brain damage or substance abuse issues are discussed in chapters 7 and 8, respectively.

Below are the stories of athletes with the types of mental health challenges that anyone might experience, but in the context of participating in a variety of spectator sports. It should come as no surprise, though, that many of these athlete narratives involve more than one type of mental health issue. Determining which category is the best fit for their stories was admittedly a largely subjective judgment.

Collectively, however, these narratives, wherever they have been placed, make significant contributions to understanding the mental health challenges athletes face in America's favorite spectator sports, as well as how things have changed and how they have remained the same or been made worse. Whether they are truly representative of all elite and aspiring elite athletes is questionable. For every story that has been told, many more remain hidden from view. Those never-told stories are likely to be somewhat different from the ones that are included here. And, as with any such media-based narrative, they only tell part of the story.

Athletes' Mental Health Narratives over the Years

Jimmy Piersall (Boston Red Sox and Broadcaster)

Just like Lou Gehrig did for amyotrophic lateral sclerosis (ALS) in 1939, Jimmy Piersall brought mental illness out of the shadows in 1955 with his memoir, *Fear Strikes Back*. Similar to Gehrig, Piersall was a high-profile athlete playing professional baseball, which then was still the American pastime. Although not nearly as talented or accomplished as Gehrig, Piersall nonetheless made the American League All-Star team twice, in 1954 and 1956, and received a Gold Glove in 1958 for his defensive skills. Furthermore, he was an eager and able chronicler of his struggles.

As with Gehrig, the movie depictions of Piersall's battle with his disability, bipolar disorder, were distorted versions of what purportedly had happened in real life. Hollywood wanted both athletes to appear heroic in the end. Additionally, the science of mental illness, as well as attempts to minimize the stigmas surrounding mental health conditions, had not yet progressed very far. Thus, the root cause of Piersall's disorder was popularly blamed on his father, who reportedly had dominated his son's early life and obsessively pushed him toward a professional baseball career. Piersall later denied that his father had been the primary reason for his illness.

At age eighteen, Piersall signed a contract with the Boston Red Sox. Two years later, in 1950, he became one of the youngest players in the big leagues. On-field behavior problems in 1952—including a fistfight with volatile New York Yankees infielder Billy Martin and Piersall's spanking the young child of a Red Sox teammate during a spring game—resulted in his being sent back to the minor leagues. His seemingly erratic behaviors continued; he was repeatedly ejected from ball games, finally receiving a three-game suspension.

Piersall was *voluntarily* institutionalized (as it was mischaracterized then) for nearly two months in a Massachusetts state mental hospital, where he was diagnosed, at least publicly, not with bipolar disorder, but with "nervous exhaustion." In those days, what was called voluntary really was not since the patient could not leave the facility. To treat that vague and seemingly insubstantial condition, Piersall received highly invasive

45

electroshock therapy. He also was prescribed lithium, a new and apparently effective drug used to treat mood swings.

Although Piersall did not play baseball for the rest of that season, he was able to return to the Red Sox the following year. He went on to complete a relatively lucrative baseball career, followed by on and off broadcasting positions after he retired. His salaries and endorsements were greatly supplemented by the income from his best-selling book and its movie rights. In 1955, the book was turned into a television drama starring Tab Hunter in the lead role. In 1957, it became a movie classic starring Anthony Perkins as Piersall and Karl Malden as his controlling father.

Throughout his life, Piersall engaged in various behavioral antics, in part, he said, because it made fans come out to see him play. Such behaviors also were consistent with a bipolar diagnosis. He later explained in his autobiography that "[p]robably the best thing that ever happened to me was going nuts. Who ever heard of Jimmy Piersall until that happened?"[9]

For years, Piersall was the only American athlete to be so directly and famously associated with having a mental illness. Nevertheless, the Jimmy Piersall story was atypical, unique, and therefore misleading. It took a long time for other athletes with mental disorders to overcome the stereotypes his groundbreaking narrative produced. Too often those athletes who came later were dismissed and stigmatized as "head cases."

Pete Harnisch (New York Mets)

The next MLB player to make national headlines due to his mental illness was New York Mets starting pitcher Pete Harnisch. In 1997, forty-two years after Piersall, Harnisch became one of the very few athletes to publicly acknowledge, to a certain extent, his mental condition while he was still a player. Until then, there was an unwritten code that sports journalists did not write about athletes' mental health issues.

Not surprisingly, Harnisch's story reeked of stigma. He called his condition, which lasted the entire season, a "depressive episode" and purportedly "recoil[ed] at being the poster boy for depression." Instead, he hid behind the hard-to-believe excuse "that his body chemistry [had been] destabilized when he abruptly quit a 13-year chewing tobacco habit."[10] Making matters worse, his unsympathetic manager, Bobby Valentine, traded him after an angry tirade at a team meeting in which Valentine reportedly called Harnisch's refusal to practice and perform due to his depression "gutless."[11]

Referring to the Harnisch story specifically, but generalizing it to spectator sports more broadly, *New York Times* columnist Robert Lipsyte concluded that "the discussion of any kind of mental illness . . . has not progressed much beyond the 1950's Jimmy ('Fear Strikes Out') Piersall story." As sports commentator and author Jon Wertheim put it, "Half a century later . . . the sports world [has] remained largely in the dark on matters of mental health."[12]

Terry Bradshaw (Pittsburgh Steelers)

Years before Harnisch's difficult experiences, NFL MVP and four-time Super Bowl champion Pittsburgh Steelers quarterback Terry Bradshaw experienced his own mental health struggles. It was not until many years later, though, in 2003, that Bradshaw revealed details about his depression and anxiety attacks. Rather than celebrating his Super Bowl accomplishments, he worried throughout his football career whether he would be able to accomplish the same level of success the following year.

As the first pick in the 1970 NFL draft, he "lost confidence" and became "sensitive to criticism" when his presumed stardom took time to evolve. Much later, he understood that depression and anxiety had been largely responsible for his overwrought feelings, which after games would, in his words, make him "hemorrhage sweat and dissolve into tears." Yet even though at the time he understood his "life was going to hell in a hand-basket," Bradshaw shunned professional help due to the stigma of mental illness in the NFL. Instead, he, and those who were close to him, pretended everything was fine.[13]

The stigma he felt around mental illness was so strong that it was not until twenty years after he retired from the NFL that Bradshaw was able to talk about those steep challenges. The impetus for this transparency was "his third divorce" and "a series of crippling anxiety attacks . . . [that]

left him lying on the floor of his apartment, calling out to a friend for help and feeling sure he would die."[14]

Bradshaw became a very successful NFL television commentator and a mental health advocate. He has shared his story countless times and acknowledged that in addition to depression he had to deal with attention deficit disorder, all of which played havoc in his personal relationships. He divorced three times, has had numerous "bouts with the media," and had such a bad relationship with Steelers head coach Chuck Noll that he was a no-show at Noll's 2014 funeral.[15]

Shayne Corson (Toronto Maple Leafs)

Shortly before Bradshaw made his grim circumstances known, near the end of a distinguished NHL career that spanned nearly twenty years, Shayne Corson publicly acknowledged that throughout his tenure as a professional athlete playing for several teams, he would often awaken "in the middle of the night panicking—my heart pounding, tears in my eyes. . . . I wouldn't know what to do."[16] His extreme anxiety was exacerbated by profound and prolonged grief at the death in 1993 of his father, with whom he "had a unique bond . . . more than the typical father and son relationship."[17]

Corson, a prized youth hockey player, was selected 8th in the first round of the 1986 NHL Draft by the Montreal Canadians. Throughout his career, though, he battled mental demons. He also had a penchant for deliberately getting into fights, often with players much bigger than himself, even when his coaches told him his fighting was not only ill advised but counterproductive. He was traded many times during his career and became unpopular with the media. His problems became more pronounced after his father's death.

Those troubles reached a peak ten years later. During the 2002 Stanley Cup playoffs, when he was playing for the Toronto Maple Leafs, Corson's anxiety became so overwhelming that he had to leave the team. Most of the reactions to his mental disorder proved to be unsympathetic and mean-spirited. "[M]embers of the press unleashed their daggers," accusing the hockey player of abandoning his team. Furthermore, unlike how he would have been treated for a physical injury, management made him forfeit the remainder of his contract, which was worth millions of dollars.[18]

Because of this incident, though, Corson sought professional help. He said in a 2019 interview that he came to understand that "while various life stresses played a role in his psychiatric condition, not properly dealing with his father's death was the cause of most of his issues." Corson began to feel better in therapy, talking to "the doctors about all the issues he'd repressed for so long."[19]

Chamique Holdsclaw (Washington Mystics, Los Angeles Sparks)

Chamique Holdsclaw was one of the very best women college basketball players ever. Throughout her mental health–shortened WNBA career, which began in 1999, she experienced severe bouts of depression. Excessive alcohol consumption and the death of her beloved grandmother made it worse.

Her first team, the Washington Mystics, including her teammates, did little to help the future Women's Basketball Hall of Fame member. They apparently viewed the symptoms of her mental disorders as character flaws. In the words of the *Washington Post*'s Sally Jenkins, Holdsclaw was "labeled . . . a quitter . . . , an enigma . . . , or a problem."[20]

Holdsclaw's depression remained mostly a secret from the public until the fall of 2004, when she left the Mystics following an extended leave of absence during that summer season. Neither she nor her team was willing to explain what was really happening to her. Publicly, she had some unspecified medical condition.

But as soon as Holdsclaw was traded that October, Mystics team officials eagerly revealed her mental illness to the media, apparently as a justification for having traded away one of the greatest female basketball players of all time. Over her last three years with the Mystics, Holdsclaw had averaged nearly 20 points and 10 rebounds a game.[21]

Her trade to the Los Angeles Sparks seemed to work out well at first, but Holdsclaw's mental condition became problematic in 2006, her second season with the team. She reportedly swallowed an entire bottle of antidepressant medication and was committed to a mental health facility with what were described as "delusions."[22] From there, her career went downhill. Although she returned to the WNBA as a member of the Atlanta Dream, it was only as a role player. Holdsclaw retired in 2010. In her 2012 autobiography, she wrote about her "mortal struggle with despair," especially as a mostly closeted gay woman in the WNBA.[23]

Retirement did not end her bouts with depression, however. Holdsclaw's situation escalated into impulsive violence, and in 2013 she was arrested for shooting a bullet into her ex-girlfriend's car in what was reported to be a domestic dispute. Unlike her experiences as an athlete, Holdsclaw was treated sympathetically by the criminal justice system. She pled guilty to felony assault and received no prison time. Instead, as part of her plea deal, she was required to undergo intensive outpatient mental health treatment over an extended period, which seemed to have been inadequate—if it existed at all—in the WNBA when she was playing.[24]

Delonte West (Cleveland Cavaliers)

Delonte West, an NBA guard for several different teams, left the Cleveland Cavaliers training camp in 2008 to receive treatment for a "mood disorder" and depression, which the twenty-five-year-old said he had been dealing with much of his life. West's mood swings reportedly became most pronounced when everything else in his life seemed to be going well. Just before training camp a year later, his condition became a public spectacle when he was caught speeding on his three-wheeled motorcycle in his home state of Maryland. At the time, West was in possession of "two loaded handguns and a loaded shotgun in a guitar case." The officer who stopped him said he "was very cooperative."[25]

The incident occurred at a time when the possession of guns by NBA players had become a volatile issue for NBA commissioner David Stern, and West had clearly violated Maryland's weapons restrictions at the time. Despite, or arguably because of, his transparency in dealing with his bipolar disorder, West became the butt of "brutal mockery" online and "tabloid fodder" in the media. Even National Public Radio (NPR) reportedly ridiculed his situation with the lede, "Delonte West . . . is apparently serious about his role as a shooting guard."[26]

Things got worse from there. In a regular column in *Bleacher Report*, a contributor called "Jabber Head" questioned whether "Delonte West [was] bipolar, or does he have aspirations of being a gun wheeling [*sic*], guitar case carrying outlaw" like Antonio Banderas's character in *Desperado*. Continuing, Jabber Head observed, "I'm no doctor, but I think they got this diagnosis wrong. Has anyone checked Delonte's DVD collection?"[27]

If that were not awful enough, West became the subject of what has been described as one of "the most famously unfounded scandals in sports history."[28] A rumor began circulating over social media that West had been sleeping with teammate LeBron James's mother. Despite the ridiculousness of the accusation, James eventually felt compelled to deny that it had ever occurred. After West retired, his bipolar disorder became much worse as he disappeared from public view. His life became a mess, so much so that when photos surfaced of him "panhandling in Dallas, Mark Cuban [owner of the Dallas Mavericks] drove to pick him up and offer help."[29]

Justin Duchscherer (Oakland A's)

In 2009, a few years after Pete Harnisch's mental health debacle with the Mets became public, another MLB pitcher, Justin Duchscherer of the Oakland A's, told his own story about struggles with clinical depression and performance anxiety. Soon after, Duchscherer, then age thirty-two, interrupted his baseball career to undergo intensive psychiatric treatment. Instead of pretending he had some physical malady, he took the risk of being open about his mental condition.

The pinnacle of his crisis came just after he had gone through a divorce and then sustained a serious elbow injury in spring training. That injury kept him out of baseball for five months for rehabilitation, which created substantial doubts about his baseball future. While he was at the airport about to fly to Sacramento for his final rehab assignment with the team's Triple-A affiliate before rejoining the A's, Duchscherer, in his words, "froze. I couldn't even get on the plane to do something I loved all my life. . . . I felt like a total failure."[30]

The Oakland A's appeared to be supportive. When asked to address questions from ESPN journalist Jerry Crasnick, A's assistant general manager David Frost said he and the team could not address "the specifics of Duchscherer's condition because of medical confidentiality laws." Frost acknowledged, though, that depression was "not something we have a ton of experience with. . . . We know it's serious and we would always say that life comes before baseball."[31]

What Frost apparently left out, though, was that if Duchscherer could not perform as an elite athlete, he would no longer be a part of the team. The A's re-signed the two-time All-Star to a low-risk contract for the next season for a fraction of what he had been earning before. Duchscherer made five starts for Oakland in the first month of the 2010 season. He posted a 2–1 record with a 2.89 ERA but went on the disabled list in May, missing the remainder of the season.

Afterward, the A's allowed Duchscherer to become a free agent, meaning they no longer had any interest in him. In 2011, he signed another minimal low-risk contract, this time with the Baltimore Orioles, but never pitched for that team. The Orioles released him in August, and that was the end of the pitcher's professional baseball career. Duchscherer said he "never doubted my ability to pitch. . . . My problem is that I'm a soft guy in a profession of hard guys."[32] And he was in the MLB, not the NFL or NHL.

Amanda Beard (Swimming)

Before Michael Phelps became famous for his mental health advocacy, another highly decorated American Olympic swimmer, Amanda Beard, helped set the stage for him with a courageous public disclosure of her emotional demons. Beard's challenges included self-destructive behaviors, self-injury, eating disorders, and substance abuse fueled by depression. It did not matter that she had twice broken the world record in the breaststroke, won a gold medal at the 2004 Olympics, and appeared on the cover of *Playboy*. She still spiraled out of control.

Her life began to turn around for the better when she married Sacha Brown, a photographer she had met at a 2005 swimsuit catalog shoot. He recommended that Beard enter therapy, which included taking antidepressants. However, she performed well below her previous standards at the 2008 Olympics—in part, it seems, because she had stopped taking her prescribed medication so drug testers would not discover her secret. In 2009, she gave birth to a son, which provided her life with a new meaning. She was happy being a mother and was able to compartmentalize motherhood from her swimming career, which had become a lower priority.[33]

In 2012, she detailed her struggles in a book titled *In the Water They Can't See You Cry* and began speaking out about the importance of public awareness of mental illness. She failed to make the US Olympic team that year and retired shortly thereafter.

Royce White (Houston Rockets)

Royce White was one of the most physically gifted athletes in the 2012 NBA Draft. Yet his draft value dropped significantly when he revealed his anxiety disorder, which manifested itself most prominently in an overwhelming fear of flying. Unlike most male athletes with mental disorders who scrupulously hid their conditions, White decided that he would be candid and transparent, which is what most mental health practitioners recommend.

White's anxiety was hardly unique in the sports world. When they were doing live broadcasts of weekly network football games, both Tony Kornheiser and John Madden were driven to game locations in luxurious buses to accommodate their fears of flying. Their networks understood that the talent of those two television personalities more than made up for the added expense of providing a workable solution to this relatively common anxiety disorder.

Unfortunately for White, most professional athletes with mental conditions tend to be treated with far less empathy and therapeutic concern. Although White was viewed by many as a top ten or five pick, on draft day he was selected 16th by the Houston Rockets. White was optimistic at first, but soon a serious rift emerged with the Rockets regarding the proper way to deal with his mental health issues, especially the provision of reasonable accommodations or modifications around flying.

The Rockets, the NBA, and most of the professional basketball media reflexively presumed that the team's front office retained a prerogative to make most decisions as they pleased, without any guidance from mental health experts. Thus, an unenlightened Rockets management refused to agree to formulate a comprehensive plan to accommodate White's special needs. Instead, they decided the team should address each disability-related issue of his when it arose, based largely on a narrow view of the economics and administrative convenience to the team. The compromise they chose was to permit White to use a car to travel, but only to some road games.[34]

White did not agree. He insisted upon a comprehensive plan that would allow him to participate in all the team's road games, which the Rockets refused to develop, much less implement. Neither party budged from their positions. In this mental health–unfriendly sports atmosphere, however, White was generally regarded as having overstepped his bounds. Despite his obvious basketball skills and talent, he was sent to play in what is now called the NBA G League but was then the NBA Developmental League (D-League).

By the fall of 2013, White had been traded to Philadelphia and soon was waived out of the NBA for good. His professional basketball legacy was summed up by the Houston Rockets management as possibly "the worst first-round pick ever."[35] With a little help from the Rockets and the league, White could well have become a very productive player; he became a mental health advocate and, sadly, an NBA pariah instead.

Jonathan Martin (Miami Dolphins)

Like Royce White, college football player Jonathan Martin was a high draft pick in 2012 and an All-American in his sport. Martin, however, came from an educationally and economically privileged background, majoring in classics at Stanford. In this and other ways, he was quite unlike most of the players in the NFL, except for the fact that he was Black.

His bouts with depression and his perceived privilege made him a target for vicious harassment by his teammates with the Miami Dolphins.

At Stanford, he was a well-respected, highly functioning member of the team. Once he arrived in the NFL, his football life changed dramatically.

Martin left the Dolphins in October 2013, early in his second NFL season, alleging he had been the victim of harassment and bullying from his offensive line mates. In particular, he singled out white teammate Richie Incognito, who in 2009 had been voted by his peers as the dirtiest player in football. Incognito had sent Martin emails that were later described as racist and threatened violence against his teammate. Also, Incognito and two other offensive linemen on the Dolphins, who were both Black, repeatedly hazed and bullied Martin. This triggered a depressive episode, which led Martin to leave the team and check himself into a psychiatric ward.[36]

Almost no one associated with the Dolphins or the NFL came to Martin's defense. Instead, criticism of Martin began to mount. Publicly, players were divided, but not in good ways. Some expressed hard-to-believe shock that this sort of bullying could happen in the NFL; others were offended by Martin's lack of courage. Very few showed any empathy at all.

Not a single player publicly supported Martin's decision to take a break from the hostile team environment that had been causing him so much psychic pain. In the NFL and throughout much of the sports media, Martin was widely viewed as weak and having let his teammates down. Dolphins general manager Jeff Ireland expressed the widely held sentiment that Martin should have "punch[ed]" Incognito.[37]

A report commissioned by the NFL, however, documented how Incognito and two teammates, Michael Pouncey and John Jerry, had harassed and bullied Martin. This included making fun of Martin's mental illness and labeling him as gay—which, like being mentally ill, is a status rarely tolerated in NFL locker rooms, serving as shorthand in NFL and other locker rooms for being weak.

Yet, while all three of his tormentors—after relatively short suspensions—continued to have productive NFL careers, Martin's life was permanently derailed by the stigma around his mental health. William Rhoden of the *New York Times* captured the prevailing sentiment, advising Martin to stay away from the game for at least a year "to sort through . . . [the] complex emotional issues that have been aggravated, not eased, by the culture of a brutal sport." Rhoden reiterated the view that Martin should have "retaliate[d]" rather than leaving his team to seek mental health care.[38]

Rhoden and others in the media suggested that Martin should seriously consider never returning to the NFL because it was unlikely the culture would ever change enough to accommodate his emotional needs. Martin signed with the San Francisco 49ers but never started again. In 2015, he left the NFL for good, posting messages on social media that he was clinically depressed and had tried to kill himself on several occasions.

In March 2018, he hit rock bottom after he was arrested and charged with making criminal threats against his NFL tormentors. On Instagram he sent them an image of a shotgun and ammunition, captioned: "When you're a bully victim & a coward, your options are suicide, or revenge." Criminal charges against him were eventually dropped.

Ronda Rousey (Mixed Martial Arts)

At the 2008 Summer Olympics, Ronda Rousey became the first American female to earn a medal in judo when she won bronze. By 2013 she had transitioned to mixed martial arts and found even more success and fame. Rousey became so famous that the Ultimate Fighting Championship (UFC) established a women's division so she could compete. During the next two years, she won her first twelve fights in spectacular fashion. Some in the media crowned her the most dominant athlete in the world. Based on her name recognition as an athlete, she launched a movie career as well, eventually including a starring role in a Peter Berg film opposite Mark Wahlberg.

In 2015, Rousey lost her first fight in an embarrassing knockout to Holly Holm. This sent Rousey into a depression, and she contemplated suicide. But this was not the first time she dealt with mental illness. Her father died by suicide when she was only eight years old, and early in her career, while competing in judo internationally and under constant pressure to make her weight class, she developed a serious eating disorder. She blamed herself for being emotionally incapable of overcoming the weight issue, which, as she revealed later, had produced a pattern of "bingeing and purging."[39]

Much of the sports world still mischaracterized her mental health as being a lack of character. In 2021, famed basketball coach turned sports commentator Larry Brown dismissed Rousey's mental health challenges as nothing more than a failure to deal with losing. He even labeled it "Rousey Disease," then applied his suck-it-up, macho pseudo-psycho-analysis to Naomi Osaka's struggles.[40] Even if fear of losing was an underlying cause of these female athletes' mental health challenges, Brown pontificated that it was obvious both women were dealing poorly with their extreme emotional turmoil and distress.

Michael Phelps (Swimming)

Unlike the experience of many athletes battling mental health demons, Michael Phelps's revelation in 2016 about his depression and anxiety was treated sympathetically in both the media and the swimming community. But his narrative was different and, in important ways, unique. Phelps is the greatest male Olympic swimmer ever, and he was poised to successfully return to the pool in pursuit of even more gold medals for the United States in Rio de Janeiro. He had seemingly overcome his demons. Moreover, he was about to be embraced as the poster athlete for mental health.

Phelps's mental health nadir had occurred two years earlier, a short time after he was arrested in Baltimore for drunk driving. As would happen to Tiger Woods a few years later, Phelps was stopped for excessive speeding—going 84 mph when the speed limit was 45. Both his mother and his coach viewed this incident as either part of a downward spiral or a cry for help. In his own words, Phelps later acknowledged that he had "lived in a bubble for a long time." In the aftermath of his shameful mistake, he did not want "to be alive anymore."[41]

It was not Phelps's first DUI. In 2004, "he was sentenced to probation and to talk to high school students about alcohol awareness."[42] This time, though, the swimmer voluntarily admitted himself to an Arizona treatment facility for more than six weeks and followed up with outpatient therapy.

His reckless behavior and alcohol abuse were apparently symptoms of his mental health disorders. Even as the nation's most recognizable mental health advocate, Phelps works continually on managing his depression and anxiety, even today. For him, it will be a lifelong process as well as an essential part of his future mission in life.

Allison Schmitt (Swimming)

Like Phelps, Allison Schmitt was a champion Olympic swimmer who was overcome by depression and later became a mental health advocate. At the age of eighteen, she won a bronze medal as part of an American relay team in the 2008 Beijing Summer Olympics. Her fame escalated in the London Olympics of 2012, but shortly thereafter, she—and her athletic career—plummeted into the depths of despair.

She won five medals in 2012, three of them gold, to place her in the annals as one of America's greatest swimmers. Inexplicably, this seemingly "upbeat . . . regular girl," who has a twin sister, experienced a severe and persistent case of the post-Olympic blues. Even though she "had great friends, a supportive family, a top-shelf training group," and the "staunch support . . . of Michael Phelps," her depression "just got worse."[43]

Schmitt recovered enough to return to Olympic form, but her love for the sport was never quite the same. At the 2016 Olympics, she was named a team captain and won two medals, gold and silver. In 2021, she won silver and bronze, making her one of the most decorated female swimmers in US history. Yet Schmitt acknowledged how difficult the COVID pandemic had been for her to handle emotionally as an athlete. Now, her main focus is as a mental health advocate and close ally of Michael Phelps.

DeMar DeRozan (Toronto Raptors)

DeMar DeRozan was one of the first of several active NBA stars to publicly acknowledge their mental health challenges after the unsettling stories of Delonte West and Royce White surfaced. The National Basketball Players Association was attempting to bring mental health out of the professional basketball shadows, but as noted earlier, the union's executive director acknowledged, "the devil is in the details."[44]

At the 2018 NBA All-Star Game and celebration, at which DeRozan was going to play, he tweeted, seemingly "out of nowhere": "This depression get the best of me." The message was "jarring" coming from a player who was "unimaginably wealthy, uncommonly famous and [had] at his disposal a virtual army of family, friends and support staff." The response, though, was "a maelstrom of support throughout social media."[45] Too often, social media can make mental health challenges worse, but here it turned out to be uplifting.

Some of DeRozan's angst lay outside of basketball. Gun violence in his home city of Compton, California, had taken the lives of family and friends, and "[t]hat difficult upbringing pushed him deeper into basketball and further away from his reality." Even though the All-Star Game was in Los Angeles, near his boyhood home, DeRozan could not get away from those "dark" feelings. In the words of Lee Michael of the *Washington Post*, DeRozan's revelations were "how the NBA [finally] got serious about mental health."[46]

Kevin Love (Cleveland Cavaliers)

Rightly or wrongly, Kevin Love is credited in many other circles with being the most important NBA player to shine a light on mental health. Shortly before DeMar Rozan's 2018 Twitter revelation, Love gave a moving account of his suffering a severe in-game panic attack. Some in the media cast this in racial terms—the story of a white NBA player receiving more attention than that of the Raptors' Black star—and there was a certain amount of truth to that observation.

At the same time, Love provided an important contribution to increasing "awareness of mental health issues." He was articulate in conveying his message on social media, writing,

> I know I could have really benefited from having someone to talk to over the years. But I didn't share—not to family, not to my best friends, not in public. Today, I've realized I need to change that. I want to share some of my thoughts about my panic attack and what's happened since. If you're suffering in silence like I was, then you know it can feel like nobody really gets it. Partly I want to do it for me, but mostly, I want to

do it because people don't talk about mental health enough. And men and boys are probably the furthest behind.[47]

FROM JIMMY PIERSALL TO NAOMI OSAKA

As these narratives illustrate, much has changed with the way known mental disorders affecting athletes are perceived and dealt with by sports organizations, the media, and fans. Yet so much more still needs to be done to make it safe for athletes to reveal their mental conditions to others in their sport and to the public. Perhaps the best illustration of where we find ourselves today is the mental health struggles of the former number-one-ranked women's tennis player in the world, Naomi Osaka.

The sports world has not come that far from the Piersall days in supporting the relatively small number of athletes who are willing to disclose their mental conditions. Osaka made worldwide headlines after withdrawing from the 2021 French Open. She revealed that she was mentally unfit to assume the press obligations expected (and often mandated) of players. Unlike Phelps, DeRozan, and Love, Osaka received widespread social media criticism and condemnation.

Osaka's mental health challenges were clearly visible for the first time at the 2018 US Open, just after she thrashed overwhelming crowd favorite Serena Williams, 6–2, 6–4. Osaka had scaled the pinnacle of athletic success, becoming arguably the best female tennis player on the planet, trying to represent both her Japanese and Haitian ancestry.

Yet the fans in New York were so obsessed with their desire for Serena to win a match the tennis legend was now incapable of winning, they booed Osaka repeatedly, despite her American upbringing. At the female champions' ceremony at center court, the twenty-year-old Osaka felt no joy. Instead, she broke down in a flood of tears and apologized to the world for having beaten Williams. Her anguish was palpable, as was her emotional fragility.

Although she won three more Grand Slam titles by 2021 and was recognized as the consensus best female player in the world, Osaka acknowledged that she had "suffered long bouts of depression" since that 2018 match. In particular, she described having "huge waves of anxiety" when she faced the media to answer questions at press conferences.

Because of this, she declined to be interviewed at a mandatory press conference at the 2021 French Open.

As happened to Royce White, when Osaka essentially asked for a reasonable modification for her mental disorder—being allowed to skip press conferences—the sports powers that be refused. In this instance, the French Open and other tennis officials insisted that Osaka comply and threatened her with disqualification when she did not. It would have been so easy for everyone involved to create an exception for Osaka based on her tenuous mental state. Instead, the tennis authorities cited a so-called time-honored, male-inspired sports principle that everyone needs to be treated alike no matter what, even though the stars of tennis are routinely granted all sorts of special privileges that lesser players are not.

Osaka refused to place herself in a position that she felt would do her emotional harm, even though she seemed to be a legitimate contender for the French title. In a social media post, she put it this way: "So here in Paris I was already feeling vulnerable and anxious so I thought it was better to exercise self-care and skip the press conferences." Thus, she withdrew from the tournament before playing a single match.

What is good for athletes and their mental health often is at odds with what is viewed as best for the mostly white men who continue to govern these major spectator sports. Stigma, stereotyping, and blatant discrimination remain obstacles for athletes with mental conditions. All Naomi Osaka wanted was to be able to skip press conferences to protect her mental health.

In response, the French Open, most of the media, and the sports establishment reflexively looked at the dispute solely from the point of view of how her request might inconvenience them or complicate their ability to generate more publicity, stories, and revenues. All this greed was couched in sportswashed lingo about treating every athlete the same way.

Yet, since Russia invaded Ukraine, Ukrainian tennis players have not been required to display even the minimum standard of sportsmanship by shaking hands with Russian or Belarusian players after a match. Instead, they have been allowed to ignore their opponents. Furthermore, Belarusan tennis star Aryna Sabalenka was allowed to skip press conferences at the French Open in 2023, citing "her mental health and well-being" because she felt unsafe due to her country's support of Russia's invasion of Ukraine.[48]

Reasonable accommodation and modification are what the ADA has required for more than thirty years. That principle has not been implemented in good faith by most sports enterprises doing business in the United States.

Serena Williams, who has battled her own emotional challenges related to a very difficult pregnancy, may have said it best: "Everyone is different, and everyone handles things differently. You have to let [Osaka] handle it the way she wants, in the best way she thinks she can."[49] That recommendation should apply to every sports enterprise dealing with athletes who have legitimate mental health or emotional well-being issues. Since 2021, Osaka has plummeted in the rankings. Her once stellar career may be in jeopardy. Most recently, she decided to withdraw from the 2023 Australian Open, this time because she was pregnant, which is likely to create additional obstacles for her to scale.

CHAPTER 5

Sports-Related "Yips," Stress, Anxiety, and Depression

ATHLETES WITH SPORTS-RELATED MENTAL DISORDERS OFTEN SEEM TO generate more sympathy and empathy within the sports world—especially among other athletes—than athletes who have mental conditions that anyone might have, but not always.

To some extent, sports-related stress and performance-related anxiety are experienced by almost every elite athlete. This is a major reason why psychologists have more elite athletes than ever as clients, and many therapists specialize in sports psychology. A few star athletes in individual sports, like tennis or golf, even travel with their psychologists in tow. Sometimes elite athletes' mental distress can be overwhelming, threatening their careers and even their lives.

When sadness, stress, and anxiety become extreme, an athlete's ability to perform can be badly compromised, sometimes permanently. Unless the athlete can overcome or control those feelings, at least enough so they can perform at elite levels, sooner or later they will face suspension or expulsion by their teams or their sports, generally without compensation or health-related benefits. This can spiral into a whole host of other problems and complications, including aberrant behaviors.

Manifestations of performance-related depression, stress, and anxiety experienced by athletes, by definition, arise from sources directly related to athletics, such as the extreme distress Naomi Osaka, Ronda Rousey, Royce White, and Ricky Williams (whose story is told later in this chapter) have experienced with respect to press conferences, body image, flying, and social interactions, respectively. Frequently, though, these performance-related concerns are an outgrowth of mental disorders and/or substance abuse issues the athlete first experienced much earlier in life. Jason Duchscherer and Kevin Love, for example, who were already dealing with mental health issues, also both experienced extreme panic attacks related to performing in their sports. (See chapter 4 for their stories.)

Athletes also have gotten into trouble, performance-wise, when they obsessively overtrained, like Olympic swimmer Simone Manuel, or become distressed after failing to meet performance expectations, like tennis superstar Novak Djokovic. And many elite athletes in many different spectator sports have endured some form of what is generally known as the "yips."

This occurs most commonly in sports requiring exceptional touch, hand-eye coordination, or balance in order to excel, such as baseball, golf, basketball, and gymnastics (where yips are called the "twisties"). What were once routine sports maneuvers become nearly impossible for affected athletes to perform consistently without making gross mistakes—or, in gymnastics, as happened to Simone Biles, threatening their safety. This type of routine-specific mental paralysis can last for hours, days, weeks, months, or years and alter, delay, or even end athletic careers. As former Northwestern softball player and sports counselor Eileen Canney Linnehan explained about her yips, hiding from them only worsens the situation: "Deal with it head on."[1]

In sports, perfectionism can propel elite athletes toward great competitive outcomes and/or make them hyperconcerned or depressed about not performing up to the standards imposed by themselves or others. This is part of what is known more generally as the "athletic personality." When it turns extremely negative, though, stress, anxiety, sadness, and self-doubt can skyrocket, producing feelings and behaviors that undermine performance and other aspects of the affected athlete's life.

Quite a few of these athletes, like tennis great Rafael Nadal or golfer Keegan Bradley, deal with this type of mental and emotional challenge by developing athletic-based rituals as part of their preparations before they perform. These rituals may look odd to the casual fan or observer, and even to other athletes, but for many competitors this way of coping seems to allow them to perform at an elite level. However, if an athlete engaged in these types of rituals all the time, on and off the field of play, it probably would be classified as obsessive-compulsive disorder, which should be treated and ameliorated, rather than as an athletic coping mechanism.

In Nadal's case, everything he brings onto the court or is provided to him, such as towels and drinks, must be set out in a way that appears to be always the same. Before he serves, he goes through a series of steps that must be replicated for each serve, often taking too much time off the clock and sometimes resulting in time warnings or even penalty point deductions. Similarly, Djokovic bounces the tennis ball in front of him repeatedly before each of his serves.

Many other prominent athletes, however, have seen their careers tempered, postponed, or derailed by sports-related obsessions, stress, anxiety, and/or overwrought perfectionism. The athletes who appear to have dealt with these sports-related mental health challenges the best are the ones who have been willing to recognize they have a problem and carried out a plan, often with the help of others, to manage the mental distress in both their athletic and personal lives, without paying too much attention to any critical social media noise. Sometimes these athletes confront their yips and other sports-related mental disorders head on; other times they embrace narratives that may not seem to be plausible under closer scrutiny but, in their minds, work well for them.

While many of the telltale symptoms of these sports-related mental manifestations, especially those involving the yips, seem to be similar across all sports, how they present themselves appears to be specific to the sport and individual athlete involved.

PROFESSIONAL BASEBALL (MLB)

Some of the most well-known examples of the yips have occurred in professional baseball, where they involved the seemingly routine maneuver of throwing the ball. It has happened to catchers and infielders other than first basemen, but not outfielders, who, like first basemen, throw relatively rarely in game situations. Pitchers are the most likely candidates for this affliction, in part because the consequences can be so harmful to their baseball careers. For pitchers, throwing is almost everything, both for baseball and softball.

Rick Ankiel (St. Louis Cardinals)

Perhaps the most fascinating story of the yips in baseball belongs to Rick Ankiel, who began his career as a pitcher for the St. Louis Cardinals organization. When the twenty-year-old phenom was called up to the major leagues for the 2000 season, he did not disappoint. He posted an 11–7 record in the regular season with nearly 200 strikeouts and a more-than-respectable 3.50 earned-run average (ERA). The *Sporting News* named him the best rookie pitcher that year.

Ankiel had pitched so well that his manager, Tony La Russa, named him to start Game 1 of the National League Division Series. After shutting out the Atlanta Braves for two innings, Ankiel inexplicably came apart in the third. He threw five consecutive extremely wild pitches and was pulled from the game. In his second start in that series, Ankiel's wildness continued, and he lasted only two-thirds of one inning.

Ankiel had severe control problems the next year as well. In just twenty-four major-league innings, he threw five more wild pitches and walked twenty-five batters. As a result, Ankiel was sent back to the minor leagues, where his pitching control problems escalated, landing him in the elementary Rookie League. There, he began to excel as a designated hitter. In 2002, Ankiel sat out the entire season due to what was officially described as a left elbow sprain. When he returned to the minors in 2003, he posted a disappointing 6.29 ERA in ten starts, then had to undergo Tommy John surgery to repair his ulnar collateral ligament.

Ankiel finally made it back to the majors in September 2004 as a relief pitcher, but he again had an unacceptably high ERA, although his control problems seemed to have been mostly tamed. In March 2005, however, after his wildness returned, Ankiel announced he was going to become an outfielder, and by 2007, he had completed that extraordinary position transition.

In his 2017 memoir, Ankiel maintained that his sudden inability to pitch beginning in the 2000 postseason was due to some "unknown" phenomenon, rather than characterizing his problem as the yips. Whatever was going on in his head, though, he had the wherewithal and support to pivot to a successful baseball career in a different position.

Aaron Barrett (Washington Nationals)

Aaron Barrett, a late round pick in the 2010 MLB Draft, was sent to one of the Nationals' minor-league affiliates to work on his fundamentals and hopefully develop into a starting pitcher in the majors. Like Ankiel, Barrett's control had suddenly disappeared.

As Adam Kilgore chronicled in the *Washington Post*, the prospect "threw nine wild pitches and walked 22 batters in 21 innings." Barrett's pitching coach devised drills in which he had Barrett practice throwing as an infielder. The coach had his pitcher repeatedly "turn[ing] double plays" to get the feel for what it "was like to make a different type of throw without thinking"—and without the anxiety of having to pitch.[2]

To a large extent the plan worked. The Nationals, however, never again felt comfortable with the idea of Barrett as starting pitcher. In that sense, he seemed to be damaged goods in their eyes, so they converted him into a relief pitcher, which, in terms of baseball status at the time, was a significant step down. This appeared to be a front-office decision, based more on the stigma around mental health issues than on common sense: Relief pitching is far more stressful than starting because it requires immediate control of one's pitches in high-pressure situations, often with runners on base.

Despite the added pressure, the conversion worked out well. Barrett became a decent major-league relief pitcher, posting his best season in 2014. In 2016, though, he had Tommy John surgery, and other injury issues followed that curtailed his MLB career.

Unlike most athletes who develop mental health disorders, Barrett speaks about his publicly, wisely embracing transparency. For many people, if they cannot speak about their conditions, it is difficult for them to move on.

Jose Altuve (Houston Astros)

One baseball player who does not want to talk about his bout with something resembling the yips is Houston Astros All-Star and former league MVP second baseman Jose Altuve. Altuve and his team have insisted he never had that condition.[3] Whatever he had, though, it was much like the yips, albeit an abbreviated version.

Beginning in Game 2 of the 2020 American League Championship Series against the Tampa Bay Rays, out of nowhere the superstar was unable to make routine throws any infielder should be able to make without thinking. His two throwing errors proved decisive in his team's one-run loss in that game. In Game 3, with the Astros leading by a run in the sixth inning, Altuve flubbed an almost certain double play when his throw to the shortstop covering second base bounced well short of his teammate's glove. Both runners were safe, rather than being out on what should have been an easy play. The Rays scored five runs to take a 3–0 lead in the series, which they hung on to win in seven games.[4]

There were good reasons to question the media narrative that Altuve had the yips. It was a particularly small sample—two games and only three bad throws—from which to draw such a conclusion. Yet the errant throws all happened at critical times, which inflated their significance. Muddying the matter further, Altuve was a leader on a team that had cheated to beat the Los Angeles Dodgers in the 2017 World Series by stealing their opponent's signs in ways that were clearly prohibited by the MLB. Thus, Altuve, once adored by fans, was probably one of the most hated superstars in baseball. It seemed as if much of the baseball world, rather than being sympathetic to his mental plight, hoped he had a condition that would harm his career as payback for his having benefited from cheating.

This outpouring of bad feelings toward Altuve did not emerge until the beginning of 2020, just after the details of the cheating scandal were first divulged. Not surprisingly, Altuve had one of his worst seasons as a major-league player, which no doubt was due, at least in part, to his being the face of a disgraced team. The psychological pressure on him to do well in the playoffs must have been immense.

His aberrant throws, while falling short of being a serious case of the yips, may well have been the result of emotional turbulence in his life, having gone from fan favorite to arch villain. His throwing problem certainly was shocking for the perennial All-Star and former Gold Glove winner.

PROFESSIONAL GOLF

The list of professional golfing greats—and not so greats—who have been stricken with the yips, or something very close to or even worse than that, is long. Even Tiger Woods, acclaimed as one of the greatest golfers of all time—if not *the* greatest—appeared to be affected by the yips when he went into a slump around 2014. It is a common psychological ailment in golf, more so than in any other sport. This is because the mechanics of golf are all about making repetitive movements routine. Any disruption of that process can make that small golf ball do strange, unintended things.

Furthermore, while in other sports there is often one specific routine that is subject to this type of disruption, in golf it can be any stroke, or every stroke all at once, but especially putting. Putting is key to professional golf success, demanding fine motor skills and touch. "Drive for show and putt for dough," so goes the golf mantra.

In golf, more so than in any other sport, the yips become much more apparent as golfers age, probably due to biochemical changes that occur as people grow older. In professional golf, careers tend to be significantly longer than in other sports; the yips are nevertheless viewed more as an athletic failing even as golfers age. Instead of allowing them to accommodate their putting yips in what seemed to be a reasonable manner, the golfing establishment decided to penalize players for trying to manage their yips, implementing special rules that placed arbitrary burdens on those golfers who had that psychological challenge and anchored their extra-long putters.

For years, many golfers would anchor their putters to their bodies in order to reduce unwanted yips-like movements that might disrupt the direction and speed of their putts. Even though—or perhaps because—the yips appear to be a common part of the aging process for golfers, the Professional Golfers' Association (PGA) Tour in 2016 outlawed the use of that effective anchoring technique, forcing quite a few players to change their putters and putting techniques.

This is perhaps unsurprising since the PGA Tour also refused to allow Casey Martin to use a cart as a reasonable accommodation for his degenerative leg disability, resulting in a landmark Supreme Court decision upholding Martin's right to use a cart. Yet twenty years later, no professional golfer has dared take advantage of that decision. Even the legendary Tiger Woods has been unwilling to ask to use a cart after his leg was badly damaged in a car accident in the twilight of his great career. If he plays on the tour, which is now infrequently, he sucks it up, endures the obvious pain he experiences on each golf course, and performs hero-ically—but relatively poorly compared to his once-unsurpassed greatness.

While there are dozens of stories of professional golfers who have battled anxiety, depression, and/or the yips during their golfing careers, several stand out.

David Duval

In the late 1990s, just as Tiger Woods was becoming the talk of golf as the game's consensus best player, David Duval assumed the role of his chief rival. From 1997 to the beginning of 1999, Duval won eleven of thirty-four tournaments and came close to winning the Masters more than once. He also won the Tour Championship in 1997 and then the Players Championship in 1999. That year, Duval was featured on the cover of *Sports Illustrated* and surpassed Woods as the number-one golfer in the world rankings.

The next year, Duval lost to Woods at the 2000 British Open in a painful-to-watch moment when he took four shots to get out of a bun-ker at St. Andrews. Yet in 2001, at the age of twenty-nine, Duval came back to win the British Open at Royal Lytham and St. Annes for his first major. His career seemed to hold so much promise. Then, suddenly, as Chip Brown wrote for the *Men's Journal* in a retrospective of the once presumed golfing great, "that was it. Slowly and all at once, the way peo-ple lose fortunes or love, he lost his game."[5]

In 2013, James McMahon of *Bleacher Report* ranked the ten worst cases of the yips in golf history. Cautioning that "[o]nly Duval knows whether it was the yips or utter indifference"—or perhaps social anxiety, depression, or a combination of things—McMahon ranked the golfer's case as the very worst, ahead of Tom Watson and Ian Baker-Finch: "[U]nlike many of the game's elite who have struggled with mental collapses . . . , Duval seemed to pretty much check out and move on from the game for several years."[6] Duval never won another PGA tournament and in 2011 lost his golfing privileges on the PGA Tour.

Charlie Beljan

Journeyman golfer Charlie Beljan has won only one PGA tournament. That was back in November 2012 at the Children's Miracle Network Hospitals Classic in Florida, where, according to Karen Crouse of the *New York Times*, Beljan became "the face of anxiety." That experience also made him a minor celebrity.

At the time, the young golfer was struggling to retain his PGA Tour card and avoid being demoted to a much lesser tour. Beljan's wife had just given birth to their first child. This was his last chance to win enough money on the major-league tour to remain eligible the next year. Failing to do so would have meant a huge cut in his potential compensation and endorsements.

During the tournament, he endured a series of extreme panic attacks, which were broadcast on television to millions of people. After the second round, his anxiety became so intense that he was rushed to a nearby hospital, where he was kept overnight to ensure that he had not had a heart attack.[7] Nevertheless, Beljan managed to win the tournament, which set the stage for several different media narratives about his condition.

The first was sportswashed macho athletic propaganda that, through sheer mental toughness, he was able to overcome his mental demons. A second, even harder to believe explanation tied his panic attacks and those of fellow player Bubba Watson to a less stigmatizing physical cause: "poor eating habits." Watson's anxiety symptoms purportedly were due to acid reflux from a diet of fast foods; for Beljan, the problem was not getting enough nourishment.[8]

The far more nuanced and believable explanation was that Beljan had a diagnosable mental disorder all along that had caused bouts of extreme anxiety for years, well before he became a professional. He also exhibited the types of "quirky" obsessive-compulsive routines that sometimes accompany this type of anxiety. In the end, Beljan garnered much praise for abandoning the poor-nutrition excuse and owning his mental health condition in public. He was transformed into an athlete and momentary media celebrity whose openness allowed the public to see him as "a genuine, caring, social person."[9]

Keegan Bradley

Keegan Bradley, the son of a golf pro and nephew of women's all-time great golfer Pat Bradley, has enjoyed a reasonably successful professional golfing career. In 2011, his rookie year on the tour, Bradley won the Byron Nelson and PGA championships. Since then, he has won only three other tournaments. In March 2013, he achieved his highest ranking, reaching number ten in the world; subsequently, his ranking fell below the top fifty.

Throughout his career, Bradley has endured a form of the yips that he describes as "jittery nerves."[10] Trying to manage those nerves has been a struggle. The way he has tried to do it has elicited mean-spirited criticisms. Like Rafael Nadal, Charlie Beljan, and Kevin Na, Bradley has an athletic routine that can be hard to watch and takes time, slowing his play.

Each shot is preceded by odd-looking, twitchy, time-consuming preparations that are difficult to describe in words and do not seem to be uniform. They certainly annoy many of his competitors and are subject to much social media ridicule. Yet, as Bradley told the Golf Channel in 2012 when his slow play was an issue, he had "never once been put on the clock on the PGA Tour."[11]

In his most successful early years, he would anchor his putter to his body, winning his lone major using that soon-to-be-controversial technique, which at that time did not violate any rules of golf. However, it offended some of the game's so-called purists, who happily accept other types of changes in clubs and balls to improve scores and make the golf industry more money. After the PGA and other governing bodies that determine golf's rules proposed to ban anchoring, Bradley was the subject of harassment from fans and members of the media who accused him of cheating, even though the new rule did not take effect until 2016.

Once he changed his putting style to accommodate the anchoring ban, his world ranking began to drop and he found it "hard . . . to remain confident in the face of ballooning scores." His job, he said, was not "to freak out," but to be mentally tough by "enjoy[ing] the challenge of coming back."[12] He seems to have been able to do that. After winning the Zozo Championship in October 2022, he broke into the top thirty and, as of July 2023, had a world ranking of fifteen.

Lexi Thompson

In 2007, at the age of twelve, Lexi Thompson became the female equivalent to a young Tiger Woods: a golfing phenom who also was a standard bearer for her race. The difference was that in women's golf at that time, there were only a few white Americans winning championships. Elite Asian female golfers had become dominant, to the chagrin of US corporate sponsors and the Ladies Professional Golf Association (LPGA).

In June 2010, Thompson turned professional. The next year, at age sixteen, she became the youngest female to win an LPGA Tour event. She followed that up by becoming the second-youngest player to win a Ladies European Tour championship. Then, in 2014, the nineteen-year-old Thompson won the Kraft Nabisco Championship, making her the second-youngest golfer ever to win an LPGA major.

Despite the great start to her career, she has never come close to achieving the Tiger Woods–like success expected of her. Thompson has won regular LPGA Tour events, but no more majors, as of 2023. In several of the Grand Slams, she has performed erratically, in painful ways that have extinguished golden opportunities for her to win more major championships.

At the 2017 ANA Inspiration—the site of her only major win, in 2014—Thompson appeared to be winning the tournament easily, but she made an unforgivable mental error for a professional. During the third round, while on the 17th green, she marked her ball incorrectly. While no one on-site objected, a television viewer called in her rule violation.

Later that day, officials assessed Thompson a four-stroke penalty, two for replacing the ball improperly and two for having signed a scorecard that was now incorrect. She still made a playoff but lost to Ryu So-yeon.

At the end of 2017, Thompson missed a "gimme" two-foot putt that cost her a victory at the season-ending CME Group Tour Championship. At the Evian Championship, another major, in September 2018, she burst into tears after making a mess of a chip shot on the final hole to miss the cut by one stroke. That flub was so bad she apparently missed most of the ball, which seemed to go nowhere. A few weeks earlier, Thompson had skipped the Women's British Open, saying she needed a mental break "while figuring myself out."

Her mental demons manifested themselves once again at the US Women's Open in June 2021. With a four-stroke advantage with only eight more holes to play in the final round, she had what was prematurely described as an "insurmountable lead." Yet she would "make three bogeys and one double on her way to a [nine-hole] 41," failing to even make a playoff.[13] Brandel Chamblee, an analyst at the Golf Channel, explained why he thought Thompson should not "have felt comfortable" with any lead, given her nervous putting. He demonstrated how Thompson had missed hitting the center of her putter "by a half an inch," then added, "I have never . . . seen a professional golfer miss the center of the putter by a wider margin than that."[14]

History repeated itself at the 2022 Women's PGA Championship. After having not won a major for eight years and not winning a single LGPA Tour event in her last fifty tries, Thompson had put herself in position to win with a torrid third round. With only three holes to play, she had a two-stroke advantage. Like so many times before, though, her short game betrayed her under the pressure of the moment.

Earlier, at the 14th hole, Thompson had missed a gimme two-foot par putt that would have given her a three-stroke lead. She recovered a stroke by birdieing 15. Then, at 16, she fell apart again, losing four strokes on that one hole alone with consecutive chipping and putting mistakes. She was now only tied for the lead. When she missed a ten-foot birdie at 18, it left her in a tie for second.

After her frustrating round, an emotionally distraught Thompson declined to attend a press interview. Like Naomi Osaka, she was criticized for protecting her mental health. Making matters worse, Thompson was fined for slow play. What will happen from here for this great and still young talent is hard to predict.

It will not be easy for Thompson to achieve emotional stability playing golf, given how much public attention her previous collapses have garnered. To be successful, she will have to be able to drown out the critical noise and harness her prodigious golfing skills. As of July 2023, she is ranked eighteen in the world.

PROFESSIONAL BASKETBALL (NBA)

Markelle Fultz (Philadelphia 76ers)

While rumors had already surfaced that the Indiana Pacers' Roy Hibbert was experiencing the yips shooting the basketball, the most prominent recent example of a player with shooting problems related to suspected psychological issues involved Markelle Fultz of the Philadelphia 76ers, the number-one pick in the 2017 NBA Draft. Fultz was seen as a player who would soon develop into a star point guard and quite possibly a superstar in the pros. All aspects of the game, especially scoring, seemed to come easily to the college basketball marvel. His shooting accuracy was one of his most valued skills, including from the highly effective three-point range.

During the summer preseason, though, his ability to shoot the basketball with a professional level of proficiency—much less like a star offensive player in the making—suddenly vanished. His lack of accuracy became such a problem that the Sixers no longer used him in games. While there was no official confirmation that Fultz had the yips or any other mental problem that prevented him from shooting accurately, there were plenty of rumors, suggestive media stories, and apparent signs that he was dealing with a mental disturbance that was being hidden from public view. In a February 2018 *Philadelphia Inquirer* story about Fultz, broadcaster Mark Jones described a preproduction meeting with Sixers head coach Brett Brown in which the coach stated that Fultz's problem was due to "psychosomatic effects with his shoulder."[15]

Officially, however, the team continued to attribute Fultz's shooting distress to a physical cause. The *New York Times* reported that the team contended Fultz had what was being described as a "scapular imbalance" from a shoulder injury that summer. Yet his personal trainer dismissed that explanation as untrue.[16]

For the longest time there was no significant improvement in his shooting, even though his reported injury had more than enough time to heal. After watching Fultz, former NBA coach Jeff Van Gundy remarked, during a nationally televised game, "That's a bad-looking shot right there . . . that does not look fluid at all." Fultz's demeanor as he sat in street clothes during games was concerning. He reportedly lacked the ability to express his emotions and kept his distance from the team. Kurt Streeter of the *New York Times* reported that "he is like a ghost. He is there, but not there, especially when it counts."[17]

After all the media attention on Fultz's not playing, the team suddenly returned him to the lineup as a reserve, again without any explanation. Sixers management reportedly prohibited Fultz from speaking about his issues with reporters. It appeared to be the type of secrecy and deception that typically characterizes mental health problems in spectator sports.

Not surprisingly, the team clung to its official narrative. Many months later, Fultz's ongoing problem was characterized as a nerve disorder "between the neck and shoulder resulting in abnormal functional movement."[18] This ignored the other indications that something psychological was going on, which even his coach had described as "psychosomatic." Whatever the problem was, his shooting woes continued for several more years through until the 2021–2022 season. The next season, though, his scoring improved significantly, along with his overall performance.

Ben Simmons (Philadelphia 76ers)
Much like Fultz, Ben Simmons was a number-one overall draft pick for the Philadelphia 76ers. Despite being 6-foot-11, the young Australian American had been a first-team All-American guard at Louisiana State

University (LSU) in 2016 because he had unique guard skills. Simmons was viewed as having extraordinary playmaking skills for an athlete his size, who looked like he could also excel at other positions in the NBA, including power forward.

His first pro year, 2016–2017, was lost to a serious injury to his right foot. In 2017–2018 he was NBA Rookie of the Year, and by 2019–2020 had become an All-NBA and All-Defensive player with a possible Hall of Fame career ahead of him. Instead, Simmons morphed into a media and fan enigma whose professional status was clearly in jeopardy.

The turning point occurred during the 2020–2021 COVID-influenced NBA playoffs, when he suddenly experienced the yips. Simmons, who had a regular-season percentage from the field that was way above average, lost his ability to shoot. According to ESPN, in "five out of the seven games" he played against the Atlanta Hawks in the second round, which the 76ers lost, Simmons "fail[ed] to attempt a single shot in the fourth quarter." His free-throw shooting was even worse and a bigger liability to his team. In those two series, Simmons set a record for free-throw futility in the playoffs "for a player with at least 70 attempts."[19] He made only about one-third of them after shooting over 60 percent during the season.

Philadelphia fans were merciless in spewing their venom at Simmons, whom they blamed for the team's early departure from the playoffs. For decades the city has been known for its loyal—but particularly nasty—sports fans. They have a well-deserved reputation for never letting up on a player once they've been convinced he is a quitter.

A sense of that fan sentiment was captured by NBA legend and commentator Shaquille O'Neal, who remarked, "When you see an athlete like Ben, who is a phenomenal athlete . . . break down in the playoffs, as athletes we go straight to, 'he's not strong enough mentally.'" Shaq then added, for emphasis, "There is a difference between mental health and mental fortitude."[20]

Simmons apparently determined that he would never again play for Philadelphia and subject himself to the added mental torment of being verbally abused by the team's fans and the local media. He demanded a trade, and when that did not come about for a variety of basketball-related reasons, he sat out most of the 2021–2022 season, "cit[ing] mental health concerns." Much like Naomi Osaka and Simone Biles, Simmons said protecting his well-being was more important to him than continuing to perform as an athlete.[21]

Unlike a few other athletes, including a number of NBA players, who had recently garnered considerably sympathy when they acknowledged their mental health struggles, Simmons became embroiled in a media-led barrage, mostly in Philadelphia, challenging the authenticity of his narrative. Simmons, along with his agent, was accused of using his mental health as "a loophole so he could still earn money while hanging tight for a ticket out of town." Louisa Thomas wrote in the *New Yorker* that "it is difficult to express skepticism without reinforcing the old stigma."[22] Stated another way: "You don't get to pick and choose which athletes you support. Criticism of one casts doubt on everyone struggling and builds upon the flawed belief that athletes must be 'mentally tough.'"[23]

Even in the supposedly more enlightened NBA, using mental health rather than physical injury to trigger contract protections requiring teams to pay athletes their full salary while they recover can be subject to speculative disbelief and scrutiny, even without hard evidence that their purported mental health issue is bogus. The 76ers refused to pay Simmons 25 percent of his contract and repeatedly fined him on top of that.

In February 2022, Simmons finally got his wish and became the centerpiece of a blockbuster trade between the 76ers and the Brooklyn Nets. After the trade, citing psychosomatic effects of the stress and anxiety surrounding his inability to shoot, which he said inflamed an ongoing back injury, Simmons was unable to play for the rest of the regular season and into the playoffs, where they were ousted by the Boston Celtics in the first round.

For many in the media, his alleged bout with a mental health problem was more circumstantial evidence to believe Simmons had been faking it all along—until Nets head coach Steve Nash and Simmons's superstar teammates Kevin Durant and Kyrie Irving publicly supported his decision not to play. They appeared to be thinking about both Simmons's welfare and the huge upside for the Nets if the supremely talented player could manage his lingering performance anxiety issues going forward. He continued to make progress, but well into the 2022–2023 season he remained a reserve with decreasing minutes.

OLYMPIC SPORTS

At the 2021 Tokyo Summer Olympics, the American sports world became better acquainted with two different psychological challenges faced by elite athletes. The first was overtraining syndrome, which also has the more common and stigmatizing term "burnout"; the other was the twisties.

Simone Manuel (Swimming)

At the 2016 Summer Olympics in Rio, Simone Manuel became the first African American woman to win a swimming gold medal; she followed that up with another gold and two silver medals. Thus, the expectations both from herself and the sports world were high when she began preparing for the 2020 Tokyo Olympics, which were postponed until 2021 due to COVID. That postponement meant Manuel had to try to attain peak performance levels twice. Early in 2021, she began experiencing symptoms of overtraining syndrome, or burnout.

This condition has both physical and mental components. The pressure to perform, losing interest in or becoming apathetic about training, an obsessive push to ignore the symptoms, and depression and anxiety surrounding obvious decreases in performance are all psychologically based. Yet there can be physical symptoms as well, including weight loss, fatigue, prolonged recovery times, and decreased athletic performance.

While rest for the mind and body—meaning not training or performing—is the most often prescribed treatment, Manuel, like most elite athletes, was intent on pushing through no matter what. "I would rather fail because I did everything I could to be successful but fell short," Simone said, "than to fail because I didn't try at all."[24] And of course, as it did for most other Olympic athletes, the COVID pandemic seriously disrupted her carefully laid-out training preparations.

At the US Olympic trials, Manuel's results were mixed but disappointing overall, given her original expectations. In the event she was best known for, the 100-meter freestyle, she failed to even make the team. In the 50-meter freestyle, though, she came in first. Manuel made the team and was selected co-captain by her teammates. Manuel's victory also qualified her for a possible role in various relay races.

Her doctor, an orthopedic specialist at the University of Texas, was cautious after the trials, warning that Manuel had "a long way to go" to become healthy again. She needed "rest. . . . [T]hat will be important for her."[25] In other words, she was not healthy and mentally fit going into the Olympics.

Manuel appeared to accept that reality when she told reporters before the games began that she was suffering from overtraining syndrome. She acknowledged at a press conference that this condition "was definitely my biggest fight. . . . I think it was something that I didn't quite notice until my body like completely crashed." She avoided the term "burnout," which has obvious stigmatizing mental health associations. Overtraining implies doing too much physical training, while burnout implies being mentally compromised—or, in athlete lingo, not mentally tough enough.

At the Tokyo Olympics, Manuel came in 11th in her individual race and earned a bronze medal in a relay in which she and her American teammates had been expected to do better. Afterward, she criticized the media for pressing to interview "athletes right after a disappointing performance before they have any time to process anything,"[26] but she appeared to be speaking about herself.

Simone Biles (Gymnastics)

Going into the Tokyo Olympics, Simone Biles, the greatest female gymnast of all time, was expected to collect as many as six gold medals for herself and the United States. Such optimism was minimized by two major emotional disruptors in her preparations: (1) her revelation that she was one of the female gymnasts who had been sexually abused by USA Gymnastics physician Larry Nassar (see chapter 9), then having to relive those awful events when she told and retold her story many times; and (2) the postponement of the Tokyo Olympics for a year because of the COVID pandemic.

The presumption always seems to be that great athletes will be able to overcome such distractions because mental toughness is an important reason why they are great. That tautology, of course, is flawed, even for legendary superstar athletes. Biles suddenly acquired what most sports call the "yips" but gymnasts refer to as the "twisties." This version of the yips involves a lack of connection between mind and body, which causes gymnasts to lose track of where they are in space when they are doing the airborne acrobatics that are essential to their routines.

Even though the condition is apparently something most elite gymnasts experience at some point in their careers, it can be extremely risky because the gymnastic skills required to be the best are inherently dangerous. Safety is largely based on being able to fully control one's body in space. When that control dissipates or disappears, so does safety, even though normally there is plenty of padding to cushion most falls.

In the first women's gymnastics competition, the all-around team event—where the United States was heavily favored, in large part due to Biles's presumed superiority to every other gymnast in the world—she messed up her first vault attempt. Instead of doing two and a half twists, she lost her place in space and could only manage to execute one and a half. She knew right away that something was terribly wrong and immediately withdrew from the rest of that team event.

The next day she carefully attributed her shocking exit to "having a little bit of the twisties."[27] The twisties quickly became a hot media topic nationwide, and Biles withdrew from her next four individual Olympic events: the all-around, floor exercise, vault, and asymmetric bars.

She acknowledged that at certain points in her career she had gotten the twisties in the "floor and vault, the scariest two [events]. But this time it's literally on every event, which sucks really bad."[28] She did return at the end of the gymnastics competition and won bronze on the less acrobatic beam, but that was a far cry from the six gold medals anticipated for her.

Much of the social media reaction "condemned her action [in withdrawing], suggesting she quit on the biggest sporting stage," even though many others were "supporting Biles."[29] The accusation was even made that she had sabotaged her team by not being willing to compete.

Later, in an interview on *Today*, she thoughtfully explained that such criticism mischaracterized her struggles by implying "that I was at no risk, and mental health isn't a serious issue."[30] After a two-year hiatus from competing in gymnastics, Biles competed in the 2023 US Classic in August, placing first in the uneven bars and balance beam and winning all-around gold.

NOVAK DJOKOVIC AND SPORTS MYTHS OF MENTAL TOUGHNESS

Sports-related yips, stress, anxiety, and sometimes depression are common feelings for elite athletes. Managing pressure from those mind-body reactions, so goes the sports propaganda, is what champions do, and there is a certain amount of truth to that. Yet many elite athletes succumb to, or are humbled by, these mental challenges at some points in their careers. It is not a sign of weakness, but rather of being human.

Mental health is an essential ingredient to long-term athletic success. When the mind falters, athletes cannot physically perform at their best. In turn, failing to perform up to expectations can be depressing. The paradox is that being an elite athlete is inherently stressful and anxiety inducing, but admitting to having, and getting help to treat, various mental or emotional conditions collides with the mental-toughness scenario that sports cultures try to cultivate and glorify.

All-time tennis great Novak Djokovic subscribes to and promotes athletic mental toughness, except when he is emotionally incapable of doing so; then, convulsive tears of relief or depression can appear to overwhelm him. As a former Association of Tennis Professionals (ATP) president and a gifted speaker, his words carry a great deal of weight in the tennis world and throughout the sports world. Thus, when he spoke about players needing to learn how to manage the pressure of playing tennis professionally in the wake of Naomi Osaka's attempt to protect her mental health by not enduring what she described as mentally damaging press conferences (see chapter 4), it sent a message.

As a player who at the time had already won twenty majors, Djokovic promoted the impression that his ability to manage mental pressure was a key to his success. Professional athletes, Djokovic said, need to "start learning how to deal with pressure" on and off the court.

"Without pressure there is no professional sport."[31] Unfortunately, that sportswashed bromide placing the ultimate responsibility on athletes to deal with that pressure all by themselves can be athletically counterproductive and mentally unhealthy.

In Djokovic's case, this was somewhat hypocritical, given how his tennis life has unfolded. If he had been willing to allow others to help him conquer his mental demons, there is good reason to believe he would have built an insurmountable Grand Slam victories lead over Rafael Nadal and cemented his legacy as the best tennis player ever years ago.

There have been two critical periods in Djokovic's tennis life when everything seemed to be going his way and then things suddenly fell apart because he seemed to self-destruct emotionally. In the process, he has frittered away multiple opportunities to win the Grand Slams that define tennis greatness. In some ways, Djokovic has proved to be his own worst enemy. His all-consuming mental lapses paired with his obsessive will to win appear to be Djokovic's version of the yips.

Even compared to Roger Federer and Nadal, both of whom are supreme competitors, Djokovic is in a class by himself when it comes to bringing every advantage he can onto the tennis court, except when he has these lapses. Like Serena Williams during her stellar career in the women's game, Djokovic, despite his bravado, has not always been able to constructively or rationally deal with the mental pressure, even though he is arguably the best tennis player ever.

Federer and Nadal found ways to cope. As a young man, Federer let his temper frequently burst out of control à la John McEnroe. Federer's father interceded by threatening to stop him from playing if he did not change his behavior. Federer evolved into a perfect gentleman on and off the court, at least where the public can see, beloved by corporate sponsors and millions of fans around the world.

Nadal has been obsessed with winning as well. He channels his compulsions into ritualistic, repetitive behaviors that look a bit strange on the court. Those behaviors do little harm except to delay his matches and occasionally cause him to receive time warnings—not lose the opportunity for multiple Grand Slam victories.

Djokovic, except for bouncing the tennis ball inccesantly before serving, appears to hold it all in, until, out of the blue, he reacts in counterproductive ways, sometimes for months at a time. In 2017, at the height of
his career after having won four Grand Slams in a row, his game and his
focus mysteriously dissipated. Publicly, his distress was tied to a reported
elbow issue, which, for a long time, he tried to treat with various natural
remedies before eventually agreeing to have the surgery he needed.

Much more than just that appeared to be going on, however. There
were rumors of marital discord. Furthermore, Djokovic inexplicably split
up with his longtime training team. He retained Andre Agassi, who later
admitted that during this period he could not motivate Djokovic to play
inspired tennis. Publicly, Djokovic attributed his malaise to unidentified
personal problems.

In February 2018, Djokovic finally had elbow surgery. Afterward he
said he "cried for two or three days. . . . I felt like I had failed myself." He
then added, "I am not a fan of surgeries or medications. . . . I believe that
our bodies are self-healing mechanisms,"[32] foreshadowing his steadfast
refusal to be vaccinated for COVID (see chapter 6).

Midway through 2018, Djokovic returned to topflight form after
reuniting with his training team. He won Wimbledon and then the US
Open. By postponing his surgery for so long, however, he had lost the
opportunity to compete at or near his best in as many as six straight
majors at a time when he was clearly the best in the world.

In 2020, after having won the Australian Open, Djokovic went into
the US Open as a clear favorite. Wimbledon had been canceled due to
the pandemic, and the French Open had been rescheduled for later that
fall. In a fourth-round US Open match, Djokovic became so frustrated
with himself after losing a point that he lost mental focus for an instant,
impulsively striking the ball, apparently in no specific direction. When it
hit a lineswoman, he was defaulted for acting recklessly, losing another
opportunity for a Grand Slam he was expected to win.

The following year, he won the first three Grand Slams and headed
to the US Open, once again the odds-on favorite. In the finals, the pressure proved too much, and Djokovic lost easily to Daniel Medvedev in
straight sets. During the match, in the concluding third set, he could be

seen crying in his towel, probably thinking he was about to lose and there was nothing he could do to change that outcome. His emotional capitulation was remarkable for an athlete who had a well-deserved reputation for winning five-set matches in Grand Slams by seemingly never giving up. This time, though, he appeared to give up completely.

Djokovic's most recent bout of mental self-destruction—refusing to be vaccinated for COVID—began well before the 2022 Australian Open. His public views about vaccination had been placed in context by his extreme reluctance to undergo elbow surgery in 2017, along with his tears of failure for having done so. In April 2020, Djokovic confirmed on Facebook that he was deeply troubled about what the vaccines might do to his superlative tennis fitness (see chapter 6). His extreme fear of necessary medical procedures appears to be irrational, since both his surgery delay and vaccine refusal prevented him from winning more Grand Slams and Masters 1000 tournaments, which has been his main objective in keeping his body supremely fit for as long as possible.

Despite many of his public statements about mental toughness, on various occasions Djokovic, like many elite athletes, has not managed his mental health very well or wisely. Being mentally tough is not the same thing as being mentally healthy. So much more support and planning are necessary to overcome mental conditions beyond just trying to gut it out.

Like so many elite athletes, Djokovic continues to eschew psychological help, instead turning to unproven alternative remedies that conform to his self-healing rituals. For a man who is as intelligent as he appears to be, this side of him is confounding. Yet despite everything, he won his twenty-third Grand Slam at the 2023 French Open and is likely poised—unless something else unexpected intervenes—to continue to surpass Nadal, who has twenty-two, and Federer, who has twenty-one.

Unfortunately, for elite athletes like Djokovic, spectator sports incubate various mental conditions. The failure to deal with mental disorders in effective ways can have much worse, more lasting, and even life-threatening consequences that go well beyond interfering with an athlete's sports legacy.

Sports-related stress, anxiety, and depression, in addition to the yips, are all things athletes at this level of competition must deal with and try to manage. When these mental health challenges become severe, seeking professional help is necessary and well advised. Too frequently such advice is not followed.

Evolving COVID Risks

Known, Suspected, and Unknown

As of July 2023, major American and international spectator sports have so far survived COVID, but not without complications, competitive disruption, bad behavior, long-term unknowns, and much uncertainty. It is likely that this highly infectious disease will be with us for a long time, in evolving forms with an array of harmful effects, not all of which are yet understood. Many Americans, including those in the sports world, seem resistant to the idea of doing all that is reasonably necessary to contain the disease and protect public health and the economy, favoring individual freedom over the common good—and common sense.

There is little doubt that domestic and international spectator sports competitions have been interrupted, suspended, canceled, and had a number of elite athletes missing at various times since the COVID pandemic began. In addition, there has been a certain amount of chaos as athletes and coaches have come down with the disease, refused to be vaccinated, or lied about their vaccination status. Whatever mechanisms have been in place to protect the health and welfare of athletes—as flawed as many of them were—too often even those protections have not been followed. There also have been local, state, and national jurisdictional disputes about which public health protocols and mandates should be obeyed and enforced.

No major spectator sport has escaped COVID-related problems, which also have had substantial economic consequences. These sports and their broadcast partners have conspired to try to project a narrative that these athletic competitions and the preparations by athletes and coaches to compete at elite levels have not been negatively affected. Those rosy sentiments are another form of sportswashing.

COVID and its variants changed spectator and other organized sports and may do so in the future should other pandemics arise. Also, there are now a whole new set of short-term and longer-term COVID health risks for a vast majority of athletes. What those risks are or may become is evolving along with the science.

Given the absence of herd immunity, domestically and globally, together with the reluctance of our most popular spectator sports to mandate vaccines, it appears more than likely that most elite athletes will have COVID at least once, and perhaps several times, during their careers, especially since public health protocols have been made less restrictive in all major American spectator sports and local jurisdictions across the United States. One foreign public health policy gap impeding the spread of the virus in several sports, but also creating some chaos, has been the stricter COVID protection requirements for athletes in Canada as compared to the United States.

What these COVID developments mean in terms of athletes' health, mental health, and emotional well-being is difficult to gauge because the likely effects—especially long term—of being infected are still being studied. Thus, exactly what those risks will turn out to be for elite athletes is mostly speculative, little known, or unknown. Nonetheless, the dearth of solid information should be concerning to athletes.

The Centers for Disease Control and Prevention and the World Health Organization both describe the long-term effects of the disease as including not only fatigue, shortness of breath, and cardiovascular problems, but also "cognitive dysfunction, brain fog, pain, . . . depression, anxiety, . . . and sleep disturbances."[1] A study published in the December 2022 issue of *Nature* warns that the virus can travel to, and wreak havoc with, any part of the human body, including the brain.[2] Millions of people are at risk for long-term effects of COVID.

For their part, major sports organizations have thus far shown little interest in finding out what the specific long-term risks are or might be for their athletes. The situation is alarmingly reminiscent of organizations' treatment of brain damage to elite athletes participating in contact and other risky sports. For nearly fifty years, the risks from CTE, other types of brain damage, and related mental disorders were kept in the shadows and often covered up by many sports organizations, especially in football and hockey, where such mental impairments have turned out to be rampant. In boxing, they were simply ignored or accepted as a cost of doing business (see chapter 7).

In recent times, domestic and international sports organizations have been able to hide behind a ready-made excuse that—much like testing athletes for performance-enhancing substances—investigating the health effects of COVID on athletes has been made far more difficult due to the disruptions in sports caused by the pandemic. Unfortunately, the most inscrutable COVID risks—and the ones most likely to be obscured—involve those to athletes' mental health, their emotional well-being, and their brains. So much more still needs to be learned, and comprehensive studies are only now just emerging. Except for a minimal contribution by the NCAA, major sports enterprises have done precious little to support additional studies focusing on the mental health of their athletes, much less those related to COVID risks.

This deficit in organizational concern and knowledge began with mental health risks related to the lockdowns and public health protocols that suspended or intermittently interrupted athletes' training schedules and sports events. It appears very likely, based on several smaller studies and the anecdotal evidence from athletes themselves, that lockdowns produced a much higher incidence of depression, anxiety, and other mental disorders when athletes were isolated from their teams, coaches, and training routines. In addition, elite athletes, like everyone else, had to deal with the fear of contracting the virus and passing it on to loved ones or teammates. In team sports, especially, these risks can be accelerated, though, because of the close proximity of athletes and coaches to each other and the aggressive or violent contact that certain sports require and promote.

Most of these mental health challenges have been ameliorated since vaccines have become available and lockdowns suspended. The remaining public health challenges appear to focus on no more than 5 percent of elite athletes: those who, like Kyrie Irving, Aaron Rodgers, and Novak Djokovic, have refused to be vaccinated because they are caught up in conspiracy theories, the web of vaccination rules that vary by jurisdiction, or (in Djokovic's case) their own skewed version of what is best for their fitness (see chapter 5).

Compared to the general population, a 95 percent vaccination rate seems impressive. Yet how many of us would feel comfortable attending hours upon hours of close-contact events, many inside, when we knew as many as 5 percent of the attendees were refusing vaccinations, and often all or most other reasonable safety measures, for a highly infectious disease?

The problem now, though, are the mental health, emotional well-being, and brain health risks—short and long term—posed to the overwhelmingly high percentage of elite athletes who have or will contract the virus. There are good reasons for elevated concern, beyond the fact that so little is known and too many athletes are either refusing to be vaccinated, lying about their vaccination status, or, more commonly, flouting commonsense public health measures.

To begin with, even before COVID, elite athletes appear to have been at greater risk than the general public for mental disorders (see chapters 4, 5, 7, and 8). Preliminary studies indicate that the mental health risks from COVID seem to increase for certain more susceptible individuals with preexisting mental conditions, which would seem to include many athletes.

Second, elite athletes who contract COVID and experience long-term impairments, which limit and diminish their ability to perform athletically as they once did, are at much greater risk for anxiety, depression, and substance abuse problems—problems they are already at a higher risk for due to various sports-related factors.

One physician in the United Kingdom concluded, based on clinical data he assembled working with the English Institute of Sport, that the idea that superior fitness will overcome long-term COVID symptoms appears to be misleading at best. He wrote in March 2022 that "[a]thletes in their prime and considered to be at their peak competitive performance struggled to return to their pre-existing fitness levels, several weeks after developing COVID-19 infection."[3]

A prime example of this is Boston Celtics superstar Jayson Tatum, who had physically and emotionally incapacitating symptoms for weeks from his first bout with COVID in the spring of 2021. He did not publicly acknowledge his difficulties until his second bout with the virus at the beginning of 2022. Once fully recovered, he was a first-string All-Star and candidate for league MVP in 2022–2023.

Third, elite athletes and major American spectator sports continue to stigmatize mental health and emotional well-being concerns, despite some incremental gains in acknowledging and treating mental conditions. With COVID-related mental health symptoms, which are not nearly as well understood or as readily apparent as most of the physical symptoms appear to be, the inclination to stigmatize such conditions is likely to be more pronounced, as has been the pattern with a wide variety of other sports-related emotional well-being concerns. Even having to acknowledge having long-term COVID symptoms can be stigmatizing.

Fourth, in the past, sports organizations have proved to be reluctant or unwilling to do all they can to protect the athletes under their umbrellas if doing so threatens a decline in profit.[4] Too often, these enterprises have minimized the risks, covered up key information about athletes being affected, and failed to take actions to properly help those athletes with respect to their mental health care and treatment needs.

Finally, COVID remains an enigma in the sense that it is evolving and quickly changing as new variants arise. This makes research more difficult and scientific and medical conclusions less reliable. As of July 2023, most studies have been relatively small in scope and limited to specific time frames involving specific variants.

THE EARLY DAYS OF THE PANDEMIC

During the first year of the pandemic, before a vaccine was commercially available, spectator sports were forced to halt their competitions and organized training sessions for months. Those that resumed later in 2020 did so in highly insulated environments with few or no fans and different rules and/or competitive matchups than in normal times. Team sports created bubbles around the areas in which games would be played, then tried to isolate players and coaches from other people, including fans, who might be carrying the virus. The NBA played all its games under one bubble. By and large, those bubbles produced reasonably good results in controlling the spread of the virus as compared to the rest of the United States. Yet there still were well-publicized disruptions and instances of reckless behavior.

In one notable example, after the Los Angeles Dodgers won the 2020 World Series, a maskless Justin Turner celebrated with his teammates and coaches—even though just hours earlier he had tested positive for COVID-19 and been told to isolate. Turner's thoughtless act of bravado was followed a few days later by exuberant Notre Dame fans rushing the field to celebrate their team's dramatic victory over the number-one ranked Clemson Tigers.

The circumstances of the game between Clemson and Notre Dame in South Bend at the beginning of the COVID-affected 2020 season would be repeated elsewhere throughout that college football season, a time before vaccines were available. Notre Dame president Reverend John I. Jenkins—who just days earlier had been seen at a White House superspreader event without a mask—allowed more than eleven thousand fans to sit in the stands, with no crowd control mechanisms in place. When the game was over, hundreds upon hundreds of jubilant fans, mostly students, crowded onto the field with little thought about the virus, physical distancing, or mask wearing.

Clemson quarterback Trevor Lawrence—by consensus the most valuable college football player going into that season—did not play in the game because he was in quarantine after having tested positive for the virus the week before. Hundreds of other college football players, coaches, and staff throughout the country were likewise sidelined due to positive test results. The epicenter of the virus outbreaks in college sports, though, appears to have been in the football-mad Southeastern Conference (SEC), which, beginning in July, experienced widespread football-related COVID-19 outbreaks, resulting in delays and postponements.

Major college football games scheduled for the weekend of November 14, for instance, had more than a dozen disruptions. In the SEC alone, this included postponements of contests between number-one Alabama and the previous year's number-one LSU, along with the games between Texas A&M and Tennessee, Georgia and Missouri, and Auburn and Mississippi State. Outside the SEC, contests involving Ohio State and Maryland, Air Force and Wyoming, Memphis and Navy, Pittsburgh and Georgia, Arizona State and California, Louisiana Tech and Rice, and UL Monroe and Arkansas State were all either canceled or postponed. The following week, even more scheduled superconference games had to be postponed or canceled.

While the NFL's coronavirus protocols were better than those in college football, things did not go smoothly there, either. The league had no set policy regarding how many fans were to be permitted to attend NFL games or how to calculate what appeared to be a safe number. Instead, each team was free to determine its own attendance policy, based in part on advice from local health officials, within the constraints of various local health requirements. Too often, though, what was deemed safe had more to do with economics and politics than science or medicine.

During the regular season, only thirteen of the thirty-two NFL teams allowed fans to attend games, and no stadium exceeded 25 percent capacity. Nevertheless, too many individuals associated with these football teams continued to ignore the health protocols the league tried, with very limited monitoring and enforcement, to implement. According to the Johns Hopkins Coronavirus Resource Center, "At the end of the regular season, 961 players and 803 personnel had confirmed positive cases at one time. No single team made it through the season unscathed." The Raiders and Steelers were penalized for violating the league's COVID protocols.[5] And this was before the playoffs began.

The NFL, with "vigilance and sacrifices," managed to quell any substantial increase in the number of new cases. The next year, however, when many of the protections were dispensed with, the number of cases began increasing again. By mid-December 2021, *USA Today* reported that COVID had "sidelined more than 60 players and several coaches over a three-day span."[6]

Even though Major League Baseball decided not to use an NBA-like bubble, it had a relatively successful summer and fall in terms of player and team personnel health after prohibiting fans from attending regular season games and limiting the number of fans allowed at the two designated stadium sites for the playoffs. According to Reuters, MLB had only ninety-one positive tests for the majority of the 2020 season and no more for the final two months of that season.[7] Even more impressively, that included no positive tests during the playoffs, until the last game of the World Series, when Turner tested positive but celebrated with his team after having been pulled from the game that clinched the championship for the Dodgers.[8]

Subsequently, though, an in-depth 2022 study published in the *Athletic* found that of the "71 hitters and 61 pitchers who were confirmed to have had COVID" during the 2021 season, there had been a significant drop in their on-the-field performance the first two weeks after they returned from the "injured list." This was calculated by comparing how they were expected to perform based on (1) preseason projections versus how they performed upon returning and (2) measurements of their pitching or hitting velocity before and after they contracted COVID. The author concluded that this study, along with what athletes and trainers in baseball and numerous other sports were saying, supported the position that "even a vaccinated professional athlete can be laid low by COVID and feel the effects for a while after the symptoms have abated."[9]

Initially, the NBA established the gold standard for spectator sports protection during the COVID pandemic with its bubble on the Disney-ESPN campus in Orlando. That worked well, not only for the restart of the NBA's regular season, but also during the playoffs, which ended when the Los Angeles Lakers, as many expected, won the delayed championship the second week in October. Reportedly no player, coach, or NBA team staff member tested positive, although an unknown number of the sixty-five hundred Disney employees working in the bubble and "guests" of the players were infected.

Despite the overwhelming success of the bubble strategy in preventing the spread of COVID among athletes and coaches, the NBA, like much of the United States, decided to throw caution to the wind for the next season, which began shortly after the COVID-delayed 2020 season had ended. The plan was to try to have as many fans attend games as local government mandates permitted, which required the league to try to enforce mandates regarding the wearing of masks, physical distancing, testing, and contact tracing. Due to virus-related travel restrictions between Canada and the United States, the Toronto Raptors had to play their games, at least initially, at Amalie Arena, home of the NHL champion Tampa Bay Lightning.[10]

ONCE VACCINES BECAME AVAILABLE

At the beginning of 2021, the first COVID vaccines became widely available to athletes but not the general public. Spectator sports went in an unexpected direction, from the point of view of protecting their athletes and business models; given the rush by sports organizations to get their athletes to the head of the line for vaccination before anyone else in comparable age and health categories, it seemed, for a rational moment, that full vaccination was going to become a prerequisite for athletes to be able to participate in their sports. This would have sent a strong signal to the rest of America that mandatory vaccination, except in rare, medically warranted circumstances, was a necessary government intrusion to keep businesses in the United States thriving while at the same time protecting public health.

Rarely have major US and international sports enterprises deliberately acted so consistently against their own economic best interests. Unfortunately, this has turned out to be one of those times. Too many athletes, coaches, and team owners—albeit still a relatively small minority—for a variety of reasons, refused to be fully vaccinated. Most of those who were noncompliant refused to become vaccinated at all or lied about being vaccinated. They convinced owners, organization leaders, and players' unions that their refusal to be properly vaccinated should be recognized and accepted as an exercise of their inviolate individual rights.

In that vein, International Olympic Committee (IOC) president Thomas Bach proposed the once-postponed Tokyo Summer Olympics should be held the following July, with no requirement that either the athletes or the "reasonable" number of fans allowed to attend be vaccinated. He prematurely promoted those games as being "the light at the end of this dark [COVID] tunnel."[11]

Thus, the idea that those in spectator sports would serve as vaccination role models for fans, young athletes, and the nation was quashed by numerous stories of athletes and coaches refusing to be vaccinated or lying about their vaccination status, and sports organizations refusing to make them comply with commonsense protective measures. Some athletes acted this way for political reasons, mimicking many politicians to the extreme right or left who have eschewed vaccination requirements of any kind.

Other athletes, like NFL quarterback Aaron Rodgers, thought that because of their superior fitness, vaccines were unnecessary and thus any side effects too potentially harmful to risk. Still others, including most notably tennis superstar Novak Djokovic, believed the vaccines might degrade their fitness. Even though they obsessed about their bodily integrity, these athletes ignored or minimized the likelihood that contracting COVID could have both short-term and potential long-term health consequences that would be far more detrimental to their health than the vaccine's potential side effects. A few Black athletes, especially in the NFL and NBA, were convinced that based on the racist American medical policies that predominated in the past, it was more than possible that these vaccines were being administered to them as scientific guinea pigs or to deliberately make them sick. This concern was buoyed by bogus claims that vaccines were causing a rise in cardiac arrest among athletes.[12]

In response to these anecdotal and scientifically dubious concerns, the sports leagues, teams, players' unions, and other organizations refused to support mandatory vaccination, even though such mandates were the best way to protect their sports businesses as well as the health of the athletes, coaches, and other people employed by those businesses. As a result, many more athletes, coaches, trainers, and other sports personnel have contracted COVID than would have been the case if strict vaccination policies had been imposed.

The quintessential melding of anti-vax conspiracy fearmongering with spectator sports came in the wake of the horrific spectacle of Buffalo Bills safety Damar Hamlin almost dying when his heart stopped following a routinely violent collision with Cincinnati Bengals wide receiver Tee Higgins in a game in January 2023. While the sports world was mostly united in its concern for Hamlin, who miraculously survived, the *Washington Post* reported that "[a]nti-vaxxers and right-wing provoca-teurs sought to link the injury . . . [to] Hamlin . . . [with] the coronavirus vaccine, without any evidence." Charlie Kick, "a pro-Trump activist," tweeted, "This is a tragic and all too familiar sight right now; Athletes dropping suddenly." That "tweet was viewed nearly 10 million times."[13]

COVID misinformation is a serious problem that has led to many unnecessary deaths since the pandemic began. Linking these outrageous theories to spectator sports gives them added gravitas, particularly since some athletes have embraced such misinformation. As Naomi Smith, a sociologist in Australia, observed, when fans and other people take it seriously, the misinformation "has a ripple effect." In this case, the ripple was the misleading and unsupported, but now popular, claim that "the coronavirus vaccine is causing people"—even supremely fit ath-letes—"to die."[14]

THE POTENTIAL LONG-TERM HEALTH EFFECTS OF COVID ON ATHLETES

Beyond the disruption in spectator sports caused by athletes contracting COVID and the inability of some unvaccinated athletes to compete in jurisdictions where vaccines have been required, looming questions remain about the long-term health effects of COVID on athletes and former athletes who have been or will be infected. Mounting evidence indicates that even relatively mild COVID cases may wreak havoc inside the body, including in the brain.

These negative, difficult to diagnose and overcome bodily and mental reactions, which can be severe, are particularly likely, preliminary studies suggest, for infected people with preexisting medical conditions, includ-ing mental disorders and brain damage. The virus can intensify symptoms of, and complicate treatments for, those conditions.

Unfortunately, elite and aspiring elite athletes are prone to an array of mental disorders or concerns associated with competing in their sports, all of which, it now seems, may be worsened by COVID. Severe competitive stress, performance anxiety, depression over not being able to perform up to expectations, substance abuse, and brain damage are mental conditions that sports can cause or worsen—ailments athletes may experience in addition to other mental disorders that anyone can have.

The American College of Sports Medicine concluded that athletes have a substantially greater risk than the general population of having a mental disorder of some kind[15] (see chapter 4). Unfortunately, a variety of systemic factors make it difficult for these affected athletes to receive the care, treatment, and support that may be needed to adequately address these challenges to their mental health and emotional well-being.

Due to stigma, stereotyping, and discrimination, most spectator sports cultures make it difficult for elite athletes, especially males, to publicly acknowledge mental and emotional challenges, much less seek help to successfully overcome them. Athletes will do almost anything to avoid being labeled a "head case" or injury prone, labels that can diminish or curtail careers. COVID has made the physical and mental health–related concerns for athletes more numerous, more difficult, and potentially more serious. Only time will tell to what extent COVID-related problems will negatively affect the health, mental health, careers, and postretirement lives of elite athletes.

Hopefully, leagues, teams, and other sports organizations will become more interested and transparent in identifying and addressing the potential long-term physical and mental effects of COVID on athletes. Unfortunately, the ways in which the NFL and NHL, for instance, sportswashed the dangers of brain damage to their male athletes (see chapter 7) and US Olympic and college organizations covered up and even lied about the sexual abuse of mostly female athletes (see chapter 9) suggest that the sincerity and transparency of major sports organizations in protecting their athletes from COVID's long-term effects deserve closer scrutiny and should not be taken for granted.

Even if spectator sports organizations were interested in investigating and addressing the long-term health effects of COVID on their athletes, possible future infectious disease disruptions would greatly complicate such efforts. The overall mental health record of spectator sports organizations has been discouraging so far, despite a few incremental gains in recent years. Adding COVID to the mix only makes things more complicated.

Sportswashing has made those mental health gains seem much more substantial and significant than they really are. When one takes stock of what remains to be done, however, to adequately improve the mental health and emotional well-being of elite and aspiring elite athletes in this new COVID environment, the challenges appear to be considerable, and the results, so far, are uninspiring.

THE MENTAL HEALTH IMPLICATIONS OF COVID: WHAT IS KNOWN, SUSPECTED, AND UNKNOWN

A study of the medical literature pertaining to pandemics and preexisting mental illness published in *Brain, Behavior, and Immunity—Health* revealed that it is critically "important" for there to be more "well-designed repeated measure case control studies" on this topic.[16] That said, a few preliminary findings have been made about the impact of COVID on people with preexisting mental health conditions, which appear to be relevant to elite athletes, aspiring elite athletes, and, most of all, former athletes.

First, according to the study, elderly individuals with cognitive disorders, such as those linked to CTE and other forms of brain damage, who contracted COVID "experienced a worsening of neuropsychiatric symptoms," primarily behavior issues such as "apathy, anger, and aberrant motor activities." Second, people with "eating disorders," which also affect female athletes perhaps more so than the general population, "reported an increase in [those] symptoms." Third, subjects "with pre-existing mental illnesses experience[d] high levels of anxiety, depression, stress, and sleep problems."[17]

A preliminary "narrative review" specifically on the mental health of "elite athletes" published in the *British Journal of Sports Medicine* in September 2020 found that, as a group, those athletes experienced "many mental health symptoms and disorders at rates equivalent to or exceeding those of the general population."[18] That study, carried out by thirteen medical researchers in the United States, Europe, Australia, and Canada, with the cooperation of the NCAA, focused on the management of such symptoms rather than measuring incidence rates. In doing so, however, that narrative study detailed "what is already known" and described "new findings" to the existing medical literature.

Those researchers found that the "COVID-19 pandemic has created several new stressors for elite athletes." Most of the scientific and medical communities have "focused on cardiac complications" rather than the mental health aspects of the disease. In addition, the COVID pandemic has necessitated "changes in the way in which management of mental health symptoms and disorders in elite athletes . . . should be delivered." That includes the "pharmacotherapy . . . of [their] mental health symptoms." This last concern encompasses "certain classes of medication, including stimulants, medications for bipolar and psychotic disorders, antidepressants and medications for substance abuse disorders."[19]

These findings about the mental health effects on athletes run counter to other preliminary findings for the general population that were published in late 2021 and early 2022. "A systematic review" of the "long-term effects of COVID-19 on mental health" in the *Journal of Affective Disorders* assessed the results from thirty-three smaller studies, which included a total of "6,743 participants, with outcomes assessed between one and six months after diagnosis."[20]

That review found that "there was *no clear evidence* of survivors experiencing worse anxiety or depression as compared to the general population levels." Nor was there "a greater prevalence of PTSD and sleep disturbances." These conclusions clashed with other studies that reported "worsening psychiatric symptoms."[21] On the other hand, there was no indication that athletes experienced less anxiety and depression, which for the general population has been elevated due to COVID.

However, a massive study of veterans published in 2022 in the *BMJ* reported results that should be far more concerning. Like athletes and former athletes, veterans have a greater incidence of CTE and brain damage than the general population, and a much higher proportion of males are part of that cohort of veterans. According to a 2022 summary of the study in *Science*, even a year after being infected with COVID-19, those veterans experienced substantially higher rates for "neuropsychiatric disorders," including "depression, suicidal thoughts, anxiety, sleep disturbance, opioid use disorder, and neurocognitive decline," also known as brain fog.[22]

Veterans who were not hospitalized for their infections still had a "40% higher risk of developing any of these [neuropsychiatric] disorders." The risks for brain fog and substance abuse were even greater. The dataset for this groundbreaking study was a "control group of 5.9 million veterans who sought care in 2017." Their mental health situations were compared to the "nearly 154,000 veterans" who had reported being infected with COVID.[23] That control group remains in place today, so further studies are not only possible, but likely.

What sets this study apart from all the others to date is, as one leading neuroscientist explained, its much larger "scale . . . as well as the quality of the statistical methods." Also, the study measured the mental health effects a year out, rather than being limited to only "a few months after infection."[24] In addition, as reported earlier in this chapter, researchers have found the virus can infect the brain directly.

The scientific evidence to date is somewhat mixed, a bit confusing, and a bit contradictory. Nevertheless, the "findings" of the largest study to date by far "suggest that people who survive the acute phase of COVID-19 are at increased risk of an array of incidents of mental disorders." It seems likely, then, that COVID negatively affects the long-term health of elite athletes, especially those with preexisting or developing mental conditions such as brain damage, extreme stress, extreme anxiety, depression, and/or substance abuse issues. The researchers concluded that "[t]racking mental health disorders among survivors of COVID-19 should be a priority."[25]

Such tracking should focus on elite athletes, as well, because there appear to be special sports-related COVID issues. Currently, the major professional leagues and other sports organizations representing elite athletes are doing very little tracking or sponsoring of other essential COVID research. As happened with CTE research in football, hockey, and other contact sports, the governing sports organizations appear to be more concerned about the costly potential health problems that in-depth research might reveal.

ATHLETES' COVID-RELATED HEALTH
AND MENTAL HEALTH NARRATIVES

Publicly-reported narratives about serious health effects of COVID on elite athletes are still quite rare, especially those dealing with mental health issues linked to the virus, and there are none yet detailing the long-term effects on former athletes. Most stories have focused on high-profile athletes who caused disruptions to their team or their sport because they either refused to be vaccinated, contracted the virus, or passed the virus on to other athletes.

As detailed in the *Annals of Medicine* in 2021, there appears to be a significant population of elite athletes who have "experienced long-term COVID-19 symptoms," both "mental and physical," despite the "limited research" to date and the reluctance of athletes to come forward publicly.[26] There is little doubt, though, that some elite athletes, despite their vastly superior physical fitness, have been negatively affected by these long-term effects. In fact, superior fitness may not be nearly as important in reducing many of those symptoms as it was once thought to be.

With respect to COVID symptoms attributable to various mental disorders, elite athletes may have been at greater risk than the general population. In part this is because at the beginning of the pandemic, lockdowns prevented athletes from training or competing, causing them to experience depression and emotional distress. Furthermore, athletes who have developed long-term COVID symptoms experience higher levels of stress, anxiety, and depression because they are unable to train properly or compete at the level they have in the past.

Some high-profile elite athletes—including NBA players Jayson Tatum and Mohamed Bamba, MLB players Yoan Moncada and Kenley Jansen, and NFL players Tommy Sweeney and Ryquell Armstead—have reported long-term physical symptoms, but unsurprisingly, avoided the question of how their physical struggles have affected their mental health.

Armstead, in what appears to be a rare event for an elite athlete, "was hospitalized twice due to complications." Asia Durr, who was the second overall pick in the 2019 WNBA Draft, said she was unable to play professional basketball for months. Durr described "days where I'm like, 'I just have to stay in the bed."[27] Undoubtedly, her emotional well-being was compromised as well.

Durr is among a handful of high-profile athletes whose stories of long-term COVID suggest that there are mental health issues that accompany physical impairment for long periods of time. As Michael Lee of the *Washington Post* explained, athletes "know how to adjust to mental challenges of recovering from injury." However, that ability is "strain[ed] when there is no timetable for a return, no sense of how the virus will affect them next." In Durr's case, she felt a huge loss in her life; "[b]asketball was always her outlet, the court her calming grounds."[28]

Another elite athlete who has suffered from severe long-term effects of COVID is former college defensive end Justin Foster, a key contributor to Clemson winning the 2020 national championship. Foster has asthma, so breathing has been a lifelong, emotionally charged issue for him.

A few months after his performance as a defensive force in Clemson's national championship, Foster contracted long COVID. Ten months later, normal daily living tasks continued to overwhelm him, both physically and emotionally, due to what he described as "short breath." Although Clemson head coach Dabo Swinney encouraged Foster to stay in the football program and develop his obvious talent, Foster gave up on his career "with sadness but no regrets. . . . I had to do what was best for my health."[29]

Five prominent elite athletes have found themselves caught up in well-publicized COVID-related stories. Three involved anti-vax controversies, mostly of the athletes' own making: Green Bay's All-Pro quarterback Aaron Rodgers, Brooklyn Nets superstar Kyrie Irving, and Novak Djokovic, arguably the best tennis player of all time. The other two are US Olympic figure skater Vincent Zhou, who tested positive for COVID during the Beijing Olympics, and Chicago Blackhawks captain Jonathan Toews, who has been battling long COVID symptoms.

These narratives illustrate several different types of COVID-related concerns elite athletes have experienced so far.

Aaron Rodgers (Green Bay Packers)

When COVID vaccines became readily available to elite athletes in early 2021, Aaron Rodgers, the likely future Hall of Fame quarterback of the Green Bay Packers, became the center of media attention after he told reporters that he had been "immunized," when in fact he had never received a vaccine. After he contracted COVID, Rodgers made a nonapology apology to "anybody who felt misled by those comments." He then tried to explain "his decision not to be vaccinated" but focused instead on the fact that he believed he had been placed in the "crosshairs of the woke mob" and "cancel culture."[30]

Months later, Rodgers attempted to explain a second time why he was not vaccinated. The quarterback now claimed, without medical substantiation, he had an allergy triggered by "one of the ingredients" of the vaccine. He contended that instead of a vaccine, over a two-month period, he took "'a diluted strand of the virus' orally before appealing for a waiver from the NFL." He argued that as an unvaccinated player, he was being discriminated against based on "crazy policies" and subjected to public "shaming." Thus, to avoid all this, he had elected to tell the media that "he was immunized."[31]

Rodgers went on to say, "I'm not some sort of anti-vax flat-earther. I'm somebody who's a critical thinker. . . . I believe strongly in bodily autonomy. Not to have to acquiesce to some woke culture or some crazed groups of individuals."[32] The NFL and the Packers, unlike the NBA with Kyrie Irving (below), took no action in response.

Kyrie Irving (Brooklyn Nets)

NBA All-Star guard Kyrie Irving also resisted being vaccinated in a very public way, but with very negative consequences for himself and his team. At first, Irving simply refused to disclose his vaccination status after reports surfaced that he opposed the vaccine. He defended his position by stating it was a private matter. He argued that he was a "human being first," implicitly suggesting that this came before being a member of any community. He made his statement "via Zoom . . . presumably because he [was] unvaccinated and thus by [local] law could not join the proceedings" in Brooklyn.[33]

Kareem Abdul-Jabbar penned a pointed essay criticizing NBA players like Bradley Beal and Irving who were refusing the vaccine. Abdul-Jabbar said these athletes seemed to view vaccination "like it's just a matter of personal preference, like ordering no onions on your burger at a drive-thru."[34] Unfortunately, that did not make much of an impression on Irving, who soon became explicit about his refusal to be vaccinated.

For months, Irving was not allowed to play home games for the Nets, costing them dearly in the standings. It was not until March 2022, when New York City mayor Eric Adams carved out a special exception for Irving to play in Brooklyn as an unvaccinated player, that the guard was able to participate in home games.

The mayor proclaimed that henceforth "professional athletes and performers working in New York City will no longer be required to show proof of vaccination against COVID-19." Reportedly, the mayor was responding to criticism that the vaccine mandate made little sense because "opposing players who are unvaccinated are allowed to play at Barclays Center and Madison Square Garden." Epidemiologist Jay Varma observed, wryly, that "vaccines work 'unless you're rich and powerful, in which case lobbying works.'"[35]

Irving's take on the whole controversy, like Rodgers's, was self-centered. On his teammate Kevin Durant's television show, Irving characterized himself as living "the life of a martyr, bro."[36] Yet Irving never explained why he refused the vaccine, which required him to turn down a contract he described as being for "four years, 100-and-something million."[37] As with his belief in anti-Semitic theories, his seemingly irrational vaccine refusal could also have been based on a conspiracy theory rather than a rational concern. He then asked to be traded—and was—because he felt unappreciated.

Novak Djokovic (Tennis)

Novak Djokovic's decision not to be vaccinated on the cusp of becoming the greatest tennis player of all time is more difficult to explain and loaded with mental health red flags The mental and emotional seeds for this seemingly irrational stance appear to have been planted well before Djokovic became a tennis superstar (see chapter 5).

CHAPTER 6

As a child growing up in Serbia in the late 1990s, Djokovic was exposed to frequent emotional turmoil, including the trauma of war. His practice sessions in a makeshift tennis court at the bottom of an empty swimming pool were often interrupted by bombings from NATO aircraft. This reportedly "crystalized his motivation" and inculcated in him an overwhelming desire to "overcom[e] adversity."[38]

Djokovic developed an unusual obsession to win, even for an elite athlete. He also incorporated what to others seem to be bizarre regimens in order to maintain his near-perfect tennis fitness, including keeping his body "pure" by declining vaccines. Other commentators have concluded he "has been cavalier and reckless in the face of a deadly pandemic."[39] Either way, he transformed his version of reality to conform to his own wishes, which was to keep his body pure.

Djokovic raised eyebrows early in his professional career by eliminating gluten and sugar from his diet. This made sense for him and seems to have helped his tennis. More disturbingly, though, he and his wife Jelena reportedly believe in "the healing power of celery juice" and cilantro. They have embraced the advice of self-described medical medium Anthony Williams, who has "no medical training whatsoever."[40] On his website, Williams promotes the healing power of cilantro, which he claims can "remove toxic heavy metals from the brain" and "other body systems and organs" and act as "an amazing liver detoxifier."[41]

In 2017, at the height of his career after having won four Grand Slams in a row, Djokovic's game and his focus mysteriously dissipated. Publicly, his distress was tied to a reported elbow issue, which, for a long time, he tried to treat with various natural remedies, until he eventually agreed to have the surgery in February 2018 (see chapter 5). Similarly, Djokovic posted on Facebook in April 2020 that he was concerned about what being vaccinated for COVID might do to his body and tennis fitness.

That June, during a series of exhibition matches, Djokovic and several other tennis players contracted COVID at a tournament Djokovic had helped organize. It was later revealed that even off-the-court masking and social distancing measures had been ignored. Sally Jenkins wrote in the *Washington Post* that Djokovic's obsessive "hunt for stand-alone greatness . . . [i]s downright anti-social,"[42] meaning he was ignoring the public good for his steadfast pursuit to be recognized as the very best tennis player ever.

Djokovic felt no compunction about trying to find a way to obtain a visa to enter Australia without being fully vaccinated, which the country's travel rules required unless visitors qualified for a special exemption. To him, avoiding vaccination appeared to be a tennis strategy, albeit seemingly irrational, much like parts of his extreme fitness and flexibility regimens. Reportedly, the Australian government reneged on an apparent deal that had been hashed out to let Djokovic play, then bounced him out of the country after holding him in detention for a few days.

Despite everything, Djokovic continued to obstinately refuse vaccination, based on his unscientific beliefs about what should or should not go into his body. As noted earlier, he subscribes to "extreme diets and fitness regimens."[43] His position on the COVID vaccine also violated the rules of ATP, of which he was the president for several years.

In Djokovic's version of reality, however, vaccines threatened his body's purity, which he views as essential to winning matches. Yet his refusal to be vaccinated for COVID precluded his participation in many of the most important matches required to build his tennis legacy. The paradox is that the overriding reason he wanted to keep his body pure was to help him win those types of matches.

Djokovic is an intelligent, articulate, supremely gifted athlete whose obsession to win has somehow become convoluted and a threat to his emotional and physical well-being. He seems incapable of changing his unorthodox views, no matter what the consequences for his legacy or who is telling him to act more reasonably. Djokovic is so intent on keeping his body a temple that he continues to refuse to be vaccinated, despite the scientific and medical evidence that it would be in the best interest of his health to do so.

His refusal cost him opportunities to compete in the 2022 Australian Open, which he had won nine times—and won again in 2023—the 2022 US Open, and any future tournaments, including Grand Slams, that are held in countries that have or may renew vaccine requirements for visitors. As a result of his convoluted thinking, Djokovic once again delayed his quest to win the most Grand Slams as well as Masters events, instead of being comfortably ahead.

Vincent Zhou (Figure Skating)

While many news outlets briefly covered the disappointment Vincent Zhou must have felt when he tested positive for COVID just before the men's singles event at the 2022 Beijing Winter Olympics, none did it better than ESPN's Elaine Teng.[44] Zhou had spent most of his life up to that point working toward competing to win an individual medal at those games. Everything the twenty-one-year-old had done was calculated to put himself in the best position to succeed with his dream. He reportedly took every precaution possible to avoid COVID-19. Zhou "tested daily" and did not "even take his mask off to chew his food."[45]

Zhou skated well in the team event, helping to earn the US team a silver medal. The next day, however, he received news that he had tested positive for the virus. A second positive test forced him to withdraw from the men's event. Thus, "[o]n the evening before the day he's been working for his whole life, Zhou [didn't] lace up his skates." Instead, he "[sat] alone in a hotel room . . . and turn[ed] off his phone."[46]

The psychological pain from that disappointment proved to be "crushing at times." It was another jolt to his "mental health," which had "been sorely tested over the years" in preparing for his moment. Zhou did not even watch his teammates compete; he said it was "too emotionally difficult," adding, "I knew I could have medaled."[47]

A month later, Zhou was trying to process what had happened. With the help of his psychologist, he came to understand that, in the skater's words, "this is very similar to grieving for the loss of a loved one." He described waking up and not being able to look at his skates: "I spent the first half of the day basically crying and not being able to do anything." Nevertheless, he also understood that it was important not "to try to suppress the feelings . . . because if I try to suppress them, they'll be stuck in there."[48]

Jonathan Toews (Chicago Blackhawks)

In February 2023, Chicago Blackhawks captain Jonathan Toews announced that he had been struggling with long Covid since before the 2020–2021 season. It has caused him to suffer from something called chronic inflammatory response syndrome, a nonspecific diagnosis for the symptoms that apparently have robbed him of his energy and left him feeling lethargic. He described the feeling as like being in "outer space."[49]

His condition caused him to miss the entire 2020–2021 season. He returned the following season but "scored a career low 12 goals and tied a career low with 25 assists," and in 2022–2023 he struggled once again. In February, Toews missed seven straight games and indicated he did not know when he would be able to return. Toews tried, he said, to "play through these symptoms," but "it has reached the point where I have no choice but to step back and concentrate on getting healthy."[50]

Rumors circulated that the three-time Stanley Cup champion would be shipped to another team at the trade deadline. Instead of trading him—which would have been difficult, given his medical condition—the team put him on the injured reserve list indefinitely. The *Chicago Tribune* opined that Toews's extended absence "not only likely erases whatever trade value he may have had, but also places his Hawks future in doubt."[51] Subsequently, the team indicated it would not be re-signing him.[52]

Sports Organizations Still Slow to Respond to COVID

COVID-19 appears to be here to stay, as are the many possible mental and physical health risks that contracting the virus may impose on elite athletes. As happened with brain damage (see chapter 7) and sexual abuse (see chapter 9), it probably will take a long time for more athlete narratives about negative COVID experiences, especially long-term concerns, to be revealed in significant numbers. In large part, this may be because the understanding of scientists and doctors about what is happening to athletes and former athletes as a result of COVID, especially concerns related to their mental health, is evolving slowly after an initial flurry of interest about cardiac-related events.

This delay is understandable, although regrettable, given how medical research in the United States tends to follow the money. Unless sports organizations, players' unions, and athletes themselves push hard for more funding for this type of research, and perhaps provide much of it themselves, knowledge about this important subject—currently still in its nascent stage—is likely to continue to develop slowly.

Nevertheless, COVID exposure for athletes may well increase as vaccine mandates and public health practices are stepped down and variants of the virus evolve. At the same time, the vacuum of information about COVID's long-term health effects on athletes and former athletes could seriously jeopardize their mental and physical well-being going forward. At this point, nobody really knows what to expect, which is a problem that should be addressed sooner rather than later.

CHAPTER 7

CTE, Other Brain Damage, and Related Erratic Behaviors

ONE OF THE—IF NOT *THE*—MOST WRITTEN ABOUT MENTAL HEALTH problems in sports has been the threat of brain injuries to athletes, especially in contact sports such as boxing, football, and hockey but also in less violent athletic events like soccer and skiing. The problem is not only damage to the health of individual athletes but also any aberrant or erratic behaviors that may present as a result. For decades, though, brain damage involving athletes was ignored, minimized, or covered up. Full transparency and adequate care and treatment for brain-damaged athletes are still a long way off.

CTE AND OTHER BRAIN DAMAGE IN ATHLETES GENERALLY
A prominent category of sports-derived health challenges for athletes is the risk of mental disorders and erratic behaviors thought to be closely linked to brain damage, especially from chronic traumatic encephalopathy (CTE), a brain condition that appears to be caused by blows to the head resulting in concussions and/or repeated subconcussive impacts. CTE is thought to appear in four different stages, each of which is progressively worse. Stage 1 includes symptoms such as headaches and loss of concentration. Stage 2 adds more severe symptoms: depression, explosive moods, and memory loss. Stage 3 includes severe cognitive difficulties with memory and with the ability to plan, problem solve, and organize. Stage 4, full-blown CTE, is characterized by extreme

symptoms such as "profound memory loss," "language deficits," and "psychotic" mood disorders.[1]

CTE is caused by injuries to the brain, but not all brain injuries result in CTE. CTE, though, has become the most prominent form of brain damage in sports. While there is still disagreement among neuroscientists about the exact symptoms of CTE, since there is no widely accepted and validated test to diagnose it in living brains, there appears to be a consensus that, at the very least, it is associated with problems related to thinking and memory, cognitive confusion, personality changes, and erratic behaviors due to misplaced aggression, depression, and/or suicidal thoughts. Yet CTE is only one major sign of a condition known more generally as traumatic brain injury (TBI).

This array of brain traumas that "sports activities, especially contact sports," cause produce "a spectrum of dysfunctions that alters the neuronal, musculoskeletal, and behavioral responses of an athlete." Making matters worse, "[m]any sports-related brain injuries go unreported" but still "trigger neurometabolic disruptions that contribute to long-term neuronal impairment."[2]

The occurrence of symptoms related to CTE and TBI appear to be most prevalent in boxing, given the relatively small number of athletes who box professionally, but it is a sport that operates like a "close[d] shop." For many decades, boxing has been able to successfully sportswash "[brain] damage and death of their athletes."[3] It is simply accepted that brain damage is an inherent risk of the sport and most boxers should understand that they will experience it in some way. This, and the relatively small percentage of elite athletes who are boxers, has proved to be a disincentive to US researchers in recent years to closely study CTE in boxers the way it is being studied in football, hockey, and soccer players.

Punch-drunk boxers have been around for as long as boxing has been a spectator sport and knockouts the favored fan outcome. Unfortunately, the only solution that makes sense to meaningfully prevent brain damage in boxing is abolishing it entirely, which is unlikely to happen—and in fact, new and arguably more dangerous combat sports, such as the Ultimate Fighting Championship and cage fighting, have become increasingly popular.

CTE-like symptoms of TBI and the erratic behaviors they seem to cause also appear to occur in football and hockey players, past and current, at alarming rates. Furthermore, CTE has become a concern in soccer and other popular team and individual contact sports. In recent years, there has been no topic related to the mental health of athletes that has captured more media attention than brain damage.

In individual sports like gymnastics, figure skating, snowboarding, skiing, and bobsledding—but not boxing, wrestling, and other combat competitions—brain damage of this sort is usually an unintended consequence of performing, especially at an elite level where athletes push themselves to be the best they can be, often exceeding the limits of reasonable safety. In certain team sports, though, most prominently football and hockey, injuries to the brain can be due to the deliberate and/or reckless acts of aggression and violence that are part of the cultures of those sports, often with devastating impacts. Soccer lacks that type of all-out aggression most of the time, but heading the ball and being hit hard in the head with the ball or the ground can produce severe concussions and repeated head traumas as well.

Preliminary studies indicate that in both football and hockey, the longer elite athletes compete in those sports, the greater the likelihood they will develop CTE. Research conducted at the Boston University Chobanian and Avedisian School of Medicine published in 2022 found a significant increase in the CTE rate for every additional year athletes at the highest levels of competition played hockey, perhaps as much as 23 percent.[4]

These results correlated with a 2017 Boston University (BU) study published in the journal *Translational Psychiatry*, which concluded that the risk of mental impairment and behavioral issues tripled for former football players who had begun playing the sport before the age of twelve. That study included more than two hundred former athletes, almost all of whom played football in college and/or the NFL.[5] Furthermore, a study published in 2023 in the scientific journal *Nature Communications* found that it is not only the number of brain impacts that increases the risk of CTE to football players, but also the "collective force" behind those impacts over time.[6]

It would be reasonable to expect a correlation between the amount of time elite soccer players participate in their sport and the likely increase in CTE symptoms, given that a leading study conducted in Glasgow, Scotland, in 2019 found that professional soccer players were three and a half times more likely than the rest of the population to die from neurodegenerative diseases. Both male and female professional soccer players have reported having symptoms, and Scott Vermillion, a former Major League Soccer (MLS) player who died of acute alcohol and prescription drug poisoning in 2020 at the age of forty-four, was later discovered to have had CTE.[7]

The same type of accumulated risk undoubtedly applies to boxing and mixed martial arts, where repetitive brain punishment is continuous, but for some reason the brains of boxers and other professional fighters do not appear to be part of any comprehensive American studies, at least not in recent years. The results of a preliminary study published in the *British Journal of Sports Medicine* in December 2022, however, examined the records of 110 retired boxers and 66 retired MMA fighters. Using a yet-to-be-validated test for diagnosing CTE in living people rather than examining the brains of deceased fighters, researchers found that 41 percent of all the subjects studied likely had the condition. For fighters over the age of 50, though, researchers found the prevalence rate exceeded by 60 percent.[8]

Each time athletes are concussed, they become more susceptible to being concussed again. In this way, the brain is like any other structure: Each head trauma weakens the structure and makes it more susceptible to injury. According to the Centers for Disease Control website:

> A person with a history of repeated mild TBIs [traumatic brain injuries] or concussions may experience a longer recovery or more severe symptoms [and] have long-term problems, including ongoing problems with concentration, memory, headache, and occasionally, physical skills, such as keeping one's balance.[9]

These cognitive problems seem to be worse in female athletes experiencing the same level of head trauma as male athletes. A 2020 systematic review of studies and other relevant research published in the *Orthopaedic Journal of Sports Medicine* concluded that female athletes are more susceptible than their male counterparts "to sport-related concussions (SRCs) and experience worse outcomes." Why this is true remains uncertain, but it could be in part that their perceived susceptibility is due to the fact that female athletes are more apt to report these types of brain injuries.[10] This does not explain why their outcomes are generally worse, however.

BRAIN DAMAGE LITIGATION AND THE LARGELY DISAPPOINTING CHANGES THAT HAVE FOLLOWED

In recent years, the NFL, NHL, NCAA, and US Soccer have all chosen to settle rather than contest lawsuits by their athletes seeking damages for mental trauma and brain injuries. Significantly, no major boxing organization in the United States has been sued over brain damage to their boxers as a class, perhaps because of the somewhat outdated legal defense of "assumption of risk" and the popular belief that everyone should know boxing is dangerous.

The 2013 NFL class action settlement, which has been plagued by claims of fraud on both sides and a race-norming scandal in which Black former players initially received less compensation than other former players, will still likely result in total awards exceeding a billion dollars.

In 2018, the NHL managed to pay out less than $20 million to its former players. John Vrooman, "a sports economics professor at Vanderbilt, . . . called the settlement a 'lopsided victory for the owners.'"[11] According to Vrooman, this was, in large part, because class action status had been denied. His conclusion that the plaintiffs had been legally outmaneuvered was reinforced more than two years later when it became known that the NHL had compensated its counsel $70.6 million to settle the suit, nearly four times as much as the $18.49 million it had paid out to the former players.[12]

The NCAA's $75 million settlement reached in 2019 was arguably an even worse outcome for its student-athletes with lasting brain damage. The payout applied to all former NCAA athletes who had played any sport at any time prior to July 15, 2016, but set aside no special or additional compensation or services for athletes with CTE-like and other brain damage symptoms. The settlement provided qualifying former college athletes up to two medical screenings and evaluations through the year 2069 to help their treating physicians provide health care, which would be at the former athletes' expense. Furthermore, those seeking a screening must first go before a panel of doctors, which the NCAA has selected, to assess whether a complete evaluation is even warranted.[13] Thus, brain-damaged college athletes are entitled—at most—to receive two diagnoses over their lifetimes, but no other follow-up care and treatment.

Similarly, US Soccer provided no compensation to its former players with CTE-like symptoms, instead agreeing, without admitting any wrongdoing, to "ban heading in games and practices," but only for players under age ten. Restrictions also were put in place for older US youth soccer players that limit how much heading can be done in practices. This falls well short of eliminating heading entirely.[14] In addition, enforcement of these guidelines is based more on an honor system than active scrutiny.

Over the years, the NFL, NHL, NCAA, and US Soccer have acted selfishly and to avoid liability when it has come to protecting and caring for their players, former players, and young players whose lives have been compromised by mental disorders linked either to football-, hockey-, or soccer-related CTE or other forms of sports-related brain damage.[15] Since at present only the brains of deceased athletes can be reliably examined for CTE, a determination as to whether such disorders should be linked to CTE must be based on expert opinions rather than established scientific facts. This makes proving causation much more difficult legally.

The present impossibility of getting a proper diagnosis in living athletes is a key problem, but it is not the only one. The cultures of these contact sports often encourage players to use overly aggressive, reckless, and even violent tactics against their opponents. Thus, the list of former and current athletes with suspected symptoms of CTE or other types of brain damage and related mental health challenges continues to grow, and likely will continue to do so until changes are made that fundamentally transform those sports and/or their cultures. So far, the improvements implemented to protect athletes from brain injury have been incremental rather than fundamental.

The NFL is a case in point. Concussion protocols during games—and supposedly during practices, when television cameras are not recording every play—appear to be inadequate and flawed, as the situation faced by Miami Dolphins quarterback Tua Tagovailoa in late 2022 (covered later in this chapter) illustrates. Thus, the NFL settlement has not done that much to motivate the league to take more meaningful steps to correct its continuing problem of brain damage to its current and future players.

The NFL knows it still has a serious brain damage problem that has not been adequately addressed. That is why it has tried to float the idea—unsuccessfully, so far—that the so-called Guardian helmet shield it mandated for players in certain positions during much of the 2022 preseason could be the holy grail of brain damage protections. The NFL gushed that the helmets had "exceeded our expectations,"[16] even though there was little evidence to support the helmet's protectiveness beyond the subjective information collected by the teams themselves; quarterbacks, running backs, and wide receivers were excluded from this preseason demonstration; a number of players at the affected positions objected to wearing the bulky helmets; and there are no indications that very many, if any, players use these helmets now.

In addition, the NFL, through the Pittsburgh Steelers, is trying to challenge the damning CTE data collected by the BU researchers. They have funded a competing project at the University of Pittsburgh Medical Center to study why only some players appear to get CTE or its symptoms. One of the main organizers of the project, neurosurgeon Dr. Joseph Maroon, who has been an adviser and consultant to the NFL's Head, Neck, and Spine Committee, in the past has characterized CTE in football players as being "rare" and "over-exaggerated."[17] This latest project appears to be a delaying gambit by the NFL, because it will be years before any results from any studies conducted by the center will be published.

CHAPTER 7

OVERLY AGGRESSIVE AND VIOLENT TACTICS, ESPECIALLY IN FOOTBALL AND HOCKEY

Football, hockey, soccer, basketball, baseball, NASCAR, and other spectator sports—especially for men and boys—provide implicit and explicit incentives for being overly aggressive and sometimes violent, including coaching deliberately intended to slow down and even incapacitate opponents, which are presented as winning strategies. In these sports, aggressive, dangerous, and violent techniques and practices are taught and passed down from one generation to the next, and the rules, as they are implemented, do not necessarily punish athletes for engaging in behaviors that unnecessarily injure their opponents or place them at heightened risk, at least not enough to make it worthwhile to stop.

Overly aggressive and violent play tends to increase in key competitions and playoffs because the more important results justify the riskier means. In addition, certain types of aggression, like throwing bean balls in baseball, have often been excused as being part of the manly tradition of those sports.

Overly aggressive play remains integral to both football and hockey, more so than in any other American or Canadian team sport. Rule changes responding to widespread brain damage to athletes playing these two sports have had limited success in curbing overly aggressive and violent play. In soccer, basketball, baseball, lacrosse, wrestling, and other contact sports, overly aggressive competition exists, but nowhere near the extent to which it occurs in football and hockey. In terms of the gross brain damage numbers combined with the elevated risks, football is the most dangerous team sport in America. It is also the most popular.

For years, frequent displays of mayhem and deliberate injuries in football were accompanied by sportswashed refrains from athletes, coaches, management, and the media that no one in the sport ever wants anyone to injure someone else deliberately. That refrain only grew louder as evidence about football's reckless disregard for health and safety piled up. Bountygate was remarkable. It suggested that in addition to the New Orleans Saints, where the scandal involving bounties being paid for injuring opponents was first uncovered, throughout the NFL deliberately injuring opponents was not only implicitly permitted but had become an institutionalized tactic and strategy that coaches and teammates encouraged and even rewarded. All-out aggression and violence were praised. There even were cash payouts, including the distribution of bounties, by coaches to players who incapacitated their opponents.[18]

Violence has long been an important element of football, not only for players, but also for fans and the sports media. Until Bountygate, though, the evidence consisted of anecdotes and images focusing on the savagery of individual players and the serious, potentially life-changing injuries that occurred as a result. Chuck Bednarik's brutal hit on Frank Gifford in 1960, which knocked him senseless, was replayed on football programs for decades. Bednarik, Dick Butkus, Jack Tatum, and many other star players became folk heroes in NFL lore because of their ability to deliver punishing and crippling hits. After Gifford died in 2015, an autopsy on his brain indicated he had CTE.

Today, the NFL still lists that deliberate act of violence that jeopardized Gifford's career and mental well-being as one of the greatest plays in professional football history. These hits continue to be celebrated, and their absence becomes a noteworthy story. Sam Fortier of the *Washington Post* reported that the 2023 Senior Bowl had special restrictions in place prohibiting "the thunderclap blows that would make a packed stadium go 'OOOH!'"[19] In Fortier's article, though, in the minds of at least some of the Senior Bowl defensive players, those restrictions unnecessarily inhibited their ability to impress the NFL scouts.

Bountygate demonstrated that NFL teams encourage deliberate bodily harm to their opponents. That scandal, along with the NFL's lies and deceptions about concussions and brain damage to its players, revealed how pathological much of the game continued to be, even with rule changes and attempts to ratchet down the violence that has historically been cause for celebration. Today, there remains substantial resistance to making America's favorite spectator sports, especially football and hockey, substantially safer by reducing overly aggressive play. Many players and fans continue to view this type of violence as justified because to them it is strategically essential and extremely entertaining.

In the past several years Ding Productions on YouTube has featured a series of videos highlighting violent hits in NFL football games.[20] Many

CHAPTER 7

of the hits that are covered appear to involve brain trauma. Deliberately hurting opponents is what purportedly helps to make football entertaining and profitable as America's favorite spectator sport. During his administration, President Donald Trump echoed that sentiment when he used his bully pulpit to castigate the NFL and its referees for penalizing players for "hit[ing] too hard. . . . They're ruining the game. . . . [Players] want to hit."[21] This point of view continues to be firmly ingrained in the American consciousness.

The leaders of professional and college team sports in the United States understand—or at least perceive—that there is a correlation between profitability and sports violence. As *Washington Post* columnist Sally Jenkins explained, in order to sportswash the violence, "the NFL and its television presenters . . . render them [the players] as avatars, not people" by using "muscle-bound cartoonized graphics."[22] In the process, the toll on the physical and mental health of athletes is being minimized in order to glorify the thrill of victory and the agony of defeat.

In many contact sports, game officials lack the incentive—and often are discouraged—from calling personal fouls as strictly as necessary to effectively curb overly aggressive, violent, and dangerous plays. A constant, at times deafening refrain is that calling too many fouls ruins games and athletic competitions for fans and players alike: "Don't allow the referees to decide the outcome," even though by not calling legitimate fouls, they are doing just that—and placing athletes' mental and physical health at greater risk in the process.

This type of subjective refereeing resembles the subjective monitoring and enforcement systems in place for controlling the use of performance-enhancing drugs in many spectator sports. Those systems are designed to create the impression that something meaningful is being done, but without employing stringently enforced rules that change deviant sport cultures, especially if such changes might substantially affect, in negative ways, the generation of revenue. Deviance, apparently, sells.

The other problem is that in contact sports, athletes who break the rules successfully without getting caught tend to be rewarded, and those who obey the rules are placed at a competitive disadvantage. In that way, it is much like American politics. The dynamic of intimidation and

120

deliberate injury has transformed what it means to be a good athlete, much like lying and embracing conspiracy theories have transformed what it means to be a good politician.

Those athletes who are unwilling to break the rules or are unable to do so without being caught become less valuable. Disincentives for safe and healthy competitions are many. The most successful violators tend to be excused and even embraced as winners. The more they win, it seems, the more they are allowed to break the rules and collect a bigger paycheck.

In the macho North American sports environment, recklessness and risk-taking thrive and are often embraced as character-building athletic traits. Thus, it should be no surprise to learn that football (NFL) and hockey (NHL) are the most popular spectator sports in the United States and Canada, respectively. The former sport is inherently dangerous, while the latter is unnecessarily so because violence—which does not have to be an emphasis in men's hockey, and too often detracts from the beauty of the sport—has been allowed to flourish, with only half-hearted restrictions.

THE INHERENT DANGERS OF TACKLE FOOTBALL

Medical and scientific evidence continues to mount that the risks of playing tackle football, by far the most popular sport in the United States, are even greater than most Americans imagine. As it was with the dangers of tobacco use, however, substantial cognitive dissonance persists, much of it perpetuated by propaganda from the NFL and its allies, including the sports media. Better helmets and rule modifications have helped make the sport incrementally safer, but tackle football as it is played today is a fundamentally dangerous sport, especially in terms of causing long-term mental impairments to a substantial percentage of players. The movement to discourage children and adolescents from playing football and look to other sports instead continues to face substantial resistance, although there are signs that this cause is picking up speed in many, but certainly not all, parts of the country.

It is significant that even though 76 percent of sports fans in a September 2017 *Washington Post*–UMass Lowell survey acknowledged that "head injuries causing long-term health problems for [NFL] players" was a "major problem," most of the adults surveyed, including 66 percent of sports fans, still believed "tackle football is safe for high schoolers." More than 40 percent of respondents, including 48 percent of sports fans, believed it was reasonably safe for children to begin playing tackle football before age fourteen.[23]

The apparent disconnect that allows fans to appreciate the health risks of football for professional players but discount those dangers when children and adolescents, even their own, are involved is disturbing. As with the obvious health risks of tobacco that were ignored for so long, cognitive dissonance and various social factors have contributed to this paradox. Perhaps the most important factor, though, is that for a long time the NFL has funded misleading public relations campaigns that take sportswashing to new levels of sophistication.

Despite the criticism of the league and its medical experts for their continuing denials and deceptions, in April 2018 the NFL named Nicholas Theodore, a Johns Hopkins neurosurgeon who had publicly expressed doubts about studies that link CTE to football, to be the chair of its Head, Neck, and Spine Committee. In addition, for years the NFL has reportedly been retaining "financially biased" in-house doctors around the country to decide whether former players who are lucky enough to be vested in their pensions should be eligible to receive disability benefits for brain damage and other lasting impairments.[24]

According to Pulitzer Prize–winning *Washington Post* investigator and reporter Will Hobson, the league and the players' union have conspired to avoid paying out legitimate disability claims. That has led ten former players to sue the NFL's benefits plan for "an overly aggressive and disturbing pattern of erroneous and arbitrary benefits denials."[25]

On top of all that, USA Football, "the N.F.L.-funded national governing body for the sport . . . , [has insisted the game] doesn't have a health and safety problem as much as it has a messaging problem."[26] Furthermore, in most high schools, football continues to play an important—and sometimes dominant—role in the social activities of students and parents alike. About a million boys—and a relatively small but increasing number of girls—play high school football each year. Girls, in fact, receive special media attention and praise when they decide to jeopardize the health of their minds and bodies by playing football with the boys.

Despite NFL propaganda, tackle football is dangerous, but especially so for children, including adolescents. While safety measures can be improved, it is unlikely that it can be made reasonably safe without transforming the sport into something that more closely resembles flag football. Studies indicate that a vast majority of former professional and college football players whose brains were examined show alarming signs of brain damage in the form CTE. Estimates indicate that at least 10 percent of current players already have the disease,[27] which is why a growing number of them are retiring early. Researchers from Boston University who studied the brains of 376 NFL players through January of 2023 found that 345—more than 90 percent—of them had CTE, compared to only about 0.6 percent for the general population.[28]

Even though these findings were based on brains that, for the most part, were submitted for study because the players involved had shown signs of brain damage and other cognitive impairments before they died, the results are extraordinary. Most neuroscientists and the federal courts have concluded that the available evidence overwhelmingly indicates that at the very least CTE is a common condition among former professional and college football players, and it may be an almost inevitable condition for most athletes who play the game for more than a few years.

What should be especially alarming to parents who allow their children to play tackle football is that the high incidence of concussions is only a part of the reason players develop brain impairments. Stanford University researchers confirmed what many neuroscientists suspected: Repeated subconcussive impacts over a football player's lifetime can be more devastating than multiple concussions. These mini concussions are the brain traumas that were once cavalierly dismissed or accepted as badges of honor, often called "dings" or "having one's bell rung." Typically, the harm from these subconcussive impacts goes mostly unnoticed until it is too late to undo the damage to the player's brain.

At all levels of competition, football players continue to get bigger, stronger, and faster, which means each concussive collision generates more force and impact on the brains of both the players being hit and those doing the hitting. The frequent scientific comparison, even for kids, is that each of these collisions—which may occur dozens of times in a game or practice session—can be like driving a car into a cement wall at 30 miles an hour, and the force of these collisions increases as the athletes become more physically imposing. As Hamlin's near-tragic circumstances showed, these collisions can even completely stop an elite athlete's heart from beating.

Tim Gay, a physicist at the University of Nebraska, gained national attention with his excellent treatise, *Football Physics*.[29] The comparisons he makes "applying Newtonian principles" to the major college and professional game are startling. For example, when two players weighing 220 pounds running at a top speed of "about 10 meters per second" collide, they generate about "1,650 pounds"—three-quarters of a ton—of force. In a helmet-to-helmet collision, the force is like "a 16-pound bowling ball dropped on [an uncovered] head from a height of 12 feet." That is why among players, the "injury rate in the NFL is 100 percent. They all get hurt."[30] And in those helmet-to-helmet collisions, the injuries are mostly to the brain.

Finally, and most alarmingly, children's brains and skulls—much like their judgment—do not fully develop until they have been young adults for quite a few years. This makes them especially vulnerable to brain injuries from concussions and subconcussive impacts. Their brains rattle around inside their skulls, rather than being somewhat cushioned by a tighter fit. Each time younger players, which means most of them, absorb a blow to their head or upper body, the harm to their brain is even greater than it would be for a mature adult. Furthermore, because children, adolescents, and young adults can absorb more punishment without displaying symptoms of brain damage, their injuries tend to be missed or more readily ignored.

The repeated head traumas elite football players get as youngsters are aggravated over those athletes' playing careers. Studies show that the longer athletes play sports where concussions and subconcussive impacts are common, the worse their mental health prospects and outcomes appear to be.

In recent months, though, the NFL has latched on to a way to try to either quell concerns indefinitely or at least kick the CTE can further down the road. Currently, as noted earlier, the Guardian Cap—a soft helmet cover designed to reduce the force of impact—is being promoted as the holy grail in preventing football-related brain damage, alongside the league's much promoted, but inconsistently applied, concussion protocols.

Guardian Caps and the NFL

The NFL's messaging in September 2022 was crystal clear. Among those position players, mostly linemen, who were mandated to wear the odd-looking and apparently clumsy feeling Guardian Cap helmet covers during most of the preseason, the incidence of concussions dropped more than 50 percent from the year before. The implications were clear as well. This new helmet could (1) greatly ease concerns about brain damage to football players and (2) boost the impression that team owners are looking out for the welfare of their players. "The performance of the cap exceeded our expectations," gushed Jeff Miller, the NFL's executive vice president of communications, public affairs, and policy, the position once held by NFL commissioner Roger Goodell during the height of the league's CTE and brain damage scandal.

If the NFL's concussion shenanigans (see discussion below) of the past were any guide, however, this announcement deserved to be scrutinized to determine whether it was another deflection, if not an outright deception. To begin with, as even Miller conceded, concerns remain among players about the sizing and awkward fit of the pillow-like casing, which, for those watching, appeared to make the heads of players wearing them move like bobblehead dolls. As Pittsburgh Steelers defensive tackle Cameron Heyward complained, "When you go to tackle, it almost feels like there's a pillow on your head." More to the point, after Philadelphia Eagles tackle Jordan Mailata sustained a preseason concussion, he lamented, "The hat's fake news. It doesn't stop anything."

For those who saw these awkward-looking protective shells on top of the supposedly already buttressed NFL helmets, it would be difficult not to come away with the impression—unless they too were deflecting—that the Guardian Cap was being rolled out as a concerted effort by the league to try to improve negative perceptions about player safety. Yet there was only meager, inconclusive evidence that those caps provided much protection for concussions, much less for repeated subconcussive impacts over a football player's career, which likely are far more dangerous. The methodology of the Guardian Cap study was not revealed publicly. Moreover, the results were based on the self-reporting of the teams themselves rather than independent sources.

Three aspects of the league's orchestrated narrative are deserving of closer examination before the American public and parents of children playing football applaud the NFL—or take seriously the football media's congratulations of the NFL. First, what do these results mean when scrutinized from a more scientific perspective? Not much since it was not an empirical study conducted or reviewed by trained empiricists. Second, given its history (discussed further below), why should anyone trust the NFL as a reliable source for information about NFL player safety? And finally, will the NFLPA, which has been unwilling to agree that COVID vaccines should be mandated for its members, be willing to agree that players should be forced to wear pillow caps on their heads? That seems doubtful.

The NFL's most recent safety campaign appears to be another deflection, which will continue to be pursued until it becomes obvious that the current version of the Guardian Cap is a no-go, or at best a stopgap measure. Even if it proved to be every bit as protective as advertised and was embraced by the players, the helmet cap still would be only an incremental improvement in brain safety, especially since collision forces continue to increase as athletes grow bigger, become stronger, and run faster.

What Do Preliminary Results about the Guardian Cap Really Mean?

Even though information indicating a more than 50 percent reduction in concussions among players using the Guardian Cap was disseminated by the NFL as if that figure was based on reliable empirical findings, this publicity exercise was far from a rigorous scientific study. To begin with, the NFL chose a time period that, for some unstated reason, ended with the second preseason game rather than including all three preseason games and the regular season, which would have been a much more meaningful sample. That is a relatively minor concern.

One can surmise that because no players were compelled to use the cap in the regular season, the NFL and the players' union must have agreed there needed to be a transition game where no one had to wear the cap. According to the NFL, two hundred players wore the Guardian Cap once the mandate was lifted, but this figure was highly deceptive. It did not identify how many of those players were cut before the regular season began and how many other players continued to wear them going forward. There was no evidence that players used the helmet in the regular season or playoffs in significant numbers, if at all, or that any are using it now.

More importantly, though, in terms of the reliability of the NFL's preliminary results, the basis for those findings are two small samplings that may not even have been random. Reportedly, there were twenty-three concussions involving players who played in the designated helmet cap positions during an equivalent period in 2021, and only eleven such concussions were reported in the NFL's 2022 sample. That difference may not be statistically significant because the sample was so small. NFL teams, which have a vested interest in promoting the purported safety advances of the league, were exclusively responsible for reporting how many concussions there had been on their respective teams during those two periods of time, approximately a year apart. This makes their reported results appear suspicious and unreliable.

In addition, there seems to be considerable inconsistency in how games are called in terms of penalties from game to game, much less from season to season, especially when relevant rule changes are announced or updated. The only given seems to be that NFL referees are supposed to change how they interpret the rules and issue penalties based on instructions from the league office, which often are not publicized. Thus, comparing those two seasons may be like comparing apples and oranges. It is more than just conceivable, given the NFL's embarrassing history, that there could have been a special behind-the-scenes effort made to protect players from collisions involving their heads during the 2022 preseason as compared to the year before in order to make the new helmet look more effective. It will take quite a few more years and a far more structured empirical study comparing players who use the caps with those who do not to reliably determine whether the newfangled helmet (or a subsequent version thereof) provides statistically significant protection for players, much less fully protects them.

It seems at least odd, and arguably suspicious, that most of the players in skill positions, who also tend to be involved in the most violent collisions, were excluded from this initial experiment. Wide receivers, running backs, and return and special team specialists were not part of the league's reported statistics, and they are at the center of the offensive-minded NFL. Quarterbacks already receive greatly enhanced protection because they are viewed as too valuable to sacrifice, even in order to satisfy the fans' and football media's craving for more violent entertainment. One can only imagine the delight of personal injury lawyers at the legal opportunities such an obvious disparity in safety measures among various positions would provide them if the ultimate helmet mandate were implemented in the way it had been rolled out in the preliminary, experimental stage.

THE NFL'S LEGACY OF CTE DEFLECTION, DECEPTION, AND LIES

For decades, the NFL did everything possible to cover up the dangers of brain damage to its players. These disturbing efforts, which were aptly described by sports journalists at the time as involving deflections, deceptions, lies, and a combination of all three, went on for decades. Now the league is earnestly asking the American public to believe it is sincerely committed to protecting the safety of players' brains when it assesses—in-house, rather than with a rigorous scientific study—the efficacy of the new helmet configuration the NFL hopes will substantially reduce negative effects of, and perceptions about, concussions and repeated sub-concussive impacts on athletes' cognitive and mental health.

A summary of a few of the more recent outrages makes the point that the NFL should not be trusted without close scrutiny and skepticism of its claims. As will be described in more detail later in this chapter, Junior Seau committed suicide in 2012 during one of his reported bouts with the effects of CTE. In 2015, when Seau was to be inducted into the NFL

Hall of Fame posthumously, his daughter, whom Seau had designated to speak on his behalf, was denied that opportunity. The NFL apparently did not want deceased players' CTE symptoms to even be referenced, much less emphasized, during those ceremonies.

Thus, in 2010, once it became obvious that there might be a string of NFL players who had died in tragic ways related to CTE being inducted into the football Hall of Fame, a remarkably suspicious rule was instituted, which apparently was still in place as of summer 2023, barring anyone but the player himself from speaking. The NFL, citing this rule, declined to make an exception to honor Seau's predeath request. As David Baker, a past Hall of Fame president, explained, "Our mission is to honor the heroes of the game. . . . We're going to celebrate his life, not the death and other issues."[31]

Similarly, the NFL successfully sportswashed Jovan Belcher's CTE-infused murder-suicide in 2012. The *New York Times* summarized what had happened this way: "With his coach looking on, a Kansas City Chiefs linebacker shot and killed himself outside the team's practice facility . . . less than an hour after he killed his girlfriend . . . ," who also was the mother of his baby daughter.[32] *Times* television critic Richard Sandomir observed later that "sports . . . has become adept at a type of cleansing more commonly associated with authoritarian governments." Belcher, like many other star athletes with suspected CTE, was simply "airbrushed from the highlights."[33]

This shameful history of obscuring and covering up brain damage—which directly involved Goodell, the NFL's chief publicist at the time—does not inspire much confidence in the objectivity or sincerity of the league when it comes to matters involving the brain health of its players. As the recent stories of NFL athletes below illustrate, even the league's much ballyhooed concussion protocols, which have been revised repeatedly, continue to malfunction when put into practice.

So much discretion continues to be placed on the teams, the coaches, the doctors whose allegiances are often conflicted, and the players themselves, who do not want to be viewed as soft or concussion-prone or have their value as athletes diminished. Even during games, when the television cameras are rolling, there are screw-ups and questionable decisions made with respect to the brain health of the players. What happens in practices is anyone's guess. A major problem is that there is a great deal of incentive for misdiagnosing head injuries of key athletes, especially quarterbacks, then clearing them to get back on the field, especially when players themselves participate in the deception in order to get back on the field as soon as possible.

What is reasonably clear, however, is that the NFL's concussion protocols are not being implemented as independent, medically based decisions. There are too many subjective factors that come into play. As Kevin Blackistone wrote in the *Washington Post*, even boxers and MMA fighters are "protected by state laws that . . . err on the side of extreme caution." When they sustain a "knockout . . . [they are kept] out of competition and even practices, for a month or more."[34] This rarely happens in the NFL. On top of all that, after experiencing slight declines the previous two years, during the 2022–2023 regular season the number of reported concussions in the NFL spiked by 18 percent.[35]

Moreover, even if these concussion protocols were judiciously implemented to protect players' health, they may have little effect on the reportedly more serious problem for NFL athletes: repeated subconcussive impacts, which do not immediately produce concussion-like symptoms but can lead to lifelong cognitive malfunctions and behavioral issues.

THE UNNECESSARY DANGERS OF HOCKEY

While no one is arguing that hockey is as unsafe as football, boxing, cage fighting, or some extreme sports, it still is near the top of the list for popular North American contact sports. The NHL had its own brain damage cover up (discussed below). Hockey, however, can be made far less dangerous without changing the fundamental nature of that sport, which involves skating and stickhandling the puck, not fighting and other acts of violence. So the NHL's reluctance to better protect hockey players by eliminating or more strictly limiting fisticuffs, sticks to the face and head, and hits that send players headfirst into the boards and onto the ice reflects an unseemly hockey culture.

One of the most dangerous aspects of the game in terms of brain injuries is body checking, which occurs when players use their hip or shoulder to crash into another player, usually the one controlling the puck. It is not permitted in women's hockey, except in certain international competitions, and it is prohibited in youth hockey up to age fourteen. However, it is allowed in men's high school, college, and professional hockey. Body checking, unlike tackling in football, is not essential to the game, as women hockey players have demonstrated.

Nevertheless, body checking, along with fighting, remains an ingrained part of the men's game. Yet a study by Toronto neurosurgeon Charles Tator "estimates that if body checking were prohibited" as much as 85 percent of the collisions in which players experience "persisting concussion symptoms such as memory problems, difficulty concentrating, anxiety, depression and sleep problems" could be avoided, along with a "99 percent reduction in the number of months suffering with symptoms." In addition, the absence of body checking would likely reduce substantially the long-term problem of hockey-related brain damage and CTE, "which can lead to aggression, paranoia and dementia."[36]

To its credit, the NHL was willing to move more quickly than the MLB in protecting its fans from errant pucks by supplementing the existing Plexiglas barriers surrounding the ice with netting. As for player safety, however, the league—and much of the sport—seems to have engaged in sportswashing rather than comprehensive and meaningful league action by promoting the importance of athletes taking personal responsibility for reducing violence in their sport.

Under NHL commissioner Gary Bettman's reign, the most notable improvement has been the creation of a league Department of Player Safety. Each game is supposed to be reviewed to ensure that rules are strictly enforced against players who cause head injuries to their opponents. Nevertheless, NHL and minor-league hockey players continue to sustain head injuries that are serious enough to keep them off the ice for multiple games, sometimes threatening their careers and even their lives. Furthermore, NHL and other hockey players regularly sustain subconcussive impacts that are difficult, if not impossible, to identify, much less count, but collectively can be deadly over a hockey player's career.

Superstar players like Sidney Crosby, Chris Pronger, and Eric Lindros have all made headlines for their ordeals in dealing with the immediate and long-term impact of brain damage. Based on postmortem tests, player advocates have estimated that about 90 percent of all NHL players will have CTE before they die, a rate comparable with that of NFL players. This is backed up by the very high percentage of CTE found in the brains of deceased former hockey players.

The longer-term impacts of CTE and other forms of brain damage have been felt most notably by former NHL enforcers, who appear to be the most likely hockey players and former players to suffer devastating effects, including addiction to painkillers and alcohol. Goons, as they are sometimes called, are not only at higher risk than most hockey players for concussions, subconcussive impacts, broken bones, and destroyed teeth, but in their roles as enforcers they are instructed to go out of their way to inflict punishment on their opponents, and thus themselves as well.

Enforces are expected to act like prize fighters on skates, willing to drop their gloves and start hitting—and be hit—in the face or head for any perceived slight, for intimidation, or simply for the fun of it. Enforcers also are not shy about deliberately injuring their opponents with vicious blindside hits that can send their victims' heads into the boards or ice with extreme force. They also are known for their proficiency in delivering scar-making cuts and contusions to their opponents' heads from high sticks and slashing.

The NHL and the hockey world have long been aware of the dangers of excess hockey aggression and violence but have marginalized its impact through propaganda and deception. Much like the NFL, NHL officials historically tried to pretend that there was no violence problem. Not so long ago, those officials gushed that the NHL was "completely satisfied with the responsible manner in which the league and players have managed player safety."[37] When that rosy statement was made in 2013, the league still had no "sound concussion protocols for responding to players injured on the ice," much less harsh penalties to deter violence on the ice.[38]

In 2015, Bettman was still maintaining in video legal depositions that because there was "no medical certainty that concussions lead to

CTE," he could think of "no reason to warn NHL players about [its] risks." He also contended that the link "between fighting in hockey and brain damage" could not be established because the "sample has been too small."[39] This led lawyer and Hall of Fame former Montreal Canadiens goaltender Ken Dryden to observe that the CTE propaganda that team owners, the league, and the NHL's paid experts were disseminating was not only "embarrassing" but also a "betrayal" of the players' trust.[40]

In March 2016, the NHL's falsehoods about the health impacts of fighting were revealed in emails written by Bettman and his key deputies in 2011. Officials had "privately acknowledged that fighting could lead to concussions and long-term health problems, including depression . . . and [abuse of] . . . pills to ease the pain." The league was aware that enforcers were known to have a higher "incidence of head injuries/concussions, which raise[d] the incidence of depression onset, which raise[d] the incidence of personal tragedies."[41] Nonetheless, Bettman has continued to deny "any connection between long-term brain damage and hits to the head," instead stressing that "the game is safer now than it ever has been."[42]

BRAIN INJURIES IN SOCCER

Warnings about CTE symptoms in soccer players have been around for years. The primary identified culprit has been repeated heading of the ball, especially by younger players. This is a concern for both male and female soccer players. Players may be concussed if they are hit in the head with a ball, by another player, or the ground. In fact, an estimated 22 percent of all soccer injuries are due to concussions. Nonetheless, those types of brain injuries occur far less frequently than subconcussive impacts from repeatedly heading a soccer ball.

In the summer of 2022, stories emerged about soccer players Scott Vermillion (profiled below), who was diagnosed with CTE after his death, and Bruce Murray, a still-living former player suspected of having CTE. Dr. Ann McKee, director of the CTE Research Center at Boston University and a neuropathologist, put it this way: "Soccer is clearly a risk for C.T.E.—not as much as football, but clearly a risk."[43]

Former American professional soccer players like Taylor Twellman, Alecko Eskandarian, and World Cup champion Brandi Chastain "have been vocal about concussions" in soccer. Twellman and Eskandarian, both former MLS players, have stated that brain traumas "ended their careers," while Chastain has "pledged to donate her brain for C.T.E. research." Cindy Parlow Cone, who is now the president of US Soccer, retired from playing professional soccer in 2006 with post-concussion syndrome. Despite these revelations, soccer is still well behind football and hockey in implementing even modest safety measures because "the research and public conversation around C.T.E. and head injuries are still emerging."[44]

This has led Chastain to urge people "to understand the gravity of the situation. . . . It needs attention." Rory Smith, soccer columnist for the *New York Times*, has argued that not only is heading dangerous, but like fighting and body checking in hockey, it is being viewed as increasingly irrelevant to the aesthetic beauty of the sport and the level of play.

When this transformation will occur is impossible to predict, Smith says, but he believes "[t]he days of heading in soccer are numbered." He hopes "the skill [will] gradually fall into obsolescence, and then drift inexorably towards extinction" without the need for "an absolute prohibition." He notes that the "connection between heading and [CTE and dementia] has been soccer's tacit shame for at least two decades, if not longer." Smith concludes that even in "a sporting sense, . . . it is easy to believe that heading's demise would be no great loss."[45]

ATHLETES WHO LIKELY WERE DAMAGED DUE TO CTE OR CTE-LIKE SYMPTOMS

While stories about athletes devastated by CTE or CTE-like brain damage symptoms are increasing in number, it is likely they represent a small but unknown percentage of a much larger problem. So far, these personal narratives have been concentrated in a few sports, especially football, hockey, and more recently soccer. This reflects both the relative number of cases that have been uncovered as well as the media and fan popularity of each of those sports. Unsurprisingly, as the most popular sport in the United States, football has received the most concussion attention by far, even more so than boxing and other forms of fighting. Yet other sports like hockey, soccer, skiing, and bobsledding have produced concerning examples as well.

Together, these narratives from various athletes chronicle a variety of mental, emotional, and behavioral concerns and tragedies, including murders and suicides, that have been linked to suspected or verified brain damage. The subjects have been mainly men, but the struggles of some female athletes have also been publicized. Sometimes, erratic behaviors that seem to accompany severe brain damage are complicated by substance abuse, which can be difficult to sort out from CTE or brain damage–related misbehaviors. Many of the athletes, especially football players who are known to have engaged in violence targeting women, may have been affected by yet-to-be-confirmed CTE symptoms.

Below are some of the more moving, remarkable, notorious, and tragic reported or confirmed narratives of athletes with brain damage that have emerged over the past twenty years or so. They include individuals who had brain damage that was diagnosed while they were alive, were diagnosed postmortem with CTE, or exhibited suspicious erratic behaviors that appeared to be related to brain damage but were never conclusively diagnosed.

Mike Webster (Pittsburgh Steelers)

By most accounts, the tragic death of the Pittsburgh Steelers' Hall of Fame center Mike Webster, who died in 2002 when he was only fifty, changed the conversation about CTE in the NFL, and in other sports as well. Greg Garber of ESPN described Webster as a former player whose life ended prematurely from drugs that caused "heart failure . . . [after an] odyssey of bizarre behavior and homelessness." Webster took "a numbing cocktail of powerful medications" to calm his nerves, for anxiety and depression, to prevent seizures, as painkillers, and for Parkinson's disease. In addition, Webster had "dementia." A dozen years after he retired in 1990, his body was found in a bed with "a bucket of vomit by his side."[46]

When he successfully sued the NFL's retirement board in 1999 for benefits based on what was described as "irreparable brain damage from repeated concussions," Webster established a precedent for other former NFL players who had played long enough to be vested in the plan to seek compensation for their concussion-related brain damage. His death provided Pittsburgh coroner and pathologist Bennet Omalu with the first opportunity to diagnose CTE in an athlete by measuring tau deposits—"abnormal accumulations of a protein called tau that collect inside neurons,"[47] which is a sign of dementia and CTE—in Webster's brain.

This was the first step in forcing the NFL to finally acknowledge that, like boxers, many football players probably have CTE. Yet, as *Reader's Digest* reported following Webster's death, until the very end, he was coaching and training his "six-foot-nine, 340-pound teenage son," Garrett, how to play football scholastically. Webster attended every one of his son's high school games.[48]

Muhammad Ali (Professional Boxing)

Muhammad Ali, perhaps the most consequential and influential American athlete of the twentieth century, later in life became an advertisement for the dangers of brain damage from boxing, even though he and his family always resisted his being characterized as punch-drunk. They preferred to explain his symptoms as being a result of his Parkinson's disease, which was diagnosed only three years after his last fight. Yet Parkinson's, like Alzheimer's disease and ALS, is directly linked to having CTE from repeated blows to the head. A boxer like Ali undoubtedly was hit in the head tens of thousands of times in his fights and when sparring in preparation for fights.[49]

Unfortunately, Ali and his family were reticent to acknowledge that he had CTE symptoms, and his brain was not examined after he died. If boxing's most well-known athlete were confirmed to have CTE, it would certainly bring attention to this problem, which affects almost every boxer later in life, and many well before that. Few high-profile boxers or their families have spoken out about the ravages of CTE, which produces "slurred speech, memory loss, shakes, violent mood swings, depression and other symptoms" in boxers.[50] As one boxing expert explained in 2021, "Boxing turned its back for nine decades and we haven't had our [Mike] Webster moment yet."[51]

John Grimsley (Houston Oilers and Miami Dolphins)

John Grimsley, a linebacker who played in the NFL from 1984 to 1993, shot and killed himself in 2008 under suspicious circumstances, which a coroner sympathetically ruled an accident rather than suicide. His wife, though, described Grimsley as having had various cognitive and emotional issues, including memory loss, mood swings, and bouts of anger "without warning or provocation."[52]

His wife also agreed that Grimsley's brain should be the first one to be examined for CTE by the researchers at the Boston University Chobanian and Avedisian School of Medicine. They found widespread tau deposits, indicating the presence of CTE and proof that Grimsley had suffered extensive brain damage. Researchers at Boston University later examined the brains of many other deceased elite athletes who had participated in various contact sports, especially football and hockey. An overwhelming percentage of them, like Grimsley, showed substantial signs of CTE.

Chris Henry (Cincinnati Bengals)

In 2009, Chris Henry of the Cincinnati Bengals became the first active NFL player to be diagnosed with CTE after he died under tragic circumstances at the height of his career. The talented wide receiver, who had a storied history of behavior problems, died in a domestic dispute with his fiancée. He mysteriously fell out of the back of his pickup truck, which his girlfriend was driving. At the time, Henry was in Charlotte, North Carolina, on leave from the team while recovering from a broken arm.

Henry had been suspended twice from the NFL for a total of ten games. He also had been arrested five times for "marijuana possession, a concealed weapon charge, a DUI, a probation violation, [and] serving alcohol to minors." The year before his death, a judge had identified Henry as "a one-man crime wave." Henry's erratic behaviors and the way he died, according to his family and friends, were totally unlike the person they had once known.[53]

His diagnosis with CTE after his death at age twenty-six sent shock waves throughout the NFL. It now seemed likely that CTE could begin to develop in football players much earlier than what was once thought to be the case.

Briana Scurry (Washington Freedom)

One of the earliest publicized stories about brain damage from concussions involving a female athlete centered on Briana Scurry, the Hall of Fame soccer goalie for the US women's national team (USWNT), which won Olympic gold in 1999 with her as the star goalkeeper. Eleven years later, while playing for the Washington Freedom (now the Spirit), Scurry experienced a devastating, career-ending injury when she was kneed in the head during a game in attempt to make a save.

Her life going forward was impacted by an array of mental and emotional symptoms—including depression, ongoing pain, memory loss, and anxiety—all of which may or may not have been a result of that one blow. There was little doubt, however, that this severe concussion was a contributing factor. Scurry was diagnosed with post-concussion syndrome. While she had a brief stint at ESPN, it did not last, and her life was a mess for over three years. Things did not improve for her until 2016, after she decided to become an advocate for female athletes' brain health.

In that role, she voices concerns about women, especially in Olympic or professional sports, not getting the care they need because head injuries are ignored or unreported, much like what happened in major contact sports for men. Like her USWNT teammate Brandi Chastain, who also experienced multiple concussions, Scurry has pledged that when she dies her brain will be donated to be examined for CTE.[54]

Dave Duerson (Chicago Bears)

Dave Duerson, the perennial Pro Bowl safety for the Chicago Bears, died by suicide, shooting himself in the chest in 2011 at age fifty. He had been experiencing severe symptoms of dementia, including memory loss and depression. He also exhibited erratic behaviors, such as an explosive temper and being abusive to his loved ones. Reportedly, Duerson's final words were, "Please, see that my brain is given to the NFL's brain bank."

A few months later, an examination at Boston University's CTE Research Center confirmed Duerson's suspicions that he had the disease.

In 2007, though, Duerson had told a Senate subcommittee that he doubted that football "players' cognitive and emotional struggles were related to football."[55] Unfortunately, such skepticism often kept symptomatic athletes and former athletes from getting the diagnosis, treatment, and care they needed. In Duerson's case, he changed his mind sometime after he was stricken with symptoms.

Bob Probert (Detroit Red Wings and Chicago Blackhawks)

From 1985 to 2002, Bob Probert gained a well-deserved reputation as one of the NHL's leading enforcers, prevailing in most of his "246 [bare-knuckle brawling] fights." Less than ten years after he retired, Probert died from heart failure. Like many enforcers, he had a long history of substance abuse—both alcohol and cocaine. As a result, he was imprisoned for ninety days and suspended for the entire 1994–1995 season while he recovered from substance abuse in a rehabilitation facility.[56]

A few months after his death, Boston University's CTE Research Center revealed that Probert's brain, like those of so many deceased NFL football players, showed that he had CTE. He was one of a string of NHL enforcers diagnosed with the disease after their deaths, including Rick Rypien, Wade Belak, Steve Montador, Todd Ewen, and most famously, Derek Boogaard, who died shortly after Probert.

Derek Boogaard (Minnesota Wild and New York Rangers)

When Derek Boogaard overdosed on painkillers in 2011 while in recovery for a hockey-induced concussion, his tragic death made national news. A few months later, his family sued the NHL, alleging that physicians affiliated with two NHL teams were partly responsible for his addiction to painkillers.

Buried in an array of legal claims was the contention that Boogaard's brain had been damaged while he was carrying out his role as an NHL enforcer. Lending support to that allegation was the conclusion of Boston University neuroscientists that Boogaard had CTE. After the original lawsuit was refiled, a more prominent claim was added describing how the NHL had been "responsible for the physical trauma and brain damage that Boogaard sustained."[57]

Although the suit was dismissed in 2017 on technical legal grounds that had nothing to do with the merits of the case, the federal judge hearing the matter went out of his way to note that "this opinion should not be read to commend how the NHL handled Boogaard's particular circumstances—or the circumstances of other NHL players who over the years have suffered injuries from on-ice play."[58]

Ryan Freel (Cincinnati Reds and Other MLB Teams)

In 2013, Ryan Freel became the first former MLB player to be diagnosed with CTE. He was examined not long after he died by suicide with a shotgun at the age of thirty-six, only two years after his retirement. He reportedly sustained as many as ten concussions over his career, missing thirty games in 2007 alone with post-concussion syndrome after colliding with a teammate. In 2006, Freel's mental condition should have raised red flags when he told a reporter at the *Dayton Daily News* that there was an imaginary companion "who lives in my head who talks to me and I talk to him."[59] In April 2009, he was once again on the disabled list after being hit in the head by an errant throw during a play to try to pick him off at second base.[60]

Freel was one of those Pete Rose–like ball players who "ran into walls, hurtled into the seats and crashed into other players trying to make catches." He also was a loving father to three girls. When the positive results of the CTE exam were announced, his wife said she was pleased because it would offer their children a way to "understand why he did what he did."[61]

Junior Seau (San Diego Chargers)

The suicide of Hall of Fame linebacker Junior Seau at age forty-three in 2012 may have been the CTE-related death that had the most jarring impact. At one point, Seau was so distressed after being arrested for domestic violence that he "drove his sport utility off a cliff." As Dave Duerson had done, Seau shot himself in the chest so his brain would remain intact. He reportedly was convinced that his erratic behaviors, including angry outbursts and isolation from family and friends, was the result of brain damage.[62]

As it turned out, Seau's suspicions were largely confirmed a few months after he died when researchers at the National Institutes of Health diagnosed him with CTE. His ex-wife, who had divorced him as a result of his erratic behaviors, wanted "everyone to know Junior did indeed suffer from CTE." She explained that all those "head-to-head collisions over the course of 20 years playing in the NFL . . . gradually . . . developed the deterioration of his brain and ability to think logically."[63]

As noted earlier, Seau's story received additional media coverage in 2015 when, leading up to and during the ceremony to induct him post-humously into the Pro Football Hall of Fame, his daughter was denied the opportunity to speak on his behalf.[64] The NFL's insensitivity brought even more attention to his having been found to have CTE at a relatively young age, perhaps even more than if the league had allowed his daughter to speak at that ceremony on his behalf.

Aaron Hernandez (New England Patriots)

Undoubtedly the most notorious and unsettling story of a football player who was found to have had CTE is that of former New England Patriots All-Pro tight end Aaron Hernandez. He hung himself in a jail cell while being tried for the third of three murders he had been charged with committing as an active NFL player. Given his long history of antisocial behaviors beginning in high school and throughout college, it is uncertain to what extent his severe symptoms from CTE were responsible for his behavior and his demise at such a young age.

Hernandez knew he had a problem, though, which is why, when his daughter was born in the fall of 2012, he acknowledged that "I can't be young and reckless . . . no more."[65] Unfortunately, that was a few months after a drive-by shooting for which he was eventually charged in the killings of two people. A year and a half later, Odin Lloyd, a close acquaintance who apparently had been blabbing to the wrong people that Hernandez was responsible for that alleged double homicide, was murdered as well, and Hernandez faced charges for that crime. At around the same time, in May 2013, Hernandez received football's Pop Warner Inspiration to the Youth Award.

Hernandez was ultimately found not guilty of the double murders because the jury reportedly deemed a key witness unreliable, but Hernandez was convicted of murdering Lloyd. After Hernandez's apparent suicide, though, his legal record was cleansed. A common law precedent provided that in the event of a defendant's death before an appeal can be concluded, any convictions must be overturned. Thus, in the eyes of the legal system, upon his death Hernandez became an innocent man.[66]

That ruling might well have ended any further scrutiny of Hernandez's football life, except his family, like the families of so many deceased players with troubled pasts, submitted his brain for testing at Boston University's CTE Research Center. Neuroscientists there found that Hernandez's brain showed substantial signs of CTE. The amount of brain damage found in the recently active twenty-seven-year-old NFL player was surprising. One researcher noted it was "the most severe case they had ever seen in someone of Aaron's age."[67] Hernandez had participated for several years in Pop Warner football before playing in high school, which apparently had substantially increased his risk for cognitive impairment and mental disorders later in his college and NFL football careers.

Jovan Belcher (Kansas City Chiefs)

Sandwiched in between Hernandez's CTE-related shooting sprees was Jovan Belcher's horrific murder-suicide. As discussed earlier, that tragedy received much less attention because the NFL was largely successful in obscuring the story. A lawsuit filed by Belcher's mother many months later on behalf of Belcher's infant daughter, however, refocused attention on the case, which was exactly what the NFL had wanted to airbrush from history.

As Dave Zirin wrote in the *Nation*, by subjecting that NFL franchise to "a discovery process under oath," Belcher's mother was about to uncover valuable pieces of "everything the NFL attempts to hide in its skeleton-stuffed closet: guns, violence against women, . . . and head injuries." The plaintiff's lawyers accused the Chiefs of negligence "in exposing Belcher to frequent head trauma and failing to offer him adequate care." Once the team became "aware of Belcher's symptoms and signs of cognitive and neuropsychiatric impairment," allegedly they did nothing to intervene.[68]

Those failures, the plaintiff's lawyers contended, "caused or contributed to cause irresistable and/or insane impulses," which led to the murder-suicide. An autopsy revealed that Belcher had advanced CTE. In the lawsuit, his mother alleged the NFL's "culture of harassment and bullying" had made her son's mental impairments much worse.[69] Reportedly, the suit was withdrawn when the plaintiffs elected, along with many other players' families, to take advantage of the NFL's CTE settlement.[70]

Chris Pronger (Philadelphia Flyers and Other NHL Teams)

Hall of Fame defenseman Chris Pronger sustained career-ending head trauma when he was felled by two severe injuries to his brain and eye, back to back, during the 2011–2012 season. Although he did not retire right away because he was still under contract, he never played another NHL game.

Since his retirement, Pronger has experienced frequent migraines, was driven into a "black hole of depression," and has had to deal with other CTE-like symptoms. Although Pronger was not an enforcer, he easily took off his gloves to fight his opponents and was known around the league for "always deliver[ing] more punishment than he received." Despite all he had been through, however, he accepted, at least in part, Bettman's argument about personal responsibility of the athletes involved. Pronger expressed the sentiment embraced by the NHL that it is up to the players, not the league, to "look out for themselves by talking about symptoms and protecting themselves on the ice."[71] That personal responsibility rationalization, however, inevitably diminishes the league's legal and moral obligation to protect its players.

Amanda Kessel (US Women's Hockey Team)

Often praised as the best American female hockey player ever, Amanda Kessel decided not to play during the 2014–2015 college season at the University of Minnesota—her final year of eligibility—due to post-concussion syndrome she experienced after being injured just before the 2014 Olympics. Kessel's coach said, "It's just not worth it for her and her health." Apparently, Kessel had a "litany of . . . ailments," including "debilitating headaches [and] light sensitivity." Kessel said there were "'some really dark times'" that were accompanied by mood swings and problems sleeping.[72]

Kessel's situation improved greatly after going to see the same doctor who was treating Pittsburgh Penguins superstar Sidney Crosby for his extended post-concussion problems. The doctor kept Kessel away from hockey for eighteen more months but instituted an active plan to treat her symptoms with workout routines including "vertical and lateral exercises" to deal with her sensory and motion problems.[73] Kessel returned to hockey action in early 2016, becoming a key member of Minnesota's national championship team. Since then, she has played in two more Olympics for the US team, in 2018 and 2022, helping them win gold and silver, respectively.

Pavle Jovanovic (US Bobsledder and "Sled Head")

Since 2013, three North American bobsledders have committed suicide: Adam Wood in 2013 at age thirty-two; Travis Bell in 2014 at age forty-two; and, most recently, Pavle Jovanovic in 2021. Jovanovic, an Olympic bobsledder for both the United States and Serbia, was only forty-three at the time of his death. The *New York Times* reported that "[d]egenerative brain problems and their debilitating effects have become an increasingly open secret within the tight-knit world of bobsled and its sister sport, skeleton, in which competitors slide headfirst on small sleds."[74] Those athletes have coined the term "sled head" to describe the brain damage and CTE-like symptoms many of them experience.

The array of symptoms include "constant headaches, a heightened sensitivity to bright lights and loud voices, forgetfulness and psychological problems." Apparently, this type of damage can be caused by "[c]atastrophic crashes" and repeated "brain rattling . . . that researchers have compared with shaken baby syndrome." Jovanovic suffered from mental and cognitive disorders following his retirement, was a heavy drinker and moody, and had anger issues. He was treated for alcoholism, depression, and bipolar disorder and was taking medication for "shakes and tremors." Despite his engineering degree, he was no longer able to do simple mathematics.[75]

After Jovanovic hung himself, his brain was examined and found to have significant levels of CTE. The *New York Times* reported that it was comparable to the levels of the disease found in the brains of Junior Seau and Aaron Hernandez.

Vincent Jackson (San Diego Chargers and Tampa Bay Buccaneers)

Three-time Pro Bowl wide receiver Vincent Jackson, who played in the NFL from 2005 to 2016, was found dead in a Florida hotel room in 2021 after his family reported him missing. He was only thirty-eight years old. In his mid-thirties, according to Dr. Ann McKee, director of Boston University's CTE Research Center, Jackson had been transformed from "a brilliant, disciplined, gentle giant . . . to [becoming] depressed, with progressive memory loss, problem-solving difficulties, paranoia, and eventually extreme social isolation."[76]

Jackson was found to have stage 2 CTE "from repetitive blows to the head." That diagnosis came shortly before a Florida medical examiner ruled his cause of death to be chronic alcoholism. The same doctor noted, however, that Jackson had CTE. Early in his career, when Jackson was with the San Diego Chargers, he had been arrested twice on DUI charges and suspended for three games.[77] This may well been the result of early symptoms of CTE-related brain damage.

Antonio Brown (Pittsburgh Steelers, Oakland Raiders, and Other NFL Teams)

From his rookie season in 2010 through 2018, superstar Antonio Brown caught more passes than any other NFL wide receiver, all for the Pittsburgh Steelers. In 2016, he sustained a serious concussion during a game. The next year he suffered what was described as a severe helmet-to-helmet impact and then another "big-hit . . . after that."[78]

In 2018, during his last year with the Steelers, Brown's behavioral problems became public. That April, Brown reportedly tossed a piece of furniture out of his apartment window, injuring an infant. Later, he was arrested for speeding and reckless driving. Toward the end of the regular season, he was benched for skipping practices.

Brown requested a trade, and in March 2019 he was sent to the Oakland Raiders, where his erratic behaviors became even more pronounced. Brown missed about ten preseason practice sessions due to frostbite he had sustained while undergoing cryotherapy for an injury. He missed many more practices after refusing to wear one of the new, somewhat more protective, league-mandated helmets that preceded the Guardian Cap. When he lost his first grievance, Brown filed another because his replacement helmet also had failed to meet NFL standards. By the time he agreed to wear the required equipment, the season was about to begin.

Raiders general manager Mike Mayock fined Brown $54,000. Brown attacked Mayock verbally and tried to physically assault him but was restrained by his teammates. After apologizing, Brown was briefly reinstated. The next day, however, he asked for and was granted a release because the Raiders said his behaviors had voided the guaranteed-payment part of his contract.

The New England Patriots immediately signed Brown to a $15 million contract, most of which was guaranteed. A few days later, Brown's former trainer filed a lawsuit against him for allegedly sexually assaulting her on three separate occasions. When another woman accused him of sexual misconduct and various text messages surfaced in which Brown had tried to intimidate his accusers before the 2019 season had even begun, the Patriots released him.

Brown did not play in the NFL for more than a year. During that hiatus in January 2020, he was involved in several police-involved domestic disputes in Florida with the mother of three of his children. Thereafter, an arrest warrant was issued because Brown allegedly attacked the driver of a moving truck his ex-girlfriend had hired, which was in front of Brown's home. He pleaded no contest to felony battery and burglary charges based on that confrontation. Brown was sentenced to community service, required to attend anger management classes, and undergo a psychological evaluation.

In April 2021, Brown's football career seemed back on track when the Super Bowl champion Tampa Bay Buccaneers, at the urging of quarterback Tom Brady, signed Brown to a one-year deal worth more than $6 million. At the beginning of the 2021 regular season, though, Brown was placed on COVID leave because he had been untruthful about his vaccination status and the NFL suspended him for three games.

The likely end to Brown's NFL career came at the end of the regular season in early January 2022. In the third quarter of a game against the New York Jets, Brown reportedly refused to play. When he was asked to leave the field, he took off his jersey, shirt, and football equipment and ran into the locker room. Buccaneers head coach Bruce Arians told the media Brown was no longer part of the team, and the Buccaneers officially released him several days later. Afterward, Will Leitch of *New York* magazine wrote, "Something hasn't been right with [Brown] for a while, and the erratic behavior does seem to track with those hits and concussions."[79]

Brown, though, claimed his injuries were from something else. Shortly after his release, the ex-football player appeared on *The Full Send Podcast* hosted by Bob Menery, ostensibly to address questions about Brown's mental health and suspected CTE. Brown brushed it all off. The athlete noted that CTE cannot be diagnosed until the player is dead, opining that he had "mental wealth. . . . Not mental health, mental wealth."

Brown then appeared with his lawyer on HBO's *Real Sports*, accusing the Buccaneers of trying to cover up their mistreatment of his physical injury. Brown contended the Bucs had offered him $200,000 if he agreed to receive intensive mental health treatment and went on the injured reserve list in lieu of being released.[80]

A year later, though, the former player produced a live video on Instagram in which he acknowledged he had CTE-like symptoms, including being overly aggressive, which he blamed on being hit by his former Steelers teammate James Harrison, who was using an improper helmet. Brown may have been trying to build a case in order to sue or otherwise receive compensation for football-related brain damage.[81]

Scott Vermillion (US Soccer)

In late 2021, Scott Vermillion, who died of an accidental drug overdose in 2020, became the first American professional soccer player to be officially diagnosed with CTE by neuropathologists at Boston University. Vermillion had played in the MLS for only about three years when he was forced to retire in his early twenties due to a severe ankle injury.

According to Vermillion's family, upon his retirement he began displaying mental and cognitive symptoms associated with CTE: depression, impulse control problems, anger, memory loss, and substance abuse. On Christmas Day 2020, at the age of forty-four, Vermillion died of acute poisoning from a mixture of alcohol and prescription drugs. A year later, his brain was examined and showed the telltale signs of CTE.[82]

Bruce Murray, who was a key member of the 1990 US World Cup team, worries that he too has developed CTE after playing soccer for many years. Murray says he has had at least four serious concussions and has experienced early signs of dementia and related behavior problems. Robert Stern, a physician specializing in head injuries of athletes at Boston University's CTE Research Center, observed that Murray's dementia is "unusual" for someone who is only fifty years old.[83]

Tua Tagovailoa (Miami Dolphins)

In a perfect storm of incompetence and neglect, the flaws in the NFL's concussion protocols were put on full display in three nationally televised football games during the 2022–2023 season. Normally, much of what happens during practices—and even in games to less scrutinized players—tends to fly under the radar. In this case, however, the player garnering all the attention was Tua Tagovailoa, a young starting quarterback who was having a breakout season for the resurgent Miami Dolphins.

In the first contest played in September on a Sunday afternoon, his team was playing division rival Buffalo Bills. In the second quarter, Tagovailoa could be clearly seen staggering to even walk off the field after he was slammed to the ground, helmet first, by a Bills player. His "gross motor instability" appeared to be a clear sign of potential brain trauma. He left the field under concussion protocols to be examined by a "neurotrauma consultant" hired by the league but not the team itself.

"Inexplicably," the quarterback "was cleared to return . . . and finished the game."[84]

Four days later, Tagovailoa was quarterbacking in a Thursday night football game in Cincinnati. He had been certified to play after suffering what he and his team were now calling a "hyperextended" back, not a concussion or brain trauma that would have required him to be placed on the injured list. During that game, Tagovailoa was tackled hard, and once again his helmet struck the ground violently. This time he could not get up under his own power. He lay motionless, supine, with "his arms and fingers splayed in front of his face." Neuroscientists identify such a display as an involuntary response triggered by some sort of brain trauma.[85] Tagovailoa should never have been allowed on the field in the first place.

The NFL and the Dolphins went into full damage-control mode. The league, at the insistence of the NFLPA, fired the medical specialist who let the quarterback return to action in the Buffalo game, creating the impression that what had happened was entirely the result of that doctor's negligence. All the team-generated press releases and comments by head coach Mike McDaniel were suspiciously upbeat. Tagovailoa himself said all the right things: He felt okay and was improving but would not be playing in the next game.

A few days later, officials from the NFL and the players' union said they were going to speak with the quarterback to get his view of what had happened as part of an internal investigation, the results of which would be announced sometime in the future. Those officials also indicated that concussion protocols would be changed to prevent what had happened to Tagovailoa from happening again.

Initially, the league and the union were not able to agree what those changes should be or how the incident should be communicated to the public. In a matter of days, though, the NFL and the union reached an accord that teams and their medical personnel should no longer have the discretion to let a player back on the field if that athlete is visually evidencing some sort of ataxia, which they narrowly defined as "abnormality of balance/stability, motor coordination or dysfunctional speech."[86] Both parties to the agreement, however, continued to voice divergent explanations of what had happened to Tagovailoa, based not on a thorough investigation, which the NFL had not yet completed, but rather their differing self-interests.

The league continued to maintain that the fired medical specialist did nothing to circumvent league protocols. He applied the criteria that were then in effect, which gave him the discretion to let Tagovailoa play, based on his expert opinion that the quarterback had not suffered a concussion in the Sunday game. The union maintained that this was an error in judgment that, based on the collective bargaining agreement, justified firing the doctor.

Tagovailoa resumed his starting quarterback duties twenty-four days later and performed well for a while. Then he had some worrisome games as his performance level dropped toward the end of the regular season. In a late December contest against the Green Bay Packers, after being "sacked from behind. . . . Tagovailoa fell backward, his head smacking the field [once] again." Nevertheless, he was allowed to continue to play, proceeding to throw "three interceptions on three consecutive possessions." He had been permitted on the field because he "did not display the obvious loss of motor skills" to necessitate his removal. The next day, Tagovailoa "reported concussion symptoms to team personnel." He was ruled out of the Dolphins' last regular season contest and the team's first—and, as it turned out, last—playoff game.[87]

For a second time, it appeared very likely that Tagovailoa had not been removed from a game after suffering a concussion-inducing blow to the head. Without addressing what happened to Tagovailoa specifically, or the apparent failure of the league's concussion protocols, NFL chief medical officer Dr. Allen Sills remarked, "I can tell you there's been a sea change over the last decade in the willingness and the understanding of players to speak out about their symptoms."[88] The obvious implication was that it is the players' responsibility to protect themselves, not the league's, which is also the position the NHL has taken.

The NFL announced that the league and the players' union had determined, without any thorough investigation, that in dealing with Tagovailoa in that Christmas Day game there had been no violations of the concussion protocols. Unlike boxing, which has specific state-imposed rules about minimum time periods of inactivity following a concussion, the NFL's concussion protocols are too subjectively imposed to adequately protect players who are unwilling, unaware, or cognitively unable to take the right steps to protect themselves.

Conclusion

As these narratives encompassing various contact sports suggest, brain damage to athletes continues to be a major mental health concern. The number of these reported brain damage cases keeps rising. Yet much of the media still tends to buy into sportswashed claims that major US sports enterprises are committed to making their athletes substantially safer.

Meanwhile these enterprises—especially the NFL, which is the wealthiest and most popular spectator sport in the United States— choose instead to pour more and more money into lawyers and public relations specialists. These legal and media professionals are retained to limit the liability of these organizations for their brain damage neglect, while working to negate any bad publicity that neglect may generate.

Unfortunately, there appear to be no solutions on the horizon that will adequately protect the brains of athletes in any of the more dangerous contact sports. The type of jarring solutions that could work, particularly fundamental changes to the competitions themselves or outright prohibitions, are unlikely to be implemented anytime soon. In the meantime, brain damage to athletes has become another cost of doing business.

The incremental, stopgap approaches that have been tried or proposed may better protect the brains of some elite and aspiring elite athletes. Way too many of them, though, will sustain serious or severe cognitive and related brain damage, which will seriously diminish the quality and length of their careers and their lives, unless more dramatic steps are taken to reimagine what a new and improved status quo in these sports should be.

CHAPTER 8

Substance Abuse and Dependency

ANOTHER MAJOR CATEGORY OF MENTAL DISORDERS ATHLETES MUST contend with is substance abuse and dependency, including misuse of performance-enhancing drugs (PEDs). The Substance Abuse and Mental Health Services Administration, which is part of the US Department of Health and Human Services, defines substance abuse as "the recurrent use of alcohol and/or drugs [that] causes clinically significant impairment, including health problems, disability, and failure to meet major responsibilities at work, school, or home." When substance abuse and other mental health disorders occur together, they are "referred to as co-occurring disorders."[1] Such combinations seem to manifest frequently with athletes.

As in American society more generally, "[d]rug abuse in athletes is a significant problem that has many potential underlying causes." It "occurs in all sports and at most levels of competition."[2] Much the same can be said about alcohol abuse. Substance abuse or dependency can occur during athletes' careers, after they retire, or both. Difficulty adjusting to retirement can trigger substance abuse.

Dependency due to withdrawal symptoms makes it much more difficult for anyone, including athletes, to substantially reduce or quit abusing a substance. Unfortunately, athletes, like other people, tend to take more and more of these substances as their tolerance increases.

Substance abuse involving athletes may occur for many reasons, as has been discussed throughout the book. Chapter 4 covered the issue of athletes self-medicating to deal with co-occurring mental disorders or emotional challenges that can happen to anyone but tend to happen to athletes more frequently. Often, however, substance abuse is specifically related to performing as an athlete. Chapter 5 discussed substance abuse that may arise when elite and aspiring elite athletes are trying to better manage competitive stress, anxiety, and other training and performance challenges. Chapter 6 mentioned substance abuse as a potential issue for athletes trying manage the COVID pandemic. Chapter 7 examined the abuse of drugs and/or alcohol in the context of athletes and former athletes who have CTE, suspected CTE, or other brain trauma or damage.

This chapter focuses on the two largest remaining categories of substance abuse that affect athletes: athletes who are attempting to manage pain, injuries, and diminishing performance as a result of those injuries, often with the assistance or encouragement of team physicians, trainers, coaches, or other people in their sport, by misusing or otherwise becoming addicted to over-the-counter painkillers or prescription drugs; and athletes who are taking any one of a variety of illicit or illegal drugs in order to enhance their athletic performance, which can have dangerous side effects and/or be addictive, transforming what began as cheating into substance abuse.

This chapter also recounts stories of prominent athletes who have had or dealt with substance abuse issues. The emphasis here is on elite athletes for whom substance abuse appears to have been a prominent—if not the most prominent—mental health challenge. Often, however, those athletes were dealing with co-occurring mental disorders or emotional challenges as well.

Athletes who take PEDs may think their illicit or illegal behavior is the best way to perform better or to compete against other athletes, who they believe are cheating as well. The difference between feeling obliged to cheat to perform better and having and developing a compulsion to take PEDs may be difficult to discern, especially in the relatively few manicured narratives that become public.

Abuse of Drugs and Alcohol to Overcome Pain and Injuries

Underlying the substance abuse and addiction challenges of athletes in popular spectator sports, especially those played mostly by males, is a macho ethos that celebrates and rewards the ability of athletes to overcome pain that would typically incapacitate most other people. This ethos is reinforced because there also is an expectation by coaches, trainers, sports management, fans, and the media that athletes should be super resistant to pain and nagging injuries. Those who are not may be disparaged as being injury prone, weak, or a head case.

This mindset is problematic in several respects. First, unrelenting pain is nature's warning to human beings that they should stop engaging in whatever activity is causing them physical distress and discomfort. By ignoring or minimizing their pain, athletes may be placing their health and well-being at risk, especially in the long term.

Second, drugs that are used to eliminate or substantially reduce athletes' pain tend to mask symptoms of injuries rather than treat the underlying cause. Hence, dedicated athletes often have many nagging injuries when they train and compete that never really heal, at least not until they have time to rest their bodies in the off-season. Too often, however, those injuries never fully heal and become permanent impairments. When that happens, athletes may become physically and/or mentally unhealthy, especially as they age.

Third, unless athletes rely on over-the-counter medications, the drugs they take tend to be opioids (like hydrocodone or oxycodone), stimulants, or other similarly powerful controlled substances that have addictive properties and may well be obtained illegally. Even marijuana, which appears to have certain medicinal benefits, can be easily misused and/or used illegally, creating other health-related and/or legal problems.

Furthermore, even over-the-counter analgesics have risks, especially if taken in higher-than-recommended dosages or before or after consuming alcohol, which appears to be common. The image of athletes swallowing a handful of pain relievers, sometimes with alcohol, is part of this macho folklore, which reflects a counterproductive sports culture reality.

What happens to athletes trying to deal with nagging injuries is somewhat analogous to driving a car that has mechanical problems until it breaks down and can no longer function properly. Sometimes the vehicle can never be driven again. Usually it requires costly repairs, but rarely can it be made as good as it once was without replacing essential parts. Similarly, playing in—or with—pain from injuries managed with drugs, particularly if it occurs frequently, is likely to shorten athletes' careers and create long-term mental and related health problems in their lives after they retire from competitive sports. Reactive treatments are almost never as effective as preventive maintenance and care.

Making matters worse health-wise, many of these painkillers and prescription drugs, especially when they are misused by taking them more frequently or in higher doses than recommended, take on the addictive qualities of recreational drugs. These drugs can make users feel relaxed and euphoric, which in common parlance is called "getting high." This side effect contributes to abuse, tolerance, and dependency, which can propel users, including athletes, down the path of addiction.

Despite strong evidence that playing with pain is unhealthy, athletes are taught from a relatively young age that to be successful they must learn how to manage their pain and injuries, whether through sheer willpower or through artificial means. Coaches, trainers, teammates, team doctors, and even parents reinforce this message in different ways. The immediate and short-term athletic performance of athletes tends to be valued much more than their long-term health and well-being. As discussed in chapter 7, brain damage is the most powerful illustration of the consequences of playing with pain and injury, but it is only one of many serious conditions that can result.

Ultimately, in American spectator sports "there remains a strong psychological imperative . . . which believes overcoming pain and injury is what real men do. . . . This bravado is greatly enhanced among elite athletes, in locker rooms and among fans."[3] As William Rhoden wrote in the *New York Times*, "We ask players to play hurt. . . . We make heroes out of those who do and vilify those who do not."[4]

The Abuse of Painkillers in the NFL and NHL

Nowhere in the North American sports landscape is the misuse of pain-killers more apparent than in football and hockey, especially in the NFL and NHL, where being considered injury prone or not tough enough can quickly disrupt or end a player's career. Team doctors and trainers in both sports, including the minor leagues and major college football and hockey programs, often have divided loyalties between the ethics of their profession and what is perceived to be best for the teams that pay their salaries. As Sally Jenkins and Rick Maese concluded, based on their in-depth investigation of the NFL for the *Washington Post* in 2013, "a central tenet of the Hippocratic oath—'Do No Harm'—[can be] turned on its head."[5] This continues to be true today.

Ironically, most NFL players who participate in this type of drug abuse understand on some level that it is unhealthy, although the "getting high" aspect of such abuse may further cloud their judgment. Players often do not trust their team's medical staff, but they do embrace the trainers who can get them what they want with no questions asked. In many ways, it may be even worse in North American hockey, where coaches and teams insist upon making injured players play, especially in big games and the playoffs, unless they are physically unable to suit up. In professional hockey, "[i]njuries that are not apparent, especially concussions and mental impairments, tend to be dismissed, marginalized, and/or stigmatized." As in football, "strong medications are dispensed by team doctors and other members of the medical and training staffs."[6]

Although the drug aspects of this play-with-pain culture in professional, college, and Olympic sports are often illegal and/or unethical, especially the dual loyalties of team physicians, the social ramifications of breaking the law and behaving poorly in this regard are minuscule compared to the perceived monetary benefits. Beyond the prosecution of a San Diego team physician in a US Department of Justice probe of illegal prescriptions written by team doctors during the Obama administration, the NFL and college football have largely escaped serious government scrutiny. In addition, civil remedies have been few and far between.

As former Miami Dolphins corner back Byron Jones—who recently had to retire with crippling injuries before he turned thirty, after once being an All-Pro—warned young players about to come into the league in 2023: "DO NOT take the pills they give you. DO NOT take the injections they give you. If you absolutely must, consult an outside doctor to learn the long-term implications."[7]

One California federal judge, in dismissing a 2017 suit by former NFL players against the league and its teams for the harm caused by painkiller abuse, decided that this matter was an issue for collective bargaining, even though those agreements do not cover former football players because they are not allowed to be members of the players' union. That same federal court had previously dismissed most of the charges in the former players' lawsuit for failing to definitely prove the medical conditions they had developed in retirement were linked to the drugs they had received in the NFL or how their "teams administered pain medication to them."[8]

The NFL Players Association filed a grievance in which it alleged that the league and its teams violated the existing collective bargaining agreement because they had "illegally stored, transported and dispensed medication" using "NFL medical personnel" to keep players on the field.[9] The NFL responded by denying those allegations, and in a meeting with the Drug Enforcement Administration, league officials claimed that each team had a strictly enforced compliance plan in place to properly prescribe these drugs—a response that appeared to be untrue based on player and media accounts.

According to the NFLPA, owners and management viewed the dissemination of powerful painkillers as strategically necessary for teams to remain competitive with other teams.[10] Ultimately, the NFL, its teams, and its doctors were never held legally accountable for encouraging and concealing rampant drug abuse among the league's players. Presumably, this type of drug abuse continues to occur today and will be the subject of future media exposés.

Similarly, in professional, minor-league, and college hockey, instances of drug abuse seem to be widespread, but legal remedies in that sport also have been almost nonexistent. The family of NHL enforcer Derek Boogaard lost its wrongful death suit against the NHL, even though Boogaard died from a fatal drug overdose while he was still in the NHL's substance abuse program fighting his addiction to painkillers (see chapter 7). In 2018, the US Court of Appeals for the Seventh Circuit affirmed that his family members had failed to state a valid claim upon which restitution could be ordered.

What the court did not know at the time it made that ruling, however, was that two years earlier, former NHL player Brendan Shanahan, in his role as a league senior vice president, wrote an email to other NHL officials acknowledging that enforcers like Boogaard "take pills . . . to sleep . . . to wake up . . . to ease the pain . . . to amp up."[11] Thus, as in the NFL, the abuse of those drugs was known at the time in the NHL and very little was being done to address that concern.

In most spectator sports, even in the various major professional leagues, once athletes are out of their sports, they have limited or no opportunity to get financial or other assistance to deal with their addictions. Most of these sports do not have pension plans that provide such benefits to former athletes. Even if they do, as mentioned already, many athletes do not qualify because either they did not or will not play long enough to become vested in those plans, or plan administrators have stringent rules and decision-making protocols in place to exclude or limit a substantial proportion of their claims.[12]

The Use of Medical Marijuana for Pain and Other Conditions

Reasonably safe alternatives to addictive painkillers that would help athletes to play with nagging and more serious injuries are not readily apparent, with one alluring potential exception: medical marijuana. There is plenty of anecdotal evidence that athletes value its use as an alternative to opioids and as a recreational outlet. In addition, as is described in more detail below, at least one well-known athlete—football player Ricky Williams—seems to have used it religiously to deal with his social anxiety disorder.

Under federal law, however—which in this case preempts state law—the use of marijuana for medical purposes remains illegal, even in the many states that have legalized it for various purposes. Because of its federal illegality, Auburn football player C. J. Harris had his invitation as a preferred walk-on revoked after it was revealed that he was taking legally prescribed "cannabis oil to treat [his] epilepsy." The NCAA, consistent with how its lawyers interpret federal law, does not permit any type of "medical exemption" for marijuana or its active ingredients, which remains true for most professional team sports as well.[13]

Whether the professional leagues, the NCAA, and Olympic organizations doing business in the United States should sanction their athletes for using marijuana has become a complicated question. Doctors and scientists appear torn over the drug's medical benefits and risks. That division in medical opinion is unlikely to be resolved anytime soon.

There is a scarcity of empirical data and other scientific and medical evidence supporting the benefits of medical and now recreational marijuana, especially in the context of athletes managing their pain, when weighed against the risks of harmful side effects, reckless behaviors, and possible addiction. It is clear, though, that marijuana use is being legalized and decriminalized in many jurisdictions, but not by the federal government. What is much less clear, however, is whether marijuana provides a therapeutic alternative to other, more toxic drugs and whether it too can become addictive, and, if so, in what circumstances.

A few years ago, Golden State Warriors head coach Steve Kerr suggested it might be a good idea for athletes, specifically professional basketball players, to be allowed to use marijuana to deal with their pain. But former NBA player and longtime assistant coach John Lucas, who is a recovering drug addict and alcoholic, vehemently disagreed, saying that marijuana "hasn't killed anybody, but . . . it kills them emotionally, spiritually, and it will make you violate all your values."[14] To date, no professional league, including the NBA, has approved marijuana use for medical purposes, and only the NHL treats marijuana use as a public health concern rather than a disciplinary matter.

USE OF PERFORMANCE-ENHANCING DRUGS

While PEDs, as a class, do not necessarily lead to a substantially elevated risk of mental disorders and behavior problems, two notable examples do: anabolic steroids—hence the term "roid rage"—and amphetamines and methamphetamines (meth), which are used as stimulants but are known, in certain cases, to produce paranoia, convulsions, hallucinations, and compulsive and repetitive behaviors.[15]

Dozens of American athletes over the years have been accused of bulking up on steroids, with a few reportedly exhibiting signs of mental disturbances, including severe behavior problems. Professional baseball players in the later part of the twentieth century, Olympic track and field sprinters, and football players have been the most publicized culprits of this type of substance abuse, in part because those three sports are covered closely by the media. Most prominently, East German female athletes were accused of—and later reported dangerous side effects from—using steroids during and in their preparations for a string of Cold War–era Olympic Games. The most notorious recent example, however, involved South African runner Oscar Pistorius, who it was thought might be using roid rage as part of his defense but did not, after he was charged with murdering his girlfriend in 2013. (His story will be discussed below.)

Steroids

Steroids are not all alike. There are five basic types, but today, "[p]rofessional and recreational athletes commonly use anabolic-andogenic steroids (AASs) to [either] enhance performance [anabolic] or improve their physical appearance [andogenic]." Anabolic steroids "include testosterone and its numerous synthetic analogs," which are the most often used steroids in US and international spectator sports.[16] Andogenic steroids are popular in bodybuilding, where Arnold Schwarzenegger drew so much scrutiny due to his remarkable physique.

The sport of bodybuilding, both for men and women, has recently been under scrutiny for widespread use of these drugs. A *Washington Post* exposé titled "Built and Broken" revealed that such abuse often was accompanied by brain damage, which is consistent with anecdotal evidence.[17] Based on visual inspection alone, the physiques of these competitors have raised eyebrows for years. The irony is that bodybuilders are not super strong and healthy; they just want to look that way. Reportedly, many have a variety of physical and mental impairments.

While the physiological effects of long-term anabolic steroid use captured most of the early attention regarding dangerous health risks—including liver damage, stunted growth and puberty disruption in children and adolescents, and impotence—only more recently have the psychological effects been more closely studied. Depression, suicide, roid rage, and psychotic behaviors have all been identified as potential side effects from their long-term use.

Like many substances, PEDs, especially steroids, can be habit forming. Harrison Pope, "a professor of psychiatry at Harvard Medical School and leading researcher on anabolic steroids, . . . noted that steroid users in particular show all the signs of biological and psychological dependence." That means that athletes, whether they are bodybuilders, football players, wrestlers, or cyclists, must "take larger quantities over time, experience withdrawal effects when not taking them, and continue to use them despite warnings to stop . . . or the emergence of adverse side effects." Pope has warned that other PEDs may be similarly habit forming.[18] Further research is necessary, he opines, to properly assess the potential addiction risks and side effects of those other PEDs.

Amphetamines and Methampetamines (Meth)

Another particularly concerning class of PEDs is amphetamines, which include methamphetamines, known on the streets as "meth." These drugs are stimulants that excite the central nervous system, making athletes more alert and less fatigued. They also make users falsely feel powerful, strong, and motivated, all attributes that, if true, would make them practice and perform better. Amphetamines are also popular recreational drugs that are "potent, long-lasting and extremely addictive."[19]

Andre Agassi wrote in his autobiography, *Open*, that he was a crystal meth user beginning in 1997, but it was unclear whether he did this entirely for recreational purposes or also to enhance his performance. In any case, he acknowledged that he failed at least one Association of Tennis Professionals drug test but was never punished under the lax monitoring and enforcement policies the ATP adhered to at the time.[20]

Continued use of amphetamines creates a "high potential for tolerance and psychological dependency," which can produce "compulsive and stereotyped behaviors." Withdrawal can cause depression. Thus, while there is some debate whether such use is "physically or psychologically addictive or both," chronic or frequent users are subject to serious mental and physical health problems.[21]

ATHLETES WITH SUBSTANCE ABUSE AND ADDICTION ISSUES

More than a few of the athletes profiled in earlier chapters, including Derek Boogaard and Michael Phelps, had co-occurring substance abuse and addiction issues accompanying their other seemingly more primary mental disorders. The athletes discussed below are profiled here because substance abuse and addiction issues appear to have been their most dominant mental health challenge. Some of them have managed to recover, typically by agreeing to seek treatment and other types of help; many have experienced significant relapses, which is not usual with addiction and dependency, sometimes with career shortening or even more tragic consequences.

The death of Len Bias from a cocaine overdose in June 1986 was instrumental in changing—not in good ways—how federal jurisdictions across the United States would deal with drug use, especially crack cocaine, treating it as a serious felony with long prison sentences rather than as a public health matter. The September after Bias's death, Congress passed the Anti-Drug Abuse Act, which President Ronald Reagan signed into law. Bias's death also brought much more media attention to athletes who were caught abusing drugs of any sort.

Len Bias (Boston Celtics and University of Maryland)

Len Bias remains the University of Maryland's best basketball player ever. He was picked second in the 1986 NBA Draft, after future Hall of Fame center Patrick Ewing, by the legendary Boston Celtics. The Celtics felt they had found the perfect player to join Larry Bird in order to beat Magic Johnson and the Los Angeles Lakers and win more championships. Bias was being compared favorably to a young Michael Jordan.

On June 20 of that year, however, Bias was found unresponsive in "his dormitory suite . . . and two hours later was pronounced dead of cardiac arrest." Medical experts stated that the cause of death "in [this]

22-year-old in apparent top physical shape" was "cocaine . . . , a heart ailment that even frequent examinations might have missed or a combination of the two."[22]

According to ESPN, two days later, an autopsy revealed that Bias had a "copious amount of cocaine in his system." That retrospective ESPN article also went to great lengths to correct two false rumors that had been widely circulated after Bias's shocking death. First, it was very unlikely, as those who wanted to protect Bias's legacy and the Maryland basketball program had claimed, that this was his "first encounter with cocaine." Later, in court, an acquaintance of his testified that Bias was the one who had introduced him to coke and that on campus the star player had served as a "'courtesy middleman' in the drug trade." Second, the doctor who performed the autopsy stated that "'most likely' [Bias] smoked cocaine rather than snorted it in powder form through the nose." Years later, it turned out, based on the acquaintance's account, the doctor was probably incorrect in concluding crack cocaine had killed Bias.[23]

The misimpression that Bias died from a first-time exposure to crack cocaine would have dire policy consequences almost immediately. Bias "became a symbol of the fight against drugs in the 1980s. But [his death] ended up ushering in a discriminatory legal system."[24] Crack cocaine, more often used by Black people, would be dealt with far more harshly than other forms of cocaine and similarly harmful opioids, which are mostly used by white people.

In addition, treatment and rehabilitation options were soon curtailed in favor of imprisonment for poor and middle-class people of color, but not for famous athletes, like Andre Agassi, and other people of means. This type of lax enforcement and special treatment for athletes set the stage for how sports organizations would manage substance abuse issues in the twenty-first century.

Josh Hamilton (Tampa Bay Rays, Texas Rangers, and Los Angeles Angels)

After being chosen first overall in the 1999 MLB Draft by the Tampa Bay Rays, Josh Hamilton did not make it to the majors until 2007. His emotional turmoil in between—including multiple serious baseball injuries in the minor leagues—put him in a psychological frame of mind in which drugs and alcohol reportedly became his primary escape and passion. He first tested positive under the MLB's substance abuse protocols in 2003, after which he entered a treatment program while he was suspended from playing professional baseball. When Hamilton violated the conditions of his MLB drug treatment program in February 2004, he was barred from baseball indefinitely.

Following that suspension, Hamilton went on a "crack binge in 2005," which separated him from "his wife, stepdaughter, and his family." Later that year, he said he had found God and seemed to be back on the path to recovery. In June 2006, the MLB reinstated Hamilton, believing he was a sincere, born-again Christian athlete. In 2007, now with the Cincinnati Reds, he had a decent year. The following season, after being traded to the Texas Rangers, Hamilton had a monster year, vying for the triple crown throughout much of the summer. As one journalist wrote, it seemed as if Hamilton had made it "[t]o hell and back."[25] Hamilton wrote an autobiography in 2008 about how he had recovered by turning to Christianity, which he called *Beyond Belief*.

For five or six years, Hamilton appeared to be sober and performed very well as a baseball player. Then, during the off-season between 2014 and 2015, as many addicts do, he relapsed. After having shoulder surgery, he began using both cocaine and alcohol again. Hamilton reported his relapse just prior to a drug test that he was required to take three times a week under the MLB's drug treatment program. As a result of his voluntary admission before testing positive, under the medically enlightened rules of that program, Hamilton was not, and could not, be formally disciplined by the league or his team—the Los Angeles Angels—and escaped criminal liability as well.

The Angels, however, traded Hamilton back to the Texas Rangers. This effectively ended his major-league career. Subsequently, Hamilton's wife divorced him amid rumors of his infidelities and multiple relapses. In 2019, he was arrested and charged with felony assault against one of his daughters.[26] Nearly three years later, in a plea deal, he was convicted of a Class A misdemeanor. Instead of jail time, Hamilton was sentenced to do community service and attend anger management counseling.

Vin Baker (Milwaukee Bucks)

Vin Baker, a star NBA player from 1993 to 2006, presented as an alcoholic seemingly out of nowhere, self-medicating for what he described as bouts of depression. His mental disorder had apparently been a problem for quite a while. These co-occurring disorders frequently incapacitated him and were difficult to keep secret, especially as his more destructive behaviors became noticeable to the media. Despite being a high draft choice who became an All-Star, Baker gained a reputation on his teams and around the league for being unreliable and unmotivated. He would be advised by a clueless coach, "Don't let the blues get you down . . . run it off."[27]

Instead, Baker drank alcohol in large quantities. It eventually cost him his NBA career, frayed his relationships with family members, and allowed him to fritter away "more than $100 million in wages and endorsement money."[28] Baker later said he was so far gone that he was smoking weed before games and popping pills afterward, as well as drinking Listerine.

Without an NBA career or a job, and with almost no money, Baker struggled until he realized he needed and wanted help. His "fifth trip to rehab . . . worked." Baker had nothing to lose. In 2018, after a stint working at Starbucks, he became an assistant coach with the Milwaukee Bucks, a position Baker still holds today. Bucks superstar Giannis Antetokounmpo considers him to be a "great friend," which undoubtedly serves Baker and his mental health needs well.[29] Being away from the pressure of having to perform as an athlete, along with having the support of an influential ally, seems to have made a big difference.

Ricky Williams (New Orleans Saints and Miami Dolphins)

Ricky Williams, a Heisman Trophy–winning running back, was the 5th overall selection in the 1999 NFL Draft by the New Orleans Saints. Beginning with his second year in the NFL, he had four consecutive seasons in which he gained at least 1,000 yards. In 2002–2003, the first year after he was traded to the Miami Dolphins, he gained 1,853 yards, won the rushing title, and became a superstar. The following year, he gained 1,372 yards.

In 2004, however, Williams shocked the football world by dropping out of the NFL, reportedly because the league had made it illegal to smoke marijuana. Williams, an avid user, was facing suspension and possible criminal prosecution for continuing his marijuana habit. This act of defiance made him the butt of jokes about his reefer madness.

It also contributed to the notion that he was a weird and unreliable teammate. After Williams returned to the Dolphins in 2005, he had to serve a four-game suspension without pay, resulting in his worst year as a professional to that point. When he failed another drug test before the 2006 season, he was suspended for the entire year.

After he returned for the 2007 season, a right shoulder injury put Williams out of action for most of that season. In 2008, he still was not performing on the football field as he had in the past. The next year, when the Dolphins' first-string running back, Ronnie Brown, had a season-ending injury, Williams stepped in and gained an impressive 1,121 yards. When his performance sagged again in 2010–2011, he retired to become a cannabis entrepreneur.

An important part of the explanation for Williams's dependence on smoking marijuana did not fully emerge until years later. As a young player with the New Orleans Saints, he had gained a reputation for being strange and distant, conducting media interviews with his helmet on and visor shades down, never seeming to interact with the fans. He also had become isolated from his friends and family. He did not know what was wrong.[30]

A therapeutic diagnosis revealed that Williams had an extreme form of social anxiety combined with bouts of depression. He used, and became dependent upon, marijuana to self-medicate. According to Williams's website, "Ricky found cannabis and everything changed. . . . Ricky [continues] smoking weed daily."[31] For him, it seems to have worked out reasonably well, all things considered.

Oscar Pistorius (Paralympic and Olympic Runner)
Oscar Pistorius first gained international fame as a record-setting, gold medal–winning Paralympian at the 2004 Summer Games in Athens, Greece. He was a double leg amputee who used special prosthetic blades

for racing. For years, however, the International Association of Athletics Federations (IAFF; now World Athletics) barred him from competing against nondisabled runners, claiming his reasonable accommodation—artificial legs—provided him with an unfair competitive advantage. Apparently, his artificial appendages allowed him to expend less energy than nondisabled runners but did not give him such an advantage when he was competing as a Paralympian. The IAFF simply ignored the countervailing physical liabilities Pistorius faced by having to race with artificial limbs.

In 2008, the Court of Arbitration for Sport (CAS) ruled that his ban should be lifted. At the 2012 London Summer Olympics, Pistorius became the first amputee in history to compete in the Olympic Games. Despite his once-presumed unfair advantage, in his specialty, the 400-meter run, he made it to the semifinals but finished last in that race.

What the IAFF could have penalized Pistorius for was using PEDs, which was never on its testing radar, at least not with him. After Pistorius's career ended in February 2013, he was arrested for murdering his girlfriend. During a search of his home, law enforcement authorities "found anabolic steroids and other PEDs."[32] The specter of Pistorius asserting a roid rage defense was floated in the media repeatedly. This possibility provided for a broader, if not a particularly nuanced, discussion about the potential psychotic effects of using those steroids, even though Pistorius did not actually use that defense and may not have been psychotic due to his steroid use. Nevertheless, the discussions underscored the dangers of using these performance-enhancing drugs.

Hope Solo (US Women's Soccer)

Hope Solo was widely recognized as the best female goalie in the world and one of—if not *the*—best of all time. She also had a very troubled career on and off the field, which was fueled by alcohol abuse, anger control issues, and speaking her mind in ways that were deemed inappropriate, especially for a woman.

The first well-publicized incident that placed Solo in an unfavorable light occurred during the 2007 World Cup. This was a couple of years after she had assumed the role of the US team's primary goalie, taking over for Briana Scurry, a great goalie in her own right. In the semifinals, when the Americans were facing Brazil, head coach Greg Ryan sat Solo on the bench and replaced her with Scurry. The US team was defeated, 4–0. Solo reportedly lost it in a "postgame tirade" and took the unusual tack of publicly criticizing her coach for benching her while implicitly dumping on Scurry, her teammate.[33]

At the 2008 Beijing Summer Olympics, Solo built upon her stellar athletic reputation by helping the US team win a gold medal with her excellent goaltending. Afterward, she and some of her teammates were interviewed on the NBC show *Today*. Thereafter, Solo let it slip that she and her teammates had been drunk when they appeared on that early morning program.[34]

Just before the 2012 London Games, Solo tested positive for a banned substance, canrenone. US antidoping authorities mostly accepted her explanation that she had unknowingly ingested that substance because it was an ingredient in her premenstrual medication. She only received a warning. Solo went on to help the US team win its second consecutive gold medal.

Leading up to the 2015 World Cup, Solo made headlines for her continuing erratic behavior. First, she was arrested for physically assaulting her half sister and nephew. Those charges were eventually dropped. At the team's summer camp, Solo apparently acted in ways she later had to apologize for, but for what was never revealed. Then, after her husband was arrested for DUI while driving a team van, Solo was suspended for thirty days, but again, no specific reason was given publicly as to why.[35]

During her suspension, Solo reportedly received therapy to address anger and other mental health issues. By the time the global tournament began, she was back in top athletic form. The US team won all its games and the world championship. Solo allowed only three goals in seven games.[36]

At the 2016 Summer Olympics in Rio, everything fell apart for Solo as she played relatively poorly. The United States was eliminated in the quarterfinals. Throughout those Olympics, Solo made questionable comments on Twitter and to the media, while displaying what was viewed as a lack of sportsmanship. US Soccer suspended Solo for six months and terminated her contract. Solo's teammates, however, claimed that this unprecedented penalty was in retaliation for their goalie being a strong voice in the team's dispute with US Soccer over equal pay. Nonetheless, Solo's tenure on the team had ended.

In 2022, following several uneventful years after her forced retirement, Solo was arrested near her home in Winston-Salem, North Carolina, just before she was to be inducted into the National Soccer Hall of Fame. She was charged with "impaired driving, resisting arrest, and misdemeanor child abuse." Solo had reportedly passed out in her car with the "engine running and her 2-year-old twins in the back seat."[37] While she awaited trial, Solo said she would be "voluntarily entering an in-patient alcohol treatment program to address . . . challenges with alcohol."[38] She asked that her induction ceremony be postponed until 2023.

Erik Ainge (New York Jets)

Former NFL quarterback and New York Jets backup Erik Ainge—the nephew of Danny Ainge, at that time the general manager of the Boston Celtics—entered the league with a long history of addiction as well as yet-undiagnosed bipolar disorder. When Ainge was only twelve, he began self-medicating for his mental distress, first with alcohol and later with cocaine and heroin. In 2007, his senior year at the University of Tennessee, Ainge also developed an addiction to painkillers. This only made his mental condition worse, and his behaviors more erratic and self-destructive. It also led to several rehabilitation stints while he was in college.[39]

Despite readily available information that Ainge had serious substance abuse issues when he arrived for his first NFL training camp in 2008, Jets management and the NFL's security force appeared to mostly ignore Ainge's situation. In the NFL, like other professional leagues, what a player does on the field is much more important than anything else. Athletes who cannot suit up or perform competently are quickly forgotten, especially if there is no physical injury present that can explain their absences or poor performances.

In November, two months into his pro career, the NFL suspended Ainge for four games—not for his life-threatening substance abuse but rather for taking steroids to enhance his performance. His mental health problems continued to be ignored. Professional sports teams—particularly in the NFL—tend to view mental conditions as something that athletes should deal with themselves. Early in 2009, though, Ainge felt bad enough that he finally checked himself into a drug detoxification center and was compelled to tell Jets management. During his stay in rehab, he was officially diagnosed, for the first time, with bipolar disorder.

After completing that program, Ainge initially kept away from drugs, but he also decided not to take the medications prescribed for his bipolar disorder. Instead, he turned to alcohol again. Since no one associated with the Jets or the league was monitoring his drinking, Ainge's alcohol problem grew worse. The NFL was testing him several times a week for drugs but not for alcohol, which is likely why he switched substances in the first place.[40]

In July 2010, just before training camp was to begin, Ainge relapsed once again, this time turning to hard drugs. As part of his rehabilitation, he was given medication to treat his bipolar disorder. Nearly a year later, in June 2011, although Ainge was still under contract, the quarterback retired. Both parties publicly maintained that Ainge was leaving the sport because of the physical injuries he had endured.[41] He later told ESPN, "I'm a drug addict. . . . I had to get help before I died."[42]

Once he was out of the NFL and relieved of the pressures of being a quarterback, Ainge began turning his life around. Although early in his retirement he relapsed again and was arrested for driving while drunk, Ainge later became the longtime host of a popular local Tennessee sports radio show, married, and had two children, a son and daughter.[43] There have been no reported instances of substance abuse involving Ainge in the news since 2013.

Rex Chapman (Charlotte Hornets, Miami Heat, Washington Wizards, and Phoenix Suns)

Rex Chapman was a standout University of Kentucky shooting guard and a better-than-average NBA swing man who made tens of millions of dollars playing basketball but never achieved the level of production in the pros that his talent in college had once suggested. A series of injuries limited his development. After he retired in 2000, he became a drug abuser, addicted to various opioids. Between 2000 and 2014, Chapman's life spiraled out of control. He spent most of his money, his wife of many years divorced him, his relationships with his children suffered, and he relapsed twice after going to rehabilitation facilities for treatment.

Chapman's life reached a turning point, however, after he was arrested for stealing from an Apple Store on nine different occasions and selling those items, worth a reported $14,000, to a pawnshop at a huge discount. Chapman claimed that because of his addiction he did not even remember committing those crimes. Ten days later, he voluntarily admitted himself into another drug treatment facility. In 2016, Chapman pled guilty to four felonies, receiving eighteen months of supervised probation in lieu of jail time. Years later, Chapman tweeted that he stole in order "to support my 14-year drug habit."[44]

His arrest, third stint in rehabilitation, and continued therapy appear to have helped him overcome his addiction and allowed him to reestablish relationships with his now-adult kids. As Chapman's daughter remarked, "I just wanted him to get better for himself. And he's done that. So I'm proud of him."[45] Chapman became a Twitter and streaming sensation, and in April 2022 he was set to host his own show on CNN+. Days after his first broadcast, CNN pulled the plug on its entire streaming service, but in 2023 Chapman reconstituted his proposed show as an Apple podcast.

Abby Wambach (US Women's Soccer)

Abby Wambach is a proudly gay and patriotic American who starred on the US Women's Soccer Team, helping the team win two Olympic gold medals and a World Cup. In her 2017 memoir, *Forward*, she acknowledged playing while being addicted to prescription drugs and abusing alcohol. During her career, Wambach did not address her substance abuse problems because, she said, "[w]hen you're a pro athlete, life is very narcissistic—everything relates back to you and how you play."[46] In addition, she acknowledged that being a gay pro athlete made her life much more difficult.

Wambach retired in 2015. Yet retirement was not kind to her, despite her fame. She continued to abuse alcohol and drugs in an attempt to deal with her pain and depression, a pattern she said had begun years earlier, after the 2007 World Cup. In her memoir, Wambach described how she would "pop a few Ambien, and then a few more, wishing I had vodka to wash them down." Her world "spun out of control . . . nearing the end of her career," including her marriage, which ended in divorce. Retirement worsened her substance abuse problems. The moment that changed her life occurred in 2016 when she was arrested for driving under the influence. Since then she has "remained sober, remarried and has tried to remain out of the national headlines."[47]

In September 2022, one of her corporate endorsements, a "nasal spray designed to treat concussions" backed by Hall of Fame quarterback Brett Favre, became embroiled in national sandal that was "at the center of a Mississippi welfare fraud case." Wambach, who had pledged to donate her brain for "concussion research," claimed she "genuinely believed this company was being transparent about a product that could spare the next generation of athletes from the severe impact of concussion injuries that I endured as a professional athlete."[48] Despite that embarrassing moment, she has made no recent headlines involving substance abuse and seemingly has regained control of her life.

Tiger Woods (Golf)

Although professional golf has been able to mostly sportswash the uglier parts of Tiger Woods's global legacy as he has intermittently limped back to the PGA Tour as its once most valued asset, his life almost came to an end in 2021 due to a likely impaired driving incident. This was not the first time his career and well-being had been jeopardized by what was reported to be suspected abuse of drugs.

Woods has had emotionally disturbed periods throughout his life that have culminated in highly publicized and embarrassing incidents involving the police. There also have been rumors about various types of substance abuse that he allegedly has engaged in to manage pain, enhance his performance, or just allow him to get a good night's sleep. What substances he may have been using when these three reported car accidents took place is mostly speculation because his public relations team and lawyers helped him effectively massage the truth when these highly publicized episodes occurred.

The first incident happened in 2009 when Woods somehow hit a fire hydrant and then a tree in front of his home. He was reportedly rendered unconscious, forcing his then-wife Elin to break into the car with a golf club. Speculation arose, however, that his injuries were caused when she attacked him with that golf club during a domestic dispute, which supposedly involved the many affairs he later admitted to having.[49]

While no toxicology report was ever released by authorities, later "a former mistress said Woods regularly took Ambien, while other sources said he had taken the drug on the night of the accident."[50] Woods pleaded guilty to a reduced charge of reckless driving rather than the initial DUI charge, but he refused to give any details, saying the matter was "private." He also checked himself into a rehabilitation center that specialized in both sex addiction and co-occurring mental disorders, including substance abuse.[51]

In 2017, Wood's drug use was verified to the public after he was arrested for DUI and a mug shot of him unshaven and in a highly disheveled state appeared in newspapers and on the internet. In a written apology, Woods claimed the incident was due to prescription medications. This time, however, a toxicology report was done and showed that when Woods was arrested, he had five different drugs in his system, including "pain killers, sleep drugs, and an ingredient active in marijuana." Once again, though, the DUI charge was dropped when he pleaded guilty to reckless driving and entered a diversion program.[52]

Four years later, in 2021, Woods was involved in a one-person crash early in the morning on his way to a golf tournament he was hosting. While speeding, he lost control of his SUV and rolled over several times, severely injuring his leg and almost losing his life. This time everything about his accident was kept under wraps. No toxicology exam was conducted, which would have been expected in such circumstances. The Los Angeles County Sheriff concluded, based on nothing more than what he said he had been told by his officers at the scene, that no drugs or alcohol had been involved. The hospital cooperated further by not taking a blood sample to test for any substances in his bloodstream.

Given Woods's history of DUIs and emotional problems, Kurt Streeter opined in the *New York Times* that "Woods somehow [has] remained swaddled in Teflon," which has created unrealistic expectations and marginalized his "human frailties." These frailties clearly involve his various emotional issues, especially his "battle [with] addiction."[53]

For years, Woods has been trying to manage the emotional turmoil in his life, erratically, as he has gone well past his Hall of Fame prime and then been severely physically impaired twice, but he is still not yet ready to retire. Since 2008 Woods has won only one major, an unexpected victory in 2019. Yet, even though today he can barely play as well as an average tour professional, Woods is so badly needed to prop up the sagging and contentious sport of professional golf that his troubled past has been almost completely airbrushed from history.

Conclusion

Drug and alcohol abuse and dependency are behaviors that locker rooms and other spectator sports environments, along with competitive pressures, often instigate, perpetuate, nurture, and/or facilitate, rather than ameliorate. For most elite athletes who use drugs or engage in erratic behaviors that violate federal and state laws as a result of substance abuse, prosecutions are relatively rare and jail time almost unheard of. However, many athletes who abuse substances shorten their professional careers and put their lives in jeopardy.

Once these athletes retire from their sports, many—like Vin Baker, Erik Ainge, and Abby Wambach—seem better able to manage their substance abuse issues, whether that means being able to control their addictive behaviors or not feeling compelled to risk their health by using PEDs. For some, though, retirement does not lessen their addictive behaviors, and not being able to compete as they once did makes things worse. Substance abuse becomes a dysfunctional way to fill a hole in their lives that athletics once filled. Hope Solo, Rex Chapman, and Tiger Woods appear to be sad examples of that phenomenon.

PART III

MENTAL HEALTH AND EMOTIONAL WELL-BEING CHALLENGES OF MARGINALIZED ATHLETES

THE OVERALL RECORD OF AMERICA'S MOST POPULAR SPECTATOR SPORTS on issues related to the mental health and emotional well-being of female, LGBTQ+, and intersex and trans women athletes has been subpar at best and often much worse than that, even compared to the neglect and ignorance too often displayed in serving the mental health needs of athletes in general. Sports enterprises have been more likely to be major contributors to the neglect, discrimination, and abuse experienced by those marginalized athletes, rather than a supportive resource to address their concerns. These problems appear to have grown worse since the COVID pandemic took hold, disrupting or periodically suspending protection, monitoring, and enforcement activities where they had existed.

Discrimination based on gender and gender identity has been rampant. Promoting diversity and inclusion, especially in the professional leagues, remains a relatively low priority. So far, only incremental improvements have been made. Gender-based injustices resulting from male privilege in America's most popular spectator sports remain well entrenched. Misogyny and homophobia are ever present, although things are changing, albeit slowly, with the ascendancy of feminine values in the operation of sports and the growing social and political sophistication of athletes. Clearly, though, there continue to be numerous gender-based injustices, including, most disturbingly, the widespread sexual and emotional abuse of female athletes.

Homophobia and gender identity discrimination remain widespread in most sports, especially in locker rooms and other private areas shielded from the public's view. Sexual abuse of some male athletes has been fueled by homophobia. Mistreating and demonizing intersex or trans women athletes, who are presumptively viewed as having an unfair competitive advantage by not being "female enough," has become a clarion call for most spectator sports, too much of the United States, and too many state legislatures.

CHAPTER 9

Female Athletes

FEMALE ATHLETES EXPERIENCE MANY OF THE SAME MENTAL HEALTH and emotional well-being challenges as male athletes. One significant difference, however, is that female athletes experience some degree of misogyny and gender discrimination virtually all the time. Additionally, pregnancy, postpartum depression, menstrual disorders, and motherhood pose special challenges for female athletes that their male counterparts do not share.

In addition, female athletes are much more likely to be harmed by the mental and emotional traumas of sexual and emotional abuse, mostly by trusted men in their sports. Making matters worse, female athletes too often lack the necessary resources to deal with these additional mental and emotional challenges because they tend to receive considerably less compensation, healthcare, disability, and other work-related benefits than do male athletes.

It is no wonder, then, that female athletes consistently report substantially greater mental health challenges—especially anxiety and depression—than their male counterparts, regardless of age. Yet their struggles with various mental health concerns, including relationships with their mostly male coaches, has received much less empirical and psychological study than the mental health issues that male athletes tend to experience.[1]

With respect to college athletes specifically, the NCAA conducted a survey at the end of 2021 involving nearly ten thousand student-athletes from all three NCAA sports divisions. While all college athletes had significant mental health concerns, the survey found significant gen-der-based differences, with female athletes experiencing substantially more feelings of (1) being overwhelmed (47 percent versus 25 percent), (2) mental exhaustion (38 percent versus 22 percent), and (3) extreme anxiety (29 percent versus 12 percent).[2]

It is no wonder that, for the most part, it is female athletes who have been speaking out about mental health in recent years, rather than hid-ing their concerns, especially female athletes of color like Simone Biles, Naomi Osaka, and Simone Manuel (see chapters 4 and 5).[3]

MISOGYNY AND DISCRIMINATION

Gender discrimination in college and high school athletics was supposed to be largely ameliorated in the 1970s with the passage of Title IX. Nonetheless, overall support, much less equity, for female athletics has been inconsistent at best. Even in college, support seems to thrive only if women's sports do not appear to take resources and attention away from the more popular and well-promoted men's sports.

For years, the NCAA women's basketball championship has been handled very differently than the men's championship. Men's teams get first-class treatment and widespread television coverage. Although there have been improvements in recent years, with the exception of a few remarkably popular contests, such as those involving Connecticut or South Carolina, women's teams receive second-class treatment and lesser television coverage. In large part, this is because the ways in which the NCAA administers the two national basketball championships and distributes the revenues that each generates greatly favor the supercon-ference men's teams.[4]

In this inherently inequitable environment, men become "the stan-dard for female athletic achievement," which too often has operated as a ploy "designed to diminish and distort women's accomplishments . . ., block opportunity, attack equal pay or discontinue women's sports altogether."[5]

Professional leagues and other enterprises—as well as the male-dominated media that control, cover, and broadcast the specta-tor sports they think Americans most like to watch—have tolerated, accepted, encouraged, and directly participated in such sexism and misogyny. Gender-based injustices targeting women are pervasive and take many different forms. Each of these injustices, though, takes some toll on the mental and emotional well-being of female athletes.

One of the major factors contributing to these injustices is the reality that most American sports for elite and aspiring elite female athletes are still run and operated by male-dominated sports enterprises. Gender tokenism continues to be accepted in the sports media as a sign of progress. Female athletes in leading professional and Olympic team sports for women—most notably soccer, basketball, and hockey—still earn a fraction of what their male counterparts receive and, like college female athletes, often must compete in substandard conditions.

Management positions, especially senior positions, in women's professional, Olympic, and college sports are still overwhelmingly dominated by men. Most of the exceptions have been manufactured when female figureheads are appointed to leadership positions after scandals involving years of corruption by a sports organization's mostly male leaders become public. This has happened with USA Gymnastics, the United States Olympic and Paralympic Committee, and US Soccer, for example, but not in any major American team sports for men, which are all led by men.

In international sports competitions in which American women and girls compete—most notably Olympic and World Cup soccer, hockey, and track and field—Title IX does not apply unless the activity takes place in the United States and involves an entity that receives federal funds. This limited coverage makes sexual abuse, harassment, other gender inequities and injustices even more difficult to challenge. The substantially lower pay and other compensation US women athletes have received in World Cup soccer and Olympic hockey and basketball, when compared to their male counterparts in those international sports, indicates that invidious gender discrimination is still being allowed.

Even the playing surfaces for World Cup matches are gender based. Men demand and receive grass fields to play on, while women are usually relegated to artificial turf, which significantly increases their risk of injury, disease, and infection.[6] In 2022, *Scientific American* reported that there is a significant difference favoring men in the measures taken to protect the safety of and improve the equipment for male soccer players versus female players at the World Cup.[7] Apparently sports science, like medicine, is sexist.

Furthermore, numerous allegations have surfaced that some men leading or affiliated with FIFA, the international governing body for soccer, have been engaging in sexual discrimination and harassment, including the organization's vice president. Several years ago, former US soccer star Hope Solo accused now-disgraced former longtime FIFA president Sepp Blatter of "groping her at an awards ceremony."[8]

Female athletes are acutely aware of widespread misogyny and sexism in US spectator sports that have been ignored, marginalized, or covered up. This is a constant concern that male athletes do not have to deal with. When Serena Williams lost in the 2018 US Open final after having clearly faced discrimination from the mostly male leaders of professional tennis due to her difficult pregnancy and maternity (see below), she accused the male referee, who had made a couple of legitimate calls against her, of sexism.

That charge resonated with her fans and many in the media because sexism is so prevalent in sports, but in that case it appeared to be a mistake, given what had occurred during the match. This placed her young, victorious, and emotionally fragile opponent, Naomi Osaka, in a very uncomfortable position. Osaka cried at the victory ceremony and apologized for having defeated Williams.

FEMALE ATHLETES, PREGNANCY, AND ABORTION

Tennis, Track and Field, and Marathon Runners
There is no mistaking that female athletes continue to experience discrimination and other undue emotional pressures if they become pregnant, after they give birth, or if they choose to have an abortion. In the long run, Williams's 2018 US Open served a greater good in highlighting discrimination in the way elite female athletes are treated when they are pregnant. Williams's stature and insistence helped pave the way for both the Women's Tennis Association (WTA) and the only Grand Slam

tournament in the United States to change their seeding policies to take pregnancy into account—but only to a limited extent, as it has turned out.

When Williams returned from her especially difficult pregnancy, she plummeted from being first in the world to a dismal #451, meaning she would not be seeded in tournaments and would have to play as a qualifier to get in, unless she received a wild card from the tournament organizers. At that time, there was no mechanism to hold women tennis players harmless when they become pregnant. After the world saw how much the very popular Williams struggled in the French Open as an unseeded player and at Wimbledon as a low seed, the US Open promised it would no longer penalize women players as severely for having been pregnant when determining seeds for that Grand Slam event.[9] But it would not eliminate those penalties entirely.

Six months later, the WTA revamped its seeding rules for all players returning from pregnancies. While not holding those players harmless, the new rules allow them to receive a higher "special ranking for up to three years following the birth of a child."[10] Williams's moral victory also began to motivate other female athletes to insist upon equitable treatment when they become pregnant.

One of the most punitive sports for women athletes in this regard has been track and field, where sponsors have reportedly added clauses to performance contracts that financially penalize athletes if they become pregnant. First-person stories from two distinguished Black US track athletes who were discriminated against during their pregnancies appeared in the *New York Times* in May 2019.

Olympian and three-time US National Champion runner Alysia Montaño explained how Nike, like other track sponsors, cut her income after corporate officials learned she was pregnant, and then extended those cuts during her maternity leave. As Phoebe Wright, another elite runner, put it, "There's no way I'd tell Nike if I were pregnant."[11]

Sprinter Allyson Felix, who won six Olympic gold medals for the United States, told a similar story. Like Williams, she had a difficult pregnancy, which in Felix's case involved a C-section. Nike, which also was her chief corporate sponsor, proposed paying her 70 percent less than what she had earned before giving birth. Because of the publicity

Williams had garnered around the issue and Montaño's and Felix's advocacy, several clothing manufacturers, most notably Nike, "came forward to announce new contractual guarantees for women who have children while being supported by their sponsorships."[12]

Despite those changes in policy by professional tennis and track and field sponsors like Nike, they were only small steps in the movement toward achieving equity for pregnant female athletes. The Boston Marathon still penalized long-distance runners who became pregnant until 2023, when Fiona English of Great Britain called out the Boston Athletic Association (BAA) for its unwillingness to accommodate her pregnancy.

English had requested that her entry approval be deferred a year and her $235 entry fee be refunded. She complained in an open letter that the BAA rejected her request because it had violated their rules, as it would have for most of the premier marathon races in the United States. Because of her letter, most of these races have changed their policies to allow deferred entries for pregnant runners.[13]

Nevertheless, there continues to be enormous pressure on female athletes, both self-imposed and financially coerced, to push them to compete while they are pregnant and during the early months of their maternity or to have an abortion to end their pregnancy so it will not interrupt or undermine their time-limited athletic careers.

The NCAA

These family planning pressures for women athletes, whether to have a child or not, can travel in opposite directions, often both at once, but ultimately it should be the right of female athletes to make highly personal reproductive decisions unencumbered by additional outside pressure from various sports enterprises and sponsors. As was first reported in 2007 in an ESPN *Outside the Lines* exposé, for years the NCAA allowed major university and college athletic programs to revoke the scholarships of female athletes who became pregnant and carried their pregnancies to term.[14]

Since 2018, the NCAA asks, but does not mandate, that the scholarships of pregnant student-athletes be "protected," along with "their ability to come back," including "their rehabilitation."[15] The NCAA has established somewhat equivocal and unenforceable guidelines about what universities and colleges should do to help female athletes if they become pregnant.[16]

While the NCAA has not directed universities and colleges to use any specific approach, its officials established a "pregnancy tool kit" as a guide. That kit recommends that member schools "assemble a 'decision-making team' of coaches, team doctors, athletic officials, family members, faith leaders and counselors" to help the pregnant athlete decide what to do about her pregnancy, as if it is a collective decision rather than a deeply personal one.[17] It would be much better for the pregnant athlete to be able to decide whom, if anyone, should be involved in such decision making.

Nevertheless, given the financial and competitive incentives to encourage athletes to terminate their pregnancies, this seemed like a less regressive, although still flawed, way of handling the matter. Now that *Roe v. Wade* has been overturned and twenty states already have abortion bans on the books—many of which are draconian intrusions into pregnant people's right to make their own decisions—the NCAA appears to have a political dilemma to contend with: Its pregnancy tool kit approach may well create additional concerns. Will the NCAA hold fast to the recommendations it has embraced in its tool kit, or will it revise that guidance to placate pro-life governmental forces? Will those decision-making committees be convened to convince pregnant athletes to carry their pregnancies to term? Will the NCAA choose not to hold its major athletic events in jurisdictions that have laws in place that make it impossible, or next to impossible, for female student-athletes to choose to terminate their pregnancies? Since the Supreme Court ruling, the organization has been silent on those issues.

Abortion has been so politically charged in college athletics that in 2009, Elizabeth A. Sorensen, an assistant professor of nursing at Wright State University, believing a review of the scientific literature was warranted, wrote an article for the *Journal of Intercollegiate Sport* "debunking the myth of pregnancy doping." The notion had been circulating, undoubtedly by men, that certain female athletes were getting pregnant so they would be able to be prescribed hormones to enhance their performance, and afterward would abort their fetuses.[18]

The political questions surrounding abortion become especially poignant for female athletes who depend on athletic scholarships at public colleges, especially those students who lack the financial resources to afford college without the support of scholarships. Moreover, "the power centers of elite women's college sports are disproportionately in states where abortion access is likely to be restricted or banned altogether." Many key college sporting events for female athletes "are held in states with some of the strictest abortion laws."[19]

What the NCAA does likely will be determined by the interests of the male-dominated superconference members who largely control the NCAA's decisions. Thus, while it is in the interest of women's college sports to at least toe the line and seriously consider prohibiting NCAA-sponsored events in those states with the more draconian abortion bans, that is unlikely to happen.

The huge financial imbalance that favors major male NCAA sports has always been the most significant factor in determining the NCAA's positions on key moral issues that affect student-athletes. If the past is any guidance, female athletes may be sorely disappointed in the NCAA's ultimate abortion policy decisions. Because of this, many elite female college athletes to be may well choose to avoid going to schools in states that have draconian abortion laws.

SEXUAL ABUSE OF FEMALE ATHLETES

The sexual abuse of mostly young female athletes by trusted coaches, trainers, and team physicians—most notably in US Olympic sports and colleges and universities under the NCAA's jurisdiction, but in other less popular spectator sports as well—has caused those athletes untold mental and emotional trauma and other damage, not only as youngsters, but throughout their athletic careers and thereafter. This appears to be an epidemic in sports for girls and women.

A growing list of American sports organizations representing elite athletes have been identified as (1) having kept such abuses secret for years, (2) failing to take appropriate actions to address those abuses, and

(3) having used various sportswashing techniques and bankrupt legal theories to deflect accountability when those abuses were finally revealed. (Sexual abuse of male athletes, which happens less frequently, is covered in chapter 10.)

US Olympic Sports

Arguably the most unsettling revelations in US spectator sports history, and surpassing even Russian state-sponsored doping internationally, has been the rampant sexual abuse of female US Olympic athletes and those competing to make Olympic teams. In recent years, systemic sexual abuse has been documented in USA Gymnastics, USA Swimming, US Figure Skating, USA Track and Field, and many other US Olympic sports, as well as in the gymnastics programs at Michigan State and other colleges. There have undoubtedly been many other instances of spectator sports–related sexual abuse of female athletes that have not yet been uncovered, or at least not revealed publicly.

These sexual abuse revelations have had two things in common: official incompetence and cover-ups by men and their male-dominated organizations and institutions. The nature and extent of this sexual exploitation has been one more powerful argument for insisting upon gender equity in all spectator sports for women that are typically dominated and controlled by men—in other words, most of them. Not only have women shown themselves to be far less likely to sexually exploit their charges, but because of their life experiences, they are far more predisposed to report such abuses once they become aware of them.

One of the few things US Olympic organizations have done when faced with sexual abuse crises of their own making is to eventually force their male chief executive to resign—typically with a bloated severance payout—and replace him with a female stand-in. Unfortunately, too often little of substance changes beyond the face of the organization. Most of the male-dominated leadership remains in place to harvest the predominant share of the revenues these female athletes generate.

Widespread sexual abuse has been going on in US sports for decades. More than twenty years ago, the *Seattle Times* conducted a detailed investigation of sexual abuse and exploitation of young athletes by male coaches in the state of Washington. During a ten-year period ending in December 2003, the investigation discovered that in that one state alone, at least "159 coaches [had been] reprimanded or fired for sexual misconduct." Of those coaches, "98 continued to coach or teach—as schools, the state and even some parents looked the other way."[20]

Typically, identification and tracking of the mostly male perpetrators of these sexual crimes has occurred only after a rare criminal conviction—and not always even then. Generally, there has been secrecy and silence. That has allowed coaches and other trusted male figures to be predators, even after having been asked to leave their positions because they have been caught engaging in sexually abusive behaviors.

A 2021 digital survey found that "[m]ore than 1 in 4 [former college] student athletes reported being sexually assaulted or harassed by someone in a position of power on campus," most frequently a coach.[21] Much of that abuse occurred because trusted men were allowed to prey upon young female athletes without much scrutiny. It seems reasonable to believe, given what has happened in the past, that many, and probably most, such crimes are never officially identified, much less reported, investigated, and prosecuted.

USA Swimming

A conspiracy of silence was instrumental in allowing numerous teenage girls, some teenage boys, and children younger than that to be sexually abused by mostly male coaches while participating in USA Swimming.[22] This was the first sex abuse scandal involving a US Olympic sport to be well publicized nationally. The most well-known swimming organization in the United States reportedly spawned an epidemic of "coaches preying upon [their athletes]."[23] Not only were these young swimmers extremely reluctant to come forward, but for years, even if they filed formal complaints, USA Swimming kept the information about the offending coaches confidential and did almost no follow-up, allowing abusers to leave one job and begin coaching other young swimmers elsewhere.[24]

It was not until 2010 that USA Swimming even began tracking coaches who had been involved in incidents of abuse, and the number of coaches publicly identified as abusers increased substantially. Since 2013, about one hundred swim coaches nationwide have been officially banned each year.[25] Tragically, though, many—perhaps most—abused and traumatized swimmers have been psychologically and circumstantially unable to come forward with their allegations until many years have passed, if at all, meaning the problem is much greater than those abusive swim coaches who have been identified.

In response to this awful problem, a group of California legislators in 2013 proposed a one-year window be created to permit survivors to sue their abusers, as well as USA Swimming and other sports organizations, regardless of how much time has passed, for "harboring" those offenders. USA Swimming reportedly hired "a powerful lobbying firm to fight . . . [the] bill." Thus, even after the legislation passed, Governor Jerry Brown exercised his veto power, based on the legal rationalization that it would be unfair to hold USA Swimming and other youth organizations liable for "things that happened decades ago."[26] California was not the only state jurisdiction that attempted to enact such legislation. New York passed that type of one-year window law, but it did not go into effect until 2022.[27]

For years, USA Swimming officials continued to deny any responsibility for facilitating sexual abuse in their sport, and the legal system mostly looked the other way. In February 2018, things changed somewhat when the *Orange County Register* published a damning exposé concluding that "U.S.A. Swimming executives were aware of sexually predatory coaches for years, but they did not take action against them or try to change the organization's permissive culture." As a result, two of the organization's "top . . . officials, including one whose job was specifically to protect athletes . . . resigned."[28] Otherwise, the male-dominated leadership of USA Swimming remained much the same, even as more swimmers were accusing their coaches of sexual abuse.

USA Gymnastics

Despite the revelations about USA Swimming, those in charge of Olympic and college gymnastics ignored obvious warning signs of rampant sexual abuse of girls and young women in their sport. USA Gymnastics, the United States Olympic and Paralympic Committee, Michigan State

University (MSU), and the NCAA all failed to protect female gymnasts. That disturbing pattern of institutional neglect continued well after key gymnastics officials knew—or had good cause to recognize—that many of their female athletes were being sexually assaulted.

The various organizations in charge of youth, Olympic, and college gymnastics built walls of silence and separation that provided them and their officials with plausible deniability, then engaged in various deceptions, sportswashing, and legal maneuvers to hide their corruption. These unconscionable behaviors were exposed nationally after Olympic medalist McKayla Maroney bravely revealed details of her 2016 sealed financial settlement with USA Gymnastics.

USA Gymnastics had compelled Maroney to agree that she would not disclose details of the abuse she had endured or reveal the identity of her abuser, team physician Larry Nassar. The USOPC, which is responsible for overseeing USA Gymnastics, claimed that its officials "had no knowledge of any confidential agreement,"[29] which seemed improbable.

On the college side of this travesty, the optics proved even more disturbing, if not as widespread. MSU gymnastics coach Kathie Klages continued to sing the praises of Nassar long after members of her team complained that the physician had sexually abused them. The university retained Nassar even though there had been sexual abuse complaints against him from female students going "as far back as the late 1990s."[30] (A more complete account of the MSU gymnastics scandal can be found below.)

Throughout this cover-up, the NCAA was invisible. Even today that organization and its members continue to show little interest in or appetite for preventing, investigating, or sanctioning allegations of sexual abuse, sexual assault, or any other type of sexual misconduct in college sports. Even after the sordid sexual abuse scandal involving Penn State football assistant coach Jerry Sandusky sparked national outrage in 2012, the NCAA failed to implement any new rules or policies governing sexual offenses involving university and college athletic programs. Similarly, until recently the USOPC had no meaningful protocols in place for dealing with sexual abuse, consistently pleading ignorance. Remarkably, the USOPC defended itself by implicitly arguing that the lines of communication with its affiliates were so poor that it had no inkling of any problems related to the sexual abuse of Olympic gymnasts, which had begun no later than the late 1990s. The organization said it was informed only after USA Gymnastics "quietly fired Nassar after reporting him to the FBI [in the summer of 2015]."[31]

That Olympic institutional ignorance encompassed not only Nassar's multiplicity of sexual crimes but also countless allegations of sexual abuse lodged against numerous coaches associated with USA Gymnastics and many other US Olympic federations, including USA Swimming. Furthermore, after the USOPC was officially notified about wanton abuse and neglect of so many young female gymnasts over such a long period of time, it still refused to sanction USA Gymnastics or its officials, much less begin a much-deserved decertification process.

This complete abdication of institutional responsibility typified how both USOPC and NCAA officials, most of whom were men, chose to operate. That these officials were clueless was the best defense they could muster. As reported on ESPN's *Outside the Lines*, the offending coaches and Nassar had been surrounded by responsible adults who enabled these predatory behaviors.[32] Sadly, many of these enablers turned out to be USOPC, MSU, and NCAA officials.

The male chief executives of both USA Gymnastics and the USOPC were eventually forced to resign, albeit with large payouts. In their places, several women—two of whom were soon fired—took over the day-to-day operations of these male-dominated sports enterprises. In addition, the USOPC changed its name for good reasons to include the Paralympics, but it also deflected attention away from the negative associations linked to the now toxic United States Olympic Committee. Signifcantly, though, its basic organizational structure remained intact. The USOC had replicated the International Olympic Committee's organizational pyramid, which the USOPC adopted as well. It is the same decentralized structure that has enabled state-sponsored doping in Russia to flourish—which makes responsibility at the top extremely difficult to assign or prove.

A second important line of authority malfunctioned repeatedly as well: University and NCAA officials facilitated Nassar's predatory behaviors at MSU. It turned out that the dysfunctional, and ultimately corrupt, lines of authority in both Olympic and college gymnastics were closely linked.

MSU paid Nassar to volunteer his services to USA Gymnastics, reportedly to promote the recruitment of top female gymnasts to MSU. Klages, a former MSU gymnastics coach, bragged that her university could provide one benefit no competing college gymnastics program had to offer: "We have Larry Nassar! . . . [R]enowned for his ability to keep Olympic gymnasts healthy—who [teaches] at Michigan State's medical school and treat[s] Spartan gymnasts."[33]

In 2014, while Klages was still holding Nassar out as a school treasure, the doctor sexually assaulted hundreds of female gymnasts and other students, including members of Klages's own team. At least two of her gymnasts had complained about Nassar's behavior in 1997, but Klages summarily dismissed their accusations as a "misunderstanding."[34]

Over many years, both USA Gymnastics and MSU ignored and even covered up obvious signs and clear indications that female gymnasts were being sexually abused. Making matters worse, both the Olympic and college lines of institutional authority were withholding critical information from each other.

For years, the USOPC knew, or should have known, that sexual abuse was prevalent in Olympic sports. In 1999, former USA Gymnastics CEO Bob Colarossi had warned that "Olympic sport governing bodies lacked basic sex abuse prevention measures." Colarossi told key USOPC officials, including Scott Blackmun, who years later would be its CEO during the gymnastics scandal, "USO[P]C can either position itself as a leader in the protection of young athletes or it can wait until it is forced to deal with the problem under much more difficult circumstances." Around the same time, *Sports Illustrated* published an extensively documented exposé "about coaches molesting children in youth sports."[35]

Yet the USOPC and its Olympic affiliates continued to do nothing. USA Gymnastics officials waited more than fifteen years to take any official action. Instead, they covered up reports of sexual abuse complaints "on 54 coaches, from 1996 to 2006 . . . [who] were accused of misconduct, including sexually assaulting their athletes." In addition, they failed

FEMALE ATHLETES

to follow up on serious sexual abuse allegations dating back to 2011 that reportedly included "a detailed account of abuse involving . . . a former coach of the year."[36]

In 2015, after USA Gymnastics was notified that Nassar had been accused of molesting many female gymnasts, its officials neither suspended Nassar as team doctor nor reported him to law enforcement authorities. Instead, they "spent five weeks on an internal investigation" that amounted to nothing.[37] For nearly two more years, USA Gymnastics officials took no further action.

In March 2017, stories in the *New York Times*, *Washington Post*, and other media outlets revealed shocking details of the apparent USA Gymnastics cover-up. Nonetheless, the organization and its board chairman, Paul Parilla, defended USA Gymnastics president and CEO Steve Penny as one of the "strongest advocates for our athletes."[38] A few days later, Penny resigned. Subsequently, when he was asked in a court deposition why he had failed to protect the female gymnasts that he should have known were in jeopardy, Penny responded, "To the best of my knowledge, there's no [legal] duty to report . . . if you are a third party to some allegation."

Despite these widespread sexual abuse revelations, the USOPC, as it had done with the sexual abuse of female athletes in most other of its affiliated sports—including "U.S.A Swimming . . . , U.S. Speedskating and more"—chose to try to preserve the status quo.[39] Rather than decertifying USA Gymnastics, the USOPC tried to deflect attention away from its own role in this unconscionable national scandal by supporting the establishment of the quasi-independent US Center for SafeSport.

A couple of months after Penny resigned, USA Gymnastics, under Parilla's direction, finally announced the results of an internal investigation it had commissioned back in 2016. The lead investigator, a former prosecutor, concluded—deliberately without naming names—that USA Gymnastics officials had failed "to notify law enforcement officials about allegations of sexual abuse by its coaches." Predictably, USA Gymnastics decided no organizational changes were warranted. Instead, the disgraced organization published nonmandatory guidelines advising "thousands of private gymnastics clubs across the country" how they might want to handle sexual abuse complaints in the future.[40]

For months, USA Gymnastics had no CEO. In December 2017 it hired Kerry Perry to restore the organization's shattered reputation. A few weeks later, more disturbing news surfaced involving the US women's gymnastics team training center owned and operated by legendary Olympic coaches Martha and Bela Karolyi. Reportedly, Nassar had sexually abused numerous female gymnasts at that training center as well. USA Gymnastics immediately cut ties with the Karolyis and their facility.[41]

After all of this, the USOPC still was not ready to decertify USA Gymnastics as it had for the far less influential US Taekwondo Union for less egregious sexual abuse problems. The chair, vice chair, and treasurer of USA Gymnastics, however, all resigned.[42]

Soon public outrage focused on Blackmun and the USOPC for failing to properly oversee USA Gymnastics and the other US Olympic federations that had mishandled so many sexual abuse cases. "[T]wo United States Senators and . . . about 30 former Olympians, athletes' representatives and child-advocacy experts" demanded his resignation.[43] Blackmun complied a few days later but received a $2.4 million buyout, which the lawyer representing "nearly 200 accusers of Dr. Nassar" described as "vile" and "despicable."[44]

A few months later, Sarah Hirshland, a former marketing executive with the United States Golf Association, replaced Blackmun as CEO. All the USOPC board members, including its chair, Larry Probst, retained their positions for the time being. Six months later, Probst resigned and Susanne Lyons, one of the few female board members, became the new chairperson. The USOPC then "praised Probst's contributions" to the organization.[45]

In an obvious legal ploy to limit its liability, USA Gymnasts filed for bankruptcy. Bankruptcy meant that USA Gymnastics' future assets could not be used to compensate the numerous female gymnasts who had sued the organization for failing to protect them from being sexually abused.

In November 2018, facing more intense congressional scrutiny, the USOPC finally initiated the lengthy process for possibly decertifying

USA Gymnastics, noting, too little and too late, that female gymnasts "deserve better."[46] The move, however, turned out to be a deceptive sportswashing gambit. Decertification is an organizational decision made by the USOPC board after there has been a hearing before a three-person USOPC panel, the results of which may or may not be made public. Hirshland foreshadowed the result when she explained that this drawn-out process has no "predetermined outcome," nor any predetermined deadlines.[47]

Three months after the decertification was initiated, Hirshland praised USA Gymnastics after it hired its fourth female CEO in the two-year period since Penny's resignation. She said that Li Li Leung, the former NBA midlevel marketing executive and American Ninja Warrior contestant, "is an accomplished professional, a former gymnast herself, and committed to transforming the culture of the sport." Hirshland then maintained that this hiring was "one of the most important aspects of USA Gymnastics' way forward"[48]—which appeared to mean a predetermined path to avoid the decertification it richly deserved.

America's female gymnasts, however, did not share Hirshland's enthusiasm. As Simone Biles complained in August 2019, it was difficult to represent USA Gymnastics because the organization had "fail[ed] us so many times."[49] A bipartisan Senate Commerce Committee investigation found that USA Gymnastics had "enabled the abuse" of many female gymnasts and that both USA Gymnastics and the USOPC failed to "'act aggressively to report wrongdoing' and officials in positions of power 'prioritized their own reputations or the reputation of a sport's national governing body over the health and safety of the athletes.'" In addition, they had "tried to conceal their negligence."[50]

Four years later, there was still no final decision about decertification. Meanwhile, USA Gymnastics continued to function as usual. After declaring bankrupcy, which greatly limited the amount of money it could be sued for, the organization finally reached a settlement agreement with the USOPC. That settlement not only offered discounted compensation to the abused gymnasts but officially ended the decertification process without there ever being any public report or findings.

Female Olympic gymnasts were sadly disappointed. What former Olympic gold medalist Dominique Moceanu had said years earlier about the sexual abuse scandal applies now: "The same people who have groomed this environment and didn't catch it to begin with. . . . [are] telling us . . . this [has been] . . . fixed"[51]—and they remain in charge.

United States Center for SafeSport

The one improvement in US Olympic sports following these sexual abuse scandals, especially with USA Gymnastics, which had generated so much national attention, was the establishment of the United States Center for SafeSport. Unfortunately, there are substantial limitations and concerns about the center beyond the fact that its reach does not include high school or college sports. To begin with, the center is structured so that it has close ties to the USOPC and the national governing bodies (NGBs) it is supposed to be monitoring and, where necessary, investigating and sanctioning. The center is dependent upon both the USOPC and, to a lesser extent, those NGBs for much of its funding, a readily apparent conflict of interest.[52]

In addition, the center's dearth of financial resources appears to be problematic. Even though the USOPC and the NGBs bring in hundreds of millions of dollars in revenue each year, which goes way up in Olympic years, the center's total budget in 2019 was just $10.5 million, $1 million of which came from non-Olympic sources.[53] That funding was woefully short of what was needed to investigate all the athlete abuse inquiries, which continued to rise, much less to closely monitor and investigate all Olympic sports in a comprehensive way.

In October 2020, Congress responded to that problem in the Empowering Olympic, Paralympic, and Amateur Athletes Act by direct- ing the USOPC to provide $20 million annually for the center's opera- tions.[54] That amount, while substantial, still appears to be inadequate to meet all the center's responsibilities and do it well. Moreover, Congress inexplicably diluted the center's power in abuse cases by making it work cooperatively with the relevant NGBs, which included sharing juris- dictional authority in many abuse situations. In other words, Congress expanded, rather than contracted, the preexisting conflict of interest.

In matters involving sexual misconduct, the center's authority remains exclusive, but with all other types of athlete abuse its authority is discretionary in concert with the responsible NGB.[55] Since its creation in 2017, the center "has been criticized for its mission and process," according to the *New York Times*. Abused athletes have charged that "SafeSport investigates . . . too slowly and leaves them in the dark." Also, "it is not truly independent and attempts to shift blame away from the national governing bodies and the U.S.O.P.C."[56]

That divided loyalty reportedly helped produce the four-year saga involving emotional abuse allegations against national team gymnastics coach Maggie Haney, recounted later in this chapter. USA Gymnastics deflected its own responsibility for such delays by blaming the revised federal law governing the Center for SafeSport. Reportedly, there have been other instances in which investigations of alleged abuse by US Olympic coaches have been slow to reach a conclusion.[57]

A bipartisan Senate commission was created in April 2021 to extensively review the USOPC and its affiliates and recommend potential changes to a Senate committee. As part of its revised oversight function, Congress theoretically has the authority to decertify any Olympic affiliate unilaterally and direct that the USOPC board of directors be dissolved. No US Olympic organization has been replaced in the past, however; nor, as of the summer of 2023, have any of them been replaced since the commission was established. Congress also mandated that athletes have somewhat more representation on boards that govern these Olympic organizations, and that these organizations file detailed annual reports about their activities and expenditures—which, incredibly, it seems they were not asked to do in the past.[58]

Michigan State University's Gymnastics Program

Michigan State University's contributions to the gynmastics scandal did not become national news until 2017, months after Larry Nassar was accused of sexually abusing female Olympic gymnasts. The *Washington Post*'s Will Hobson reported that MSU officials had ignored "verbal complaints about Nassar" as far back as the "late 1990s."[59] In 2014, Nassar was investigated after a female MSU student filed a sexual assault complaint against him. Michigan State Police and the university, through its flawed Title IX process, decided not to press charges. Remarkably, MSU did not advise USA Gymnastics about that complaint, even though the university was paying Nassar to volunteer as an Olympic team doctor.

In 2016, well after the FBI had finally begun its reportedly reluctant investigation of Nassar, and even after USA Gymnastics had dismissed the physician, another female student at MSU filed a sexual abuse complaint against the doctor. When that happened, Nassar's MSU "colleagues and superiors offer[ed him] support." This included assistance from the university's "public relations staff [which] counseled Nassar on how to handle reporters' questions about accusations of abuse."[60]

Nine months later, as noted earlier, an ESPN *Outside the Lines* investigation revealed that MSU knew about and ignored Larry Nassar's abusive behaviors toward female gymnasts. He carried out his sexual abuse with the help of supposedly responsible adults associated with the university, described as "medical professionals, administrators and coaches at Michigan State University, and gymnasts' parents, whom he groomed just as effectively as those he violated."[61]

The *Detroit News* soon reported that "multiple M.S.U. officials, including trainers and assistant coaches, had been told of inappropriate behavior by Nassar over two decades." MSU president Lou Anna Simon was aware in 2014 that an unnamed university sports doctor was the subject of a Title IX investigation but had been "cleared." The university's board of trustees "continu[ed to] support . . . Dr. Simon" while they awaited results of an inquiry into whether university officials "had ignored or covered up complaints about . . . Nassar."[62]

Three days later, Simon submitted her resignation letter, which read in part, "I am sorry that a trusted, renowned physician was really such an evil, evil person who inflicted such harm under the guise of medical treatment." Simon denied any cover-up, saying she had decided to leave due to "outside pressure."[63] The university made the decision much easier by giving her a retirement package worth nearly $3 million and the title of "president emeritus."[64]

When Simon testified before Congress nearly a year later, she and a lawyer representing the university claimed that "'no MSU official believed that Nassar committed sexual abuse' before a victim contacted police in 2016." Nevertheless, MSU still "agreed to pay $500 million to settle lawsuits brought by Nassar victims."[65] The university also shelled out just under $20 million more in legal fees, including to defend Simon against charges that she had lied to police.[66]

The NCAA finally, but very briefly, took official notice of this national scandal in January 2019, following the resignations of MSU's women's gymnastics coach Kathie Klages and athletic director Mark Hollis. Parroting Simon, Hollis claimed his program "ha[d] been attacked by [an] evil . . . individual," asserting that his department's "first priority has always been [student-athletes'] health and safety."[67]

The NCAA decided not to pursue "potential violations of [its] rules regarding sexual assault cases at Michigan State"—because it had no such rules. Even though Klages had just been arraigned on two counts of lying to police, the NCAA quickly ended its non-investigation by once again doing nothing.[68]

Thus, it fell upon Michigan's attorney general and the state courts to try to send a message to MSU well after the fact. Eventually, the former deans of MSU and its College of Osteopathic Medicine were convicted of "neglect and misconduct in office," minor offenses, for mishandling the sexual misconduct complaints against Nassar.[69] In addition, both MSU's former gymnastics coach and president were tried for lying to police. Klages was initially convicted, but her conviction was overturned by the Michigan Court of Appeals in a split decision on technical evidentiary grounds related to the timing of her original false statement about what had happened in 1997 and the investigation conducted nearly twenty years later in 2018.[70] Simon was never convicted.

After agreeing to pay more than $500 million to "hundreds of victims and [for] related legal costs," the university proceeded to create more walls of silence. Its lawyers asserted attorney-client privilege regarding key documents needed to complete the investigation. MSU also reneged on its commitment to pay for, and participate in, an "independent review of sex assaults committed by Nassar." In addition, both the university and its interim president, John Engler, refused to cooperate with state officials. The state attorney general's office indefinitely suspended its two-year investigation into the MSU's "handling of complaints against . . . Larry Nassar."[71] The case was never reopened.

The NCAA and Sexual Abuse

The NCAA does not consider the prevention of sexual assault and other forms of sexual abuse to be its responsibility. Following the sex abuse scandal at Penn State, the NCAA failed to mandate that college athletics programs implement basic sexual abuse prevention and reporting protocols. Unlike Olympic sports, there is not even a pseudo-independent Center for SafeSport in college athletics—or much congressional appetite to get involved.

The primary mechanism for dealing with sexual abuse and other sexual misconduct in college sports is Title IX. Unfortunately, that statute has been only marginally effective in preventing, monitoring, and/or investigating these on-campus abuses, in large part because the affected universities have a vested interest in protecting themselves.

When the NCAA has been sued by sexually abused female student-athletes charging the organization with deliberately shirking its duties, the organization and its officials have successfully hidden behind the defense that it "has no legal duty to protect NCAA student-athletes from such predatory conduct."[72] This defense works because the organization has no rules in place that specifically prohibit such conduct.

Unfortunately, what happened at MSU is not an outlier. There have been numerous other reported instances of sexual abuse of female student-athletes by coaches, trainers, team physicians, and male student-athletes. San José State University, for example, agreed to pay $1.6 million to thirteen female student-athletes who alleged a school trainer subjected them to "'unwelcome sexual touching' of their breasts, groins, buttocks and pubic areas during treatment in campus training centers." Ten other student-athletes who had made similar allegations rejected that settlement.[73]

Longtime college track coach John Rembao, who has coached at numerous schools, was accused by three Texas high school girls, whom he coached on the side, of sexual abuse between 2013 and 2016. Because the class action lawsuit against Rembao was not filed until March 2021, it had to be dismissed under that state's very short statute of limitations.

The allegations had been reported "within weeks of the abuse" to the universities that employed Rembao. Yet no one investigated, much less acted to sanction, Rembao. As one former female student-athlete who was a victim of such abuse wrote, the "NCAA must do more to protect student-athletes from sexual abuse."[74] Presently, it is doing almost nothing.

EMOTIONAL ABUSE OF FEMALE ATHLETES IN OLYMPIC AND OTHER SPORTS

Track and Field and Gymnastics

Sexual abuse is not the only type of abuse that female athletes face. Emotional and physical abuse occur far too frequently as well. In November 2019, celebrated track star Mary Cain accused her coach, the celebrated runner Alberto Salazar, of extreme body shaming and "extreme training methods" that reportedly resulted in her breaking "five bones, miss[ing] her period for three years and [having] suicidal thoughts due to disordered eating." Eight female track athletes supported Cain's accusations, complaining about Salazar's abusive training methods. All of this was documented in a *Sports Illustrated* exposé condemning the "toxic culture" surrounding Salazar's Oregon-based Nike program.[75]

Nike eventually shuttered the abusive national training center because Salazar was caught doping. Thereafter, though, Nike had to rededicate the building on its Beaverton campus that had been named for Salazar. In January 2020, the Center for SafeSport suspended Salazar from coaching while it launched a belated investigation into abuse allegations dating back to 2008. Salazar faced a lifetime ban and was already serving a four-year suspension as a long-distance runner for doping.[76] Salazar eventually was barred from coaching for life, based on findings that it was "more likely than not" that he had "sexually assaulted an athlete on two different occasions."[77]

While all of this was going on, elite female gymnasts, including Olympic champion Laurie Hernandez, spoke out about emotional abuse they had endured while being instructed by US Olympic and national team coach Maggie Haney. In 2016, several female gymnasts lodged complaints against Haney for both verbal and emotional abuse. At least six athletes and their families filed complaints with USA Gymnastics.[78]

According to the *Orange County Register*, Haney "screamed, swore at, threatened, bullied, and harassed gymnasts on a regular basis." In addition, "she told injured gymnasts to remove their boot casts and to continue training and competing." Haney's lawyer maintained throughout that these charges were "patently false,"[79] although later Haney admitted to having used harsh training methods.

Like other emotional abuse cases in Olympic sports, this matter "was not given a high priority." Haney did not receive "a formal notice of the allegations against her" until June 2017. For nearly three more years, there was no hearing held under SafeSport protocols. Incredibly, USA Gymnastics claimed it had been unable to get a commitment from *any* former elite gymnast to participate on the three-person hearing panel it was supposed to convene under the center's elastic requirements.[80]

Haney continued to coach for USA Gymnastics until January 2020, when she was "placed on interim suspension." After a hearing panel was finally convened in late April, its members found that Haney had violated the organization's code of ethical conduct, and USA Gymnastics suspended Haney for eight years. An arbitrator then reduced the suspension to five years because of sloppy due process lapses, including the failure to provide proper notice in each of the cases involving four of Haney's accusers. Haney was allowed to appeal—not to the Center for SafeSport, but to USA Gymnastics directly.[81] Thus, through that process, USA Gymnastics' reported complicity in Haney's abusive conduct was never investigated.

Women's College Basketball: North Carolina and Other Universities

Emotional abuse occurs in college sports programs as well. In 2019, University of North Carolina (UNC) Tar Heels Naismith Hall of Fame women's basketball coach Sylvia Hatchell was accused of abusing her players. The university hired an outside law firm to investigate.[82]

As the university's representative, athletic director Bubba Cunningham insisted upon interpreting the undisclosed results of that investigation for the media and public. Without revealing specific details, Cunningham made a vague statement that the investigation "led us to conclude that the program needed to be taken in a new direction."[83] Hatchell was forced to resign for what Cunningham described as "racial insensitivity," but the former coach received a large settlement.

The emotional abuse issues that could have created substantial liability for the university, including forcing female athletes to play hurt, were summarily dismissed. The university contended, without offering any evidence, that no one on the medical staff or the women's team had "surrender[ed] to pressure to clear players before they were medically ready."[84]

Despite the allegations and her forced resignation, a few months later Hatchell was allowed to host a UNC-sponsored basketball camp "for children between 8 and 18 years old, one last time." In addition, the UNC women's basketball museum reportedly continues to display a "plaque with her picture and a brief biography which include[s] her accomplishments as a coach at the university."[85]

Similar allegations of emotional abuse surfaced in Syracuse University's women's basketball program, which were allegedly ignored by the athletic department and the university. Reportedly, because no legal or administrative actions were being taken, there was a "mass exodus" of players to other schools.[86] At the University of Florida, however, women's basketball coach Cameron Newbauer chose to resign in 2021 after numerous athletes on his team described "a toxic culture" and "verbal abuse," especially toward Black players.[87]

Women's Swimming: University of California

Teri McKeever, who coached the University of California's women's swim team for twenty-nine years, including to four national team titles, was fired in January 2023 for alleged "harassment, bullying, and verbally abusive conduct" of team members.[88] McKeever's dismissal followed a so-called independent law firm investigation into the coach and her swim program. The former coach's lawyer, however, indicated that McKeever planned to file a suit for gender discrimination in lieu of a financial settle-ment, which the university, bucking the trend, had not provided her with.

The university's athletic director, Jim Knowlton, cited "numerous vio-lations of university policies that prohibit race, national origin, and dis-ability discrimination" as the main reason McKeever was fired. Knowlton also noted that the nearly five-hundred-page investigative report, which was not publicly shared, had "detail[ed] verbally abusive conduct that is antithetical to our most important values."[89]

The investigation was in response to an exposé about the swim pro-gram in the *Orange County Register* that revealed numerous female swim-mers at the university had alleged emotional and verbal abuse, including racist remarks, body shaming, and constant pressure on them to train and compete. The complaints against McKeever went back as far as 2001.

Some athletes reported developing serious mental health conditions as a result of McKeever's emotional abuse. Even though these athletes had supported their concerns with medical records, they said the coach refused to believe them. One of those swimmers alleged that when she told McKeever the pressure on her was too intense and she had thought about killing herself, the coach "laughed in [her] face" and said, "Do you know how pathetic that is? How stupid it is? How selfish that is?" That athlete was one of "at least six Cal women's swimmers since 2018 who [said they had] made plans to kill themselves or obsessed about suicide" as a result of McKeever's "bullying."[90]

US Women's Soccer and the National Women's Soccer League

One of the most publicized and thoroughly investigated scandals involv-ing the sexual and emotional abuse of elite female athletes occurred in the National Women's Soccer League (NWSL). A series of revelations in October 2021 resulted in the resignations or firings of four head coaches, called managers, as well as the commissioner; the cancellation of matches; and an independent investigation by former US Attorney General Sally Yates. Furthermore, an article in the *Athletic* detailed alle-gations by current and former players on the North Carolina Courage that former manager Paul Riley had been "emotionally abusing players and coercing them into sex."[91]

The Yates investigation and report strove to be independent, despite being financed by the United States Soccer Federation (US Soccer). The law firm's mandate, as articulated in the report, was "to conduct an independent investigation concerning allegations of sexual abuse and other misconduct in the NWSL. Our mandate was to follow the facts wherever they led."[92] Unfortunately, that apparently did not include investigating the NWSL and US Soccer officials for their complicity in allowing this abuse and neglect of players to continue.

Furthermore, the investigators lacked the "power to compel compliance from third parties." That included "teams and coaches, whether for the purpose of collecting documents or conducting interviews."[93] This was a substantial limitation and one that is typical with this type of in-house-financed investigative report. Both the NWSL and US Soccer could have demanded that those third parties comply or be banned from participating in the NWSL and US Soccer in the future, but, like other sports organizations under investigation, they did not choose to do so.

Nonetheless, the Yates report, although obviously incomplete, was damning in many respects. Her investigation "revealed a league in which abuse and misconduct—verbal and emotional and sexual misconduct— had become systemic, spanning multiple teams, coaches, and victims." The report found that such abuse was "rooted in a deeper culture in women's soccer, beginning in youth leagues, that normalizes verbally abusive coaching and blurs boundaries between coaches and players." Most disturbingly, the report said players reported "a pattern of sexually charged comments, unwanted sexual advances, and sexual touching, and coercive sexual intercourse."[94]

While all of this was going on, abusive coaches were being moved from team to team. According to investigators, NWSL and US Soccer officials did nothing. Furthermore, the report found no one associated with those teams, the league, or the federation "demanded better coaches." Nor did they "identify and inform others of coaches' misconduct."[95] Like most sport-financed investigative reports, the names of many of the officials who were in positions to act and failed to do so were not specifically identified, although a few of the most egregious individual participants and teams were named.

This led two owners from the Portland Thorns and the Chicago Red Stars to remove themselves from team matters until the NWSL released its own, presumably massaged, findings. Neither owner indicated that he planned to sell his team.

Becky Sauerbrunn, the captain of the US women's national soccer team and a player for the Thorns, was not impressed. She opined, with considerable justification, that "every owner and executive and U.S. Soccer official who has repeatedly failed the players and failed to protect the players, who have hidden behind legalities and have not participated fully in these investigations, should be gone."

Instead, US Soccer followed the USOPC's example and embraced its own "Safe Soccer" rubric, vaguely promising that its newly created "Participant Safety Taskforce [would] implement additional measures [as needed] across the soccer ecosystem."[96]

As the gymnastics and swimming sexual abuse scandals proved, this pattern of abuse and neglect has become all too familiar in women's spectator sports, not only in soccer. Sally Jenkins of the *Washington Post* put it this way: "Some of America's greatest young female athletes were serially coerced and groped, called [humiliating names], and suffered retaliation from the clammy-handed male coaches they rejected." She went on to ask the obvious question that few in Congress have been pursuing in a comprehensive manner: "[H]ow many times" do these abuses need to be documented that "recit[e] the[se] stomach-turning 'systemic' cycles"? They have occurred in "Gymnastics. Swimming. Skiing and snowboarding. Taekwondo, Equestrian, for God's sake."[97]

As the *Post*'s editorial board summed up: "The indignities suffered by female athletes are by now . . . sadly familiar."[98] There has been an epidemic of sexual and emotional abuse in US women's sports, and very little in the way of meaningful, systemic reforms have been implemented to deal with this widespread problem.

Conclusion

Just before Christmas 2022, Jenn Abelson, another investigative reporter for the *Washington Post*, documented new allegations of abusive conduct. This time it was about James Ayotte, who coaches female bodybuilders.

He reportedly encouraged them to do strenuous workouts, take perfor-mance-enhancing drugs, and dangerously restrict their calorie intake.

One of Ayotte's clients, a thirty-six-year-old female athlete, after allegedly following his instructions against her family's warnings, "col-lapsed days before a November competition [and was placed] on life support." Abelson concluded that this tragedy was "a stark example of how [female] bodybuilders are risking their lives, and sometimes dying, because of extreme measures that are encouraged by coaches, rewarded by judges and ignored by leaders of the industry."[99]

Sexual, emotional, and physical abuses of female athletes never seem to end. New scandals continue to be revealed and documented in a broad array of women's spectator sports. With only a few exceptions, the peo-ple most responsible for these abuses and allowing them to happen have been men. This leads to the obvious recommendation that women should lead athletics for female athletes, not only to bring about gender equity, but to deal more effectively with the epidemic of abusive conduct these athletes continue to be confronted with.

CHAPTER 10

LGB Athletes and Sports Homophobia

DISCRIMINATION AND OTHER INJUSTICES BASED ON HOMOPHOBIA remain well entrenched in American spectator sports. Arguably, homophobia has been, and continues to be, the most culturally inculcated and neglected pathology in American spectator sports. Only a relatively few openly gay professional and Olympic athletes—especially gay men—have emerged from the closet of secrecy during their careers. Homophobia inevitably wreaks havoc on the mental health and emotional well-being of many LGB athletes throughout their athletic careers. It also has consequences for young male athletes who are sexually abused since homophobia often works to prevent the abuse from being revealed or properly investigated.

For many years, the American Psychiatric Association listed homosexuality as a mental disorder, so the close connection between homophobia and the emotional well-being of those who are the subjects of that discrimination is very real, even though being LGB should never have been labeled a disorder in the first place. Jonathan Martin, for instance, was viewed as being gay, although he never has confirmed that belief. Yet this perception contributed to his mental health challenges, which were exacerbated by bullying from his Miami Dolphins teammates (see chapter 4). Not surprisingly, diagnosed depression and suicide for LGB athletes are considerably higher than for the rest of the US population.

Although elite athletes themselves seem to be somewhat more receptive to having teammates, opponents, and other competitors who are LGB than they were in the past, homophobia continues to be widespread in most major professional team sports for men—football, basketball, baseball, hockey, and, to a lesser extent, soccer. Various forms of discrimination against gays, lesbians, and other members of LGBTQ+ communities still thrive in the rest of the spectator sports world as well. In professional tennis, one of the major stadiums at the Australian Open continues to be named for Margaret Court, who has repeatedly made ugly, religiously inspired, public pronouncements condemning LGBTQ+ communities.

In a six-country study of the United States and five former British Commonwealth nations, the United States topped the list with regard to athletes experiencing homophobia in their sports. That 2015 survey research study found that of the nations studied, the United States had the highest percentage of gay male athletes who reported being threatened and derided. In none of the participating countries did lesbian, gay, and bisexual athletes feel safe playing team sports.[1] Yet there still are no US spectator sports–related reports cards measuring this type of prejudice like there are for discrimination based on gender and race. Homophobia remains shrouded in secrecy, as well as ignorance, in part because this type of discrimination has been deemed to be protected by the First Amendment, mostly on Christian religious grounds.

Fear, combined with intolerance and dislike of people who are perceived to be different in terms of gender identity or sexuality, can become a particularly toxic mixture in locker rooms and other private areas where male athletes and coaches gather. A vast majority of athletes remain reluctant to call out their fellow athletes for being blatantly homophobic. Homophobia is the most ingrained prejudice in men's spectator sports today.

That locker room prejudice seems to carry over to other sports-related issues involving LGBTQ+ populations (see chapter 11). A vast majority of the relatively few gay male athletes who have been willing to reveal their sexual orientation openly chose to wait until after their playing days ended. Many athletes still do not feel comfortable publicly affirming that they are LGB, at least while they are likely to receive substantial sums of money from corporate sponsors for being role models. They assume, with good reason, coming out will reduce—and maybe all but eliminate—their earnings.

Unenlightened attitudes by fans and members of the sports media have contributed to this homophobic discrimination and stereotyping. Even a former athlete having a gender-diverse child can bring out the worst in some fans. In late 2019, former basketball great Dwyane Wade found this out from social media attacks after he decided to do the right thing by publicly supporting his child, who came out as a trans girl at the age of twelve.[2] Wade acknowledged that in order to be a good father, he had to change his own attitude to help his child: "I had to look myself in the mirror and say: How are you going to act? It ain't about him. He knows who he is. It's about you. Who are you?"[3]

In 2012, Steve Czaban, a popular sports talk radio host for an ESPN affiliate in Washington, DC, was briefly suspended from his show after referring to a junior college basketball player who was in the process of transitioning to another gender as an "it."[4] Similarly, ESPN baseball analyst Curt Schilling used his personal social media account to support North Carolina's transphobic "bathroom bill" to compel trans people to use the bathrooms and locker rooms that conform to their gender assigned at birth. According to a report in the *New York Times*, "[His] post showed an overweight man wearing a wig and women's clothing with parts of the T-shirt cut out to expose his breast." The accompanying message read: "LET HIM IN! to the restroom with your daughter or else you're a narrow-minded, judgmental, unloving racist bigot who needs to die."[5]

Being "Outed" as a Gay Athlete

One of the more controversial LGB issues in sports has been whether athletes and other popular figures who are members of those groups but still in the closet should be "outed." When an elite male athlete or former athlete's identity is revealed in this way, it can be personally devastating, both emotionally and economically. It also can be cruel. Most in the sports media today still operate under the journalistic ethic that one's sexual orientation is a private matter, unless the subject is being openly hypocritical about their identity.

There are more than a few in the LGBTQ+ communities, however, who strongly believe that the outing of star male athletes is necessary for confronting homophobia. Sportswriter L. Z. Granderson embraced that position in an article he wrote for *ESPN The Magazine* in 2013. He argued that "[t]he gossip-obsessed media's silence on gay-athlete rumors [has been] deafening." Unless star athletes are exposed as being gay, Granderson explained, that "invisibility allows prejudice to fester." It was time, he opined, that the "charade ends. . . . The media [should cover] gay athletes with the same intensity and integrity . . . [as] straight athletes."[6]

For years it was presumed that a male athlete with the incredible courage to come out during his career could break down homophobic barriers in any of the four major American professional team sports for men. To date this has not happened in a way that signals broad social acceptance, as the unfortunate experiences, detailed later, of Jason Collins and Michael Sam in the NBA and NFL, respectively, prove. The best that can be said is that there seem to be a few more players in US men's professional leagues who feel comfortable not actively hiding their LGB identity from their teammates and close friends.

Also, more teams are trying to reach out to the LGBTQ+ communities to attract fans. Thus, Gay Pride events associated with professional sports franchises are no longer a rarity, although they are far from universal, and such recognition, where it is granted, tends to be limited to a day or two annually.

Changing Attitudes in the Sports Media

The year 2013 seemed to be one in which sports journalists and editors became more comfortable publicly expressing relatively evolved attitudes about homophobia and other forms of LGB discrimination. This awakening emerged when rumors began to circulate that the first professional athlete in a major team sport would be coming out very soon.

Mike Wise, then of the *Washington Post*, did a timely retrospective on Dave Kopay, the former professional football player who, after he retired in 1975, revealed that he was gay. Kopay wrote a very well-received book about his experiences as a closeted gay man in a league filled with homophobic athletes. He explained that it had been necessary for him, like many other gay NFL players, to "lie about his sexual orientation. . . . Otherwise, there [was] a good chance [he would] never have [had] an NFL career."[7]

Wise pointed out that during the 2013 NFL Draft combine, discussion about whether a player "like[s] girls" was still common for athletes whose sexuality might be in question. Notre Dame linebacker Manti Te'o's sexual orientation became part of the discussions about his character prior to the draft in part because he had helped to perpetuate a highly publicized hoax about having a dying girlfriend to impress the Heisman Trophy voters, which had backfired by creating questions about his sexuality. Although Te'o became the starting inside linebacker for the San Diego Chargers, he was taunted with homophobic barbs by opponents.[8] He retired in 2021 after an abbreviated NFL career.

Phil Taylor of *Sports Illustrated* posed the question in 2013 whether "the major pro leagues [were] ready for the first openly gay athlete."[9] Taylor hoped the reaction would be that it was no "big deal at all," or at least not "as devastating as expected." Taylor noted that a number of athletes in the NFL and NBA, as well as their players' associations, had indicated that they would support a gay player, but he acknowledged that "homosexual athletes at all levels still faced bullying and other mistreatment."[10]

Howard Bryant of *ESPN The Magazine* tied the reluctance of professional teams and their management to embrace gay athletes to widespread homophobic attitudes and language in sports. American society, he said, has made both "misogyny and homophobia . . . acceptable . . . , [and thus encourages] language [that accepts these prejudices] . . . in the locker room." These attitudes appear to be heightened among male professional athletes. As Bryant observed, upon hearing the rumors of a gay basketball player coming out, NBA All-Star Roy Hibbert, for example, went into a "weird post-game rant" proclaiming there would be "no homo" in his sport.[11]

Bryant explained that focusing on whether teams would welcome a gay athlete was putting the cart before the horse. Homophobic slurs have been a staple of locker room talk for years, and "[t]he culture is moving much faster than the language." Words used behind closed doors by athletes in major American professional team sports are still in a "Neanderthal stage," Bryant observed. A "change in language doesn't happen overnight. . . . [B]eing labeled as soft will always be Kryptonite [to male athletes]."[12]

In 2014, *New York Times* opinion columnist Frank Bruni, who occasionally writes about sports, ridiculed locker room homophobia and bigotry, especially by "straight" athletes in football. He noted that virtually "every straight man . . . [has] been naked . . . in front of many gay men." That experience has left them "uninjured, uncorrupted, intact. The earth still spins. The sun rises and sets." The gay athlete isn't "beaming special gay-conversion gamma rays." Homophobic locker room "anxiety depends on stereotypes of gay men as creatures of preternatural libido. . . . [I]t's illogical" and "based on bigotry."[13]

THE NATIONAL BASKETBALL ASSOCIATION

Jason Collins

The rumors circulating in 2013 turned out to be true, but the result was hardly groundbreaking. Jason Collins, a reserve center with the NBA's Washington Wizards, became the first active athlete in one of America's four major professional sports to publicly acknowledge that he was gay. As dignified as Collins appeared to be in dealing with the media crush, his declaration was not a Jackie Robinson type of moment. After pretending to be straight for most of his career, Collins had waited until the end of his playing days to speak out.

His story emerged when *Sports Illustrated* advertised that in its next issue the magazine would be publishing Collins's firsthand account of being gay in the NBA. This acknowledgment was historic because unlike former NBA reserve center John Amaechi, who had "waited until retirement [in 2007] to divulge [his] sexuality publicly," Collins was still in the league—but, as it turned out, not for long.[14] While Amaechi did not hide that he was gay, he never spoke about it publicly, except to one of his teammates.[15]

For most of his basketball career Collins pretended to be straight, until a year earlier, when he had come out "to his family and close friends." He also had hinted at his sexuality by choosing to wear the number 98 on his

Boston Celtics uniform "to mark the year that Matthew Shepard, a gay student at the University of Wyoming, was murdered."[16] Collins claimed that until 2012 even his twin brother, Jarron, did not know that he was gay, nor did his longtime girlfriend, former Stanford women's basketball player Carolyn Moog. Collins had said nothing, even when he "called off their engagement in 2009." As Moog put it, for thirty-three years of his life Collins incorrectly "identif[ied himself] out of fear."[17]

As compared to the other three major American team sports, the NBA has been somewhat more tolerant and understanding about sexual and gender diversity, but as Wade demonstrated, it has been a slowly evolving process, especially with fans. According to Amaechi, "overt homophobia" and "derogatory" locker room language have become "far less prevalent" than in the past.[18]

Kobe Bryant, who was once admonished, but not suspended for uttering homophobic slurs, joined other prominent players who tweeted their good wishes to Collins. NBA commissioner David Stern's sportswashed response emphasized that he was not surprised by the "overwhelming positive reaction." He opined that "[o]ur players are . . . knowledgeable and sophisticated on this issue. . . . [O]ur teams understand it completely.'" President Barack Obama called Collins to say that he was "impressed by his courage."[19]

Nonetheless, not all the reactions within the NBA community and the adjacent sports world were so enlightened. Chris Broussard, who at the time was an NBA analyst for ESPN, condemned Collins for "walking in open rebellion to God and Jesus Christ." Columnist Mike Wise responded that Broussard and others like him were "heterosexual religious zealots . . . [trying] to play God."[20]

After the initial hullabaloo subsided, Collins found it very difficult to find an NBA team willing to sign him. The Wizards had released him, but not before the front office went out of its way to tell members of the media the "revelation that he is gay [would] have no influence on [its off-season] plans for him." After the Wizards cut Collins, they disparaged him in this way: "Bringing back a 34-year-old . . . center with limited skills was never among the team's priorities."[21]

Harvey Araton of the *New York Times* opined that "something more sinister [was] at work."[22] Eventually Collins did receive ten-day contracts at drastically reduced compensation to play with the Brooklyn Nets for a few games. The following year Collins received no offers and was forced to retire. There have been no openly gay active NBA players since.

THE NATIONAL FOOTBALL LEAGUE

Football Homophobia Generally

If the NBA has a reputation for being a somewhat less repressive—relatively speaking—major US professional league for a gay male athlete to come out in, the NFL has a long history to support the view that it is the worst. Homophobia has been rampant in professional football seemingly forever. A comparison of the experiences of Jason Collins and Michael Sam, detailed below, highlights this distinction.

However, there also appears to be a dichotomy between major college football, which has grown somewhat less hostile to gay athletes, and the NFL. Even large universities that compete for an opportunity to play in major bowl games tend to be more proactive than NFL franchises in trying to protect the rights of their LGB athletes. This does not mean that athletes who are part of the frequently homophobic football cultures at those large universities rarely discriminate against those athletes or that their team status is placed in jeopardy for venting their homophobic prejudices. Rather, if college players or coaches discriminate in public, they are much more likely to encounter social condemnation for their words or actions from the students and academic communities that surround them.

In the NFL, though, attitudes about gay players and the LGBTQ+ communities have been disappointing. Between 1989 and 2006, when Paul Tagliabue was commissioner, as a private citizen he actively supported gay rights in public forums after his son came out as a gay man. Tagliabue's public advocacy, however, never extended to the NFL. The league's reluctance, until recently, to take a firm stand has also extended to Tagliabue's successor, Roger Goodell, whose brother is gay.

Homophobic NFL Personalities

For every supportive statement made by NFL players, coaches, and other personalities associated with the league—of which there have been relatively few—many more homophobic sentiments have been expressed, along with conspicuous silence in the face of overt homophobia. During Super Bowl week in January 2013, San Francisco 49ers cornerback Chris Culliver used his media day opportunity to speak out against having a teammate who was gay.

Culliver was reportedly responding to a news story that "former 49ers offensive lineman Kwame Harris had been named in a police report detailing a dispute between him and his ex-boyfriend." Culliver took his personal stand, against the wishes of his team management, which is one of the few NFL franchises that has publicly supported "the L.G.B.T. community." Culliver promised that "we don't got no gay people on the team. They gotta get up out of here if they do." Culliver later issued a perplexing apology explaining that his comments were "thoughts in my head . . . not how I feel."[23]

A few months later, former Washington football great and frequent loose cannon Dexter Manley joined Culliver in espousing homophobia. During a local radio interview, Manley contended that his rival, former Dallas Cowboys Hall of Fame quarterback Troy Aikman, now the lead football color analyst for ESPN Sports, "was a queer." Manley, who was a plaintiff in the NFL concussion lawsuit, later blamed his comment on a lapse in judgment caused by recent "brain surgeries."[24]

Reckless and irresponsible attacks on Aikman's sexuality have been repeated periodically for twenty years or more. Adding fuel to those rumors were suggestions that his broadcast partner Joe Buck is gay. Aikman has consistently maintained that such rumors are "ridiculous. . . . [I]t is not my lifestyle."[25]

Similarly, in 2014 NFL MVP quarterback Aaron Rodgers responded to media stories that he had broken up with his boyfriend by maintaining, "I really like women."[26] This did not convince a *USA Today* commentator, who decided that because the quarterback "has long kept his life . . . guarded," Rodgers's response had "a touch of incredulity," and thus made it a matter for public discussion and vitriolic criticism.[27]

Perhaps the most distasteful homophobic utterances in recent years were revealed in the private emails of former Los Vegas Raiders head coach and ESPN football announcer and commentator John Gruden, which surfaced in 2021 in connection with Dan Snyder and the Washington Commanders' ongoing sexual harassment scandal. Many of those emails were part of an exchange Gruden had with former Commanders president Bruce Allen. In them, the ESPN personality wrote highly offensive things, calling Goodell a "faggot" and a "clueless pussy" and saying the Rams should not have been "pressured . . . to draft 'queers' . . . [like] Michael Sam."[28]

Testing the NFL Waters: Wade Davis and Brendon Ayanbadejo
For the NFL, 2012 turned out to be the year in which gay professional football players became part of the public conversation. It began with Wade Davis, a journeyman NFL cornerback who retired in 2004 after never having played in a game. Eight years later, he talked "about being gay in the macho N.F.L." Davis said he kept his sexuality a secret growing up because his Baptist religion still viewed being gay as an abomination. When he arrived in the NFL, he continued the charade because he believed that "being gay was going to ruin [his] chances as a free agent."[29]

That same year, two active NFL players made waves by coming out in support of same-sex marriage. The first was Baltimore Ravens linebacker and special teams player Brendon Ayanbadejo, who was born in Nigeria to biracial parents. His public stand "caught the attention of . . . a Maryland state delegate who oppose[d] same-sex marriage" and was also a Baptist minister. He demanded that Ravens owner Steve Biscotti order Ayanbadejo "to cease and desist such injurious actions," which Biscotti, to his credit, refused to do.[30]

Soon thereafter, Minnesota Vikings punter Chris Kluwe issued what was described in the media as "a profanity-laced response" decrying the Maryland delegate's bigotry. The fact that two players had spoken out in support of same-sex marriage was interpreted by some as a sign that the NFL's "homophobic culture" was changing.[31]

That interpretation turned out to be premature at best. Minnesota soon released Kluwe. The Oakland Raiders signed him, but only briefly.

Adrian Peterson, Minnesota's superstar running back, publicly opined that Kluwe's release had nothing to do with the punter's support for same-sex marriage, which, as a Baptist, Peterson strongly opposed.[32]

Peterson's reaction exposed a troubling connection between the homophobic culture in sports and athletes who are members of certain Christian denominations. In Peterson's case, he also used his religious beliefs to defend himself from criminal charges that he physically abused his kids.[33] Both Ayanbadejo and Davis had been negatively affected by those with Baptist religious beliefs as well.

In a league in which devout Christianity has a strong foothold, it should not have been surprising that a significant number of NFL players would be opposed to LGBTQ+ rights. When such religious intolerance is combined with the NFL's homophobic locker room culture, it creates a powerful mixture. It also establishes a substantial disincentive for teams to draft, acquire, or retain players who, like Kluwe, are perceived to be gay even though they appear to be straight.[34]

Chris Kluwe

In 2013, shortly before Michael Sam became the first openly gay college football player drafted into the NFL, a new controversy surfaced involving former Vikings punter Chris Kluwe. As a married man, Kluwe did not acknowledge being gay himself but, like Ayanbadejo, said he formed his ideas about gay rights growing up with progressive parents in California.

After he was released by Minnesota, Kluwe accused Vikings special teams coach Mike Priefer of "harassment and homophobia." Priefer "'vehemently' denied those allegations," adding, "I do not tolerate discrimination. . . . I personally have gay family members who I love." Kluwe said later that former head coach Leslie Frazier and general manager Rick Spielman had texted him about the incident, asking Kluwe to "please fly under the radar."[35]

Ultimately, the Minnesota Vikings endorsed Kluwe's version of events. Priefer initially received a three-game suspension after "an independent investigation . . . showed that Priefer made a homophobic remark." Priefer, contrary to his denials, had been overheard "comment[ing] about 'putting all the gays on an island and nuking it.'"[36] Kluwe was disappointed by Priefer's brief suspension, which was reduced to only two games. (One can only imagine what would have happened to Priefer if he had said he wanted to put all Black people on an island and nuke it.)

Based on Kluwe's experiences, Phil Taylor of *Sports Illustrated* conceded that his prior opinion that an NFL player who came out as openly gay would produce very "little backlash . . . might have been . . . dead wrong." Taylor acknowledged that "even rumors of homosexuality can affect a player's career." He wrote about the experience of Arizona Cardinals defensive back Kerry Rhodes, who, after being rumored to be gay in 2013, became unemployed even though he had been a starter for "virtually his whole career."[37]

Michael Sam

Months before Kluwe's situation came to its disappointing close, the football world was focused on Michael Sam, the Southeastern Conference's co-Defensive Player of the Year and a first-team All-American. In February 2014, in advance of the NFL's draft, Sam announced: "I am an openly proud gay man."[38]

Nearly a year earlier, the defensive end had revealed his sexual orientation to his University of Missouri Tigers teammates, many of whom already knew or suspected. Thus, "Sam set himself on a path to become the first openly gay player in the National Football League." Initially, he seemed destined for "a prosperous pro career."[39] Eight of the previous nine SEC defensive players of the year had been drafted in the first round and the ninth was selected at the beginning of the second.[40] Goodell praised Sam for his "courage."[41]

Nonetheless, homophobic ugliness in response to Sam already had begun to surface within the NFL. A week earlier, three-time Pro-Bowl linebacker and Bountygate villain Jonathan Vilma had railed that "he did not want a gay teammate. 'I think he would not be accepted. . . . Imagine if he's the guy next to me and, you know, I get dressed, naked, taking a shower . . . and it just so happens he looks at me. How am I supposed to respond?'" Vilma's blatant homophobic discrimination, which according to Yahoo Sports made him "the poster boy of intolerance,"[42] was so inconsequential to the league that in 2020, after he retired, Vilma became a regular NFL broadcaster. Apparently ESPN let Vilma's vile comments slide because he had clarified his "poor choice" of words, saying instead, "No one in the NFL for the past however many years has experienced this before, so this is all new to everybody."[43]

More ominously for Sam's status in the league, though, "several scouts [had] asked Sam's agent . . . whether Mr. Sam had a girlfriend or whether [the agent] had seen him with women."[44] Another unenlight-ened NFL employee compared the process of introducing a gay player to league locker rooms to the "chemical imbalance . . . [of using] steroids, Adderall and painkillers."[45] An unnamed NFL assistant coach added that having a gay teammate would disrupt the highly "sensitive heartbeat of the locker room."[46] Jason Reid wrote in the *Washington Post* that Sam would be a target of bullying and intolerance.[47]

The league office, understanding the potential legal and public rela-tions implications, sent a memo to its teams "that the sport's existing policies prohibit them from discriminating against players based on . . . sexual orientation."[48] Given the practices of teams in the past, as well as the lack of any enforcement mechanism, the reminder seemed more like sportswashing than an enforceable, culture-changing threat.

Almost immediately, Sam's once-vaunted draft status dropped pre-cipitously. Instead of being a likely first-round selection, it was being reported that he was "projected by some talent evaluators as a mid-round selection." Doubts had surfaced whether "the NFL [was] fully prepared" to draft an openly gay player. Many teams would "surely pass on Sam," meaning they would not draft him in any round or even sign him as a free agent.[49]

On draft day Sam was finally selected at the end of the last round as the 249th pick, out of 256 possible choices, by the St. Louis Rams. Based on his football talent, this was shocking. It seemed as if the only reason he was drafted at all was to blunt criticism of the league for allowing such obvious discrimination.[50]

Unsurprisingly, many of those who make a living from the NFL tried to develop misleading narratives to excuse and justify what happened to

Sam in the draft process. First, it was floated that his performance at the NFL scouting combine had been "mediocre," although the consensus was that he "later performed well in individual team tryouts."[51]

Second, allegedly his "size—6 feet 2 and 261 pounds—made him an awkward fit at defensive end or outside linebacker."[52] Yet other NFL players have made careers as in-betweeners; some have made All-Pro, including DeMarcus Lawrence, who was smaller than Sam and drafted as a defensive end out of Boise State at the beginning of the second round of that same draft.

As a result of all the media attention, Sam became a national curiosity and celebrity. Like many high-profile college football players coming into the league, Sam decided to take advantage of his enhanced profile. He signed a contract with Oprah Winfrey to tape a documentary of his early professional football life. Sam explained that "[i]f seeing my story helps somebody accept who they are and to go for their dreams too, that's great."[53]

The proposed *Oprah* program format was not that dissimilar to what the NFL has done every year since 2001 in allowing players on a selected team to be filmed throughout that season, including in locker rooms. *Hard Knocks*, as it is called, is produced by the league in cooperation with HBO. Almost immediately, though, Sam's involvement with Oprah was transformed into a referendum on his lack of athletic motivation and character.

Media critics pounced, pontificating that they had objected because Sam was promoting a cause as opposed to an NFL-approved off-the-field product. "Sam should be focusing more on football and less on making himself a celebrity," wrote Scott Pierce of the *Salt Lake Tribune*. Sam should "cut ties with Oprah, or risk [not] making the team," claiming that by promoting gay rights, he was "putting himself over the team."[54]

Sam and the Rams apparently succumbed to the pressure. The Oprah Winfrey Network released a statement saying that Sam's agent added, "[T]his will allow for Michael to have a total focus on football, and ensure no distractions to his teammates."[55]

Despite his decision to focus on football, these false narratives had been repeated enough times that a growing consensus formed that

Sam, as a gay player, was too much of a liability for any team to allow him play in the NFL. William Rhoden of the *New York Times* put it this way: "[T]he odds of [Sam] making the team were stacked against [him]."[56] Indeed they were, but not due to his lack of talent.

Tony Dungy, a former head coach, Pro Football Hall of Fame member, and football commentator who is much admired around the NFL, opined that he "would not have drafted Sam. 'It's not going to be totally smooth . . . things will happen.'" Dungy added that he would not have "want[ed] to deal with" Sam being on his team.[57]

Dungy was well known for "promot[ing] . . . Christian faith and values [that support] intolerance of homosexuality."[58] In January 2023, NBC News reported that Dungy was "facing renewed criticism for his history of anti-LGBTQ statements" after he "shared a debunked myth to his nearly 950,000 followers that U.S. schools are providing litter boxes for students who identify as cats." This was a transphobic response to proposed Mississippi legislation that would "mandate menstrual products in boys bathrooms."[59]

Just as the 2014 preseason was underway, an ESPN reporter created new controversy with her article stating that multiple Rams players were concerned about having to shower with Sam. According to an unidentified teammate quoted in the story, "'Sam [was] respecting our space' . . . [by] waiting to take a shower, as not to make his teammates uncomfortable."[60] Rams star defensive lineman Chris Long responded with a tweet to ESPN, which stated that as to the issue of Sam showering with teammates, "[e]veryone but you is over it."

In late August, what had appeared to be destined ever since he was drafted at the end of the seventh round became a reality when the Rams released Sam. Rams head coach Jeff Fisher, who let Sam go, said he had been "pulling for Mike . . . [who] did everything we asked him to do"[61]— except not be openly gay. The Dallas Cowboys signed Sam to their practice squad but released him outright in October. He never played another minute in the NFL. Sam later tweeted that he had retired to protect his mental health.

Carl Nassib

In June 2021, a few months before his head coach, John Gruden, was identified as having sent homophobic email rants, Los Angeles Raiders defensive end Carl Nassib came out on social media, becoming the second active player to do so in NFL history. Initially, Roger Goodell and a few players congratulated him on his courage.[62]

Nevertheless, an overwhelming majority of players, including most of the league's stars, kept silent.[63] In addition, like the NBA's Jason Collins, Nassib did not feel comfortable revealing his status publicly until he had been in the league for a number of years. He may well have been influenced by the experience of Michael Sam, who had been cut and run out of the league before he could establish himself.

Predictably, as had happened to both Collins and Sam, Nassib's team released him after less than a year later, purportedly to save $8 million on the Raiders' salary cap. It took a long time for Nassib to find another team. Even though he was an edge rusher, one of the most valued positions in football, more than a year passed until he signed with the Tampa Bay Buccaneers, in August 2022, at a steep discount on his previous salary. Nassib was relegated to third string on the depth chart, according to ESPN. Despite his demotion, Nassib pledged $100,000 for LGBTQ+ mental health.

Unfortunately, as historic as Nassib's breakthrough may have seemed, what happened afterward indicates that homophobia in the NFL continued to be a major problem. With Sam, Te'o, and now Nassib, the message was sent that a player's status and longevity in the league are likely to be jeopardized should he publicly reveal that he is gay or otherwise be perceived as gay.

HOMOPHOBIA IN OTHER AMERICAN SPORTS

What happens to LGB athletes in American professional sports depends a great deal on the culture of the sport and the gender of the athletes involved. Women's sports generally, as well as men's soccer, appear to be far less intolerant in this way. That probably is why women's soccer, Major League Soccer, and the WNBA all had openly gay athletes before the

NBA, NFL, MLB, and NHL. Even professional boxing had an openly gay athlete in its midst in 2012.

Megan Rapinoe (US Women's Soccer)

The first high-profile, active openly gay American professional athlete was US women's soccer superstar Megan Rapinoe, who came out publicly when she was an emerging star in 2012.[64] Rapinoe's sexuality has never been much of an issue. Her acceptance has been widespread, especially after she helped lead the US team to World Cup gold medals in 2015 and 2019. The same could be said for Rapinoe's fiancée, former WNBA superstar Sue Bird. That is a contrast to the experience of her former teammate Abby Wambach, who appears to have struggled emotionally with her sexual orientation.

In 2019, Rapinoe became only the fourth woman in history to win *Sports Illustrated*'s Athlete of the Year—and the first who did not have to share the award with a male athlete. More so than any other openly gay athlete to date, Rapinoe has the stature, political awareness, intelligence, and personality to become the Jackie Robinson of the LGBTQ+ spectator sports world. At the same time, though, Rapinoe is a woman, and her experience has been special. It would be difficult, if not impossible, to replicate her welcoming experience in a team sport for men.

Orlando Cruz (Boxing)

In 2012, at the age of thirty-one, featherweight boxer and 2000 Puerto Rican Olympian Orlando Cruz became the first openly gay fighter in the particularly homophobic sport of professional boxing. Cruz described himself as a "proud Puerto Rican gay man" and said that he hoped people would "look at me for the human being I am." The huge emotional risk that he took was reflected in the fact that in preparing to come out, Cruz reportedly "met with a psychologist and others" to prepare himself "for the fallout from his announcement."[65]

Cruz revealed that once he made his announcement, his own father refused to speak to him "for a year." Four years later, though, Cruz was fighting to "become boxing's first openly gay champion." He dedicated that fight to all those who had perished or been injured as a result of a mass shooting in June 2016 at Pulse, a gay nightclub in Orlando, Florida. "Cruz himself lost four friends" on that night. He then proceeded to win that fight in a knockout.[66]

The *New Yorker*, however, noted in a 2016 piece featuring Cruz that the boxer was not the first openly gay fighter. Emile Griffith, the great welterweight and middleweight champion, had publicly revealed strong clues to his identity in a 2008 taped interview, but for years it had been widely known in boxing circles that Griffith was bisexual. He reportedly punched Benny Paret to death because Paret had hurled "anti-gay slurs" at him. In referring to that tragedy, Griffith observed, "I kill a man, and most people forgive me. . . . However, I love a man, and many say this makes me an evil person."[67]

A major difference between Cruz and Griffith, though, is that due to the intense homophobia in the United States and this sport during his boxing career, Griffith hid his identity from the public until well after he had retired as a fighter.[68]

Robbie Rogers (MLS)

As Sam Borden chronicled in the *New York Times*, former US national soccer team member Robbie Rogers "revealed . . . that he was gay" in 2013. Even though he was only twenty-five and still playing professionally in England, he decided to retire from international soccer, in part to protect his mental health. Rogers thought it best not to remain in the British public eye as an active male professional athlete who is gay. If he were to play professional soccer again, he said "almost surely" it would be in the United States with the MLS, noting that the "sports culture" in England "in terms of gay rights . . . may lag behind that of the United States." While he was unwilling to label international soccer as "homophobic," he acknowledged that "there's definitely still work to be done."[69]

Two months later, Rogers signed a contract with the Los Angeles Galaxy, which made him the first openly gay male professional athlete to play for a major American team. As *Sports Illustrated* explained, "MLS is the kind of progressive league that would welcome a trail-blazing athlete like Rogers." When players have been caught "using antigay slurs . . . , the league has been consistent in its punishments, issuing three game suspensions in each case."[70] No such rules exist in other major American male team sports.

Collin Martin (United Soccer League)

In 2018, Collin Martin succeeded Rogers as the only actively gay male player in US Soccer. His coming out was memorialized in 2021 when, as a player for the San Diego Loyal of the United Soccer League, he was the recipient of an alleged homophobic slur. His head coach, celebrated US soccer player Landon Donovan, took his players off the field in protest, forfeiting a contest the Loyal were leading, 3–1.[71]

This was a revelation in the sense that it was a team-driven effort in an American professional men's team sport to collectively protest homophobia in order to support a gay teammate. In 2022, Martin opined that he had "no regrets" about coming out. Many of his teammates on the Minnesota United already knew, and he had a boyfriend, whom he openly went out with as well.

He explained, though, that being a gay soccer player and the subject of homophobic taunts was a burden on his mental health and well-being. It was especially tough knowing that the stand his team and coach took in forfeiting the game when they walked off in protest may have cost them a trip to the playoffs.

"I alluded to it as a living nightmare," he said. Since he was a child, Martin "was always fearful about his sexuality interfering with his team's performance." As a kid, "especially in high school . . . when I thought I was potentially going to have to hide this big fact that I was gay and still try to progress in sport, the last thing I wanted was anyone to know I was gay."[72]

Brittney Griner (WNBA)

Women's basketball is another team sport that has been ahead of the curve in its acceptance of lesbian athletes. Not so long ago, though, and even today, that acceptance is more like tolerance, which often is packaged in a Christian doctrine of loving one's teammates even though they have sinned.

Kate Fagan has written poignantly about her experience on the University of Colorado's women's basketball team when she came out around 2002. Although being gay on the Boulder campus was no big deal, Fagan had to navigate the religion-based prejudices of her coach and many of her teammates. They accepted her as a player capable of redemption: "Love the sinner . . . , hate the sin."[73]

Ten years later, though, after Fagan had become a respected sports columnist, she wrote about a different dynamic. In locker rooms for both men and women, players were practicing their versions of the military's "don't ask, don't tell" policy. Yet by the time women's basketball great Brittney Griner "casually" came out in early 2013 to begin her professional career after being the first player chosen in the WNBA draft, her revelation was a nonevent—that is, until 2022 when she was imprisoned in Russia and became a political pawn in a US–Russian prisoner exchange. It was only then that her sexual orientation became an issue for certain conservative politicians who believed a straight white man should have been freed instead of her.

In 2013, though, the "sports world shrug[ged]." Sam Borden's *New York Times* article pointed out that "such nonchalance" existed "[b]ecause it was a woman. . . . [I]f it was a man who did the same thing . . . [everyone's] head would have exploded." There also have been "subdued response[s]" when other high-profile female athletes have come out, including "tennis legend Martina Navratilova . . . , basketball's Sheryl Swoopes and soccer's Megan Rapinoe."[74]

Much of the reason for that difference is unsettling: "Stereotypes that top female athletes are [all] gay continue to persist." As one women's basketball coach remarked, the attitude tends to be, "Oh, it's just another lesbian [athlete]." Thus, spectator sports have tended to embrace other equally preposterous homophobic stereotypes like "there are no gay male athletes, [but] every female athlete is a lesbian."[75]

Nevertheless, throughout much of her life, Griner struggled with mental health issues related to her being different from the other kids. In 2021, she had to leave the WNBA bubble "because of mental health reasons and . . . [pursued] counseling."[76] This was before she went to Russia to play basketball and became a political pawn. Now that she is back, her readjustment to WNBA life undoubtedly has been difficult emotionally.

LGB RIGHTS: THE SOCHI WINTER OLYMPICS

When it comes to intolerance and bigotry toward LGB athletes, few industrialized nations, if any, surpass Russia. While hosting the 2014 Winter Olympics in Sochi, Vladimir Putin showcased what government-inspired intolerance is capable of producing in the sports world. The US Olympic movement, not the IOC, turned out to be the primary mediating force against Russia's oppression of its LGBTQ+ communities.

In the United States, aside from its male figure skaters, for whom being gay is not uncommon and generally accepted in the skating world—even though the first openly gay male skaters did not compete in the Olympics until 2018—the Olympian who has probably had the greatest influence on public perceptions about gay male athletes is the incomparably gifted diving champion Greg Louganis. "For more than a decade, beginning in the late 1970s, Louganis was the closest thing to perfection the diving world had ever witnessed." He won "five world and 47 national titles . . . four Olympic golds and one silver . . . by often eye-popping margins."[77]

During those years, like other gay athletes, he deliberately kept his sexual orientation secret from the public, but as he acknowledged later, his "teammates . . . certainly [knew] . . . [and m]ost of [them] . . . refused to room with [him]." Louganis's influence on LGB rights followed years of his own public silence and the negative reactions to his 1995 autobiography, which revealed that he was gay and HIV positive and had endured bouts with depression and substance abuse. He lost all but one of "his corporate sponsors . . . and was deluged with criticism from the media and general public."[78]

Twenty years later, though, he became an outspoken and generally admired advocate for LGB rights, as well as the public face of America's opposition to Putin's reactionary antigay policies. Louganis held press conferences, gave interviews, and even wrote an op-ed piece published in the *Los Angeles Times*. He counseled active engagement with the Russian people in the face of repression, as opposed to a boycott of the games.

President Obama responded by appointing three openly gay athletes to the US delegation to Sochi: tennis great Billie Jean King, Olympic figure skating gold medalist Brian Boitano, and Caitlin Cahow, a two-time medalist on the US Olympic women's hockey team. It was a historic symbolic gesture underscoring America's supposed aspirational unity on gay rights.

While all of this was happening, though, US spectator sports were still reacting badly to the first active athletes coming out in the NBA and NFL. The Sochi Olympics forced Americans who might otherwise have continued to oppose gay rights to take another look at the issue in the context of Russian oppression. Many—but certainly not all—American sports fans came to understand why homophobic discrimination is a human rights issue.

Yet in Russia, it appears that this type of discrimination and oppression against the LGBTQ+ communities has only grown worse. In December 2023, Putin signed into law a statute that greatly enhanced prohibitions against any activities viewed as promoting LGBTQ+ rights in his country. That law has had a direct impact on sports, as US teams with Russian athletes are reluctant to participate in Gay Pride events that require Russian athletes to participate. In 2023, the Chicago Blackhawks, as a team, declined to wear Gay Pride warmup uniforms due to concerns that it might place Russian Blackhawks players and their families in jeopardy.[79]

SEXUAL ABUSE OF MALE WRESTLERS AT OHIO STATE
Homophobia is an important reason why what happened to wrestlers, football players, and other male athletes at Ohio State years ago was ignored for so long, and the media coverage thereafter was relatively subdued. Another reason was the involvement of a powerful member of Congress, who was an alleged enabler. This political dynamic simultaneously enhanced national interest in the story while apparently unleashing influential efforts to smother it. The much bigger story at Ohio State, when the former wrestlers' allegations went national in the summer of

2018, was whether former Ohio State football coach Urban Meyer had misled the sports media about domestic violence committed by one of his assistants.

That April, NBC News reported that Ohio State was initiating an investigation into whether former team physician Dr. Richard Strauss, who died by suicide in 2005, had sexually abused numerous members of the wrestling team. That abuse included "shower[ing] with students and touch[ing] them inappropriately during appointments." Jim Jordan, at the time one of the most powerful Republican members of Congress, had been "an assistant wrestling coach at Ohio State from 1986 to 1994," when much of the alleged sexual abuse had taken place.[80]

A few months later, three former Ohio State wrestlers went public with accusations that Jordan knew about the abuse. Jordan's representative claimed the Congressman "never saw any abuse, never heard any abuse and never had any abuse reported to him during his time at Ohio State." One former wrestler accused Jordan of lying: "It boggles my mind that [Jordan] would take the position he has taken. . . . [He] knew this— there's no ifs, ands or buts."[81] Days later, seven more former Ohio State wrestlers opined that Jordan, as the assistant wrestling coach, must have known that Strauss had been "sexually preying on students."[82]

Four of those former Ohio State wrestlers sued the university for deliberately failing to take steps to stop Strauss's sexually abusive behavior. They alleged that university and athletic department officials knew of the "rampant sexual abuse and culture of sexual abuse . . . [b]ut . . . turned a blind eye to the abuse."[83] Those allegations "spann[ed] two decades." More than one hundred former Ohio State students were reportedly alleging that Strauss, who was "a team doctor and professor at the school . . . committed some form of sexual misconduct with them." It also was revealed that the university's athletic department had required every wrestler to submit to a physical exam with Strauss as a precondition of "being allowed to compete."[84]

According to *Rolling Stone*, Jordan was "explicitly nam[ed]" in that lawsuit. Allegedly, "Jordan made jokes and comments about Strauss's history of predatory behaviors to the other wrestlers, and . . . was dismissive to athletes who came forward with complaints about [Stauss's] conduct." One wrestler stated he had "spoke[n] to Jordan directly about the abuse."[85]

In May 2019, Ohio State released the results of an investigation that a law firm hired by the university had conducted. It concluded that Strauss sexually abused at least "177 male students . . . from 1979 to 1996, and school officials failed to take appropriate action despite being aware of numerous reports of the physician's misconduct." The victims included forty-eight wrestlers and student-athletes in fifteen or more sports, as well as other students who had used the student health center. Male students routinely complained about "excessive—and seemingly medically unnecessary—genital exams, regardless of the medical condition the student-patients presented."[86]

The investigative report, which included interviews with more than five hundred people, conspicuously avoided mentioning Jordan by name. It did find, however, that "[t]wenty-two [unnamed Ohio State] coaches . . . said they were aware of rumors or complaints regarding Strauss." Jordan maintained, unconvincingly, that the investigation "confirms everything I've said before. I didn't know about anything."[87]

Jordan's observation appears to be untrue. Nowhere in the report was it stated or even implied that Jordan's innocence had been confirmed. To the contrary, the investigation documented that complaints and rumors regarding Strauss's sexual abuse of athletes was well known throughout Ohio State's athletic department. That must have been particularly true in the wrestling program, where Jordan, as the assistant coach, had a key role in interacting with and counseling wrestlers.

The university reached a settlement of a reported $47 million with 185 of the "roughly 400" men who had lodged sexual abuse complaints. Out of another fund, which has since been closed, the university claims to have settled with forty-five other former students for amounts that have not been revealed. Most of the other alleged victims elected, unwisely, as it turns out, to go to federal court. In 2021, all those cases were dismissed because of a two-year statute of limitations on such claims. The federal judge hearing the matter stated that the plaintiffs were out of luck unless the Ohio legislature provided them with compensation. Compared to similar settlements of sexual abuse cases involving large numbers of students at other major universities, the total amount recovered by the injured parties at Ohio State was very small.[88]

THE UNIVERSITY OF MICHIGAN SEXUAL ABUSE SCANDAL

In 2022, the University of Michigan agreed to a $490 million settlement in an abuse case in which Robert Anderson, a university doctor, reportedly sexually molested more than one thousand people, including former football players, from 1966 to 2003. Those members of the university community, including many students, said they had "repeatedly complained about the doctor [who died in 2008] to coaches, trainers and administrators, to no avail."[89]

What happened to the Michigan football players who were abused became overshadowed by another controversy: whether legendary head coach Bo Schembechler, like Jim Jordan with the wrestlers at Ohio State, had ignored complaints by his players and other members of the football community regarding the doctor's predatory behavior. Unlike the Ohio State investigation by a law firm hired by the university, which did not mention coaches by name, the Michigan investigation named Schembechler.

According to *Sports Illustrated*, the Michigan report specified "multiple individuals, including members of his football team, claim[ed] to have approached Schembechler about [the doctor's] misconduct." Thus, the entire sexual abuse scandal became about Schembechler and his "legacy. . . . What little attention the survivors received from the Michigan community came mostly in the form of ridicule" and disparaging comments intended to protect Schembechler's place in Michigan football history. Revelations about the "massive institutional failure that occurred over the course of nearly four decades" were "quickly brushed aside and forgotten."[90]

Both the NCAA and the Big Ten Conference failed to investigate, much less respond to, either the Ohio State or the Michigan sexual abuse travesties. As the NCAA has done with other sexual abuse scandals in college athletic programs, it showed little or no interest in mandating effective prevention, monitoring, and enforcement protocols to address sexual abuse and other forms of sexual misconduct (see chapter 9).

Apparently, managing the organizational fallout from this and other sexual abuse scandals to protect universities with major college sports programs, rather than trying to prevent these abuses from happening, continues to be the the the NCAA's top priority.

CONCLUSION

Homophobia has been a persistent and pervasive part of American spectator sports, especially in the most popular team sports for men. Attitudes are changing, but slowly. Most of the meaningful progress has been in sports for women, individual sports, and less popular team sports for men, like soccer. The more aggressive and violent the sport, the more intolerant it is likely to be when it comes to protecting the well-being of gay athletes.

Contact sports especially cling to the prejudice that being gay is a sign of physical weakness. In addition, those athletes who are gay are far more likely to stay in the closet until they are about to retire, after their athletic careers end, or throughout all or most of their lives.

A very different set of prejudices, however, surround transgender athletes, especially if they have transitioned from male to female, which will be discussed in depth in the next chapter. These athletes are subject to attack or discrimination from state legislatures and many women athletes and their supporters, while they often lack support from key elements of the LGBTQ+ communities.

CHAPTER 11

Intersex and Trans Athletes

"Not Female Enough"

CERTAIN PHYSICAL TRAITS ARE SUPPOSED TO DISTINGUISH MEN FROM women in spectator sports. They are not always the same, however, and some do not make much sense in the context of evolving gender identification and medical ethics. Gender injustices, in the form of discrimination against intersex and transgender athletes, exist largely because men have—or are presumed to have—certain natural athletic advantages over women, while it is men who mostly define what those masculine advantages are and how they should be viewed.

The term "intersex" refers to people who have atypical sex characteristics for their assigned gender at birth, whether male or female, that don't fit into typical definitions of "masculine" and "feminine." People with intersex variations are born with sexual characteristics that seem to be masculine and feminine at the same time, not at all masculine or feminine, or neither masculine nor feminine.[1] "Transgender" means people whose assigned gender at birth, whether male or female, does not conform with their internal sense of what their gender identity is and should be.

It has been almost unheard of—until very recently, that is—for a person who identifies as male to be disqualified from a sport because he is presumed to have overly feminine characteristics. With the enactment of certain state laws that prohibit all transgender athletes from participating or limit their participation in youth and scholastic sports, however, that presumption is changing. Traditionally, though, it has long been accepted, especially by men, that women are "the weaker sex."

By comparison, athletes identifying as female who are perceived to be different in masculine ways typically must overcome the presumption that they should be disqualified from competing in sports for female athletes. In fact, this prejudice is so well ingrained that a 2022 *Washington Post*–University of Maryland poll found that most Americans are against allowing trans women "to compete with other women and girls in high school sports and . . . college and professional sports."[2]

While there have been disagreements as to how women and men differ—or are perceived to be different—physiologically in ways that affect athletic performances, the traditional, binary gender medical literature has established certain parameters that are widely accepted, while others are in flux or remain ambiguous. It is widely accepted scientifically, though, that each of these identified gender-specific traits exist on biological continua and that, given the state of the science today, no one characteristic should be used to define who qualifies as female.

With respect to spectator sports, though, singular gender criteria, including one's gender assigned at birth or minutely determined testosterone levels, are often viewed as necessarily determinative. Such views often are fueled by skewed, masculine-infused notions of traditional Christian religious values and unfair competitive advantage.

Based on several medical textbooks, two reporters writing for the *Washington Post*'s Health and Science Section in 2014 explained, in layperson's language, what those texts identified as major perceived binary gender differences.[3] They focused on five key physiological characteristics, four of which generally are deemed to provide significant athletic advantages, based on collective expert opinions rather than reliable empirical testing.

The first key difference is so-called male musculature, "particularly in the upper body." This is deemed, without definitive empirical evidence, to be due to "testosterone and other hormones," which apparently produce "more muscle" and, as a result, "more power."[4]

Second, as the reporters explained, a man's heart is typically larger than a woman's. This advantage allows those bigger hearts to "send more blood . . . [and] oxygen-carrying hemoglobin [to working muscles]." In terms of endurance, it is thought that on average a male's "aerobic capacity . . . is typically 15 to 25 percent greater." This comparison does not account the for the fact that women tend to be smaller than men. Thus, their blood generally does not have to travel as far. In addition, on average, women have significantly less blood than men that the heart needs to pump.[5]

Third, mature women typically have and need more estrogen. As a result, they tend to store more body fat, particularly in the hips and breasts. It is thought that this fat is likely to be a drag on performance because it appears that the leaner one is, the stronger one tends to be pound for pound.

This body fat may be an important reason why adolescent female athletes who compete in sports such as figure skating and gymnastics before their bodies start producing higher levels of estrogen—like former Olympic figure skater Tara Lipinski, for instance—are sometimes able to prevail over far more experienced female athletes in their sports. It also is why coaches and trainers can be overly concerned, to the point of being abusive, about female athletes keeping their weight down, which can cause those competitors a great deal of emotional damage (see chapter 9).

Fourth, because women typically have wider pelvises, the bones that lead to their knee joints are more angled. This is thought to create significantly more stress during strenuous athletic activities. That difference, according to those reporters, makes women as a group "five or six times as susceptible to knee injuries as males."[6] Whether this susceptibility is different for intersex and transgender women has never been studied empirically, however.

The one area in which women as a group seem to have a natural physiological advantage—Novak Djokovic not withstanding—is range of motion or flexibility. Many of their joints tend to be more lax due to anatomical differences and perhaps hormones as well. This characteristic is deemed to give women "the edge in [sports such as] gymnastics and figure skating."[7] Again, whether this advantage is different for intersex and transgender women has not been studied empirically.

When contemplating the physiological differences that are thought to differentiate female and male athletes, it is important to reemphasize that, almost without exception, these traits exist naturally on continua from relatively low to relatively high. This means there are noteworthy overlaps in which certain women naturally have more of a so-called performance-enhancing trait than so-called average men, while certain men have less of that trait than so-called average women.

In addition, it is critically important to recognize that all elite athletes tend to have certain physiological or cognitive advantages that help them excel athletically, which an overwhelmingly percentage of other people, both male and female, lack. This type of genetic advantage typically plays a substantial role in making them elite. Which of those characteristics, along with various social and economic advantages, are deemed to be unfair is largely subjective and can differ substantially from sport to sport. Those decisions are not necessarily based on what is best for society or what has been established empirically but rather what has traditionally been deemed to be best for the sport by those in charge, who are mostly men.

UNFAIR COMPETITIVE ADVANTAGE AND RELATED RESTRICTIONS
In many sports, women still are required to play by somewhat different rules than their male counterparts, although far less so than in the past. This is based on the traditional sexist notion that women are the weaker sex. Consequently, men traditionally have been discouraged from playing organized sports with women once adolescence kicks in. The question of who should be allowed to be a female competitor complicates these preexisting binary gender biases, often in arbitrary and disturbing ways.

Recent notions of sex verification, especially in Olympic sports, presumptively equate naturally high testosterone levels in intersex women with their having "an unfair advantage" due to what for a long time was labeled "hyperandrogenism" and is now medically defined in a more nuanced manner as unfair differences due to disorders of sex development (DSDs).

Neither of these theories, however, has been verified by reliable and definitive empirical proof. Yet in the view of the male-centered Olympic and global antidoping community, as well as among those who adopt this masculine testing model, athletes deemed to be affected by this recently created medical disorder are expected to compete as men rather than women, undergo highly intrusive inspections and treatments to correct this made-up condition, or not compete at all.

The fact that affected female-identifying intersex athletes with naturally high testosterone levels typically have mostly female characteristics, which reduce any competitive advantage to well below that of most male athletes, is ignored. Focusing on testosterone alone can be an arbitrary distinction given the fact that almost all elite athletes have at least one physical characteristic that separates them from most other people.[8] Such athletic advantages may include "lean body mass, . . . superb vision, big lungs, flexibility, long legs or testosterone."[9]

It is important to keep in mind that virtually every star athlete—whether it is Michael Phelps, LeBron James, Tom Brady, Serena Williams, Novak Djokovic, or Simone Biles—has at least one such physical trait that separates them from almost everyone else in the world. Why should naturally occurring testosterone levels be treated differently than lung capacity, reflexes, pattern recognition, flexibility, speed, power, or a combination of these traits? The focus on testosterone alone as the primary physiological difference for determining an unfair competitive advantage based on gender has been fraught with ambiguity and unfairness and has led to invidious discrimination and massive exploitation.

The social and scientific boundaries of gender identity for both intersex and trans people continue to expand in much of the world, especially among younger generations of Americans. This growing, albeit contested, acceptance does not seem to have carried over much to athletics, which still tend to view this evolution through a narrow and outdated masculine prism of unfair competitive advantages that are often peculiar to a particular sport. Thus, what increasingly should be viewed as part of scientific natural selection, social freedom of choice, and/or best for society remains a threat and mystery to male-dominated sports hierarchies that still want to determine and micromanage what it means to be a female athlete. To them, inclusion appears to have no value or very small value as compared to their view of how the female athlete should be defined.

Deciding who should be allowed to be a woman in American sports is seen as the prerogative of those male-dominated sports organizations that are obviously uncomfortable with these shifting gender boundaries, as well as female athletes who benefit from narrowly drawn boundaries that help maximize their individual athletic success. The science they cite is often ambiguous and evolving. For years, those female athletes who were labeled "lesbian" were falsely presumed to have an unfair competitive advantage as well.

Major women's groups, including the Women's Sports Foundation and the National Women's Law Center, recognize that forcing intersex athletes to undergo intrusive sex verification protocols and prohibiting transgender women from participating in women's sports are inherently discriminatory and threaten the rights of all women. This is especially true for Black and brown girls and women, who reportedly are more likely to have their sex or gender identities scrutinized.[10]

Even the IOC has recognized that something is drastically wrong in the sports world gender-wise, but it is unwilling to forcefully lead the push to change the arbitrary rules. Instead, the IOC encourages, but does not mandate, that the Olympic sports federations under its oversight and control, including all of those in the United States, not automatically bar athletes who identify as female "from competition on the exclusive ground of an unverified, alleged, or perceived unfair advantage due to their sex variations, physical appearance and/or transgender status."[11]

Unfortunately, this leaves a great deal of discretion in the hands of the male-dominated organizations that cling to outdated notions of unfair competitive advantage—one of the most subjective concepts in sports. If an advantage can be promoted, bought, or sold by corporate sponsors, it usually is deemed acceptable.

Most sports, for example, place few if any limits on the amount of money and other resources athletes are allowed to receive in order to help them train, be nutritionally fit, and purchase the best coaching and equipment. Similarly, there are few restrictions in professional, Olympic, or college sports on athletes having access to more resources than their opponents. Most resource limitations, where they do exist, including salary caps and the now-flexible rules of amateurism, are there to benefit owners, sports entrepreneurs, athletic departments, and other sports organizations, not the athletes themselves or the public.

Yet female-identifying intersex athletes who naturally produce minutely more testosterone than most other women are treated like—or sometimes worse than—the many athletes who introduce illicit or illegal performance-enhancing substances into their bodies. Female athletes who produce a little too much testosterone naturally, measured in tiny amounts, are directed to either reduce those levels artificially, typically in intrusive pharmaceutical ways, or compete against men.

The difference is that nearly 100 percent of the female athletes being tested are condemned by the results, but with performance-enhancing drugs, it seems that only some—and arguably relatively few—offending athletes are detected. This type of sex verification testing is equivalent to presuming that any athlete who is Russian must be cheating; thus, they should be tested differently from all other athletes.

In order to facilitate this testosterone mania, some years ago an Orwellian medical diagnosis known as hyperandrogenism was initially established to justify compelling women and girls with slightly higher levels of this naturally produced hormone to accept invasive "treatments." Now that disease has been replaced by a vague collection of symptoms known as disorders of sex development.

By classifying these conditions as medically abnormal, those who have them are deemed "sick" and in need of treatment. This same type of bogus medical labeling was used years ago in order to treat homosexuality or being a disobedient wife as diseases. Historically, such biased medical labeling also undermined care and treatment for those with mental disorders by locking them up in prison-like institutions rather than providing humane care and treatment in their communities.

On the other hand, trans women who have what are considered to be normal female testosterone levels still may be, and generally are, precluded or restricted from competing as women in high school, college, Olympic, and professional sports. A growing number of states have enacted or are considering bills that would absolutely ban athletes "from playing on sports teams that do not correspond to their sex assigned at birth," even if the assignment at birth was incorrect or is medically or psychologically disputable.[12]

A double standard exists regarding testosterone levels that disadvantages female athletes with higher-than-normal testosterone levels, including both intersex and transgender female athletes. To date, there is little "relevant research to speak of" that examines presumed advantages "transgender or cisgender . . . athletes have . . . [based on] size, strength, skill, speed and endurance."[13]

At the same time, there is a compelling argument that as a matter of basic social fairness, all athletes who sincerely self-identify as women should be allowed to compete as women unless it can be clearly and convincingly established that they, as individuals, have an unnatural unfair competitive advantage that cannot be mitigated to meet reasonably determined standards. As the experiences of people with disabilities illustrate, allowing for reasonable accommodations to promote inclusion and diversity should be viewed as more socially important than maintaining these sports-imposed notions and distinctions about what it means to have an unfair competitive advantage.

In April 2023, the Biden administration, through the rule-making authority of the US Department of Education (DOE) under Title IX, dove into this controversy with a compromise that still allows for more nuanced forms of discrimination. The rules proposed by the DOE would, if adopted, place restrictions on the ability of school sports programs that receive federal financial assistance to "limit or deny a student's eligibility to participate on a male or female athletic team consistent with their gender identity."[14] These rules, which are an improvement on the highly discriminatory policies of the Trump administration, would seem to apply to both transgender and intersex athletes, although the DOE refers only to transgender athletes.

Under this compromise, covered schools and their athletic programs would be expected to ensure that all students, including those who identify as transgender—and arguably intersex—have an equal opportunity to participate in school sports. Yet these same schools would be able to deny those students equal opportunities as long as they employ "sex-related eligibility criteria" that (1) consider the specific needs of "each sport, level of competition, and grade or education level"; (2) are "substantially related to achievement of an important educational objective," such as "prevention of sports-related injury" or "to promote 'fairness in competition'"; and (3) "minimize harms to students whose opportunity to participate on a male or female team consistent with their gender identity would be limited or denied."[15]

This controversy centers in large part on how one views the legal foundation underlying Title IX. Is it a federal act intended to prohibit discrimination "on the basis of sex . . . in any educational program or activity involving federal financial assistance" where sex is viewed as binary, either male or female, as those who claim to be protecting women's sports assert?[16] Or is sex supposed to be viewed more accurately to include intersex and transgender as well as traditional gender identities?

The proposed rules try to split the baby in half, combining both the traditional and modern views of what sex means in the context of gender. In addition, the proposed compromise would not apply to professional or Olympic sports and international competitions. Furthermore, the proposed rules could be easily bypassed for high school and college sports that are characterized as "competitive." Thus, for elite athletes, the proposed rules would have very limited or no applicability. The proposed restrictions, for the most part, would apply to less competitive school sports and arguably many, but certainly not all, youth sports that receive federal funds. Highly competitive youth sports programs, even if they were covered, would appear to be exempt once they have adopted eligibility criteria that satisfy the three federal requirements.

Furthermore, the proposed rules say little about invasive testing protocols used to verity sex-related eligibility criteria other than that any criteria used should "minimize harms to [those] students." It appears that the DOE chose that language intentionally rather than incorporating the more rigorous and well-defined "least restrictive alternative" concept from its rules governing programs for persons with disabilities. Nor is there any requirement that schools and other covered sports programs provide alternative athletic competitions for athletes who are disqualified by the criteria that satisfy these federal rules.

CHAPTER II

Despite all the discretion these proposed rules give to schools and their sports programs, Republican lawmakers from states with legislation that ban all transgender athletes from participating in women's and girls' sports are defiant and highly critical of the DOE. The governor of South Dakota, for instance, railed, "We will defend our laws. Only girls will play girls' sports,"[17] which may explain why the Biden administration was so cautious and equivocal in proposing its rules.

THE NORTH CAROLINA LGBTQ+ DISCRIMINATION LAW: THE NCAA AND NBA

The confusion and bad faith that can be interjected into the sex identity process in sports when state legislatures, as opposed to the federal government, become involved is illustrated by the events that took place in North Carolina in 2016. This happened after the state passed anti-transgender legislation known as the "bathroom bill" and two major sports organizations doing business in the state responded. The result demonstrates how sensitivity to gender identity and sexual orientation has evolved but can be stymied by sports-related self-interests.

In the crosshairs of this dispute were the NCAA and the NBA, in a state where basketball is revered. As Barry Svrluga of the *Washington Post* explained, "North Carolina [was] caught at the intersection of sports [and] politics,"[18] which produced an uncomfortable series of compromises that ultimately undermined LGBTQ+ rights.

The North Carolina bathroom bill was one of a number of callous measures undertaken in an attempt to deprive "lesbian, gay, bisexual, and transgender people" of their civil rights. The statute in question included a provision that compelled "transgender people to use bathrooms in public facilities that aligned with their sex at birth,"[19] much like other more recent laws dictating trans athletes' participation in team sports. The bathroom bill provision affected a smaller number of LGBTQ+ people than the statute in its entirety.

The NCAA came out against the bathroom bill relatively quickly. Like many other corporations and organizations, it promised not to hold any NCAA-sponsored events in North Carolina, including the men's basketball tournament games in 2017 and 2018, unless the law was changed.

244

NCAA president Mark Emmert said that in upholding its "values," the organization was taking a firm stand in support of "anti-discrimination protections for athletes and fans."[20]

Similarly, the NBA voted not to hold its February 2017 All-Star Game in Charlotte "to protest" the North Carolina law that had "eliminated anti-discrimination protections for lesbian, gay, bisexual and transgender people." The NBA indicated that if the law was changed, the All-Star Game could still be played in Charlotte in 2019.[21]

The two most influential basketball coaches in the state at the time, Roy Williams of North Carolina and Mike Krzyzewski of Duke, both now retired, used the term "stupid" to describe the transgender bathroom provision. Williams added that the law was "discriminatory," noting that "[i]t's harmful to us," while Coach K "called the situation 'embarrassing.'"[22] Their chief concerns, though, appeared to be that the statute would generate negative publicity and cost their basketball programs a significant amount of money. It also might harm alumni donations, television ratings, and recruiting, while also potentially depriving them of home team advantage in the NCAA basketball tournament.

In March 2017, behind closed doors, the key political parties to the dispute reached a compromise that fully protected college and professional basketball in North Carolina. The bathroom bill provision was repealed, and local governments were barred from passing similar ordinances—but only until 2020. The so-called compromise also failed to address the other discriminatory provisions in the law that would continue to negatively impact LGBTQ+ communities in North Carolina.

The NCAA issued a confusing statement saying it was "'reluctantly' lift[ing] its ban on holding championship events in North Carolina" because the state had "minimally achieved a situation where . . . N.C.A.A. championships may be conducted in a nondiscriminatory environment." Chad Griffin, president of the LGBTQ+ advocacy group Human Rights Campaign, opined that the "N.C.A.A. simply let North Carolina lawmakers off the hook."[23]

A few days later, the NBA followed the NCAA's lead and lifted its own boycott, paving the way for Michael Jordan's Charlotte Hornets to host the 2019 All-Star Game. NBA commissioner Adam Silver readily acknowledged that the state of North Carolina and other jurisdictions were continuing to discriminate. He hoped, but did not promise or insist, that his league would "be part of a larger national effort toward securing LGBT equality."[24]

While Silver indicated that he personally would help to bring this about, NBA owners did not join in, nor did the league itself. Nor, for that matter, did any other major spectator sports league or the NCAA. When it comes to homophobia and LGBTQ+ rights, not actively engaging in invidious discrimination and acts of intolerance, holding one or two LGBTQ+ events a year, and then looking the other way when various types of LGBTQ+ discrimination happen on their watch is about as far as most American spectator sports have been willing to go.

FEMALE ATHLETES WITH HIGH TESTOSTERONE LEVELS

Demanding that female athletes artificially decrease their natural testosterone production for non-health-related reasons makes about as much sense as requiring Usain Bolt, Michael Phelps, or basketball players who are seven feet or taller, of which there are many, to shorten their abnormally long limbs so their strides and/or reach no longer provide them with unfair competitive advantages. Serena Williams was celebrated because she served like, and often better than, male professional tennis players. Should she have been required to reduce her muscle mass so she would serve like other women?

Discrimination based on hyperandrogenism and now DSDs has been sanctioned in the sports world because these manufactured medical conditions affect only women who are categorized as "abnormal" based on their having one or more masculine characteristics, usually associated with higher testosterone production. The unfair competitive advantage rubric allows this type of discrimination to be misleadingly considered medically reasonable, ethical, and socially acceptable.

As noted earlier, there are certain characteristics that experts believe, but for the most part have not proved, distinguish men from women. At the same time, there are obvious emerging areas of gender ambiguity involving atypical physical characteristics or physiological or psychological needs to alter one's gender identity. These are controversial in sports in large part because all men are presumed to have certain natural athletic advantages over women.

No elite American or Olympic male athlete, though, has ever been disqualified from a sport because he has an overly feminine characteristic that might well be an advantage in sports, especially gymnastics or figure skating. By comparison, female athletes who are perceived to be different in masculine ways are often subjected to discrimination and emotional abuse. The tennis player and transgender pioneer Renée Richards faced both notoriety and condemnation in the mid-1970s when she had gender-affirming surgery, after which she was never permitted to play sanctioned tennis competitively as a woman.

If prejudice against trans athletes in major spectator sports was only about unfair competitive advantage, then there would be no objection to trans females with appropriate testosterone levels participating in women's and girls' sports. Unfortunately, there remains another big stumbling block: prejudice against both intersex and transgender people that is facilitated by flawed and outdated definitions of unfair competitive advantage.

Two researchers from Stanford University and Barnard College, respectively, have been studying this gender issue involving intersex and trans female athletes for years. In 2012, they wrote that the IOC's policy of banning "women with naturally high testosterone levels . . . [was neither] fair [nor] as rational as possible."[25] They opined that the presumption should be that if an athlete with high testosterone claims to be a woman and has competed as such, she should be treated as a woman. The only exception should be if it can be shown definitively that the person in question is not a woman based on a variety of measures or has enhanced her performance by taking substances that have increased her testosterone or other relevant hormone levels.

As a basic "human right of self-expression" and to have control over their own bodies, people should be allowed to define their gender, even in competitive sports. Currently, in terms of testosterone levels, there is "no clear or objective way to draw a bright line between male and female." Moreover, "[t]estosterone is not the master molecule of athleticism. . . . [T]here is no [scientific] evidence that successful athletes have higher testosterone levels than less successful ones." There is great "variation in how bodies make and respond to testosterone—and testosterone is but one element of an athlete's physiology."[26]

These types of variations make it difficult, if not impossible, to reliably and accurately predict how an individual athlete's testosterone level will affect his or her performance. In the past, gender determination—whether a person is male or female—was narrowly based on X and Y chromosomes, which, at the time, appeared to be reasonably definitive but turned out to have serious scientific limitations and ambiguities. Furthermore, as with the testing of other alleged performance-enhancing substances, the reliability and accuracy of testosterone testing, and analyses of the results, appear to vary considerably.

Another major concern is that testosterone testing, as presently carried out, is used to support gender discrimination and "gender-bashing . . . , [including] the name-calling and the insinuations that an athlete is 'too masculine'" or not feminine enough. Ultimately, "sex testing will always be discriminatory . . . [because] men will most likely continue to enjoy freedom from scrutiny." The idea that women have to be protected from unfair competition—overwhelmingly by men—is another form of sexism, which does little "to advance equality."[27]

Testosterone testing creates an unfair—and often irrebuttable—presumption of cheating. Generally, any female athlete who appears to have unacceptably high levels based on a test score is presumed to be male for athletic purposes. There are very limited means at her disposal to disprove the notion that she has an unfair competitive advantage, given the rules that are in place. The consequences for that athlete can be career altering in very harmful ways and even place her health in serious jeopardy.

After the two aforementioned gender researchers wrote about significant flaws in testosterone testing of female athletes in 2012, what was revealed next made a bad situation worse. It turned out that the IOC and several of its national affiliates had allowed the testosterone rules to be implemented in authoritarian ways.

A number of those athletes who fell in this perceived gray area of being "not female enough" based on this one physical trait were given an ultimatum: They could either consent to lower their testosterone level through genital surgery or the administration of powerful drugs, or be "placed under a permanent ban from elite women's sports." Those decisions were based on what was benignly termed a "therapeutic proposal" prepared by medical teams assembled at the behest of a "sport's governing bod[y]" in various nations, including Uganda, South Africa, and India. That ban also continued indefinitely if the proposed therapy proved unsuccessful in lowering "the athlete's testosterone level to what the governing bodies consider appropriate."[28]

Reliance on this "therapeutic proposal" was nothing more than a license to invade a woman's body and her civil rights. In order to develop such a proposal, which is anything but therapeutic, the athlete is compelled to agree to submit to invasive medical exams and procedures, including "blood tests, genital inspections, magnetic resonance imaging, x-rays and psychosexual history." Furthermore, drug therapies to reduce high testosterone levels have their own health risks, including "nasty side-effects, such as increased risk of blood clots."[29]

Surgery, however, is even worse. A few years earlier, "four female athletes, ages 18 to 21" from several developing countries were compelled to consent to a therapeutic proposal in which doctors "proposed removing the women's gonads and partially removing their clitorises." The young athletes had agreed to be sexually mutilated in order to continue competing and ensure "their future in sports," which could provide them with wealth and fame.[30]

More recently, Annet Negesa, who hoped to compete in the 800-meter run for Uganda in the 2020 Tokyo Summer Olympics (which was delayed until July 2021 due to the COVID pandemic), recounted her harrowing experience. She was pressured to undergo dangerous, irreversible surgery to reduce her "naturally elevated testosterone levels" that would have disqualified her from competing as a woman. Negesa, who identifies as a woman, was born with both male and female genitalia.[31] She was not the only high-profile elite intersex athlete to be affected in this way, nor the most publicized.

Naturally Occurring High Testosterone Levels: Caster Semenya
After these awful therapeutic abuses were revealed, the Olympic movement pulled back somewhat on its testosterone testing abuses, at least
for a while. Some women with naturally occurring high testosterone
levels, including most prominently Olympic champion Caster Semenya
of South Africa, who was assigned female at birth and identifies as a
woman, were permitted to compete in the 2016 Summer Games in Rio.
Semenya had been born with the XY male chromosome and testes rather
than ovaries but also with enough other traits to be considered female,
which is how she has lived and competed all of her life.

Behind the scenes, though, the IOC, the World Anti-Doping
Agency (WADA), the Court of Arbitration for Sport (CAS), and the
International Association of Athletics Federations (IAAF)—all organizations controlled by men—were readying themselves for a somewhat
more nuanced gender identity attack leading up to the 2020 Summer
Games in Tokyo. In 2019, the highly partisan CAS—which is not really
a court at all, but rather an administrative arm of the IOC—issued an
ambiguous and divided decision about what it means to be female in
sports. The CAS ruled that Semenya and athletes like her would no
longer be allowed to run in certain races, coincidentally those from
400 through 800 meters, Semenya's signature distances.

The IAAF, the Olympic affiliate lording over track and field, opined
that the ban should include longer races up to a mile as well, but not
shorter distances. Curiously, testosterone is not deemed to significantly
affect the outcome of sprints. The *New York Times* reported that the IAAF
concluded—apparently without conclusive proof—that in middle-dis-
tance and longer races, certain intersex female athletes like Semenya
"gain an unfair advantage . . . because they have additional muscle mass,
strength and oxygen-carrying capacity." The CAS recommended, but did
not mandate, that "the IAAF consider deferring application of its testosterone rule beyond 800 meters 'until more evidence is in.'"[32]

This was because the authors of the only independent empirical
study finding a causal link between increased testosterone and improved
athletic performance, which was published in 2017, had to publish a
correction in 2021 noting that their study had been "exploratory" and

"could have been misleading by implying a causal inference." Nevertheless, World Athletics (as the former IAAF has been known since 2019) clung to its discriminatory belief, based on research the organization had funded that "supported a causal relationship between elevated serum testosterone levels and the performance of elite female athletes." Later World Athletics, through its health and science office, acknowledged that "an independent and randomly controlled trial was needed" to prove that such a causal relationship existed.[33]

Nevertheless, Semenya's ban was to continue until the Olympic champion had reduced her body's naturally occurring testosterone to appropriate levels, as determined by those who control the male-dominated Olympic sports world. As Monica Hesse explained in the *Washington Post*, "Competitive athletics are full of biological advantages, both massive and minute." Here Semenya had to be able to show that the amount of testosterone in her blood fell below 5 nanomoles, "which is one-billionth of a mole." Yet if "Semenya has 4.99 nanomoles . . . the integrity of female athletics will be preserved."[34]

When asked whether she would comply, Semenya said, "Hell, no." Instead, she appealed CAS's divided ruling to the Swiss Federation Tribunal, which is that nation's supreme court.[35] The IOC, WADA, and CAS are all headquartered in Switzerland, so it was no big surprise when that the nation's high court ruled against her. As a result, Semenya had to try to compete in the 5,000 meters in Tokyo in 2021 and the Worlds in 2022. In both competitions, she failed to even qualify.

The Scientific Evidence and Medical Ethics

Whether these minute differences in testosterone levels are being measured accurately is uncertain at best, especially given the fact that different WADA-sanctioned labs and different so-called testing experts have produced different results when trying to measure the levels of other performance-enhancing substances. Furthermore, there is no reliable evidence that these higher testosterone levels have a significant impact on performance. The presumption about significantly better performances has been based on studies that many medical experts—including endocrinologists from Harvard Medical School[36] and physicians of the

World Medical Association (WMA)[37]—have warned are scientifically flawed.

The CAS, along with the male-dominated World Athletics—under the leadership of Lord Sebastian Coe—has required Semenya and other intersex athletes like her to take powerful drugs to reduce their testosterone levels. While genital mutilation is no longer permitted, these therapeutic proposals are alarming.

Exactly what combination of medications should be used, at what dosages, and at the risk of what harmful side effects—including other disqualifying performance-enhancing properties—has been left to the athletes' personal physicians to try to decipher, with the patient-athletes serving as guinea pigs. Even the CAS noted that it had "serious concerns" about whether such a testosterone policy could be applied fairly.[38]

There was and continues to be no definitive scientific proof or standard that supports the view that testosterone levels above this arbitrary maximum are performance enhancing even for middle- and long-distance runners. More importantly, the WMA, through its president, expressed "strong reservations about the ethical validity of these regulations." The *Guardian* reported that the WMA's council had advised "physicians around the world not to take part in implementing the IAAF's new [gender policy]. . . . [C]ompelling [these] female athletes to take hormone suppressants [would be] contrary to international medical ethics and human rights standards."[39]

The CAS expressed its own ethical uncertainty. After issuing a split 2–1 decision, all three CAS members joined together to advise, "We believe the IAAF should pause and consider carefully . . . the correct way to proceed."[40]

Coe, president of World Athletics, however—one of the leading proponents for forcing female athletes to artificially limit their naturally occurring testosterone if they want to be given the privilege to compete in *his* sport as females—has revealed no such willingness to reconsider. He pontificated early on—misleadingly, if not untruthfully—that "[a]thletics has two classifications: it has age, it has gender. We are fiercely protective about both. And I am grateful the court for arbitration for sport upheld that principle."[41]

More recently, Coe has begun insisting without conclusive proof "that testosterone is the key determinant in performance." Thus, he claims, it is his responsibility to "protect the integrity of women's sport." Coe then leaped to the misogynistic conclusion that without this type of "gender separation, no woman would ever win another sporting event."[42]

Coe's views about intersex and transgender female athletes are not only antiquated but discriminatory as well. Unfortunately, as one CAS official put it, the Olympic movement believes "discrimination is a necessary, reasonable and proportionate means of achieving the IAAF's aim of preserving the integrity of female athletics"[43]—as defined by wealthy men.

TRANSGENDER ATHLETES

In 2015, the Olympic decathlon and Wheaties box All-American hero formerly known as Bruce Jenner displayed considerable courage by publicly announcing his transition. The narrative Caitlyn Jenner established on national television and social media was unique for the time and suggested that attitudes about trans people might be evolving. Nonetheless, there was no shortage of vicious gossip about Jenner, both before and after her announcement.[44] Fortunately, she did not have to compete as a transgender female Olympic athlete, which in many ways is considerably more difficult.

Much of the early national discussion surrounding transgender athletics in the United States focused on three states—Texas, Connecticut, and Idaho—that had passed different laws to be adhered to by scholastic and other publicly supported sports in those jurisdictions. The underlying controversy has been propelled by groups that do not want transgender athletes to compete in scholastic sports, applying outdated notions of unfair advantage and/or religious doctrines to justify discrimination. In terms of science, though, "[t]here is little or no scientific research regarding the performance of elite transgender athletes, experts say."[45]

In Texas, the discussion focused on high school wrestling for girls where the state school system compels trans athletes to compete according to the gender they were assigned at birth. High school wrestler Mack Beggs, who was assigned female at birth, received testosterone injections during his transition.[46] Beggs, who was required to compete as a girl, proceeded to win two state girls' wrestling titles in the 110-pound division.[47] Nonetheless, he was vilified and harassed for doing what the state agency that governs Texas sports had directed. While his testosterone level was not abnormal for a girl, there was a subjective perception by some wrestling coaches that Beggs "strong and lean" physique provided him with an unnatural "strength advantage,"[48] as if there were no other strong and lean female athletes.

Beggs also competed as an amateur under the auspices of USA Wrestling. The US Anti-Doping Agency (USADA) disqualified him from those amateur competitions because of the small, therapeutically required doses of testosterone he received as part of his transition. The USADA ruled that Beggs would have to forfeit all his prior matches as well. Thereafter, Beggs competed as a male wrestler with a therapeutic-use exemption that permitted him to take testosterone injections. That outcome, Beggs said, was how he had wanted to compete in the first place but was prevented from doing so by Texas school authorities.[49]

By comparison, Connecticut, had a far more evolved policy that allowed students to compete athletically according to their gender identity. This policy of inclusion allowed Andraya Yearwood, a female transgender track star, to win state titles in the 100- and 200-meter sprints for girls. Like Beggs, she was harassed and demeaned.[50]

The most serious attack on female transgender athletes in Connecticut came from the federal government. In May 2020, the DOE, then under Secretary Betsy DeVos's direction during the Trump administration, issued guidance based on its reinterpretation of Title IX. The federal agency informed the state of Connecticut that under that statute, it could no longer allow transgender girls to compete in girls' sports. To do so, the letter contended, would deny female athletes with equal educational opportunities, such as "advancing to the final in [athletic] events . . . [and gaining] awards, medals, recognition, and the possibility of greater visibility to colleges."[51]

The Connecticut Interscholastic Athletic Conference disagreed, responding that the federal guidance, if implemented, would "deprive high school students of the meaningful opportunity to participate in . . .

inter-scholastic sports, based on sex-stereotyping and prejudice sought to be prevented by Title IX and Connecticut state law."[52] As LGBTQ+ advocate Sam Brinton explained, the decision to use Title IX "to exclude transgender athletes completely warps this landmark civil right law into a tool of discrimination."[53] The DOE under the Biden administration has reversed course by making it clear that under Title IX transgender and intersex female athletes are entitled to equal access to school sports programs, although, as discussed earlier, its proposed rules for implementing that principle would leave a great deal of discretion to the schools.[54]

In a law that went into effect in March 2020, Idaho "became the first state . . . to bar transgender girls . . . from participating in sports consistent with their gender identity." The so-called Fairness in Women's Sports Act not only bars sports for girls from being "open to students of the male sex," but compels all athletes wishing to compete as girls to undergo "genital and hormonal testing if their biological sex is challenged."[55]

Cross-country runner Lindsay Hecox, who wanted to continue to compete in her sport at Boise State University as a transgender woman after she transitioned following her senior year in high school, became the face of this Idaho statute. She sued the state to be able to try out for the college cross-country team, consistent with the NCAA's previous policy of allowing trans athletes to compete after they have completed a year of hormone treatments.[56] A federal court temporarily enjoined Idaho from enforcing its law, stating that the "categorical bar . . . stands in stark contrast to the policies of elite athletic bodies that regulate sports both nationally and globally."[57]

In 2021, the same issue of female transgender participation in sports became centered on the NCAA rules. Initially the organization had a comparatively enlightened policy that required a "trans woman competitor in any sport to have a year of hormone therapy."[58] Lia Thomas, a trans female swimmer at the University of Pennsylvania, met that requirement, so she was allowed to compete for Penn's women's team. She won several swim events, apparently rankling certain female swimmers and the powers that be in the NCAA. In January, during her only year on the team, the NCAA suddenly changed its policy. Henceforth, the NCAA would allow the "national governing bodies of each sport" to make their own self-serving and often different rules to determine who is eligible to compete.[59]

USA Swimming introduced a new policy, influenced by WADA and the USADA, that required trans female swimmers be on testosterone-suppressing treatment and have a level of under 5 nanomoles/liter for thirty-six months. The organization, which had facilitated the sexual abuse of so many female swimmers (see chapter 9), contended that these rules had nothing to do with Thomas's particular situation. Suspiciously, though, under that new rule, she would have been denied eligibility to compete because her treatment, at the time, had been for only thirty-four months. The NCAA interceded, however, and allowed Thomas to compete in the March college swimming championships. Thomas prevailed in only one race out of the three she entered.[60]

Some of Thomas's teammates and competitors objected to her being allowed to participate. Riley Gaines, who swam for Kentucky, expressed her dissatisfaction in this way: "If our priorities are fairness . . . , why are we completely neglecting that for one person or a small group of people?" Thomas responded that "[t]rans women are a very small minority. . . . The NCAA rules regarding trans women . . . have been around for 10-plus years. And we have not seen any massive wave of trans women dominating."[61]

While few athletic bodies for elite athletes continue to embrace categorical transgender bans as they once did, there are no universal standards or consensus as to what the standards should be and to whom they should apply. The science remains largely unsettled, but the recent push is toward discrimination under the political guise of religious freedom, fairness, and women's rights.

Reasonable solutions to this controversy are readily available, though. Two considerations seem most germane: (1) what the individual trans athlete prefers, and (2) what medical science can reliably and definitively contribute in determining whether that particular individual's situation would necessarily create an unfair competitive advantage. Stereotypes, religious beliefs, prejudices, or inflammatory rhetoric, such as which showers and bathrooms "they" will use, should have nothing to do with these decisions. Nor should outdated notions of what constitutes an unfair competitive advantage.

Trans athletes who want to compete as women or girls should be allowed to do so in youth, high school, and intramural sports, where inclusion is far more important than so-called notions of fairness to girls, or whenever there are no rules in place limiting them from participating. The burden should be on those trying to restrict participation of trans female athletes to present clear, unambiguous medical and scientific evidence that a particular trans female athlete has an unfair competitive advantage over the other female athletes she is competing against. Any such rules should be implemented in ways that (1) do not jeopardize the health of transgender female athletes and (2) are the least intrusive means of protecting competitive fairness.

WHO SHOULD BE ALLOWED TO COMPETE AS FEMALE ATHLETES?

The favored masculine analyses for the question of who should be allowed to compete as female athletes tend to explain gender-based differences in organizationally selfish and often disturbing ways. Recent notions of sex verification, especially in Olympic sports, equate naturally high testosterone levels in women with an illicit unfair competitive advantage. In the view of the IOC, the USOPC, WADA, and the USADA—and those sports organizations that follow this outdated masculine testing model—athletes afflicted with the newly created medical conditions known as DSDs are expected to consent to highly intrusive treatments, compete as men, or not compete at all.

Scientifically, the Olympic policy of banning intersex women who have naturally higher testosterone levels, which are measured in minuscule amounts, is neither fair nor rational. In an open society, the presumption should be that any athlete, with or without a higher testosterone level, already competing as a woman should be presumed to be woman. Any exceptions should require the governing sports authority to prove definitively that each individual female-identifying intersex or trans athlete should not be considered a woman based on either multiple, unambiguous scientific measures or clear and convincing evidence that the athlete has cheated by illicitly taking substances to artificially boost her testosterone or other relevant hormone levels beyond what is medically necessary. Otherwise, intersex and trans athletes, like any other athletes, should be allowed to define their gender—or absence of gender—for themselves.

With respect to testosterone levels, there is very little definitive scientific demarcation, beyond the opinions of experts hired by various sports authorities, that conclusively separates men from women. The evidence remains ambiguous as to whether athletes with these slightly higher testosterone levels even perform better, much less in which sports, and in sports like track and swimming, at what distances. In addition, men and women, traditionally defined, both vary considerably within their respective genders in regard to how their bodies manufacture, store, and use testosterone.

Because of these and probably other variables, it is difficult—if not impossible—to reliably predict how a female athlete's testosterone level will affect her performance in a particular sport or sporting event. Presuming there is—and has been—some reliable way to manage this controversy reasonably and fairly, and that sports organizations run by men have this knowledge, is another example of sportswashing an issue that has broader and more vital social and political implications.

A major concern is that testosterone testing, as presently carried out, justifies gender discrimination by creating a presumption that female-identifying intersex or trans athletes are overly masculine, whatever that means. Generally, gender testing in sports is inherently discriminatory because it originates with a presumption of impropriety. Once they are deemed to have tested positive for minutely higher testosterone levels, the affected athletes are forced to overcome a second, corollary presumption that they must have an unfair competitive advantage.

These presumptions lead to decisions that can alter intersex and trans athletes' sports careers in very negative ways and seriously jeopardize their emotional and physical health. This is too great a price to pay in order to maintain the self-serving belief that these presumed gender-based competitive advantages in spectator sports for women are automatically unfair and disqualifying, whereas advantages based on other genetic characteristics, economics, and/or privilege are not.

With respect to transgender athletes specifically, the current rules as to who may compete as girls or women are inconsistent and often at odds and contradictory, as the Texas, Connecticut, Idaho, NCAA, and Olympic experiences demonstrate. The idea that transgender males could and should be banned from youth and scholastic sports as well is irrational and malicious. The common theme is that there are many Americans, including those in various Republican-controlled state legislatures, who simply do not want transgender athletes to be allowed to compete—or, for that matter, to exist at all.

Conclusion

SPECTATOR SPORTS ARE BROKEN

There is a widening gap between the ideals of sport competition and how spectator sports really function, especially in protecting athletes' mental health and emotional well-being. The heart of this problem is the single-minded pursuit, by almost everyone involved, to make more and more money. To fully understand how and why American spectator sports have become broken in this way, several fundamental elements of the problem are considered.

While each spectator sport has its own unique characteristics, five familiar elements are common to all of them. What role each element plays, combined with how they interact and overlap, largely determines the ways and means by which these spectator sports malfunction.

1. the owners, management, and other organizational leaders, who run and profit from these sports enterprises

2. the athletes themselves and, where applicable, players' unions

3. the media that broadcast and otherwise cover these athletic events, increasingly paid for and directed by the sports themselves

4. the fans of each sport

5. the general public, including politicians and government officials

When these five elements are in social harmony, which is relatively rare, Americans benefit. When one or more of them goes askew for a variety of possible reasons, spectator sports can easily act in ways that are contrary to the interests of their athletes, the public, and even their fans. The more out of whack each of these elements becomes from the professed ideals of the sport, the greater the likelihood that bad behaviors and corruption will follow. Increasingly, highly specialized programs for young athletes aspiring to be elite have taken on many of the unhealthy and corrupting characteristics of the professional, Olympic, and big-time college sports these young athletes hope one day to participate in and benefit from.

With respect to the mental health and emotional well-being of elite and aspiring elite athletes, which are the subjects of this book, those elements have rarely, if ever, been in sync in healthy ways. As the stories of those affected athletes that have been made public illustrate, usually something has gone terribly wrong due to stigma, stereotyping, prejudice, outright discrimination, ignorance, and/or incompetence involving one, and typically more than one, of these actors. Almost always, though, the enterprises in charge of operating and profiting from the sport have a major responsibility for incubating these unhealthy attitudes and practices.

MENTAL AND EMOTIONAL DISHARMONY

The mental and emotional health and well-being of elite athletes in professional, Olympic, and major college sports, and younger athletes aspiring to be elite, is a topic that encompasses a variety of pathologies across numerous American spectator sports. Such pathologies exist, albeit often somewhat differently, in each major spectator sport doing business in the United States. Collectively, however, they send a strong signal that something is terribly wrong with how major sports enterprises in the United States function in dealing with the mental and emotional welfare of the athletes who make the sports possible.

This reality worsened in early 2020 when COVID unexpectedly changed life in the United States and the rest of the world. The COVID pandemic has contributed new, emerging, and unknown mental health and emotional well-being concerns for American athletes and their sports to deal with, while making it more difficult to adequately address these many other mental health and emotional well-being concerns.

At the same time, there have been some encouraging indications that the mental health of athletes, narrowly construed, is finally emerging from the dark ages that have been around in spectator sports since well before the Jimmy Piersall days. Major sports enterprises have become, or have been motivated to become, better—or at least more nuanced—in how they address the short-term mental health and emotional well-being of their athletes, if for no other reason than to get these valuable assets back into action as quickly as possible while minimizing any bad publicity that could impinge upon revenues and wealth building.

Nonetheless, this so-called renaissance has been limited in scope, size, and depth. The overall mental health and emotional well-being of athletes in America's most popular spectator sports remains an ongoing weak spot that deserves to be a continuing social concern. There is a litany of potential long-term, life-changing mental health problems, including from COVID, that many former elite and aspiring elite athletes have faced, are facing, or will have to face in the future.

The cultures of spectator sports have not evolved nearly enough to conclude that substantial progress has been made. There have been some incremental steps forward and a few backward, but mostly the status quo has been maintained by all those involved, including the athletes, teams, leagues, and other sports enterprises; sports media; fans and the general public; politicians; and local, state, and federal governments.

Substantial improvements have been made instead to the two most important tools spectator sports rely on to promote and better manage their self-interests: (1) public relations and propaganda strategies, including sportswashing; and (2) legal strategies to protect and enhance their legal privileges. The self-interest of these American sports enterprises rarely coincides with improving the overall mental health and emotional well-being of their athletes in the long term, and too often these values collide.

When they do collide, the perceived interests of the sports enterprises generally prevail, except in major team sports for men, where strong players' unions can help shape the outcomes, but not always in good ways. Unfortunately, but perhaps understandably, those players' unions tend to prioritize immediate compensation in the form of salaries and benefits over future postretirement healthcare and related benefits for former players, who are not even allowed to be members of those unions. Nowhere is that inequity more evident than in the NFL, the most popular sport in the United States, which is why their former players have continued to bring class action lawsuits against the league and its pension plan, which is operated by both the owners and the players' union.

Like many people, elite athletes experience a variety of mental disorders, and these create numerous serious challenges, many of which do not work out well for the athletes involved. The total incidence rate for those athletes with respect to mental disorders appears to be somewhat higher than that of the general population because of the addition of several sports-related mental conditions.

First, athletes experience stress and anxiety when they try, sometimes obsessively, to be the best they can be. Conversely, they may experience depression, stress, and anxiety when they fail to meet their own standards or the implicit or explicit standards of their teams, teammates, coaches, relatives, friends, fans, and/or corporate sponsors.

Second, a whole new class of short-term and long-term mental conditions now exist, are emerging, or may emerge later as a result of infections from COVID and its many variants. There is a looming health crisis because "long COVID continues to haunt millions of people," including by "crossing the blood-brain barrier, infecting and replicating in the human brain."[1] Athletes with preexisting mental disorders, of which there are many, would seem to be particularly susceptible.

Yet major spectator sports have done little to try to identify which and how many athletes or former athletes might be particularly susceptible and how they will be treated and cared for. Furthermore, spectator sports still have no mandates in place that require athletes be vaccinated so they do not become infected themselves or infect other athletes.

Third, one of the most devastating types of mental disorders for many elite athletes in contact sports is brain damage and other mental disorders closely linked to concussions and regular, repeated subconcussive impacts. The causes and severity of such brain damage, including CTE, varies depending upon which sport is involved. Boxing and other combat sports, football, and hockey are the sports that seem to produce the most severe damage. In those and other contact sports, a growing number of concerning and even tragic stories involving brain-traumatized athletes continue to be reported.

Fourth, a variety of substance abuse and dependency disorders and related problems appear to be quite common for elite and aspiring elite athletes. Much like brain damage, substance abuse appears to be endemic in professional football and hockey, where illicit, improper, and sometimes blatantly illegal pain and injury management practices have been encouraged for years. Throughout the spectator sports world, though, athletes also often try to self-medicate to deal with the stress, anxiety, and depression related to either the pressure to perform up to expectations or failure to do so. In addition, too many athletes continue to abuse performance-enhancing substances, which also can be addictive and have other dangerous side effects.

Finally, there are certain mental health and emotional well-being challenges that marginalized elite athletes experience that are different from, and in addition to, the challenges other athletes contend with. It is important to recognize that traditionally, American spectator sports were structured for cisgender male athletes. Thus, anyone who does not fit that profile is at a disadvantage and may experience various forms of discrimination.

Cisgender female athletes are the largest group of elite competitors with mental health and emotional well-being issues that are different from those experienced by cisgender men. The most obvious set of challenges involve pregnancy, abortion, and motherhood, including discriminatory policies put in place by those who control women's sports, mostly men. Way too many predominantly younger female athletes have had to deal with the potential lifelong traumas and damage resulting from widespread sexual and emotional abuse. Trusted coaches, trainers, physicians, and other people—again, mostly men—charged with making them better or healthier athletes have abused and/or neglected them.

A second group of elite athletes with special emotional well-being challenges are the estimated 5 percent of athletes who are LGB. These athletes are surrounded by homophobia, which is deeply ingrained in American men's sports. Stigma, secrecy, stereotypes, and discrimination have had a profound negative impact on the mental health and emotional well-being of gay and lesbian athletes, especially in football, hockey, and other team sports. Rather than taking constructive steps to try to extinguish this homophobia, for the most part these male-dominated sports organizations have either catered to this prejudice or ignored it, so as not to disrupt perceived team or sport harmony.

The most vilified and threatened group of athletes, though, whose emotional well-being challenges are therefore the most severely tested, also is the very smallest: intersex and transgender athletes, especially those who identify as women. For political and religious reasons, these athletes have been pitted against other female athletes, based largely on male-centered views of what constitutes an unfair competitive advantage and how sex and gender verification should be implemented and enforced.

LESSONS LEARNED
The mental health and emotional well-being challenges of elite and aspiring elite athletes are numerous and wide ranging. At the same time, there are many differently organized and run professional, Olympic, and major college spectator sports to consider. Thus, universal solutions for such an array of pressing mental health and related emotional concerns would be difficult to conceptualize and articulate. The lessons to be learned, however—including those from the narratives of athletes experiencing such challenges—often apply to multiple sports and can be guides for meaningful areas of improvement going forward. They reflect the major topics addressed in this book.

Lesson 1: Sports Organizations Should Prioritize Protecting the Mental Health of Their Athletes
American professional, Olympic, and major college spectator sports are generally broken when it comes to adequately protecting the health and welfare of the elite athletes who make all these business enterprises possible. This is particularly true with respect to athletes' mental health and

emotional well-being, which have been hidden away, minimized, and/or ignored for far too long.

Economic incentives push and pull the most popular sports enterprises toward revenue generation and wealth building, too often to the exclusion of athletes' mental health and emotional well-being, especially once those athletes retire. There is considerable divergence as to how these different sports enterprises operate, but a common denominator is doing what is deemed most economically profitable for those who run and control those enterprises.

Taking care of athletes' mental and emotional well-being, beyond doing what is necessary for them to be able to perform now, has been a secondary consideration at best. The mechanisms that should be in place to provide long-term mental health care to athletes in America's major spectator sports are either inadequate or nonexistent, especially for female and LGBTQ+ athletes.

Lesson 2: Spectator Sports Organizations Have an Obligation to Protect the Long-Term Mental Health of Their Athletes and Former Athletes

Because athletic careers are relatively short compared to other types of employment, labor-management health incentives are skewed to the detriment of former athletes. This has been especially true for a vast majority of non-star elite athletes who do not earn large salaries and hefty corporate endorsements over many years or who play in sports where average salaries and other compensation tends to be much lower. Most spectator sports for women fit that description.

When it comes to long-term health care, particularly involving mental health and emotional well-being, most elite and aspiring elite athletes are expected to take care of themselves, especially once they retire from their sport. Even those major team sports that provide pensions and health benefits to former players do so only for athletes who play long enough to vest in those plans and too often deliberately try not to compensate eligible former players for legitimate mental health–related benefits.

Former athletes are often treated like expendable commodities, while the organizations that should be protecting them are viewed more like public charters deserving of special public support and funding. Yet rarely, if ever, has that public support been used to provide adequate long-term mental health care for athletes and former athletes.

Sports organizations that reap these public benefits should be strongly encouraged, if not mandated, to devise and implement plans that will adequately protect the long-term health of their athletes, especially those former athletes whose health or mental health were—or may be—damaged as a result of their participation in those sports.

Lesson 3: Women Should Have a Larger Role in Operating and Managing Spectator Sports

When it comes to matters involving health, mental health, and emotional well-being, women in sports generally appear to be far more receptive than men to the notion of reducing profits and wealth building in order to protect the welfare of athletes and former athletes. Feminization of America's most popular spectator sports—meaning giving women a larger role in operating and managing these sports—is not only the right thing to do, but it appears to be a necessary and desirable trend for improving athletes' mental health, not only in women's sports, but in men's sports as well.

Yet token advancements of women and female figureheads in spectator sports are still far more common than actual equity, even in most women's sports. True equity will take time, and may not happen at all, but the health and mental health of all elite athletes is a big reason to hope gender equity will come sooner rather than later and be pushed in that direction by social forces bigger than spectator sports themselves.

Lesson 4: The Special Legal Status Sports Organizations Enjoy Should Create an Obligation That They Adequately Protect the Mental Health and Emotional Well-Being of Their Athletes

Allowing America's major sports organizations a great deal of leeway in determining how legal matters will be interpreted, implemented, and enforced in their sports, and granting them special legal privileges without insisting upon stricter accountability and specific protections for athletes and former athletes, has long been detrimental to all these athletes.

No amount of sportswashing can fully hide or obscure the national scandals, abuses, and neglect that have victimized the mental health and emotional well-being of so many elite athletes, especially those who are female, LGB, intersex, or transgender.

Spectator sports in the United States have done little to demonstrate that they are worthy of the special legal and public privileges they have been given—and much to prove that they are not. Their failures are apparent in issues involving the mental health and emotional well-being of athletes and former athletes in their sports. The privilege of being given special legal status and/or public funding and support should be accompanied by an obligation to adequately protect and provide for the mental health and emotional well-being of all their athletes and former athletes, especially those who likely have ongoing mental disorders, brain damage, or addiction issues as a result of participating in their sport.

Lesson 5: Reasonable Accommodations/Modifcations Should Be Widely Implemented in Sports to Better Protect Vulnerable Athletes

A cornerstone of providing protections for people with mental, physical, and sensory disabilities in the United States has been widespread, but far from universal, implementation of the notion of reasonable accommodations or modifications to help them achieve equity and reduce inequities. In spectator sports, this concept has been resisted tooth and nail wherever it has arisen, especially when it is perceived to come into conflict with the male-defined concept of what constitutes an unfair competitive advantage or the presumed prerogatives of ownership.

Many of the problems athletes experience involving their mental health and emotional well-being could be solved, or at least ameliorated, if teams, leagues, players' unions, and sports organizations tried to rationally and fairly implement reasonable accommodations and modifications to help those athletes who are challenged with mental health and emotional well-being concerns.

Why shouldn't a partially disabled Tiger Woods be allowed to use a golf cart when it would be a win-win for everyone involved? Why shouldn't Naomi Osaka be able to skip press conferences to protect her mental health? Why shouldn't Serena Williams have maintained her ranking while she was out of tennis on maternity leave? Why shouldn't Royce White have been able to take alternative transportation, rather than having to fly, in order to play in NBA games? (After all, the NBA allowed Kyrie Irving to decline being vaccinated for COVID, even though that meant he missed at least half of his team's games.)

Lesson 6: Sports Organizations Should Spend Far More of Their Resources on COVID Research

COVID presents a substantial threat to the well-being of spectator sports and the athletes who make them possible. As happened with CTE and other forms of brain damage in contact sports, the extent of the potential human damage from COVID may not be known for years. Spectator sports organizations in the United States can do two things now to minimize COVID harm to their sports and their athletes. First and foremost, they can insist that all their athletes, coaches, trainers, and other employees be fully vaccinated. Second, they can start spending significant amounts of money to help determine what the long-term impact of COVID is likely to be on athletes' and former athletes' health, mental health, and emotional well-being.

Lesson 7: Women and Female Athletes Should Operate and Manage Sports for Women

Male-dominated sports enterprises, which continue to control women's sports, have been particularly resistant to implementing improvements that would make it easier for female athletes to make and carry out critical personal decisions about pregnancy, maternity, and other female health-related issues. A number of those enterprises have been neglectful, sometimes willfully so, in protecting female athletes from sexual and emotional abuse by coaches and other trusted individuals—mostly men—in their sports, who have often traumatized those athletes starting when they were young. Once again, the feminization of these sports can go a long way toward creating sports cultures that are more responsive to the special needs of female athletes, especially if the affected athletes have a much stronger voice in deciding who should represent their interests.

Lesson 8: Efforts to Include LGBTQ+ Communities and Their Members Should Be Greatly Expanded in Sports

Homophobia, particularly in male spectator sports, is still deeply rooted, but no longer universal. Yet homophobic language by athletes is rarely, if ever, publicly condemned by other athletes or coaches. The very few male athletes who have come out of the closet early in their professional athletic careers paid a steep price for their courage, yet those who remain silent and in the shadows are often viewed as having turned their backs on the LGBTQ+ communities.

Given the widespread homophobia in spectator sports, especially men's sports, it is no wonder that so many young male athletes who have been sexually abused have chosen to remain silent for years, often forever. LGBTQ+ as well as gender diversity in men's spectator sports would undoubtedly help to reduce homophobia in those sports, as would strictly enforced rules to punish overt acts of homophobia or homophobic slurs, as is being done when racist diatribes and transgressions are publicly identified.

Gay Pride days are a small step forward, but they underscore the fact that the sponsoring sports enterprises view such events as being special rather than everyday. Furthermore, many spectator sports organizations still do not sponsor such events. Gay pride needs to be built into the cultures of these sports. Much like Jackie Robinson's legacy in Major League Baseball, however, these events need to be enhanced by organizational pronouncements and programs that specifically condemn bigotry and intolerance against LGBTQ+ athletes and communities.

Lesson 9: Reasonable Accommodations/Modifications Should Be Employed to Include Intersex and Transgender Athletes into Sports That Correspond with Their Gender Identities

Discrimination against transgender and intersex athletes continues to be practiced and/or condoned by a significant percentage of Americans and arguably may have even increased in recent years. The athletic fulcrum of this social intolerance is the presumption that as the "weaker sex," female athletes cannot possibly compete at high enough levels to defeat women who have any male characteristics that are deemed to give them even a slight competitive advantage. Male-dominated sports organizations, especially those with Olympic ties, have equated possessing these presumed advantages with cheating by taking performance-enhancing substances.

Thus, most elite athletes who are viewed as being "not female enough" are subjected to antidoping testing protocols, and if testosterone in their blood exceeds specified minuscule levels—which have never been empirically verified as being scientifically meaningful—they are not allowed to compete as women until they reduce those levels by so-called therapeutic medical interventions. That is the best-case scenario. Under various new state laws, many transgender and intersex female athletes could be automatically banned from competing.

There is a more sensible and humane alternative, however: employ reasonable accommodations and modifications to allow this very small percentage of athletes, who identify as women, to compete as women in spectator sports, unless it can be clearly and convincingly established scientifically that they as individuals have a clear-cut athletic advantage due to their gender status or they are cheating by taking drugs that are not medically prescribed or are being prescribed improperly.

PARTING WORDS

Despite the incremental progress that has been seen recently in talking about the mental health and emotional well-being of athletes in American spectator sports, there remains a wide gap between those words and meaningful changes. An overwhelming majority of athletes and former athletes whose mental and emotional well-being have been compromised in some way by participating in their sports are still reluctant to speak out, especially while they are participating in their sports.

More importantly, the sports organizations and even players' unions, which ostensibly are there to protect these athletes and former athletes, continue to place making money, increasing wealth, and other organizational interests above the mental health and well-being of those athletes. In addition, the economic assistance and legal favoritism these organizations receive from local, state, and federal governments almost never includes money for, or an obligation to provide, adequate mental health care and treatment to vulnerable athletes, much less former athletes once they retire from their sports.

NOTES

INTRODUCTION

1. Ewen Callaway et al., "COVID and 2020: An Extraordinary Year for Science," *Nature*, December 2022, https://www.nature.com/immersive/d41586-020-03437-4/index.html.

CHAPTER 1

1. P. David Howe, *Sport, Professionalism, and Pain: Ethnographies of Injury and Risk* (New York: Routledge, 2004), cited in John W. Parry, *The Athlete's Dilemma: Sacrificing Health for Wealth and Fame* (Lanham, MD: Rowman and Littlefield, 2017), 22.

2. Parry, *The Athlete's Dilemma*, 227.

3. Howe, *Sport, Professionalism, and Pain*, cited in Parry, *The Athlete's Dilemma*, 229.

4. Ken Belson and Jenny Vrentas, "Hamlin's Injury Highlights Precarious Position of Many Young N.F.L. Players," *New York Times*, January 29, 2023, https://www.nytimes.com/2023/01/29/sports/football/nfl-contracts-injuries-young-players.html.

CHAPTER 2

1. S. W. Pope, *Patriotic Games: Sporting Traditions in the American Imagination, 1876–1926* (New York: Oxford University Press, 1997), 65.

2. *Federal Baseball Club v. National League*, 259 U.S. 200 (1922).

3. See John W. Parry, *Mental Disability, Violence, and Future Dangerousness: Myths behind the Presumption of Guilt* (Lanham, MD: Rowman and Littlefield, 2013).

4. John W. Parry, *The Athlete's Dilemma: Sacrificing Health for Wealth and Fame* (Lanham, MD: Rowman and Littlefield, 2017), 253.

5. American College of Sports Medicine, "The American College of Sports Medicine Statement on Mental Health Challenges for Athletes," August 9, 2021, https://www.acsm.org/news-detail/2021/08/09/the-american-college-of-sports-medicine-statement-on-mental-health-challenges-for-athletes.

6. Sharon Masling, "The Conversation Is Changing for Athletes' Mental Health," *Sports Business Journal*, May 31, 2022, https://www.sportsbusinessjournal.com/SB-Blogs/COVID19-OpEds/2022/05/31-Masling.aspx.

7. In response to *NFL's Concussion Injury Litigation*, No. 19–2085 (3d Cir. 2020).

8. NFL Concussion Settlement website, https://www.nflconcussionsettlement.com, accessed November 27, 2022.

9. Will Hobson, "Former NFL Players Sue over Disability Claims, Accuse Plan of 'Disturbing' Denials," *Washington Post*, February 9, 2023, https://www.washingtonpost.com/sports/2023/02/09/nfl-disability-plan-lawsuit/.

10. Masling, "The Conversation Is Changing for Athletes' Mental Health."

Chapter 3

1. Michael Rosenberg, "Sportswashing Is Everywhere, but It's Not New," *Sports Illustrated*, December 29, 2022, https://www.si.com/olympics/2022/12/29/sportswashing-olympics-world-cup-daily-cover.

2. Rosenberg, "Sportswashing Is Everywhere."

3. Rosenberg, "Sportswashing Is Everywhere."

4. Robert Weintraub, "Play (Hard) Ball: Why the Sports Beat Must Evolve," *Columbia Journalism Review*, September/October 2017, https://archives.cjr.org/feature/play_hard_ball.php.

5. Ruth Graham, "Players Rely on an Unseen Teammate: Their Faith," *New York Times*, January 8, 2023, https://www.nytimes.com/2023/01/08/pageoneplus/quotation-of-the-day-players-rely-on-an-unseen-teammate-their-faith.html.

Chapter 4

1. *New York Times* Editorial Board, "The Solution to America's Mental Health Crisis Already Exists," *New York Times*, October 4, 2022, https://www.nytimes.com/2022/10/04/opinion/us-mental-health-community-centers.html.

2. Louisa Thomas, "A Year That Changed How Athletes Think about Mental Health," *New Yorker*, December 20, 2021, https://www.newyorker.com/culture/2021-in-review/a-year-that-changed-how-athletes-think-about-mental-health.

3. Alyson Meister and Maude Lavanchy, "Athletes Are Shifting the Narrative around Mental Health at Work," *Harvard Business Review*, September 24, 2021, https://hbr.org/2021/09/athletes-are-shifting-the-narrative-around-mental-health-at-work.

4. Jackie MacMullan, "NBA and Players Aim to Erase Stigma Surrounding Mental Health," ESPN, March 19, 2018, https://www.espn.com/nba/story/_/id/22806905/nba-players-aim-erase-stigma-surrounding-mental-health.

5. American College of Sports Medicine, "The American College of Sports Medicine Statement on Mental Health Challenges for Athletes," August 9, 2021, https://www.acsm.org/news-detail/2021/08/09/the-american-college-of-sports-medicine-statement-on-mental-health-challenges-for-athletes.

6. Thomas, "A Year That Changed How Athletes Think about Mental Health."

7. Cindy Chang et al., "Mental Health Issues and Psychological Factors in Athletes: Detection, Management, Effect on Performance and Prevention: American Medical Society for Sports Medicine Position Statement—Executive Summary," *British Journal of Sports Medicine* 54, no. 4, https://doi.org/10.1136/bjsports-2019-101583.

8. Matt Schudel, "H. Wayne Huizinga, Florida Billionaire and Sports Franchise Owner, Dies at 80," *Washington Post*, March 23, 2018, https://www.washingtonpost.com/local/obituaries/h-wayne-huizenga-florida-billionaire-and-sports-franchise-owner-dies-at-80/2018/03/23/813dfafc-2eae-11e8-8ad6-fbc50284fce8_story.html.

9. Richard Goldstein, "Jimmy Piersall, Whose Mental Illness Was Portrayed in 'Fear Strikes Out,' Dies at 87," *New York Times*, June 4, 2017, https://www.nytimes.com/2017/06/04/sports/baseball/jimmy-piersall-died-mental-illness.html.

10. Robert Lypsyte, "Backtalk; Harnisch a Reluctant Role Model," *New York Times*, November 22, 1998, https://www.nytimes.com/1998/11/22/sports/backtalk-harnisch-a-reluctant-role-model.html.

11. Jon Wertheim, "Prisoners of Depression," *Sports Illustrated*, September 8, 2003, https://vault.si.com/vault/2003/09/08/prisoners-of-depression-mental-illness-still-carries-a-powerful-stigma-in-pro-sports-but-there-are-signs-that-teams-are-finally-facing-the-problem-and-trying-to-help-troubled-athletes.

12. Wertheim, "Prisoners of Depression."

13. Wertheim, "Prisoners of Depression."

14. Christopher Snowbeck, "Behind Bradshaw's Bravado Was Depression," *Pittsburgh Post-Gazette*, October 28, 2003, https://www.post-gazette.com/news/health/2003/10/28/Behind-Bradshaw-s-bravado-was-depression/stories/200310280062.

15. Brady Langmann, "Terry Bradshaw Is Finally Becoming Himself," *Esquire*, January 27, 2022, https://www.esquire.com/entertainment/tv/a38900889/terry-bradshaw-interview-depression-legacy-going-deep/.

16. Kostya Kennedy, "Brotherly Love: Beset by Panic Attacks, Toronto's Shayne Corson Turned to Linemate and In-Law Darcy Tucker for Help," *Sports Illustrated*, October 22, 2001, https://vault.si.com/vault/2001/10/22/brotherly-love-beset-by-panic-attacks-torontos-shayne-corson-turned-to-linemate-and-in-law-darcy-tucker-for-help.

17. Peter Mendelsohn, "'You're Not Alone': How Shayne Corson Found Hope in His Battle with Mental Health," *Athletic*, September 10, 2019, https://theathletic.com/1183302/2019/09/10/youre-not-alone-how-shayne-corson-found-hope-in-his-battle-with-mental-health/.

18. Wertheim, "Prisoners of Depression."

19. Mendelson, "You're Not Alone."

20. Sally Jenkins, "Chamique Holdsclaw Confronts Her 'Little Secret' of Depression," *Washington Post*, May 17, 2012, https://www.washingtonpost.com/sports/othersports/chamique-holdsclaw-confronts-her-little-secret-of-depression/2012/05/17/gIQAoUe7WU_story.html.

21. William C. Rhoden, "On the Court, Finding an Outlet, and a Voice," *New York Times*, February 26, 2012, https://www.nytimes.com/2012/02/27/sports/basketball/chamique-holdsclaw-is-sharing-her-struggles-off-the-court.html.

22. Mame M. Kwayie, "Chamique Holdsclaw Speaks on Her Depression," *Ebony*, August 14, 2014, https://www.ebony.com/chamique-holdsclaw-speaks-on-her-depression-354/.

23. Jenkins, "Chamique Holdsclaw Confronts Her 'Little Secret' of Depression.".

24. Rachel Axon, "Chamique Holdsclaw Pleads Guilty to Assault," *USA Today*, February 27, 2013, https://www.usatoday.com/story/sports/wnba/2013/06/14/chamique -holdsclaw-pleads-guilty-to-assault/2425383/.

25. Associated Press, "Cavs' West Arrested in Maryland," ESPN, September 18, 2009, https://www.espn.com/nba/news/story/_/id/4485441.

26. Alex Reimer, "Delonte West's Mental Illness, Once Treated as a Joke, Was Never a Laughing Matter," *Forbes*, January 21, 2020, https://www.forbes.com/sites/alexreimer /2020/01/21/delonte-wests-mental-illness-used-to-elicit-laughs/.

27. Jabber Head, "Diagnoses: Delonte West Watched Desperado One Too Many Times," *Bleacher Report*, October 10, 2009, https://bleacherreport.com/articles/269465 -diagnoses-delonte-west-watched-desperado-one-too-many-times.

28. Reimer, "Delonte West's Mental Illness."

29. Brady Langmann, "What Happened to Delonte West Tells a Larger Story about How We Treat Athletes," *Esquire*, January 19, 2021, https://www.esquire.com/sports/ a34209617/delonte-west-nba-homeless-now/.

30. Jerry Crasnick, "Putting the Pieces Back Together," ESPN, November 24, 2009, https://www.espn.com/mlb/columns/story?columnist=crasnick_jerry&id=4686519.

31. Crasnick, "Putting the Pieces Back Together."

32. Matt Vensel, "Depressed Duchscherer Is 'a Soft Guy in a Profession of Hard Guys,'" *Baltimore Sun*, April 14, 2011, https://www.baltimoresun.com/sports/bal -sportsblitz-duchscherer-depression0414-story.html.

33. Karen Crouse, "For Champion Swimmer, a Simpler Time," *New York Times*, July 31, 2010, https://www.nytimes.com/2010/08/01/sports/01swimmer.html.

34. Michael A. McCann, "Do You Believe He Can Fly? Royce White and Reasonable Accommodations under the Americans with Disabilities Act for NBA Players with Anxiety Disorder and Fear of Flying," *Pepperdine Law Review* 41, no. 2 (2014), https:// digitalcommons.pepperdine.edu/plr/vol41/iss2/7.

35. Dan Favale, "Daryl Morey Says Royce White 'Could' Be Worst 1st-Round Draft Pick Ever," *Bleacher Report*, January 26, 2014, https://bleacherreport.com/articles /1937127-daryl-morey-says-royce-white-could-be-worst-first-round-nba-draft-pick -ever.

36. Mike Chiari, "Jonathan Martin–Richie Incognito Investigative Report Released," *Bleacher Report*, February 14, 2014, https://bleacherreport.com/articles/1960345-jonathan -martin-richie-incognito-investigation-report-released.

37. ESPN News Services, "Fins GM Suggested 'Punch,'" ESPN, November 7, 2013, https://www.espn.com/nfl/story/_/id/9938868/jeff-ireland-miami-dolphins-suggested -jonathan-martin-physically-confront-richie-incognito.

38. William Rhoden, "In Report on Bullying, the Vile and the Gripping," *New York Times*, February 15, 2014, https://www.nytimes.com/2014/02/16/sports/football/in -report-on-bullying-the-vile-and-the-gripping.html.

39. Josh Gross, "Ronda Rousey Finds Time, Energy for Charity," ESPN, March 12, 2013, https://www.espn.com/blog/mma/post/_/id/17068/ronda-rousey-finds-time -energy-for-charity.

40. Larry Brown, "Analysis: Naomi Osaka Suffering from Ronda Rousey Disease," *Larry Brown Sports* (blog), June 1, 2021, https://larrybrownsports.com/tennis/naomi -osaka-suffering-ronda-rousey-disease/579713.

41. *Guardian* Sport, "Michael Phelps Did Not Want to 'Be Alive Anymore' after DUI Arrest," *Guardian*, November 10, 2015, https://www.theguardian.com/sport/2015/nov /10/michael-phelps-did-not-want-to-be-alive-anymore-after-dui-arrest.

42. Associated Press, "Michael Phelps Pleads Guilty to DUI," ESPN, December 19, 2014, https://www.espn.com/olympics/swimming/story/_/id/12052498/gold-medalist -michael-phelps-pleads-guilty-dui.

43. Bonnie D. Ford, "Out of the Blue," ESPN, July 16, 2016, https://www.espn.com /espn/feature/story/_/id/17125857/us-olympic-swimmer-allison-schmitt-takes-aim -stigma-depression.

44. MacMullan, "NBA and Players."

45. Doug Smith, "Raptors' DeRozan Hopes Honest Talk on Depression Helps Others," *Toronto Star*, February 26, 2018, https://www.thestar.com/sports/raptors/2018/02 /25/raptors-derozan-hopes-honest-talk-on-depression-helps-others.html.

46. Michael Lee, "How the NBA Got Serious about Mental Health," *Washington Post*, April 19, 2022, https://www.washingtonpost.com/sports/2022/04/19/nba-mental-health -demar-derozan/.

47. Cindy Boren, "'Everything Was Spinning': Kevin Love Opens Up about His In-Game Panic Attack," *Washington Post*, March 6, 2018, https://www.washingtonpost .com/news/early-lead/wp/2018/03/06/everything-was-spinning-kevin-love-opens-up -about-his-in-game-panic-attack/.

48. Chuck Culpepper, "A Belarusian Tennis Star, a Ukrainian Reporter, a Tense Media Session," *Washington Post*, June 2, 2023, https://www.washingtonpost.com/sports/2023 /06/02/aryna-sabalenka-french-open-ukraine-war/.

49. Steven Wine, "Serena Williams Says Naomi Osaka Must Find Her Own Way to Handle Media Scrutiny," *Chicago Sun-Times*, June 1, 2021, https://chicago.suntimes.com /2021/6/1/22463063/serena-williams-naomi-osaka-must-find-her-own-way-to-handle -media-scrutiny.

CHAPTER 5

1. David Walstein, "Hiding from Yips Will Only Make It Worse," *New York Times*, July 26, 2023, https://www.nytimes.com/2023/07/26/sports/baseball/yips-eileen-canney -linnehan.html.

2. Adam Kilgore, "Washington Nationals Prospect Aaron Barrett Overcomes 'Yips' to Regain Control of Career," *Washington Post*, February 23, 2014, https://www .washingtonpost.com/sports/nationals/washington-nationals-prospect-aaron-barrett -overcomes-yips-to-regain-control-of-career/2014/02/23/96f034d4-9cde-11e3-975d -107dfef7b668_story.html.

3. Stephanie Apstein, "How Jose Altuve Got Thrown Off," *Sports Illustrated*, March 26, 2021, https://www.si.com/mlb/2021/03/26/jose-altuve-thrown-off-daily-cover.

4. Tyler Kepner, "Jose Altuve, the Yips, and Some Sympathy for the Astros," *New York Times*, October 14, 2020, https://www.nytimes.com/2020/10/14/sports/baseball/astros -jose-altuve-rays.html.

5. Chip Brown, "What the Hell Happened to David Duval?" *Men's Journal*, December 4, 2017, https://www.mensjournal.com/entertainment/what-the-hell-happened-to-david -duvall-19691231.

6. James McMahon, "Ranking the 10 Worst Cases of the Yips in Golf History," *Bleacher Report*, May 29, 2013, https://bleacherreport.com/articles/1654754-ranking-the -10-worst-cases-of-the-yips-in-golf-history.

7. Karen Crouse and Bill Pennington, "Panic Attack Leads to Hospital on Way to Golfer's First Victory," *New York Times*, November 13, 2012, https://www.nytimes.com /2012/11/13/sports/golf/charlie-beljans-panic-leads-to-hospital-and-then-pga-title .html.

8. Emily Kay, "Bubba Watson, Charlie Beljan Blame Panic Attacks on Poor Eating Habits," SB Nation, January 3, 2013, https://www.sbnation.com/golf/2013/1/3/3833464 /bubba-watson-charlie-beljan-blame-panic-attacks-on-poor-eating-habits.

9. Karen Crouse, "A Fun-Loving, Carefree Spirit Becomes the Face of Anxiety," *New York Times*, January 3, 2013, https://www.nytimes.com/2013/01/04/sports/golf/charlie -beljan-lives-a-life-of-high-anxiety-and-low-golf-scores.html.

10. Bill Pennington, "To Calm His Jittery Nerves, Keegan Bradley Embraces Them," *New York Times*, July 15, 2016, https://www.nytimes.com/2016/07/16/sports/golf/keegan -bradley-british-open.html.

11. Jason Sobel, "Bradley Can Relate to Na's Slow Play Backlash," Golf Channel, May 15, 2012, https://www.golfchannel.com/news/keegan-bradley-can-relate-kevin-nas-slow -play-backlash.

12. Pennington, "To Calm His Jittery Jittery Nerves."

13. Nick Piastowski, "Why Brandel Chamblee Sensed Lexi Thompson Was Going to Struggle on Sunday," *GOLF*, June 6, 2021, https://golf.com/news/brandel-chamblee-lexi -thompson-putting/.

14. Piastowski, "Why Brandel Chamblee Sensed Lexi Thompson Was Going to Struggle on Sunday."

15. Keith Pompey, "Something Obviously Bothers Sixers Rookie Markelle Fultz That Has Nothing to Do with His Shoulder," *Philadelphia Inquirer*, February 18, 2018, https:// www.inquirer.com/philly/sports/sixers/sixers-markelle-fultz-shoulder-shot-hitch-mental -injury-bryan-colangelo-20180210.html.

16. Kurt Streeter, "Markelle Fultz's Lonely Search for His Jump Shot," *New York Times*, March 9, 2018, https://www.nytimes.com/2018/03/09/sports/basketball/markelle-fultz -philadelphia-76ers.html.

17. Streeter, "Markelle Fultz's Lonely Search for His Jump Shot."

18. Benjamin Hoffman, "Sixers Guard Markelle Fultz out Indefinitely with Nerve Disorder," *New York Times*, December 4, 2018, https://www.nytimes.com/2018/12/04/ sports/markelle-fultz-injury-76ers.html.

19. ESPN, "Ben Simmons Timeline: All of the Major Happenings with the Phila- delphia 76ers Star in 2021–2022," February 18, 2022, https://www.espn.com/nba/story

/_/id/32877959/ben-simmons-line-all-major-happenings-philadelphia-76ers-star-2021 -2022.

20. Matthew Sullivan, "'I've Heard It All': Shaq Questions Simmons' Mental Health Battle in Brutal Swipe," Fox Sports, February 17, 2022, https://www.foxsports.com.au/ basketball/nba/ive-seen-real-mental-health-shaquille-oneal-blasts-ben-simmons/news -story/fd0d783f423e274c0b090f592849ec23.

21. Julie Kliegman, "Ben Simmons's Mental Health Is Not a Joke," *Sports Illustrated*, February 15, 2022, https://www.si.com/nba/2022/02/15/ben-simmons-mental-health -brooklyn-nets.

22. Louisa Thomas, "A Year That Changed How Athletes Think about Mental Health," *New Yorker*, December 20, 2021, https://www.newyorker.com/ culture/2021-in-review/a-year-that-changed-how-athletes-think-about-mental-health.

23. Kliegman, "Ben Simmons's Mental Health Is Not a Joke."

24. Pat Forde, "Simone Manuel Had to Conquer More Than Her Competitors to Make the Tokyo Olympics," *Sports Illustrated*, July 13, 2021, https://www.si.com/olympics/2021 /07/13/simone-manuel-tokyo-olympics-50-freestyle-overtraining.

25. Forde, "Simone Manuel Had to Conquer More Than Her Competitors."

26. Brendan Cole, "Piers Morgan Criticizes Manuel in Latest Olympics Comments," *Newsweek*, August 7, 2021, https://www.newsweek.com/piers-morgan-simone-manuel -simone-biles-olympics-interview-mental-health-1617186.

27. Ashitha Nagesh, "Simone Biles: What Are the 'Twisties' in Gymnastics?" BBC, July 29, 2021, https://www.bbc.com/news/world-us-canada-57986166.

28. Kayla Blanton, "Simone Biles Says She Still Has the 'Twisties' and 'Literally Cannot Tell Up from Down' in the Air," *Prevention*, July 30, 2021, https://www.prevention .com/health/a37179324/simone-biles-twisties-olympics-instagram/.

29. Steph Doehler, "Role Model or Quitter? Social Media's Response to Simone Biles at Tokyo 2020," *International Journal of Sports Communication* 16, no. 1 (2022): 64–79, https://doi.org/10.1123/ijsc.2022-0143.

30. *Today*, "Simone Biles: 'I'm Trying to Navigate My Own Unique Mental Health Journey,'" October 21, 2021, https://www.today.com/video/simone-biles-i-m-trying-to -navigate-my-own-unique-mental-health-journey-124255813897.

31. Rebecca Klapper, "Novak Djokovic Says Athletes Must 'Start Learning How to Deal with the Pressure,'" *Newsweek*, July 28, 2021, https://www.newsweek.com/novak -djokovic-says-pro-athletes-must-start-learning-how-deal-pressure-1613959.

32. Yahoo Sport Australia, "'I Cried for Days': Djokovic Reveals 'Guilt' of Elbow Surgery," November 9, 2018, https://au.sports.yahoo.com/cried-days-djokovic-reveals-guilt -elbow-surgery-110236103.html.

CHAPTER 6

1. Zeynep Tufekci, "If You're Suffering after Being Sick with Covid, It's Not Just in Your Head," *New York Times*, August 25, 2022, https://www.nytimes.com/2022/08/25/ opinion/long-covid-pandemic.html.

2. Ewen Callaway et al., "COVID and 2020: An Extraordinary Year for Science," *Nature*, December 2022, https://www.nature.com/immersive/d41586-020-03437-4/index.html.

3. James Hull, "The Road to Recovery for Athletes with Long Covid," Physiological Society, March 24, 2022, https://www.physoc.org/blog/the-road-to-recovery-for-athletes-with-long-covid/.

4. See John Weston Parry, *The Athlete's Dilemma: Sacrificing Health for Wealth and Fame* (Lanham, MD: Rowman and Littlefield, 2017).

5. Mark Maske, "Midway Through Its Season, the NFL Knows Its Biggest Coronavirus Challenges Lie Ahead," *Washington Post*, November 7, 2020, https://www.washingtonpost.com/sports/2020/11/06/nfl-coronavirus-season-schedule/.

6. Mike Jones, "Opinion: With COVID-19 Cases on the Rise, NFL's Best Hope Is to Revert to Vigilance and Sacrifices of 2020," *USA Today*, December 15, 2021, https://www.usatoday.com/story/sports/nfl/columnist/mike-jones/2021/12/15/nfl-covid-cases-protocols-positive-tests-team-players/8911311002/.

7. Reuters Staff, "54 Days without a Positive Covid Test," October 23, 2020, https://www.reuters.com/article/us-baseball-mlb-covid-19-testing-idUSKBN2782CT.

8. ESPN News Services, "Justin Turner of Dodgers Pulled from World Series after Positive COVID-19 Test," ESPN, October 29, 2020, https://www.espn.com/mlb/story/_/id/30206824/justin-turner-los-angeles-dodgers-pulled-world-series-positive-covid-19-test.

9. Eno Sarris, "How Does COVID Impact MLB Players' Performance? What Athletes, Trainers and the Stats Say," *Athletic*, August 26, 2022, https://theathletic.com/3488516/2022/08/26/mlb-players-covid-return-effects/.

10. Steve Ashburner, "NBA Outlines Health and Safety Protocols for 2020–21 Season," NBA.com, December 5, 2020, https://www.nba.com/news/nba-establishes-health-and-safety-protocol-for-2020-21-season.

11. Motoko Rich and Matthew Futterman, "Despite Uncertainly Olympics Promoted as Light at the End of the Pandemic Tunnel," *New York Times*, November 19, 2020, https://www.nytimes.com/2020/11/19/sports/olympics/tokyo-olympics-covid-postponed.html.

12. Angelo Fichera, "Claims Baselessly Link COVID Vaccines to Athlete Deaths," AP News, January 9, 2023, https://apnews.com/article/fact-check-covid-vaccines-athlete-deaths-1500-989195878254.

13. Cat Zakrzewski and Lauren Weber, "COVID Misinformation Spikes in the Wake of Damar Hamlin's On-Field Collapse," *Washington Post*, January 4, 2023, https://www.washingtonpost.com/technology/2023/01/03/covid-misinfo-damar-hamlin-collapse/.

14. Zakrzewski and Weber, "COVID Misinformation Spikes."

15. American College of Sports Medicine, "The American College of Sports Medicine Statement on Mental Health Challenges for Athletes," August 9, 2021, https://www.acsm.org/news-detail/2021/08/09/the-american-college-of-sports-medicine-statement-on-mental-health-challenges-for-athletes.

16. Kishen Neelam et al., "Pandemics and Pre-Existing Mental Illness: A Systematic Review and Meta-Analysis," *Brain, Behavior, and Immunity—Health* (2021), https://doi.org/10.1016/j.bbih.2020.100177.

17. Neelam et al., "Pandemics and Pre-Existing Mental Illness."

18. Claudia L. Reardon et al., "Mental Health Management of Elite Athletes during COVID-19: A Narrative Review and Recommendations," *British Journal of Sports Medicine* (2020), https://doi.org/10.1136/bjsports-2020-102884.

19. Reardon et al., "Mental Health Management of Elite Athletes during COVID-19."

20. Nicole Wallbridge Bourmistrova et al., "Long-Term Effects of COVID-19 on Mental Health: A Systematic Review," *Journal of Affective Disorders* 299 (2022): 118–25, https://doi.org/10.1016/j.jad.2021.11.031.

21. Bourmistrova et al., "Long-Term Effects of COVID-19 on Mental Health."

22. Meredith Wadman, "COVID-19 Patients Face Higher Risks of Brain Fog and Depression, Even 1 Year after Infection," *Science*, February 16, 2022, https://www.science.org/content/article/covid-19-patients-face-higher-risk-brain-fog-and-depression-even-1-year-after-infection.

23. Wadman, "COVID-19 Patients Face Higher Risks of Brain Fog and Depression."

24. Wadman, "COVID-19 Patients Face Higher Risk of Brain Fog and Depression."

25. Xan Xie, Evan Xu, and Ziyad Aly-Aly, "Risks of Mental Health Outcomes in People with COVID-19: Cohort Study," *BMJ*, February 16, 2022, https://doi.org/10.1136/bmj-2021-068993.

26. Rosie K. Lindsay et al., "What Are the Recommendations for Returning Athletes Who Have Experienced Long Term COVID-19 Symptoms?" *Annals of Medicine* 53, no. 1 (2021): 1935–44, https://doi.org/10.1080/07853890.2021.1992496.

27. Sydney Umeri, "How Elite Athletes Have Struggled with the Long-Term Effects of COVID," SB Nation, March 3, 2021, https://www.sbnation.com/nba/2021/3/3/22292213/athletes-covid-recovery-stories-jayson-tatum-mo-bamba-asia-durr.

28. Michael Lee, "Slowed and Sidelined, Some Athletes Struggle to Return from Long-Haul COVID," *Washington Post*, April 19, 2021, https://www.washingtonpost.com/sports/2021/04/19/athletes-long-haul-covid-justin-foster/.

29. Lee, "Slowed and Sidelined."

30. Around the NFL Staff, "Aaron Rodgers Takes 'Full Responsibility' for Comments about COVID-19 Vaccination Status," NFL.com, November 9, 2021, https://www.nfl.com/news/aaron-rodgers-full-responsibility-misleading-comments-covid-19-vaccine.

31. Chris Schad, "Aaron Rodgers Explains Why He Chose to Say He Was 'Immunized' over Unvaccinated," *Sports Illustrated*, August 28, 2022, https://www.si.com/fannation/bringmethesports/nfl-news-and-rumors/aaron-rodgers-explains-why-he-chose-to-say-he-was-immunized-over-unvaccinated.

32. Doug Farrar, "Aaron Rodgers Admits Lying about COVID Vaccination Status Last Year," *Touchdown Wire*, August 28, 2022, https://touchdownwire.usatoday.com/2022/08/28/aaron-rodgers-joe-rogan-covid-vaccinated/.

33. Sally Jenkins, "Kyrie Irving Wants to Leave a Legacy. With His Stance on Vaccination, He Just Might," *Washington Post*, September 27, 2021, https://www.msn.com/

en-us/news/us/kyrie-irving-wants-to-leave-a-legacy-with-his-stance-on-vaccination-he
-just-might/ar-AAOSQdn.

34. Jenkins, "Kyrie Irving Wants to Leave a Legacy."

35. Emma G. Fitzsimmons and Sopan Deb, "'Kyrie Carve Out' in Vaccine Mandate Frees Irving to Play in New York," *New York Times*, March 23, 2022, https://www.nytimes.com/2022/03/23/sports/kyrie-irving-nyc-vaccine-mandate.html.

36. Brian Lewis, "Nets' Kyrie Irving on Being in Middle of Vaccine Debate: 'Life of a Martyr,'" *New York Post*, May 4, 2022, https://nypost.com/2022/05/04/nets-kyrie-irving-on-being-in-middle-of-vaccine-debate-life-of-a-martyr/.

37. Nick Friedell, "Brooklyn Nets' Kyrie Irving: Gave Up 4-Year, $100 Million-Plus Extension to Be Unvaccinated," ESPN, September 26, 2022, https://www.espn.com/nba/story/_/id/34672230/gave-4-year-100m-plus-extension-unvaccinated.

38. Jocelyn Gecker and Jerome Pugmire, "Rising above Reality: How Djokovic Bends His Mind to Succeed," AP News, January 15, 2022, https://apnews.com/article/coronavirus-pandemic-novak-djokovic-sports-health-australia-37993234c4814893c1abfedf5cdaf884.

39. Gecker and Pugmire, "Rising above Reality."

40. Arwa Mahdawi, "Stalk of the Town: The Shaky Science behind the 'Global Celery Movement,'" *Guardian*, April 9, 2019, https://www.theguardian.com/food/2019/apr/09/anthony-william-medical-medium-green-celery-juice.

41. Anthony Williams, "Cilantro—Life Changing Food," Medical Medium, February 11, 2021, https://www.medicalmedium.com/blog/cilantro-life-changing-food.

42. Sally Jenkins, "Novak Djokovic Is Driven by an Obsession, but That Always Has a Cost," *Washington Post*, January 17, 2022, https://www.washingtonpost.com/sports/2022/01/17/novak-djokovic-vaccination-philosophy/.

43. Liz Clarke, "Like Novak Djokovic, Many Elite Athletes Go to Extremes to Gain an Edge," *Washington Post*, January 10, 2022, https://www.washingtonpost.com/sports/2022/01/10/novak-djokovic-vaccine-health-diet/.

44. Elaine Teng, "Figure Skater Vincent Zhou Worked His Whole Life for the Beijing Olympics. COVID-19 Had Other Plans," ESPN, March 24, 2022, https://www.espn.com/olympics/story/_/id/33216401/figure-skater-vincent-zhou-worked-whole-life-beijing-olympics-covid-19-had-other-plans.

45. Teng, "Figure Skater Vincent Zhou Worked His Whole Life."

46. Teng, "Figure Skater Vincent Zhou Worked His Whole Life."

47. Teng, "Figure Skater Vincent Zhou Worked His Whole Life."

48. Teng, "Figure Skater Vincent Zhou Worked His Whole Life."

49. Ben Pope, "Jonathan Toews Rejoins Blackhawks as Training Camp Begins: 'It's a Good Feeling,'" *Chicago Sun-Times*, September 23, 2021, https://chicago.suntimes.com/blackhawks/2021/9/23/22690224/jonathan-toews-blackhawks-returns-training-camp-covid-cirs-nhl.

50. Jaylon Thompson, "Chicago Blackhawks Captain Steps Away from Team Due to Long COVID Symptoms," *USA Today*, February 20, 2023, https://www.usatoday.com/story/sports/nhl/blackhawks/2023/02/20/jonathan-toews-steps-away-chicago-blackhawks-due-long-covid/11303922002/.

51. Phil Thompson, "Jonathan Toews Asks for 'Patience' as He Struggles with COVID and CIRS Symptoms," *Chicago Tribune*, February 19, 2023, https://www.chicagotribune.com/sports/blackhawks/ct-chicago-blackhawks-jonathan-toews-illness-20230219-iujaul45gzfppgd3sarugfa3gq-story.html.

52. Associated Press, "Blackhawks Say Toews Will Not Return to Team Next Season," Fox Sports, April 14, 2023, https://www.foxsports.com/articles/nhl/blackhawks-say-toews-will-not-return-to-team-next-season.

CHAPTER 7

1. Shaziya Allarahka, "What Are the Four Stages of CTE?" Medicine Net, August 1, 2022, https://www.medicinenet.com/what_are_the_four_stages_of_cte/article.htm.

2. Vipin V. Dhote et al., "Sports-Related Brain Injury and Neurodegeneration in Athletes," *Current Molecular Pharmacology* 15, no. 1 (2022): 51–76, https://doi.org/10.2174/1874467214666210910114324.

3. Donald McRae, "'Boxing Is a Mess': The Darkness and Damage of Brain Trauma in the Ring," *Guardian*, May 27, 2021, https://www.theguardian.com/sport/2021/may/27/time-to-find-out-who-cares-boxing-brain-damage-tris-dixon; see also Tris Dixon, *Damage: The Untold Story of Brain Trauma in Boxing* (London: Hamilcar Publications, 2021).

4. Andrew Thurston and Gina Digravio, "8 Major Findings and Headlines from BU CTE Researchers in the Past Year," Boston University, May 24, 2022, https://www.bu.edu/articles/2022/8-major-findings-from-bu-cte-researchers-last-year/.

5. M. L. Alosco et al., "Age of First Exposure to American Football and Long-Term Neuropsychiatric and Cognitive Outcomes," *Transactional Psychiatry* 7 (2017), https://www.nature.com/articles/tp2017197.

6. Daniel H. Daneshvar et al., "Leveraging Football Accelerometer Data to Quantify Associations between Repetitive Head Impacts and Chronic Traumatic Encephalopathy in Males," *Nature Communications* 14 (2023), https://www.nature.com/articles/s41467-023-39183-0; see also Ken Belson and Benjamin Mueller, "Collective Force of Head Hits, Not Just the Number of Them, Increases Odds of CTE," *New York Times*, June 20, 2023, https://www.nytimes.com/2023/06/20/sports/football/cte-study-concussions-brain-tackle.html.

7. Andrew Keh, "A Diagnosis Brings C.T.E. into American Pro Soccer," *New York Times*, June 28, 2022, https://www.nytimes.com/2022/06/28/sports/soccer/cte-soccer.html.

8. Aaron Ritter et al., "Traumatic Encephalopathy Syndrome: Application of New Criteria to a Cohort Exposed to Repetitive Head Impacts," *British Journal of Sports Medicine*, 57, no. 7 (2023): 389–94, https://doi.org/10.1136/bjsports-2022-105819.

9. Centers for Disease Control and Prevention, "Traumatic Brain Injury and Concussion," https://www.cdc.gov/traumaticbraininjury/index.html, accessed July 17, 2023.

10. Neil K. McGroaty, Symone M. Brown, and Mary K. Mulcahey, "Sport-Related Concussion in Female Athletes: A Systematic Review," *Orthopaedic Journal of Sports Medicine* 8, no. 7 (2020), https://doi.org/10.1177/2325967120932306.

11. Emily Kaplan, "NHL Reaches Settlement in Concussion Lawsuit," ESPN, November 12, 2018, https://www.espn.com/nhl/story/_/id/25256208/nhl-reaches-settlement-concussion-lawsuit.

12. Danield Kaplan, "NHL Paid $70.6 Million in Legal Fees for Concussion Settlement That Paid Players $18.49 Million," *Athletic*, April 29, 2021, https://theathletic.com/2549607/2021/04/29/nhl-paid-70-6-million-in-legal-fees-for-concussion-settlement-that-paid-players-18-49-million/.

13. Craig Lyons, "$75 Million NCAA Settlement to Fund Concussion Screening for 4 Million Former Athletes," *Lansing State Journal*, August 15, 2019, https://www.lansingstatejournal.com/story/news/2019/08/15/ncaa-concussion-settlement-athlete-medical-testing/2012186001/.

14. Keh, "A Diagnosis Brings C.T.E. into American Pro Soccer."

15. See John Weston Parry, *The Athlete's Dilemma: Sacrificing Health for Wealth and Fame* (Lanham, MD: Rowman and Littlefield, 2017), chaps. 13–17.

16. NFL, "Guardian Cap Debuts at Training Camps League Wide," NFL Player Health and Safety, July 27, 2022, https://www.nfl.com/playerhealthandsafety/equipment-and-innovation/engineering-technology/guardian-cap-debuts-at-training-camps-league-wide.

17. Ken Belson, "An N.F.L. Doctor Wants to Know Why Some Players Get C.T.E and Others Don't," *New York Times*, May 18, 2023, https://www.nytimes.com/2023/05/18/sports/football/pittsburgh-sports-brain-bank.html.

18. Parry, *The Athlete's Dilemma*, 171–76.

19. Sam Fortier, "Senior Bowl Restrictions Can Challenge Big Hitters," *Washington Post*, February 4, 2023, https://www.washingtonpost.com/sports/2023/02/03/senior-bowl-big-hits/.

20. Ding Productions, "NFL 'Brutal' Hits," video, YouTube, January 28, 2021, https://www.youtube.com/watch?v=622zSYBbHmE; "20 Biggest Hits in NFL History," video, YouTube, March 11, 2022, https://www.youtube.com/watch?v=6c4mtfRry0Y.

21. Peter King, "Trump Calls on NFL Owners to Fire Players Who Protest, and Mocks Efforts to Make the Game Safer," *Sports Illustrated*, September 23, 2017, https://www.si.com/nfl/2017/09/23/trump-nfl-fire-players-who-protest-during-anthem.

22. Sally Jenkins, "The Breathtaking Violence of an Ordinary NFL Hit," *Washington Post*, January 13, 2023, https://www.washingtonpost.com/sports/2023/01/12/nfl-physics-violence/.

23. Adam Kilgore and Scott Clement, "Poll: Nine in 10 Sports Fans Say NFL Brain Injuries Are a Problem, but 74 Percent Are Still Football Fans," *Washington Post*, September 6, https://www.washingtonpost.com/sports/poll-nfl-remains-as-popular-as-ever-despite-head-injuries-other-concerns/2017/09/06/238bef8a-9265-11e7-8754-d478688d23b4_story.html.

24. Will Hobson, "How the NFL Avoids Paying Disabled Players—with the Union's Help," *Washington Post*, February 8, 2023, https://www.washingtonpost.com/sports/2023/02/08/nfl-disability-players-union/.

25. Will Hobson, "Former NFL Players Sue the NFL over Disability Claims, Accuse Plan of 'Disturbing' Denials," *Washington Post*, February 9, 2023, https://www .washingtonpost.com/sports/2023/02/09/nfl-disability-plan-lawsuit/.

26. Ken Belson, "Football True Believers Circle the Wagons and Insist the Sport Is Just Fine," *New York Times*, January 30, 2018, https://www.nytimes.com/2018/01/30/sports/football/nfl.html.

27. Chris Nowinski, "Troubling Trend," *Sports Illustrated*, July 2, 2018, https://vault.si .com/vault/2018/07/16/troubling-trend.

28. Boston University CTE Research Center, "BU Researchers Find CTE in 345 of 376 Former NFL Players Studied," Boston University Chobanian and Avedisian School of Medicine, February 6, 2023, https://www.bumc.bu.edu/camed/2023/02/06/researchers -find-cte-in-345-of-376-former-nfl-players-studied/.

29. Timothy James Gay, *Football Physics: The Science of the Game* (New York: Random House, 2017).

30. Jenkins, "The Breathtaking Violence."

31. SI Wire, "Hall of Fame Won't Allow Junior Seau's Family to Speak at His Induction," *Sports Illustrated*, July 24, 2015, https://www.si.com/nfl/2015/07/24/junior-seau -hall-of-fame-induction-family-speech.

32. Marc Santora and Judy Battista, "Chiefs Player Kills Woman and, at Stadium, Himself," *New York Times*, December 2, 2012, https://www.nytimes.com/2012/12/02/ sports/football/police-chiefs-player-shot.html.

33. Richard Sandomir, "O.J. Who? Rogues Vanish from Annals of Sport," *New York Times*, January 5, 2014, https://www.nytimes.com/2014/01/06/sports/ncaafootball/oj -who-rogues-vanish-from-annals-of-sport.html.

34. Kevin B. Blackistone, "State Agencies Can Suspend Concussed Fighters. Why Not NFL Players?" *Washington Post*, October 9, 2022, https://www.washingtonpost.com/ sports/2022/10/07/nfl-concussions-policy/.

35. Kevin Seifert, "NFL Says Regular Season Concussions Increased 18 Percent in 2022," ESPN, February 3, 2023, https://www.espn.com/nfl/story/_/id/35582897/nfl-says -regular-season-concussions-increased-18-2022.

36. *Toronto Star* Editorial Board, "How to Reduce Brain Injuries in Youth Hockey," *Toronto Star*, October 9, 2022, https://www.thestar.com/opinion/editorials/2022/10/09/ how-to-reduce-brain-injuries-in-youth-hockey.html.

37. Jeff Z. Klein and Stu Hackel, "In the N.H.L., a Stricter Standard for Safety's Sake," *New York Times*, December 29, 2013, https://www.nytimes.com/2013/12/29/sports/ hockey/in-the-nhl-a-stricter-standard-for-safetys-sake.html.

38. Parry, *The Athlete's Dilemma*, 202.

39. John Branch, "N.H.L. Commissioner Gary Bettman Continues to Deny C.T.E. Link," *New York Times*, July 26, 2016, https://www.nytimes.com/2016/07/27/ sports/nhl-commissioner-gary-bettman-denies-cte-link.html.

40. Ken Dryden, "The National Hockey League Is Skating around Brain Injuries," *Washington Post*, June 24, 2018, https://www.washingtonpost.com/opinions/the-national -hockey-league-is-skating-around-the-brain-injury-problem/2018/06/24/9d173d58 -763c-11e8-b4b7-308400242c2e_story.html.

41. John Branch, "In Emails, N.H.L. Officials Conceded Concussion Risks of Fights," *New York Times*, March 29, 2016, https://www.nytimes.com/2016/03/29/sports/hockey/nhl-emails-link-concussions-fighting-bettman.html.

42. John Branch, "The Tragic Diagnosis They Already Knew: Their Brother Died with C.T.E.," *New York Times*, May 3, 2018, https://www.nytimes.com/2018/05/03/sports/nhl-cte-jeff-parker.html.

43. Michael Popke, "Can a Player's Posthumous Diagnosis of CTE Convince Soccer to Take Precautions?" Sports Destination Management, July 18, 2022, https://www.sportsdestinations.com/sports/soccer/can-players-posthumous-diagnosis-cte-convince-30560.

44. Keh, "A Diagnosis Brings C.T.E. into American Pro Soccer."

45. Rory Smith, "Does Soccer Still Need the Header?" *New York Times*, July 23, 2022, https://www.nytimes.com/2022/07/22/sports/soccer/soccer-headers.html.

46. Greg Garber, "A Tormented Soul," ESPN, January 28, 2005, https://www.espn.com/nfl/news/story/_/id/1972285.

47. National Institute on Aging, "What Happens to the Brain in Alzheimer's Disease?" https://www.nia.nih.gov/health/what-happens-brain-alzheimers-disease.

48. Meryl Gordon, "Before 'Concussion': An Inside Glimpse of NFL Player Mike Webster's Utterly Tragic Final Days," The Healthy *@Reader's Digest*, September 4, 2019, https://www.thehealthy.com/neurological/mike-webster-brain-injury/.

49. McRae, "Boxing Is a Mess."

50. McRae, "Boxing Is a Mess."

51. Ted Sears, "The Dreaded Subdural Hematoma," *The Sweet Science*, July 12, 2022, https://tss.ib.tv/boxing/featured-boxing-articles-boxing-news-videos-rankings-and-results/73338-the-dreaded-subdural-hematoma.

52. Mark Fainaru-Wada and Steve Fainaru, "League of Denial," *Sports Illustrated*, October 7, 2013, 64–68.

53. Paul Daugherty, "Doc: Redemption for Bengals' Bad Boy, Chris Henry," *Cincinnati Enquirer*, December 14, 2014, https://www.cincinnati.com/story/sports/columnists/paul-daugherty/2014/12/13/former-bengal-chris-henry-remembered-5-years-after-death/20205991/.

54. See Caitlan Dewey, "Her Biggest Save," *Washington Post*, November 2, 2013, https://www.washingtonpost.com/sf/national/2013/11/02/her-biggest-save/; Amie Just, "Briana Scurry Embraces New Role as Women's Brain Health Advocate," *Washington Post*, June 19, 2016, https://www.washingtonpost.com/sports/briana-scurry-embraces-new-role-as-womens-brain-health-advocate/2016/06/19/17aad636-33d4-11e6-8758-d58e76e11b12_story.htm.

55. Alan Schwartz, "Duerson's Brain Trauma Diagnosed," *New York Times*, May 2, 2011, https://www.nytimes.com/2011/05/03/sports/football/03duerson.html.

56. Alan Schwartz, "Hockey Brawler Paid Price, with Brain Trauma," *New York Times*, March 2, 2011, https://www.nytimes.com/2011/03/03/sports/hockey/03fighter.html.

57. John Branch, "Derek Boogaard: A Brain 'Going Bad,'" *New York Times*, May 12, 2013, https://www.nytimes.com/2011/12/06/sports/hockey/derek-boogaard-a-brain-going-bad.html.

58. *Boogaard v. National Hockey League*, 255 F. Supp 3rd 753 (N.D. Ill. 2017).

59. Associated Press, "Ryan Freel, Concussion-Plagued Baseball Player, Dies at 36," *New York Times*, December 24, 2012, https://www.nytimes.com/2012/12/25/sports/baseball/ryan-freel-concussion-plagued-baseball-player-dies-at-36.html.

60. See Associated Press, "Ryan Freel"; ESPN News Services, "Ryan Freel Had CTE, Parents Say," ABC News, December 15, 2013, https://abcnews.go.com/Sports/ryan-freel-cte-parents/story?id=21227773.

61. ESPN News Services, "Ryan Freel."

62. Mary Pilon and Ken Belson, "Seau Suffered from Brain Disease," *New York Times*, January 10, 2013, https://www.nytimes.com/2013/01/11/sports/football/junior-seau-suffered-from-brain-disease.html.

63. Pilon and Belson, "Seau Suffered from Brain Disease."

64. Matt Schiavenza, "The Tragic Legacy of Junior Seau," *Atlantic*, August 9, 2015, https://www.theatlantic.com/entertainment/archive/2015/08/the-tragic-legacy-of-junior-seau/400856/.

65. Pete Thamel and Greg Bedard, "A Murder in Massachusetts," *Sports Illustrated*, July 1, 2013, https://vault.si.com/vault/2013/07/01/a-murder-in-massachusetts.

66. Michael McCann, "Aaron Hernandez Found Not Guilty of Boston Double Murder: Breaking Down Jury's Decision," *Sports Illustrated*, April 14, 2017, https://www.si.com/nfl/2017/04/14/aaron-hernandez-not-guilty-boston-murder.

67. Ken Belson, "Aaron Hernandez Had Severe C.T.E. When He Died at Age 27," *New York Times*, September 21, 2017, https://www.nytimes.com/2017/09/21/sports/aaron-hernandez-cte-brain.html.

68. Dave Zirin, "Jovan Belcher's Murder-Suicide: Did the Kansas City Chiefs Pull the Trigger?" *Nation*, January 6, 2014, https://www.thenation.com/article/archive/jovan-belchers-murder-suicide-did-kansas-city-chiefs-pull-trigger/.

69. Zirin, "Jovan Belcher's Murder-Suicide."

70. Gary Mihoces, "NFL Concussion Suit: Belcher's Daughter Opted In," *USA Today*, October 13, 2014, https://www.usatoday.com/story/sports/nfl/2014/10/13/nfl-concussion-suit-belchers-daughter-opted-in/17231511/.

71. Brian Cazeneuve, "Chris Pronger Has a Headache," *Sports Illustrated*, June 30, 2015, https://www.si.com/nhl/2015/06/30/si-vault-chris-pronger-has-headache-2013-feature-story-brian-cazeneuve.

72. Chris Bumbaca, "Concussion Nearly Derailed Her Career. Now Amanda Kessel Is Starring Again for US Women's Hockey Team," *USA Today*, February 11, 2022, https://www.usatoday.com/story/sports/olympics/beijing/2022/02/11/amanda-kessel-usa-hockey-concussions-womens-hockey/6748317001/.

73. Bumbaca, "Concussion Nearly Derailed Her Career."

74. Matthew Futterman, "Olympic Bobsledder Who Killed Himself Likely Had C.T.E.," *New York Times*, September 29, 2021, https://www.nytimes.com/2021/04/08/sports/olympics/bobsled-cte-concussions-sledhead.html.

75. Futterman, "Olympic Bobsledder Who Killed Himself Likely Had C.T.E."

76. *Athletic* Staff, "Family of Former Bucs WR Vincent Jackson Says Brain Researchers Diagnosed Him with Stage 2 CTE," *Athletic*, December 16, 2021, https://theathletic

.com/4184018/2021/12/16/family-of-former-bucs-wr-vincent-jackson-says-brain
-researchers-diagnosed-him-with-stage-2-cte/.

77. Jenna Laine, "Vincent Jackson Died from Chronic Alcohol Use, Medical Examiner Says," ESPN, December 23, 2021, https://www.espn.com/nfl/story/_/id/32925482/vincent-jackson-died-chronic-alcohol-use-medical-examiner-says.

78. Will Leitch, "Antonio Brown and the Specter of CTE," *New York*, January 3, 2022, https://nymag.com/intelligencer/2022/01/antonio-brown-and-the-specter-of-cte.html.

79. Leitch, "Antonio Brown and the Specter of CTE."

80. *Athletic* Staff, "Antonio Brown Claims Bucs Offered Him $200K for Mental Health Treatment in Order to Cover Up Mistreatment," *Athletic*, January 26, 2022, https://theathletic.com/4183159/2022/01/26/antonio-brown-claims-bucs-offered-him-200k-for-mental-health-treatment-in-order-to-cover-up-mistreatment/.

81. See Victor Mather, "Antonio Brown's Tumultuous N.F.L. Career," *New York Times*, September 11, 2019, updated January 22, 2020, https://www.nytimes.com/2019/09/11/sports/football/antonio-brown-career.html; Christopher Booher, "Antonio Brown Asked about Mental Health, CTE During Wild Podcast: 'I've Got Mental Wealth,'" *Sports Illustrated*, January 8, 2022, https://www.si.com/nfl/lions/news/antonio-brown-asked-about-mental-health-cte-podcast-interview.

82. Keh, "A Diagnosis Brings C.T.E. into American Pro Soccer"; Jimmy Golen, "CTE Diagnosed in Ex-MLS Player Vermillion, a 1st for League," AP News, June 28, 2018, https://apnews.com/article/sports-health-soccer-major-league-high-school-ad6e8e9e10aca1f3533d8067a8463d77.

83. Steven Goff, "Bruce Murray Spent Years Heading the Ball. He Worries It Took a Toll," *Washington Post*, July 5, 2022, https://www.washingtonpost.com/sports/2022/07/05/bruce-murray-dementia-cte/.

84. Jerry Brewer, "NFL Protocols Couldn't Protect Tua Tagovailoa from Careless Humans," *Washington Post*, September 30, 2022, https://www.washingtonpost.com/sports/2022/09/30/tua-injury/.

85. Dan Diamond, "Tua Tagovailoa's Head Injury Spurs Scrutiny of NFL Concussion Protocol," *Washington Post*, September 30, 2022, https://www.washingtonpost.com/health/2022/09/30/tua-concussion-protocol-nfl/.

86. Marcel Louis-Jacques, "Tua Tagovailoa Ruled Out Again; Dolphins to Start Skylar Thompson," ESPN, October 12, 2022, https://www.espn.com/nfl/story/_/id/34782013/tua-tagovailoa-ruled-again-dolphins-start-skylar-thompson.

87. Elena Bergeron, "Without Updated Tools, N.F.L. Is Still Finding Concussions Too Late," *New York Times*, December 31, 2022, https://www.nytimes.com/2022/12/31/sports/football/tua-tagovailoa-nfl-concussions.html.

88. Bergeron, "Without Updated Tools."

CHAPTER 8

1. Substance Abuse and Mental Health Services Administration, "Mental Health and Substance Use Disorders," https://www.samhsa.gov/find-help/disorders, accessed January 18, 2023.

2. Claudia L. Reardon and Shane Creado, "Drug Abuse in Athletes," *Substance Abuse Rehabilitation* 5 (2014): 95–105, https://doi.org/10.2147%2FSAR.S53784.

3. John Weston Parry, *The Athlete's Dilemma: Sacrificing Health for Wealth and Fame* (Lanham, MD: Rowman and Littlefield, 2017), 7.

4. William C. Rhoden, "In Putting the Team First, Players Put Themselves at Risk," *New York Times*, October 25, 2015, https://www.nytimes.com/2015/10/25/sports/baseball/in-putting-the-team-first-players-put-themselves-at-risk.html.

5. Sally Jenkins and Rick Maese, "Do No Harm: Who Should Bear the Costs of Retired NFL Players' Medical Bills?" *Washington Post*, May 9, 2013, https://www.washingtonpost.com/sports/redskins/do-no-harm-who-should-bear-the-costs-of-retired-nfl-players-medical-bills/2013/05/09/2dae88ba-b70e-11e2-b568-6917f6ac6d9d_story.html.

6. Parry, *The Athlete's Dilemma*, 25.

7. Cindy Boren, "Dolphins' Jones Says NFL Career Has Left Him Unable to Run or Jump," *Washington Post*, February 26, 2023, https://www.washingtonpost.com/sports/2023/02/26/dolphins-byron-jones/.

8. Rick Maese, "Federal Judge Deals Blow to Former Players' Drugs Lawsuit against the NFL," *Washington Post*, May 17, 2017, https://www.washingtonpost.com/sports/redskins/judge-deals-blow-to-ex-players-drugs-lawsuit-against-nfl/2017/05/16/b0b45a1a-3a62-11e7-a058-ddbb23c75d82_story.html.

9. Rick Maese, "Players Union Complains to NFL about Handling of Opioids and Other Drugs," *Washington Post*, May 9, 2017, https://www.washingtonpost.com/sports/redskins/players-union-complains-to-nfl-about-handling-of-opioids-and-other-drugs/2017/05/09/6f638c54-34b6-11e7-b4ee-434b6d506b37_story.html.

10. Sally Jenkins, "What Happens to a Company That Dopes Its Workers? If It's an NFL Team, Not Much," *Washington Post*, May 9, 2017, https://www.washingtonpost.com/sports/redskins/what-happens-to-a-company-that-dopes-it-workers-if-its-an-nfl-team-not-much/2017/05/09/572672a4-34df-11e7-b412-62beef8121f7_story.html.

11. John Branch, "In Emails, N.H.L. Officials Conceded Concussion Risks of Fights," *New York Times*, March 29, 2016, https://www.nytimes.com/2016/03/29/sports/hockey/nhl-emails-link-concussions-fighting-bettman.html.

12. Will Hobson, "How the NFL Avoids Paying Disabled Players—with the Union's Help," *Washington Post*, February 8, 2023, https://www.washingtonpost.com/sports/2023/02/08/nfl-disability-players-union/.

13. Jacob Bogage, "A Football Recruit Uses Medical Cannabis for Epilepsy. He Says It Cost Him a Roster Spot," *Washington Post*, June 1, 2018, https://www.washingtonpost.com/news/early-lead/wp/2018/06/01/an-auburn-football-recruit-uses-medical-cannabis-for-epilepsy-he-claims-it-cost-him-his-roster-spot/.

14. Calvin Watkins, "John Lucas Disagrees with Steve Kerr's Thoughts on Marijuana Use for Pain," ESPN, December 5, 2016, https://www.espn.com/blog/houston-rockets/post/_/id/3201/john-lucas-disagrees-with-steve-kerrs-thoughts-on-marijuana-use-for-pain.

15. ESPN, "Drugs and Sports: Amphetamines," Special Section, September 6, 2021, https://www.espn.com/special/s/drugsandsports/.

16. Daria Piacentino et al., "Anabolic-Androgenic Steroid Use and Psychopathology in Athletes: A Systematic Review," *Current Neuropharmacology* 13, no. 1 (2015): 101–21, https://doi.org/10.2174/1570159x13666141210222725.

17. Bonnie Berkowitz and William Neff, "Built and Broken: What Bodybuilders Do to Their Bodies—and Brains," *Washington Post*, December 8, 2022, https://www.washingtonpost.com/investigations/interactive/2022/bodybuilding-health-risks/.

18. Nick Zagorski, "Misuse of Steroids, Other Performance Enhancers Slips under Radar," *Psychiatric News*, February 24, 2022, https://doi.org/10.1176/appi.pn.2022.03.10.42.

19. ESPN, "Drugs and Sports: Amphetamines."

20. Martyn Herman, "Andre Agassi Crystal Meth Revelations Shock Tennis World," Reuters, October 28, 2009, https://www.reuters.com/article/us-agassi-idUSTRE59R4NK20091028.

21. ESPN, "Drugs and Sports: Amphetamines."

22. Keith Harriston and Sally Jenkins, "Maryland Basketball Star Len Bias Dead at 22," *Washington Post*, June 20, 1986, https://www.washingtonpost.com/wp-srv/sports/longterm/memories/bias/launch/bias1.htm.

23. Michael Weinreb, "The Day Innocence Died," ESPN, http://www.espn.com/espn/eticket/story?page=bias&redirected=true, accessed January 23, 2023.

24. Jonathan Gelber, "How Len Bias's Death Helped Launch the US's Unjust War on Drugs," *Guardian*, June 29, 2021, https://www.theguardian.com/sport/2021/jun/29/len-bias-death-basketball-war-on-drugs.

25. Matthew Irby, "To Hell and Back: The Josh Hamilton Story," *Bleacher Report*, May 30, 2008, https://bleacherreport.com/articles/26169-to-hell-and-back-the-josh-hamilton-story.

26. Emma Baccelleri, "Katie Hamilton Will Speak for Herself, Thank You," *Sports Illustrated*, July 8, 2021, https://www.si.com/mlb/2021/07/08/katie-hamilton-where-are-they-now-2021.

27. Jon Wertheim, "Prisoners of Depression," *Sports Illustrated*, September 8, 2003, https://vault.si.com/vault/2003/09/08/prisoners-of-depression-mental-illness-still-carries-a-powerful-stigma-in-pro-sports-but-there-are-signs-that-teams-are-finally-facing-the-problem-and-trying-to-help-troubled-athletes.

28. Dan Wolke, "Bucks Assistant Vin Baker Lost Millions to Addiction, Found Salvation in a Starbucks," *Los Angeles Times*, July 10, 2021, https://www.latimes.com/sports/story/2021-07-10/bucks-vin-baker-redemption-story-addiction-lost-millions.

29. Wolke, "Bucks Assistant Vin Baker Lost Millions to Addiction."

30. See Anxiety and Depression Association of America, "Ricky Williams: A Story of Social Anxiety Disorder," November 20, 2009, https://adaa.org/living-with-anxiety/personal-stories/ricky-williams-story-social-anxiety-disorder; Francisco Alvarado, "Ricky Williams Is the Greatest Pot Smoker to Wear a Miami Dolphins Uniform," *Miami New Times*, December 18, 2018, https://www.miaminewtimes.com/news/the-real-marijuana-story-of-ricky-williams-10954869.

31. Monty602, "Naomi Osaka's Boundary Setting Invokes Memories of Ricky Williams' Struggles with Insensitive Media," Canal Street Chronicles, June 7, 2021, https:

//www.canalstreetchronicles.com/2021/6/7/22517607/naomi-osakas-boundary-setting
-invokes-memories-ricky-williams-struggles-insensitive-media.

32. Patrick Hruby, "Oscar Pistorius and the 'Roid Rage' Defense: It's No
Get-Out-of-Jail-Free Card," *Washington Times*, February 18, 2013, https://www
.washingtontimes.com/news/2013/feb/19/oscar-pistorius-and-roid-rage-its-no-get-out
-jail-/.

33. Jeff Carlisle, "Hope Solo's Painful Journey," ESPN, June 27, 2011, https://www.espn
.com/sports/soccer/news/_/columnist/carlisle_jeff/id/6691703/hope-solo-overcoming
-physical-emotional-issues-women-world-cup-soccer.

34. Gabe Zaldivar, "Team USA Goalkeeper Hope Solo Admits to Being Drunk
on 'Today' Show," *Bleacher Report*, July 13, 2012, https://bleacherreport.com/articles
/1257664-team-usa-goalkeeper-hope-solo-admits-to-being-drunk-on-today-show.

35. Ashley Coleman, "Troubled Soccer Star Hope Solo Reveals She Is Seeing a Therapist for 'Anger' Issues as She Rejoins Team USA Following 30-Day Suspension," *Daily
Mail*, March 26, 2015, https://www.dailymail.co.uk/news/article-3013348/Troubled
-soccer-star-Hope-Solo-reveals-s-seeing-therapist-anger-issues-rejoins-Team-USA
-following-30-day-suspension.html.

36. See Molly Langmuir, "The Audacity of Hope Solo," *Elle*, July 2019, https://www
.elle.com/culture/a27891036/hope-solo-soccer-fifa-womens-world-cup/.

37. Michael Levenson, "Hope Solo, Former U.S. Soccer Star, Charged with Impaired
Driving," *New York Times*, April 1, 2022, https://www.nytimes.com/2022/04/01/us/hope
-solo-arrest.html.

38. Miranda Siwak, "Hope Solo Voluntarily Enters In-Patient Alcohol Treatment after
Arrest," *Us Weekly*, April 30, 2022, https://www.usmagazine.com/celebrity-news/news/
hope-solo-enters-in-patient-alcohol-treatment-after-dui-arrest/.

39. Rich Cimini, "Ainge: 'I Had to Go Get Help before I Died,'" ESPN, March
31, 2011, https://www.espn.com/new-york/columns/story?columnist=cimini_rich&id
=6267822.

40. Cimini, "Ainge."

41. Associated Press, "Jets' Ainge Announces Retirement; Cites Injuries," ESPN, June
23, 2011.

42. Cimini, "Ainge."

43. Local8Now, "Crimetracker: Former Vol QB Arrested for DUI," July 28, 2013.

44. See Seth Davis, "After Addiction and Arrest, Ex-UK Star Rex Chapman Trying to
Rebuild His Life," *Sports Illustrated*, July 27, 2015, https://www.si.com/college/2015/07
/28/rex-chapman-kentucky-nba-painkillers-theft.

45. Brandon Sneed, "Rex Chapman Isn't Sure He Deserves Good Things," *New
York Times*, April 4, 2015, https://www.nytimes.com/2022/04/04/sports/basketball/rex
-chapman-cnn-basketball.html

46. Sam Borden, "Abby Wambach, Retired U.S. Soccer Star, Reflects on Her Addiction," *New York Times*, October 10, 2016, https://www.nytimes.com/2016/10/11/sports/
soccer/abby-wambach-addiction-alcohol-painkillers.html.

47. Hannah Withiam, "Abby Wambach's New Life after Drug, Alcohol Rock Bottom," *New York Post*, March 21, 2018, https://nypost.com/2018/03/21/abby-wambachs-found-peace-purpose-in-drug-free-life-after-soccer/; see also Borden, "Abby Wambach."

48. Mark Fainaru-Wada, "Abby Wambach Plans to Exit Drug Company Linked to Brett Favre Welfare Fraud Case," ESPN, October 13, 2022, https://www.espn.com/nfl/story/_/id/34695437/abby-wambach-plans-exit-drug-company-linked-brett-favre-welfare-fraud-case.

49. Larry Dorman and Joseph Berger, "Woods Says Car Accident Is His Fault, but Private," *New York Times*, November 29, 2009, https://www.nytimes.com/2009/11/30/sports/golf/30woods.html.

50. Jaime Diaz, "The Sad Story of Tiger Woods Grows Even Sadder," *Golf Digest*, May 29, 2017, https://www.golfdigest.com/story/the-sad-story-of-tiger-woods-grows-even-sadder.

51. Diaz, "The Sad Story of Tiger Woods Grows Even Sadder."

52. Erik Ortiz, "Tiger Woods DUI Arrest: Golfer Had Five Drugs in His System, Toxicology Report Shows," NBC News, August 15, 2017, https://www.nbcnews.com/news/sports/tiger-woods-dui-arrest-golfer-had-five-drugs-system-toxicology-n792856.

53. Kurt Streeter, "Tiger Woods and Another Terrible Turn of Fate," *New York Times*, April 9, 2021, https://www.nytimes.com/2021/02/25/sports/golf/tiger-woods-accident.html.

CHAPTER 9

1. Anne S. Walters, "Female Athletes and Mental Health: An Under-Resourced Relationship," *Brown University Child and Adolescent Letter*, September 6, 2021, https://doi.org/10.1002/cbl.30579.

2. NCAA, *NCAA Student-Athlete Well-Being Survey*, May 2022, https://ncaaorg.s3.amazonaws.com/research/other/2020/2022RES_NCAA-SA-Well-BeingSurvey.pdf.

3. See also Char Adams, "Young Black Athletes Are Launching a Mental Health Revolution," NBC News, July 23, 2021, https://www.nbcnews.com/news/nbcblk/young-black-athletes-are-launching-mental-health-revolution-rcna1490.

4. Billy Witz, "As Women's Basketball Grows, Equity Is Trying to Catch Up," *New York Times*, March 29, 2023, https://www.nytimes.com/2023/03/29/sports/ncaabasketball/womens-basketball-equity.html.

5. Howard Bryant, "Equal Forces from Serena Williams to the UConn Huskies, Female Athletes Have Set Their Own Marks for Greatness. So Stop Weighing Them against the Men's Game," *ESPN The Magazine*, May 23, 2016, 80.

6. Juliet Macur, "Inaction and Inequality on Women's World Cup Turf Issues," *New York Times*, December 5, 2014, https://www.nytimes.com/2014/12/05/sports/soccer/inaction-and-inequality-on-womens-world-cup-turf-issue.html.

7. Tanya Lewis, "Sexist Science in Soccer Harms Women in an Epic Own Goal," *Scientific American*, November 18, 2022, https://www.scientificamerican.com/article/sexist-science-in-soccer-harms-women-in-an-epic-own-goal/.

8. Tariq Panja, "A #MeToo Wave Hits Global Soccer as the Women's World Cup Begins," *New York Times*, June 7, 2019, https://www.nytimes.com/2019/06/07/sports/metoo-soccer-sexual-harassment.html.

9. Liz Clarke, "U.S. Open Plans to Factor Pregnancy into Seeding," *Washington Post*, June 23, 2018, https://www.washingtonpost.com/news/sports/wp/2018/06/23/u-s-open-to-change-seeding-process-in-wake-of-serena-williamss-pregnancy-leave/.

10. Liz Clarke, "After Outcry over Serena's Rankings, WTA Alters Rules," *Washington Post*, December 18, 2018, https://www.washingtonpost.com/sports/2018/12/18/after-outcry-over-serena-williamss-rankings-wta-alters-rules-moms-returning-competition/.

11. Alysia Montaño with Lindsay Crouse, "Nike Told Me to Dream Crazy, Until I Wanted a Baby," *New York Times*, May 12, 2019, https://www.nytimes.com/2019/05/12/opinion/nike-maternity-leave.html.

12. Allyson Felix, "Allyson Felix: My Own Nike Pregnancy Story," *New York Times*, May 22, 2019, https://www.nytimes.com/2019/05/22/opinion/allyson-felix-pregnancy-nike.html.

13. Cindy Boren, "A Pregnant Runner's Open Letter to the Boston Marathon Helped Spur Change," *Washington Post*, February 3, 2023, https://www.washingtonpost.com/sports/2023/02/02/pregnant-runner-boston-marathon/.

14. Lindsay Rovegno, "Athletes Often Forced into Heartbreaking Decisions," ESPN, May 13, 2007, cited in Nancy Hogshead-Maskar and Elizabeth A. Sorensen, *Pregnant and Parenting Student-Athletes: Resources and Model Policies*, NCAA Gender Equity, June 2018, https://www.uncp.edu/sites/default/files/2018-06/NCAA%20Pregnant%20and%20Parenting%20Students%20Resources%20and%20Model%20Policies.pdf.

15. Kevin B. Blackistone, "NCAA Should Make a Stand against States with Strict Abortion Laws," *Washington Post*, June 11, 2019, https://www.washingtonpost.com/sports/colleges/almost-half-the-ncaas-athletes-are-women-it-needs-to-make-a-stand-for-them/2019/06/10/cd52be66-8b8a-11e9-adf3-f70f78c156e8_story.html.

16. See Hogshead-Maskar and Sorensen, *Pregnant and Parenting Student-Athletes*.

17. Molly Hensley-Clancy, "With the NCAA Silent on Abortion Bans, College Sports Face Confusion," *Washington Post*, July 28, 2022, https://www.washingtonpost.com/sports/2022/07/27/college-sports-ncaa-abortion-bans/.

18. Elizabeth A. Sorensen, "Debunking the Myth of Pregnancy Doping," *Journal of Intercollegiate Sport* 2, no. 2 (2009): 269–85, https://doi.org/10.1123/jis.2.2.269.

19. Hensley-Clancy, "With the NCAA Silent on Abortion Bans."

20. *Seattle Times*, "Coaches Who Prey," Special Section, December 14–17, 2003, https://special.seattletimes.com/o/news/local/coaches/index.html.

21. N'dea Yancey-Bragg, "1 in 4 College Athletes Say They Experienced Sexual Abuse from an Authority Figure, Survey Finds," *USA Today*, August 26, 2021, https://www.usatoday.com/story/news/nation/2021/08/26/college-athlete-report-sexual-assault-common-survey/8253766002/.

22. Kelli Anderson, "Justice Underserved," *Sports Illustrated*, October 21, 2013, https://vault.si.com/vault/2013/10/21/justice-underserved.

23. Gary Smith, "Stand Up and Speak Out," *Sports Illustrated*, December 17, 2012, https://vault.si.com/vault/2012/12/17/stand-up-speak-out.

24. Smith, "Stand Up and Speak Out."

25. Smith, "Stand Up and Speak Out."

26. Smith, "Stand Up and Speak Out."

27. Douglas Wigdor, "Statute of Limitations on Sexual Assault Eliminated for One Year in New York following Passage of the Adult Survivors Act," *Forbes*, May 25, 2022, https://www.forbes.com/sites/douglaswigdor/2022/05/25/statute-of-limitations-on -sexual-assault-eliminated-for-one-year-in-new-york-following-passage-of-the-adult -survivors-act/?sh=45e988a546fd.

28. Matt Stevens, "2 U.S.A. Swimming Officials Resign amid Accusations of Ignored Abuse," *New York Times*, February 24, 2018, https://www.nytimes.com/2018/02/24/ sports/usa-swimming-resignations.html.

29. Will Hobson, "McKayla Maroney Sues USA Gymnastics, Saying It Tried to Buy Her Silence on Abuse," *Washington Post*, December 20, 2017, https://www.washingtonpost .com/sports/mckayla-maroney-sues-usa-gymnastics-saying-it-tried-to-buy-her-silence -on-abuse/2017/12/20/1e54b482-e5c8-11e7-a65d-1ac0fd7f097e_story.html.

30. Will Hobson, "Doctor at Center of USA Gymnastics Scandal Left Warning Signs at Michigan State," *Washington Post*, April 25, 2017, https://www.washingtonpost.com /sports/olympics/doctor-at-center-of-usa-gymnastics-scandal-left-warning-signs-at -michigan-state/2017/04/25/eed48834-2530-11e7-a1b3-faff0034e2de_story.html.

31. Hobson, "McKayla Maroney Sues USA Gymnastics."

32. John Barr and Dan Murphy, "Nassar Surrounded by Adults Who Enable His Pred-atory Behaviors," ESPN, January 16, 2018, https://www.espn.com/espn/otl/story/_/id /22046031/michigan-state-university-doctor-larry-nassar-surrounded-enablers-abused -athletes-espn.

33. Hobson, "Doctor at Center of USA Gymnastics Scandal."

34. Hobson, "Doctor at Center of USA Gymnastics Scandal."

35. Will Hobson and Steven Rich, "USOC Was Alerted to Sex Abuse Problems Long before Taking Action," *Washington Post*, March 7, 2017, https://www.washingtonpost .com/sports/olympics/documents-usoc-alerted-to-sex-abuse-problems-long-before -taking-action/2017/03/06/8ca2a89e-0230-11e7-ad5b-d22680e18d10_story.html.

36. Juliet Macur, "Ex-Gymnastics Chief's Career: Swift Success Marred by Years of Scandal," *New York Times*, March 17, 2017, https://www.nytimes.com/2017/03/17/sports /olympics/macur-steve-penny-usa-gymnastics-scandal.html.

37. Macur, "Ex-Gymnastics Chief's Career."

38. Will Hobson, "USA Gymnastics CEO Steve Penny Resigns in Wake of Sex Abuse Scandal," *Washington Post*, March 16, 2017, https://www.washingtonpost.com/sports/ olympics/usa-gymnastics-ceo-steve-penny-resigns-in-wake-of-sex-abuse-scandal/2017 /03/16/fe4f27de-0a77-11e7-93dc-00f9bdd74ed1_story.html.

39. Macur, "Ex-Gymnastics Chief's Career."

40. Will Hobson, "Following Sex Abuse Report, USA Gymnastics Pledges Stronger Oversight of Clubs," *Washington Post*, June 28, 2017, https://www.washingtonpost.com/ sports/olympics/following-sex-abuse-report-usa-gymnastics-pledges-stronger-oversight -of-clubs/2017/06/27/a7c799cc-5b4a-11e7-9fc6-c7ef4bc58d13_story.html.

41. Victor Mather, "U.S.A. Gymnastics Cuts Ties with Karolyi Ranch Training Center," *New York Times*, January 18, 2018, https://www.nytimes.com/2018/01/18/sports/usa-gymnastics-karolyi-ranch.html.

42. Cindy Boren, "USA Gymnastics Leaders Resign over Nassar Scandal," *Washington Post*, January 23, 2018, https://www.washingtonpost.com/news/early-lead/wp/2018/01/22/as-victims-continue-to-speak-out-three-of-usa-gymnastics-top-leaders-resign-over-larry-nassar-scandal/.

43. Rebecca R. Ruiz and Matthew Futterman, "Scott Blackmun Steps Down as Head of U.S.O.C. under Pressure from Nassar Case," *New York Times*, February 28, 2018, https://www.nytimes.com/2018/02/28/sports/scott-blackmun-usoc-nassar.html.

44. Jere Longman, "U.S. Olympics Chief Received $2.4 Million Severance amid Scandal," *New York Times*, July 3, 2019, https://www.nytimes.com/2019/07/03/sports/olympics-scott-blackmun.html.

45. Liz Clarke, "Larry Probst to Step Down as USOC Board Chair," *Washington Post*, September 10, 2018, https://www.washingtonpost.com/sports/olympics/larry-probst-to-step-down-as-usoc-board-chair/2018/09/10/a79fe0f8-b53a-11e8-a7b5-adaaa5b2a57f_story.html

46. Juliet Macur, "Olympic Committee Moves to Revoke U.S.A. Gymnastics' Governing Body," *New York Times*, November 5, 2018, https://www.nytimes.com/2018/11/05/sports/usa-gymnastics-usoc.html.

47. Laura Green, "What's Next for USA Gymnastics as the USOC Tries to Decertify It?" *Sports Illustrated*, November 6, 2018, https://www.si.com/olympics/2018/11/07/usa-gymnastics-larry-nassar-usoc-decertification.

48. Alice Park, "Can Anyone Save USA Gymnastics at this Point? New CEO Li Li Leung Is Determined to Try." *Time*, June 13, 2019, updated June 17, 2019, https://time.com/5606251/li-li-leung-usa-gymnastics-interview/.

49. Danielle Allentuck, "Simone Biles Set a New Standard. Can U.S.A. Gymnastics Do the Same?" *New York Times*, August 12, 2019, https://www.nytimes.com/2019/08/12/sports/simone-biles-gymnastics-championship.html.

50. Liz Clarke, "Senate Panel: Negligence by Olympic, USA Gymnastics Officials Enabled Abuse by Ex-Team Doctor Nassar," *Washington Post*, July 30, 2019, https://www.washingtonpost.com/sports/olympics/panel-to-introduce-legislation-to-reform-us-olympic-and-paralympic-committee/2019/07/30/7472683e-b266-11e9-8f6c-7828e68cb15f_story.html.

51. Marisa Kwiatkowski, Mark Alesia, and Tim Evans, "A Blind Eye to Sex Abuse: How USA Gymnastics Failed to Report Cases," *Indianapolis Star*, August 4, 2016, updated June 24, 2020, https://www.indystar.com/story/news/investigations/2016/08/04/usa-gymnastics-sex-abuse-protected-coaches/85829732/.

52. Eddie Pells, "Sex-Abuse Reports on Rise; SafeSport Center Seeks More Money," *AP News*, September 17, 2019, https://apnews.com/a154938aef9a4361a7fefbe784425fd3.

53. Pells, "Sex-Abuse Reports on Rise."

54. Rick Maese, "Olympics Reform Bill Passes House, Promising Sweeping Change after Abuse Scandals Rocked Sports," *Washington Post*, October 1, 2020, https://www.washingtonpost.com/sports/2020/10/01/olympics-reform-bill-house-abuse/.

55. Jared Anderson, "Digging in on SafeSport's Investigative Process, Ban Terminology," SwimSwam, October 17, 2018, https://swimswam.com/digging-in-on-safesports-investigative-process-ban-terminology/.

56. Kevin Draper and Matthew Futterman, "Disgraced Running Coach Was Barred for Life for Alleged Sexual Assault," *New York Times*, January 31, 2022, https://www.nytimes.com/2022/01/31/sports/alberto-salazar-sexual-assault.html.

57. Juliet Macur and Danielle Allentuck, "Gymnasts Push for Lasting Change after Coach Is Suspended for Abuse," *New York Times*, May 20, 2020, https://www.nytimes.com/2020/05/20/sports/olympics/gymnastics-haney-abuse-safesport.html.

58. 116th Congress (2019–2020), S.2330: Empowering Olympic, Paralympic, and Amateur Athletes Act of 2020, https://www.congress.gov/bill/116th-congress/senate-bill/2330/text.

59. Hobson, "Doctor at Center of USA Gymnastics Scandal."

60. Hobson, "Doctor at Center of USA Gymnastics Scandal."

61. Barr and Murphy, "Nassar Surrounded by Adults Who Enabled His Predatory Behavior."

62. Stephanie Saul, "Calls Grow for Michigan State University President to Resign over Nassar Case," *New York Times*, January 19, 2018, https://www.nytimes.com/2018/01/19/us/michigan-state-nassar.html.

63. Matthew Haag and Marc Tracy, "Michigan State President Lou Anna Simon Resigns Amid Nassar Fallout," *New York Times*, January 24, 2018, https://www.nytimes.com/2018/01/24/sports/olympics/michigan-state-president-resigns-lou-anna-simon.html.

64. David Jesse, "Study: MSU's Simon Raked in $855,000 in Total Compensation in 2017," *Detroit Free Press*, July 16, 2018, https://raejphillips.wordpress.com/2018/07/16/study-msus-simon-raked-in-855000-in-total-compensation-in-2017-3/.

65. Will Hobson, "Former Head of USA Gymnastics Pleads the Fifth on Larry Nassar Questions from Congress," *Washington Post*, June 5, 2018, https://www.washingtonpost.com/news/sports/wp/2018/06/05/former-head-of-usa-gymnastics-pleads-the-fifth-on-larry-nassar-questions-from-congress/.

66. Matt Mencarini, "MSU to Pay for Lou Anna Simon's Defense as Legal Bills for Larry Nassar Scandal Near $20M," *Lansing State Journal*, January 23, 2019, https://www.lansingstatejournal.com/story/news/local/2019/01/23/larry-nassar-lou-anna-simon-msu-michigan-state-bills/2645371002/.

67. Chris Solari, "Michigan State Athletic Director Mark Hollis Resigns in Wake of Larry Nassar Scandal," *Detroit Free Press*, January 26, 2018, https://www.freep.com/story/sports/college/michigan-state/spartans/2018/01/26/michigan-state-university-mark-hollis-resigns/1068989001/.

68. Dan Murphy, "Michigan State: NCAA Finds No Rule Violations in Sexual Assault Cases," ESPN, August 30, 2018, https://www.espn.com/college-sports/story/_/id/24523562/michigan-state-says-cleared-violations-larry-nassar-scandal-ncaa.

69. Associated Press, "Ex-MSU Dean Gets Jail for Neglect, Misconduct," ESPN, August 7, 2019, https://www.espn.com/college-sports/story/_/id/27340567/ex-msu -dean-gets-jail-neglect-misconduct.

70. Kim Kozowolski, "Court Vacates Conviction of Former MSU Gymnastics Coach Kathie Klages," *Detroit News*, December 21, 2021, https://www.detroitnews.com/story /news/local/michigan/2021/12/21/kathie-klages-larry-nassar-conviction-vacated-lying -to-police-michigan-state-university/8985174002/.

71. Associated Press, "Investigation into Michigan State's Handling of Larry Nassar Suspended," NBC News, December 24, 2019, https://www.nbcnews.com/news/us-news /michigan-state-investigation-handling-larry-nassar-suspended-n1106976.

72. Summer-Solstice Thomas, "It Could Have Been Me: The NCAA Must Do More to Protect Student-Athletes from Sexual Abuse, *Fortune*, November 3, 2021, https:// fortune.com/2021/11/03/ncaa-sexual-abuse-student-athletes/.

73. Vimal Patel, "San Jose State to Pay $1.6 Million to 13 Students in Sexual Harass-ment Case," *New York Times*, September 21, 2021, https://www.nytimes.com/2021/09/21 /sports/san-jose-sexual-harassment-settlement.html.

74. Thomas, "It Could Have Been Me."

75. Chris Chavez, "Inside the Toxic Culture of the Nike Oregon Project 'Cult,'" *Sports Illustrated*, November 13, 2019, https://www.si.com/track-and-field/2019/11/13/mary -cain-nike-oregon-project-toxic-culture-alberto-salazar-abuse-investigation.

76. Ben Pickman, "Alberto Salazar Placed on SafeSport's Temporarily Banned List after Alleged Verbal Abuse," *Sports Illustrated*, January 31, 2020, https://www.si.com/track -and-field/2020/02/01/alberto-salazar-safesport-suspension-mary-cain.

77. Draper and Futterman, "Disgraced Running Coach Was Barred for Life."

78. Scott M. Reid, "Delays in Maggie Haney Case by USA Gymnastics Have Both Sides Upset," *Orange County Register*, October 25, 2019, https://www.ocregister .com/2020/04/23/usa-gymnastics-mistake-in-maggie-haney-abuse-case-leads-to-more -frustration/.

79. Reid, "Delays in Maggie Haney Case."

80. Reid, "Delays in Maggie Haney Case."

81. Juliet Macur, "Suspension Reduced for Gymnastics Coach Accused of Emotional and Physical Abuse," *New York Times*, December 9, 2020, https://www.nytimes.com /2020/12/09/sports/olympics/maggie-haney-gymnastics-abuse.html.

82. Alan Blinder, Richard Fausset, and Marc Tracy, "U.N.C. Women's Basketball Coach Sylvia Hatchell Faces a Reckoning," *New York Times*, April 6, 2019, https://www.nytimes .com/2019/04/06/sports/sylvia-hatchell-unc-racially-insensitive-comments.html.

83. Will Hobson, "UNC Women's Hoops Coach Sylvia Hatchell Resigns amid Alle-gations of Berating Players, Racial Remarks," *Washington Post*, April 20, 2019, https: //www.washingtonpost.com/sports/colleges/they-make-me-sick-unc-womens-hoops -coach-berated-injured-players-parents-say/2019/04/18/7259c7c0-6146-11e9-9412 -daf3d2e67c6d_story.html.

84. Hobson, "UNC Women's Hoops Coach Sylvia Hatchell Resigns."

85. Jonathan M. Alexander, "Sylvia Hatchell, Hosting Camp at UNC, Denies Allegations That Led to Her Departure," *Durham Herald-Sun*, July 12, 2019, https://www.newsobserver.com/sports/article232490392.html.

86. Meredith Cash, "The Syracuse Women's Basketball Team Is in Disarray as Almost the Entire Team Transferred in an End-of-Season Mass Exodus," Yahoo Sports, April 26, 2021, https://sports.yahoo.com/syracuse-womens-basketball-team-disarray-184603123.html.

87. Shalise Manza Young, "Florida Basketball Abuse Is Latest Example of How Women Athletes Are Constantly Betrayed by Those Expected to Protect," Yahoo Sports, September 27, 2021, https://uk.news.yahoo.com/florida-basketball-abuse-is-latest-example-of-how-women-athletes-are-constantly-betrayed-by-those-expected-to-protect-001553116.html.

88. Scott M. Reid, "UC Berkeley Swimmers Allege Coach Teri McKeever Bullied and Verbally Abused Them for Years," *Orange County Register*, May 24, 2022, https://www.ocregister.com/2022/05/24/cal-swimmers-allege-coach-teri-mckeever-bullied-and-verbally-abused-them-for-years/.

89. Reid, "Berkeley Swimmers."

90. Reid, "Berkeley Swimmers."

91. Kurt Streeter, "Female Soccer Players Are Done Taking Abuse. Let's Stop Dishing It Out," *New York Times*, October 8, 2021, https://www.nytimes.com/2021/10/03/sports/soccer/women-soccer-league-abuse.html.

92. Sally Q. Yates, *Report of the Independent Investigation of the U.S. Soccer Federation concerning Allegations of Abusive Behavior and Sexual Misconduct in Women's Professional Soccer*, King and Spalding, October 3, 2022, https://assets.bwbx.io/documents/users/iqjWHBFdfxIU/rkHnb7fgThLU/v0.

93. Yates, *Report*.

94. Yates, *Report*.

95. Yates, *Report*.

96. Matt Bonesteel, "U.S. Soccer Vows Improved Vetting, Training, Transparency after Yates Report," *Washington Post*, January 31, 2023, https://www.washingtonpost.com/sports/2023/01/30/ussf-yates-recommendations/.

97. Sally Jenkins, "Another 'Report' on Abuse in Women's Sports. When Is Enough Enough?" *Washington Post*, October 3, 2022, https://www.washingtonpost.com/sports/2022/10/03/yates-report-womens-soccer-abuse/.

98. *Washington Post* Editorial Board, "Abuse of Women's Soccer Players Is a Sadly Familiar Story," *Washington Post*, October 5, 2022, https://www.washingtonpost.com/opinions/2022/10/05/womens-soccer-abuse-report-sally-yates/.

99. Jenn Abelson, "Coached until She Collapsed, an Aspiring Bodybuilder Is Now on Life Support," *Washington Post*, December 20, 2022, https://www.msn.com/en-us/news/us/coached-until-she-collapsed-an-aspiring-bodybuilder-is-now-on-life-support/ar-AA15tOdR.

CHAPTER 10

1. Sean Gregory, "U.S. Ranks Worst in Sports Homophobia Study," *Time*, May 9, 2015, https://time.com/3852611/sports-homophobia-study/.

2. Muri Assunção, "Dwyane Wade Explains Decision to Keep the 'Hate Out' of Trans Daughter's Life by Turning off Comments on Social Media," *New York Daily News*, October 7, 2022, https://www.nydailynews.com/snyde/ny-dwyane-wade-keep-hate-out-trans-daughter-zaya-zayre-comment-social-media-20221007-qjwb4xm3hba6fcxbmfiqzmi3ri-story.html.

3. Philip Ellis, "Dwyane Wade Just Made a Powerful Statement about Being a Father to an LGBTQ+ Child," *Men's Health*, December 20, 2019, https://www.menshealth.com/entertainment/a30296136/dwyane-wade-father-lgbtq-child/.

4. 2 Benjamin Freed, "ESPN Radio Hosts Suspended after Terrible Anti-Transgender Rant," DCist, December 11, 2012, https://dcist.com/story/12/12/11/espn-radio-hosts-suspended-after-te/.

5. Richard Sandomir, "Curt Schilling, ESPN Analyst, Is Fired over Offensive Social Media Post," *New York Times*, April 20, 2016, https://www.nytimes.com/2016/04/21/sports/baseball/curt-schilling-is-fired-by-espn.html.

6. L. Z. Granderson, "To Ask or Not to Ask," *ESPN The Magazine*, May 30, 2013, https://www.espn.com/espn/story/_/id/9315552/reporters-need-address-athlete-sexuality-avoid-homophobia-media-espn-magazine.

7. Mike Wise, "Dave Kopay Knows What Questions Should Be Asked by NFL," *Washington Post*, March 2, 2013, https://www.washingtonpost.com/sports/redskins/dave-kopay-knows-what-questions-should-be-asked-by-nfl/2013/03/02/2a12ebd2-82c1-11e2-b99e-6baf4ebe42df_story.html.

8. Wise, "Dave Kopay Knows."

9. Phil Taylor, "A Storm That May Not Come," *Sports Illustrated*, April 15, 2013, https://vault.si.com/vault/2013/04/15/a-storm-that-may-not-come.

10. Taylor, "A Storm That May Not Come."

11. Howard Bryant, "More Than Words," *ESPN The Magazine*, June 24, 2013, 14; Hunter Felt, "NBA Is Right to Fine but Not Suspend Roy Hibbert for 'No Homo' Slur," *Guardian*, June 3, 2013, https://www.theguardian.com/sport/2013/jun/03/roy-hibbert-fined-gay-slur.

12. Bryant, "More Than Words."

13. Frank Bruni, "Panic in the Locker Room!" *New York Times*, February 10, 2014, https://www.nytimes.com/2014/02/11/opinion/bruni-panic-in-the-locker-room.html.

14. Howard Beck and John Branch, "With the Words 'I'm Gay,' an N.B.A. Center Breaks a Barrier," *New York Times*, April 29, 2013, https://www.nytimes.com/2013/04/30/sports/basketball/nba-center-jason-collins-comes-out-as-gay.html.

15. Chris Sheridan, "Amaechi Becomes First NBA Player to Come Out," ESPN, February 9, 2007, https://www.espn.com/nba/news/story/_/id/2757105.

16. Jennifer Medina, "Jason Collins Took Personal Steps before Coming Out Publicly," *New York Times*, April 30, 2013, https://www.nytimes.com/2013/05/01/sports/jason-collins-took-personal-steps-before-coming-out-publicly.html.

17. Bernie Augustine, "Jason Collins' Girlfriend: I Never Suspected NBA Player Was Gay," *New York Daily News*, May 1, 2013, https://www.nydailynews.com/sports/basketball/jason-collins-girlfriend-no-clue-gay-article-1.1331903.

18. John Amaechi, "The Real Locker-Room Shocker," *Time*, May 13, 2013, https://content.time.com/time/subscriber/article/0,33009,2142497,00.html.

19. Beck and Branch, "With the Words 'I'm Gay.'"

20. Mike Wise, "Jason Collins's Religious Critics Need to Practice What They Preach," *Washington Post*, April 30, 2013, https://www.washingtonpost.com/sports/wizards/jason-collins-religious-critics-need-to-practice-what-they-preach/2013/04/30/3129e752-b1df-11e2-9a98-4be1688d7d84_story.html.

21. Michael Lee, "Wizards' Plans Not Affected by Jason Collins Announcement," *Washington Post*, April 30, 2013, https://www.washingtonpost.com/news/wizards-insider/wp/2013/04/30/wizards-never-planned-to-bring-back-jason-collins/.

22. Harvey Araton, "Jason Collins, Openly Gay and Still Unsigned, Waits and Wonders," *New York Times*, October 10, 2013, https://www.nytimes.com/2013/10/11/sports/basketball/jason-collins-openly-gay-and-still-unsigned-waits-and-wonders.html.

23. Benjamin Hoffman, "Contrary to 49ers Stance, Culliver Says He Wouldn't Accept a Gay Teammate," *New York Times*, January 30, 2013, https://archive.nytimes.com/fifthdown.blogs.nytimes.com/2013/01/30/contrary-to-49ers-stance-culliver-says-he-wouldnt-accept-a-gay-teammate/.

24. Dan Steinberg, "Dexter Manley Apologizes for Insulting Troy Aikman on WTOP (updated)," *Washington Post*, October 28, 2013, https://www.washingtonpost.com/news/dc-sports-bog/wp/2013/10/28/dexter-manley-insults-troy-aikman-on-wtop/.

25. Richard Deitsch, "Man behind the Mic: Fox NFL Analyst Troy Aikman on Broadcasting, More," *Sports Illustrated*, January 14, 2015, https://www.si.com/nfl/2015/01/14/troy-aikman-fox-nfl-analyst-qa.

26. Phil Taylor, "Act of Intolerance," *Sports Illustrated*, January 13, 2014, https://vault.si.com/vault/2014/01/13/act-of-intolerance.

27. Mike Foss, "Aaron Rodgers Denies Rumors That He Is Gay," *USA Today*, December 31, 2013, https://ftw.usatoday.com/2013/12/aaron-rodgers-denies-rumors-that-he-is-gay

28. Ken Belson and Katherine Rosman, "Raiders Coach Resigns after Homophobic and Misogynistic Emails," *New York Times*, October 28, 2021, https://www.nytimes.com/2021/10/11/sports/football/what-did-jon-gruden-say.html.

29. Tim Rohan, "For Football's Sake, Closely Guarding Sexual Orientation," *New York Times*, June 9, 2012, https://www.nytimes.com/2012/06/10/sports/football/for-footballs-sake-closely-guarding-sexual-orientation.html.

30. Adam Himmelsbach, "Players' Support of Gay Marriage Alters N.F.L.'s Image," *New York Times*, September 9, 2012, https://www.nytimes.com/2012/09/09/sports/football/players-support-of-gay-marriage-alters-nfl-image.html.

31. Himmelsbach, "Players' Support of Gay Marriage."

32. ESPN News Services, "Adrian Peterson against Gay Marriage," *ESPN*, May 28, 2013, https://www.espn.com/nfl/story/_/id/9315572/adrian-peterson-minnesota-vikings-says-gay-marriage.

33. James Strong, "Adrian Peterson, Christianity and Child Abuse," *Birmingham Times*, October 9, 2014, https://www.birminghamtimes.com/2014/10/adrian-peterson-christianity-and-child-abuse-2/.

34. Michael McCann, "Loaded Questions," *Sports Illustrated*, March 25, 2013, 16.

35. Ken Belson, "Support for Gay Rights Led to Harassment, Ex-Viking Says," *New York Times*, January 2, 2014, https://www.nytimes.com/2014/01/03/sports/football/support-for-gay-rights-drew-harassment-ex-viking-says.html.

36. Ben Goessling, "Vikings Respond to Kluwe Allegations," WABC News, July 19, 2014, https://abc7ny.com/sports/vikings-respond-to-kluwe-allegations/199345/.

37. Taylor, "Act of Intolerance."

38. Kent Babb, "Michael Sam's Announcement Prompts NFL to Examine What It Considers a 'Distraction,'" *Washington Post*, February 10, 2014, https://www.washingtonpost.com/sports/michael-sams-announcement-prompts-nfl-to-examine-what-it-considers-a-distraction/2014/02/10/e5f6d088-9293-11e3-84e1-27626c5ef5fb_story.html.

39. John Branch, "N.F.L. Prospect Michael Sam Proudly Says What Teammates Knew: He's Gay," *New York Times*, February 10, 2014, https://www.nytimes.com/2014/02/10/sports/michael-sam-college-football-star-says-he-is-gay-ahead-of-nfl-draft.html.

40. S. L. Price, "Moment of Truth," *Sports Illustrated*, February 17, 2014, https://vault.si.com/vault/2014/02/17/moment-of-truth.

41. ESPN News Services, "Commish Welcomes Michael Sam," ESPN, February 12, 2014, https://www.espn.com/nfl/story/_/id/10447810/roger-goodell-welcomes-michael-sam-says-good-him.

42. Shutdown Corner, "Saints Linebacker Jonathan Vilma Clarifies Homophobic Views Prior to Michael Sam's Announcement," Yahoo News, February 11, 2014, https://news.yahoo.com/blogs/nfl-shutdown-corner/saints-linebacker-jonathan-vilma-clarifies-homophobic-views-prior-151112471--nfl.html.

43. Mike Triplett, "Vilma Clarifies His Opinion of a Gay Teammate," ESPN, February 10, 2014, https://www.espn.com/blog/new-orleans-saints/post/_/id/5057/vilma-clarifies-opinion-on-accepting-gay-teammate.

44. Branch, "N.F.L. Prospect Michael Sam."

45. Branch, "N.F.L. Prospect Michael Sam."

46. Bruni, "Panic in the Locker Room!"

47. Jason Reid, "Is the NFL Ready for Michael Sam?" *Washington Post*, February 20, 2014, https://www.washingtonpost.com/sports/redskins/is-the-nfl-ready-for-michael-sam/2014/02/20/85858a0c-9a48-11e3-b931-0204122c514b_story.html.

48. Mark Maske, "Recent NFL Memo to Teams Reinforces Anti-Discrimination Policies," *Washington Post*, February 17, 2014, https://www.washingtonpost.com/news/football-insider/wp/2014/02/17/recent-nfl-memo-to-teams-reinforces-anti-discrimination-policies/.

49. Price, "Moment of Truth."

50. Ken Belson, "In Historic Pick, Rams Take Michael Sam in Final Round of Draft," *New York Times*, May 10, 2014, https://www.nytimes.com/2014/05/11/sports/football/michael-sam-picked-by-st-louis-rams-in-nfl-draft.html.

51. Belson, "In Historic Pick."

52. Kent Babb, "St. Louis Rams Draft Michael Sam, Who Could Become First Openly Gay Active NFL Player," *Washington Post*, May 10, 2014, https://www.washingtonpost .com/sports/st-louis-rams-draft-michael-sam-who-could-become-first-openly-gay -active-nfl-player/2014/05/10/f66d9bbe-d874-11e3-95d3-3bcd77cd4e11_story.html.

53. Sam Frizell, "Oprah's Michael Sam Documentary Put on Hold," *Time*, May 17, 2014, https://time.com/103699/michael-sam-own-documentary-rams-oprah/.

54. Scott Pierce, "Michael Sam Should Forego Reality TV Show and Concentrate on Football," *Salt Lake Tribune*, May 14, 2014, https://archive.sltrib.com/article.php?id =57944506&itype=CMSID.

55. Frizell, "Oprah's Michael Sam Documentary Put on Hold."

56. William C. Rhoden, "Michael Sam Has a Spot in History, If Not with the Rams," *New York Times*, August 30, 2014, https://www.nytimes.com/2014/08/31/sports/football /michael-sam-still-an-inspiration-after-his-release.html.

57. Jason Whitlock, "Dungy Wrong about Michael Sam," ESPN, July 25, 2014, https: //www.espn.com/nfl/story/_/id/11252669/tony-dungy-michael-sam-nfl.

58. Whitlock, "Dungy Wrong about Michael Sam."

59. Matt Lavietes, "Tony Dungy's Anti-LGBTQ History Gets Renewed Attention after Controversial Tweet," NBC News, January 25, 2023, https://www.nbcnews.com/ nbc-out/out-news/tony-dungy-tweet-nfl-homophobic-football-transphobic-rcna67322.

60. Cindy Boren, "ESPN Says It Regrets Michael Sam Shower Report That Drew Criticism," *Washington Post*, August 27, 2014, https://www.washingtonpost.com/news/ early-lead/wp/2014/08/27/espn-says-it-regrets-michael-sam-shower-report-that-drew -criticism/.

61. Jonathan Cohn, "ESPN's Report on Michael Sam's Shower Habits Was Delin-quent Journalism," *New Republic*, August 27, 2014, https://newrepublic.com/article /119237/espn-report-michael-sam-shower-habits-was-delinquent-journalism.

62. NFL Communications, "Statement from NFL Commissioner Roger Goodell on Raiders DE Carl Nassib," 2021, https://nflcommunications.com/Pages/Statement-from -NFL-Commissioner-Roger-Goodell-on-Raiders-DE-Carl-Nassib.aspx.

63. Jimmy Traina, "Star NFL Players' Lack of Public Support for Carl Nassib Was Disappointing," *Sports Illustrated*, June 22, 2021, https://www.si.com/extra-mustard/2021 /06/22/nfl-star-players-silent-on-carl-nassib-coming-out-as-gay.

64. Kate Fagan, "Waiting for the One," *ESPN The Magazine*, October 8, 2012, https: //www.espn.com/espnw/news-commentary/story/_/id/8448590/kate-fagan-turning-tide -gay-rights-movement-sports-espn-magazine.

65. Dan Rafael, "Orlando Cruz a 'Proud Gay Man,'" ESPN, October 5, 2012, https: //www.espn.com/boxing/story/_/id/8460484/puerto-rican-featherweight-orlando-cruz -comes-proud-gay-man.

66. John Florio and Ouisie Shapiro, "Orlando Cruz Fights to Become Boxing's First Openly Gay Champion," *New Yorker*, November 25, 2016, https://www.newyorker .com/sports/sporting-scene/orlando-cruz-fights-to-become-boxings-first-openly-gay -champion.

67. Florio and Shapiro, "Orlando Cruz Fights."

68. See Donald McRae, *A Man's World: The Double Life of Emile Griffith* (London: Simon and Schuster, 2015).

69. Sam Borden, "Freed of a Secret's Burden, a Soccer Player Looks Ahead," *New York Times*, March 29, 2013, https://www.nytimes.com/2013/03/29/sports/soccer/robbie-rogers-feels-free-after-revealing-he-is-gay.html.

70. Grant Wahl, "Out and About," *Sports Illustrated*, May 13, 2013, https://vault.si.com/vault/2013/05/13/out-and-about.

71. Cindy Boren, Des Bieler, and Steven Goff, "San Diego Pro Soccer Team Walks Off after Opponent Allegedly Targets Openly Gay Player with Slur," *Washington Post*, October 2, 2020, https://www.washingtonpost.com/sports/2020/10/01/san-diego-loyal-gay-slur/.

72. Alex Reimer, "Collin Martin Says He Had Mixed Feelings When His Team Forfeited a Game after He Was Called an Anti-Gay Slur," *Outsports*, June 30, 2022, https://www.outsports.com/2022/6/30/23189758/collin-martin-san-diego-loyal-soccer-gay-slur.

73. Fagan, "Waiting for the One."

74. Sam Borden, "Female Star Comes Out as Gay, and Sports World Shrugs," *New York Times*, April 19, 2013, https://www.nytimes.com/2013/04/19/sports/ncaabasketball/brittney-griner-comes-out-and-sports-world-shrugs.html.

75. Borden, "Female Star Comes Out as Gay."

76. Doug Feinberg, "Phoenix Mercury's Brittany Griner Opens up about Getting Counseling," *USA Today*, February 4, 2021, https://apnews.com/article/health-brittney-griner-basketball-mental-health-9c2b379ca0ee3cf37d700cb0d847c0d0.

77. Rebecca Shore, "Flying with Ease," *Sports Illustrated*, July 9, 2012, https://vault.si.com/vault/2012/07/09/flying-with-ease.

78. Shore, "Flying with Ease."

79. ESPN News Services, "Blackhawks Won't Wear Pride Warmup over Security Concerns," *ESPN*, March 22, 2023, https://www.espn.com/nhl/story/_/id/35920976/chicago-blackhawks-wear-pride-themed-jerseys.

80. Amy Harmon and Thomas Kaplan, "Sexual Abuse Accusations at Ohio State Could Tar Powerful Republican," *New York Times*, July 3, 2018, https://www.nytimes.com/2018/07/03/us/politics/jim-jordan-sexual-abuse-accusations.html.

81. Harmon and Kaplan, "Sexual Abuse Accusations at Ohio State."

82. Eric Levitz, "Eighth Former OSU Wrestler Says Jim Jordan Knew about the Sexual Abuse," *Intelligencer*, July 10, 2018, https://nymag.com/intelligencer/2018/07/eighth-ex-osu-wrestler-says-jordan-knew-about-sexual-abuse.html.

83. Peter Szekely, "Ex-Ohio State Wrestlers Sue School Claiming It Ignored Sexual Abuse," *Reuters*, July 17, 2018, https://www.reuters.com/article/us-wrestling-ohio-lawsuit-idUSKBN1K72F7.

84. Catie Edmondson, "More Than 100 Former Ohio State Students Allege Sexual Misconduct," *New York Times*, July 20, 2018, https://www.nytimes.com/2018/07/20/us/politics/sexual-misconduct-ohio-state.html.

85. E. J. Dickson, "Rep. Jim Jordan, Alleged Campus Sexual Abuse Ignorer, Attacks Michael Cohen's Character," *Rolling Stone*, February 27, 2019, https://www.rollingstone.com/culture/culture-news/jim-jordan-michael-cohen-congress-800948/.

86. Rick Maese, "Ohio State Team Doctor Sexually Abused 177 Students over Decades," *Washington Post*, May 17, 2019, https://www.washingtonpost.com/sports/2019/05/17/ohio-state-team-doctor-sexually-abused-students-over-decades-report-finds/.

87. Catie Edmondson, "Jim Jordan Claims Vindication, but Inquiry Says Talk of Abuse at Ohio State Rampant," *New York Times*, May 17, 2019, https://www.nytimes.com/2019/05/17/us/politics/jim-jordan-sexual-abuse-ohio-state.html.

88. Kantele Franklin, "Suits against Ohio State over Sex Abuse by Doc Are Dismissed," AP News, September 22, 2021, https://apnews.com/article/sports-health-courts-education-ohio-9ed6895f0c35cd9b928f51a26638053f.

89. Nick Anderson and Susan Svrluga, "University of Michigan Agrees to $490 Million Settlement in Sex Abuse Scandal," *Washington Post*, January 19, 2022, https://www.washingtonpost.com/education/2022/01/19/michigan-settlement-robert-anderson-sex-abuse/.

90. Christopher Breiler, "Horrific Details of Sexual Abuse at Michigan Largely Ignored amid Debates over Legacies," *Sports Illustrated*, July 12, 2021, https://www.si.com/college/michigan/football/university-of-michigan-football-doctor-robert-anderson-bo-schembechler.

CHAPTER 11

1. Laura Inter and Mara Cristina Toledo, "What Is Intersex?" Suffolk University, Our Bodies Ourselves, accessed July 21, 2023, https://www.ourbodiesourselves.org/health-info/what-is-intersex/.

2. Tara Bahrampour, Scott Clement, and Emily Guskin, "Most Americans Oppose Trans Athletes in Female Sports, Poll Finds," *Washington Post*, June 14, 2022, https://www.washingtonpost.com/dc-md-va/2022/06/13/washington-post-umd-poll-most-americans-oppose-transgender-athletes-female-sports/.

3. Bonnie Berkowitz and Alberto Cuadra, "Fit but Unequal," *Washington Post*, February 25, 2014.

4. Berkowitz and Cuadra, "Fit but Unequal."

5. See Claire Sissons, "How Much Blood Is in the Human Body?" *Medical News Today*, updated February 14, 2023, https://www.medicalnewstoday.com/articles/321122.

6. Berkowitz and Cuadra, "Fit but Unequal."

7. Berkowitz and Cuadra, "Fit but Unequal."

8. Katrina Karkazis and Rebecca Jordan-Young, "The Trouble with Too Much T," *New York Times*, April 10, 2014, https://www.nytimes.com/2014/04/11/opinion/the-trouble-with-too-much-t.html.

9. Rebecca Jordan-Young and Katrina Karkazis, "Sex Verification: You Say Your're a Woman? That Should Be Enough," *New York Times*, June 17, 2012, https://www.nytimes.com/2012/06/18/sports/olympics/olympic-sex-verification-you-say-youre-a-woman-that-should-be-enough.html.

10. National Women's Law Center, "Fulfilling Title IX Promise: Let Transgender and Intersex Students Play," June 14, 2022, https://nwlc.org/resource/fulfilling-title-ixs-promise-let-transgender-and-intersex-students-play/.

11. International Olympic Committee, "IOC Framework on Fairness, Inclusion and Non-Discrimination on the Basis of Gender Identity and Sex Variations," November 16, 2021, https://stillmed.olympics.com/media/Documents/Beyond-the-Games/Human-Rights/IOC-Framework-Fairness-Inclusion-Non-discrimination-2021.pdf.

12. Dan Levin, "A Clash across America over Transgender Rights," *New York Times*, March 12, 2020, updated June 15, 2020, https://www.nytimes.com/2020/03/12/us/transgender-youth-legislation.html.

13. Julie Kliegman, "Understanding the Different Rules and Policies for Transgender Athletes," *Sports Illustrated*, July 6, 2022, https://www.si.com/more-sports/2022/07/06/transgender-athletes-bans-policies-ioc-ncaa.

14. See US Department of Education, "Fact Sheet: U.S. Department of Education's Proposed Change to Its Title IX Regulations on Students' Eligibility for Athletic Teams," April 6, 2023, https://www.ed.gov/news/press-releases/fact-sheet-us-department-educations-proposed-change-its-title-ix-regulations-students-eligibility-athletic-teams.

15. US Department of Education, "Fact Sheet."

16. See, e.g., David French, "The Legal Foundation of Women's Sports Is under Fire," *New York Times*, June 25, 2023, https://www.nytimes.com/2023/06/25/opinion/womens-sports-under-fire.html.

17. Katie Rogers, "Biden Plan for Transgender Title IX Rules Began on Inauguration Day," *New York Times*, April 7, 2023, https://www.nytimes.com/2023/04/07/us/politics/transgender-athletes-schools-title-ix.html.

18. Barry Svrluga, "In North Carolina, Sticking to Sports Means Confronting Controversial Law," *Washington Post*, February 8, 2017, https://www.washingtonpost.com/sports/colleges/in-north-carolina-sticking-to-sports-means-confronting-controversial-law/2017/02/08/c39fb43c-ee34-11e6-b4ff-ac2cf509efe5_story.html.

19. Marc Tracy, "N.C.A.A. Ends Boycott of North Carolina after So-Called Bathroom Bill Is Repealed," *New York Times*, April 4, 2017, https://www.nytimes.com/2017/04/04/sports/ncaa-hb2-north-carolina-boycott-bathroom-bill.html.

20. Ray Glier, "N.C.A.A. Leader Mark Emmert Says Discrimination Policy Is Clear," *New York Times*, March 17, 2017, https://www.nytimes.com/2017/03/17/sports/ncaabasketball/ncaa-discrimination-north-carolina-mark-emmert.html.

21. Scott Cacciola and Alan Binder, "N.B.A. to Move All-Star Game from North Carolina," *New York Times*, July 21, 2016, https://www.nytimes.com/2016/07/22/sports/basketball/nba-all-star-game-moves-charlotte-transgender-bathroom-law.html.

22. Tracy, "N.C.A.A. Ends Boycott."

23. Tracy, "N.C.A.A. Ends Boycott."

24. Scott Cacciola, "Charlotte Eligible to Host 2019 N.B.A. All-Star Game, Commissioner Says," *New York Times,* April 17, 2017, https://www.nytimes.com/2017/04/07/sports/basketball/charlotte-eligible-to-host-19-nba-all-star-game-commissioner-says.html.

25. Jordan-Young and Karkazis, "Sex Verification."

26. Jordan-Young and Karkazis, "Sex Verification."

27. Jordan-Young and Karkazis, "Sex Verification."

28. Karkazis and Jordan-Young, "The Trouble with Too Much T."

29. *Economist*, "What Caster Semenya's Case Means for Women's Sport," May 9, 2019, https://www.economist.com/international/2019/05/09/what-caster-semenyas-case-means-for-womens-sport.

30. *Economist*, "What Caster Semenya's Case Means for Women's Sport."

31. Geneva Abdul, "This Intersex Runner Had Surgery to Compete. It Has Not Gone Well," *New York Times*, December 16, 2019, https://www.nytimes.com/2019/12/16/sports/intersex-runner-surgery-track-and-field.html.

32. Jere Longman and Juliet Macur, "Caster Semenya Loses Case to Compete as a Woman in All Races," *New York Times*, May 1, 2019, https://www.nytimes.com/2019/05/01/sports/caster-semenya-loses.html.

33. Jere Longman, "Scientists Correct Study That Limited Some Female Runners," *New York Times*, August 18, 2021, https://www.nytimes.com/2021/08/18/sports/olympics/intersex-athletes-olympics.html.

34. Monica Hesse, "We Celebrated Michael Phelps's Genetic Differences. Why Punish Caster Semenya for Hers?" *Washington Post*, May 2, 2019, https://www.washingtonpost.com/lifestyle/style/we-celebrated-michael-phelpss-genetic-differences-why-punish-caster-semenya-for-hers/2019/05/02/93d08c8c-6c2b-11e9-be3a-33217240a539_story.html.

35. Jacob Bogage, "Caster Semenya Appeals Testosterone Ruling to Swiss Supreme Court," *Washington Post*, May 29, 2019, https://www.washingtonpost.com/sports/2019/05/29/caster-semenya-appeals-testosterone-ruling-swiss-supreme-court/.

36. Hida Viloria, "Stop Trying to Make Caster Semenya Fit a Narrow Idea of Womanhood. It's Unscientific and Unethical," *Washington Post*, May 3, 2019, https://www.washingtonpost.com/opinions/2019/05/03/stop-trying-make-caster-semenya-fit-narrow-idea-womanhood-its-unscientific-unethical/.

37. Longman and Macur, "Caster Semenya Loses Case."

38. Sean Ingle, "Caster Semenya to Run in Doha as Sebastian Coe Welcomes CAS Ruling," *Guardian*, May 2, 2019, https://www.theguardian.com/sport/2019/may/02/caster-semenya-doha-sebastian-coe-iaaf-cas-ruling-athletics.

39. Ingle, "Caster Semenya."

40. Longman and Macur, "Caster Semenya Loses Case."

41. Ingle, "Caster Semenya to Run in Doha."

42. Sean Ingle, "Caster Semenya Out of World 5,000m as Coe Signals Tougher Female Sport Rules," *Guardian*, July 21, 2022, https://www.theguardian.com/sport/2022/jul/21/caster-semenya-out-of-world-5000m-as-coe-signals-tougher-female-sport-rules.

43. Sean Ingle, "Semenya Loses Landmark Legal Case against IAAF over Testosterone Levels," *Guardian*, May 1, 2019, https://www.theguardian.com/sport/2019/may/01/caster-semenya-loses-landmark-legal-case-iaaf-athletics.

44. Jacob Bernstein, "The Bruce Jenner Story Goes from Gossip to News," *New York Times*, February 4, 2015, https://www.nytimes.com/2015/02/05/fashion/the-bruce-jenner-story-goes-from-gossip-to-news.html.

45. Gillian R. Brassil and Jere Longman, "World Rugby Bars Transgender Women, Baffling Players," *New York Times*, October 26, 2020, https://www.nytimes.com/2020/10/26/sports/olympics/world-rugby-transgender-women.html.

46. Kent Babb, "Transgender Wrestler Mack Beggs Identifies as a Male. He Just Won the Texas State Girls Title," *Washington Post*, February 25, 2017, https://www.washingtonpost.com/sports/highschools/meet-the-texas-wrestler-who-won-a-girls-state-title-his-name-is-mack/2017/02/25/982bd61c-fb6f-11e6-be05-1a3817ac21a5_story.html; Katie Barnes, "They Are the Champions," *ESPN The Magazine*, June 28, 2018, https://kebarnes.com/2021/02/09/they-are-the-champions/.

47. Barnes, "They Are the Champions."

48. Babb, "Transgender Wrestler Mack Beggs."

49. Barnes, "They Are the Champions."

50. Barnes, "They Are the Champions."

51. Associated Press, "Connecticut Transgender Policy Found to Violate Title IX," *ESPN*, May 28, 2020, https://www.espn.com/espn/story/_/id/29234386/connecticut-transgender-policy-found-violate-title-ix.

52. Associated Press, "Connecticut Transgender Policy."

53. Michael Levenson and Neil Vigdor, "Inclusion of Transgender Athletes Violates Title IX, Trump Administration Says," *New York Times*, June 16, 2021, https://www.nytimes.com/2020/05/29/us/connecticut-transgender-student-athletes.html.

54. National Women's Law Center, "Fulfilling Title IX Promise."

55. Roman Stubbs, "As Transgender Rights Debate Spills into Sports, One Runner Finds Herself at the Center of a Pivotal Case," *Washington Post*, July 27, 2020, https://www.washingtonpost.com/sports/2020/07/27/idaho-transgender-sports-lawsuit-hecox-v-little-hb-500/.

56. Stubbs, "As Transgender Rights Debate Spills into Sports."

57. Gillian R. Brassil and Jere Longman, "Who Should Compete in Women's Sports? There Are 'Two Almost Irreconcilable Positions,'" *New York Times*, August 18, 2020, https://www.nytimes.com/2020/08/18/sports/transgender-athletes-womens-sports-idaho.html.

58. Kliegman, "Understanding the Different Rules."

59. Kliegman, "Understanding the Different Rules."

60. Kliegman, "Understanding the Different Rules."

61. Katie Barnes, "Former University of Pennsylvania Swimmer Lia Thomas Responds to Critics: 'Trans Women Competing in Women's Sports Does Not Threaten Women's Sports,'" *ESPN*, May 31, 2022, https://www.espn.com/college-sports/story/_/id/34013007/trans-women-competing-women-sports-does-not-threaten-women-sports.

Conclusion

1. *Washington Post* Editorial Board, "Opinion: Long COVID Haunts Millions of People," *Washington Post*, February 8, 2023, https://www.washingtonpost.com/opinions/2023/02/08/long-covid-challenges-economy-health-care/.

Bibliography

Abdul, Geneva. "This Intersex Runner Had Surgery to Compete. It Has Not Gone Well." *New York Times*, December 16, 2019. https://www.nytimes.com/2019/12/16/sports/intersex-runner-surgery-track-and-field.html.

Abelson, Jenn. "Coached until She Collapsed, an Aspiring Bodybuilder Is Now on Life Support." *Washington Post*, December 20, 2022. https://www.msn.com/en-us/news/us/coached-until-she-collapsed-an-aspiring-bodybuilder-is-now-on-life-support/ar-AA15tOdR.

Adams, Char. "Young Black Athletes Are Launching a Mental Health Revolution." NBC News, July 23, 2021. https://www.nbcnews.com/news/nbcblk/young-black-athletes-are-launching-mental-health-revolution-rcna1490.

Alexander, Jonathan M. "Sylvia Hatchell, Hosting Camp at UNC, Denies Allegations That Led to Her Departure." *Durham Herald-Sun*, July 12, 2019. https://www.newsobserver.com/sports/article232490392.html.

Allarahka, Shaziya. "What Are the Four Stages of CTE?" Medicine Net, August 1, 2022. https://www.medicinenet.com/what_are_the_four_stages_of_cte/article.htm.

Allentuck, Danielle. "Simone Biles Set a New Standard. Can U.S.A. Gymnastics Do the Same?" *New York Times*, August 12, 2019. https://www.nytimes.com/2019/08/12/sports/simone-biles-gymnastics-championship.html.

Alosco, M. L., et al. "Age of First Exposure to American Football and Long-Term Neuropsychiatric and Cognitive Outcomes." *Transactional Psychiatry* 7 (2017). https://www.nature.com/articles/tp2017197

Alvarado, Francisco. "Ricky Williams Is the Greatest Pot Smoker to Wear a Miami Dolphins Uniform." *Miami New Times*, December 18, 2018. https://www.miaminewtimes.com/news/the-real-marijuana-story-of-ricky-williams-10954869.

Amaechi, John. "The Real Locker-Room Shocker." *Time*, May 13, 2013. https://content.time.com/time/subscriber/article/0,33009,2142497,00.html.

Amar, Vikram David. "Why It's Hard for 'Independent' Investigations Like the One concerning Ohio State's Football Coach Urban Meyer to Be Meaningfully Independent." *Verdict*, September 4, 2018. https://verdict.justia.com/2018/09/04/why-its-hard-for-independent-investigations-like-the-one-concerning-ohio-states-football-coach-urban-meyer-to-be-meaningfully-independent.

American College of Sports Medicine. "The American College of Sports Medicine Statement on Mental Health Challenges for Athletes." August 9, 2021. https://www.acsm.org/news-detail/2021/08/09/the-american-college-of-sports-medicine-statement-on-mental-health-challenges-for-athletes.

Anderson, Jared. "Digging in on SafeSport's Investigative Process, Ban Terminology." SwimSwam, October 17, 2018. https://swimswam.com/digging-in-on-safesports-investigative-process-ban-terminology/.

Anderson, Kelli. "Justice Underserved." *Sports Illustrated*, October 21, 2013. https://vault.si.com/vault/2013/10/21/justice-underserved.

Anderson, Nick, and Susan Svrluga. "University of Michigan Agrees to $490 Million Settlement in Sex Abuse Scandal." *Washington Post*, January 19, 2022. https://www.washingtonpost.com/education/2022/01/19/michigan-settlement-robert-anderson-sex-abuse/.

Anxiety and Depression Association of America. "Ricky Williams: A Story of Social Anxiety Disorder." November 20, 2009. https://adaa.org/living-with-anxiety/personal-stories/ricky-williams-story-social-anxiety-disorder.

Apstein, Stephanie. "How Jose Altuve Got Thrown Off." *Sports Illustrated*, March 26, 2021. https://www.si.com/mlb/2021/03/26/jose-altuve-thrown-off-daily-cover.

Araton, Harvey. "Jason Collins, Openly Gay and Still Unsigned, Waits and Wonders." *New York Times*, October 10, 2013. https://www.nytimes.com/2013/10/11/sports/basketball/jason-collins-openly-gay-and-still-unsigned-waits-and-wonders.html.

Around the NFL Staff, "Aaron Rodgers Takes 'Full Responsibility' for Comments about COVID-19 Vaccination Status." NFL.com, November 9, 2021. https://www.nfl.com/news/aaron-rodgers-full-responsibility-misleading-comments-covid-19-vaccine.

Ashburner, Steve. "NBA Outlines Health and Safety Protocols for 2020–21 Season." NBA.com, December 5, 2020. https://www.nba.com/news/nba-establishes-health-and-safety-protocol-for-2020-21-season.

Associated Press. "Blackhawks Say Toews Will Not Return to Team Next Season." Fox Sports, April 14, 2023. https://www.foxsports.com/articles/nhl/blackhawks-say-toews-will-not-return-to-team-next-season\.

———. "Cavs' West Arrested in Maryland." ESPN, September 18, 2009. https://www.espn.com/nba/news/story/_/id/4485441.

———. "Connecticut Transgender Policy Found to Violate Title IX." ESPN, May 28, 2020. https://www.espn.com/espn/story/_/id/29234386/connecticut-transgender-policy-found-violate-title-ix.

———. "Ex-MSU Dean Gets Jail for Neglect, Misconduct." ESPN, August 7, 2019. https://www.espn.com/college-sports/story/_/id/27340567/ex-msu-dean-gets-jail-neglect-misconduct.

———. "Investigation into Michigan State's Handling of Larry Nassar Suspended." NBC News, December 24, 2019. https://www.nbcnews.com/news/us-news/michigan-state-investigation-handling-larry-nassar-suspended-n1106976.

———. "Jets' Ainge Announces Retirement; Cites Injuries." ESPN, July 28, 2013.

———. "Michael Phelps Pleads Guilty to DUI." *ESPN*, December 19, 2014. https://www.espn.com/olympics/swimming/story/_/id/12052498/gold-medalist-michael-phelps-pleads-guilty-dui.

———. "Ryan Freel, Concussion-Plagued Baseball Player, Dies at 36." *New York Times*, December 24, 2012. https://www.nytimes.com/2012/12/25/sports/baseball/ryan-freel-concussion-plagued-baseball-player-dies-at-36.html.

Athletic Staff. "Antonio Brown Claims Bucs Offered Him $200K for Mental Health Treatment in Order to Cover Up Mistreatment." *Athletic*, January 26, 2022. https://theathletic.com/4183159/2022/01/26/antonio-brown-claims-bucs-offered-him-200k-for-mental-health-treatment-in-order-to-cover-up-mistreatment/.

———. "Family of Former Bucs WR Vincent Jackson Says Brain Researchers Diagnosed Him with Stage 2 CTE." *Athletic*, December 16, 2021. https://theathletic.com/4184018/2021/12/16/family-of-former-bucs-wr-vincent-jackson-says-brain-researchers-diagnosed-him-with-stage-2-cte/.

Assunção, Muri. "Dwyane Wade Explains Decision to Keep the 'Hate Out' of Trans Daughter's Life by Turning Off Comments on Social Media." *New York Daily News*, October 7, 2022. https://www.nydailynews.com/snyde/ny-dwyane-wade-keep-hate-out-trans-daughter-zaya-zayre-comment-social-media-20221007-qjwb4xm3hba6fcxbmfiqzmi3ri-story.html.

Augustine, Bernie. "Jason Collins' Girlfriend: I Never Suspected NBA Player Was Gay." *New York Daily News*, May 1, 2013. https://www.nydailynews.com/sports/basketball/jason-collins-girlfriend-no-clue-gay-article-1.1331903.

Axon, Rachel. "Chamique Holdsclaw Pleads Guilty to Assault." *USA Today*, February 27, 2013. https://www.usatoday.com/story/sports/wnba/2013/06/14/chamique-holdsclaw-pleads-guilty-to-assault/2425383/.

Babb, Kent. "'Michael Sam's Announcement Prompts NFL to Examine What It Considers a 'Distraction.'" *Washington Post*, February 10, 2014. https://www.washingtonpost.com/sports/michael-sams-announcement-prompts-nfl-to-examine-what-it-considers-a-distraction/2014/02/10/e5f6d088-9293-11e3-84e1-27626c5ef5fb_story.html.

———. "St. Louis Rams Draft Michael Sam, Who Could Become First Openly Gay Active NFL Player." *Washington Post*, May 10, 2014. https://www.washingtonpost.com/sports/st-louis-rams-draft-michael-sam-who-could-become-first-openly-gay-active-nfl-player/2014/05/10/f66d9bbe-d874-11e3-95d3-3bcd77cd4e11_story.html.

———. "Transgender Wrestler Mack Beggs Identifies as a Male. He Just Won the Texas State Girls Title." *Washington Post*, February 25, 2017. https://www.washingtonpost.com/sports/highschools/meet-the-texas-wrestler-who-won-a-girls-state-title-his-name-is-mack/2017/02/25/982bd61c-fb6f-11e6-be05-1a3817ac21a5_story.html.

Baccelleri, Emma. "Katie Hamilton Will Speak for Herself, Thank You." *Sports Illustrated*, July 8, 2021. https://www.si.com/mlb/2021/07/08/katie-hamilton-where-are-they-now-2021.

Bahrampour, Tara, Scott Clement, and Emily Guskin, "Most Americans Oppose Trans Athletes in Female Sports, Poll Finds." *Washington Post*, June 14, 2022. https:

//www.washingtonpost.com/dc-md-va/2022/06/13/washington-post-umd-poll
-most-americans-oppose-transgender-athletes-female-sports/.

Barnes, Katie, "Former University of Pennsylvania Swimmer Lia Thomas Responds to
Critics: 'Trans Women Competing in Women's Sports Does Not Threaten Wom-
en's Sports.'" ESPN, May 31, 2022. https://www.espn.com/college-sports/story/_/
id/34013007/trans-women-competing-women-sports-does-not-threaten-women
-sports.

————. "They Are the Champions." *ESPN The Magazine,* June 28, 2018, https://kebarnes
.com/2021/02/09/they-are-the-champions/.

Barr, John, and Dan Murphy. "Nassar Surrounded by Adults Who Enabled His Predatory Behavior." ESPN, January 16, 2018. https://www.espn.com/espn/otl/story/_/
id/22046031/michigan-state-university-doctor-larry-nassar-surrounded-enablers
-abused-athletes-espn.

Beck, Howard, and John Branch. "With the Words 'I'm Gay,'" an N.B.A. Center Breaks
a Barrier." *New York Times,* April 29, 2013. https://www.nytimes.com/2013/04/30/
sports/basketball/nba-center-jason-collins-comes-out-as-gay.html.

Belson, Ken. "Aaron Hernandez Had Severe C.T.E. When He Died at Age 27." *New York
Times,* September 21, 2017. https://www.nytimes.com/2017/09/21/sports/aaron
-hernandez-cte-brain.html.

————. "An N.F.L. Doctor Wants to Know Why Some Players Get C.T.E and Others
Don't." *New York Times,* May 18, 2023. https://www.nytimes.com/2023/05/18/
sports/football/pittsburgh-sports-brain-bank.html.

————. "Football True Believers Circle the Wagons and Insist the Sport Is Just Fine."
New York Times, January 30, 2018. https://www.nytimes.com/2018/01/30/sports/
football/nfl.html.

————. "In Historic Pick, Rams Take Michael Sam in Final Round of Draft." *New
York Times,* May 10, 2014. https://www.nytimes.com/2014/05/11/sports/football/
michael-sam-picked-by-st-louis-rams-in-nfl-draft.html.

————. "Support for Gay Rights Led to Harassment, Ex-Viking Says." *New York Times.*
January 2, 2014. https://www.nytimes.com/2014/01/03/sports/football/support
-for-gay-rights-drew-harassment-ex-viking-says.html.

Belson, Ken, and Benjamin Mueller. "Collective Force of Head Hits, Not Just the Number of Them, Increases Odds of CTE." *New York Times,* June 20, 2023. https://
www.nytimes.com/2023/06/20/sports/football/cte-study-concussions-brain-tackle
.html.

Belson, Ken, and Katherine Rosman. "Raiders Coach Resigns after Homophobic and
Misogynistic Emails." *New York Times,* October 28, 2021. https://www.nytimes
.com/2021/10/11/sports/football/what-did-jon-gruden-say.html.

Belson, Ken, and Jenny Vrentas. "Hamlin's Injury Highlights Precarious Position of Many
Young N.F.L. Players." *New York Times,* January 29, 2023. https://www.nytimes
.com/2023/01/29/sports/football/nfl-contracts-injuries-young-players.html.

Bergeron, Elena, "Without Updated Tools, N.F.L. Is Still Finding Concussions Too
Late." *New York Times,* December 31, 2022. https://www.nytimes.com/2022/12/31
/sports/football/tua-tagovailoa-nfl-concussions.html.

Berkowitz, Bonnie, and Alberto Cuadra. "Fit but Unequal." *Washington Post*, February 25, 2014.

Berkowitz, Bonnie, and William Neff. "Built & Broken: What Bodybuilders Do to Their Bodies—and Brains." *Washington Post*, December 8, 2022. https://www.washingtonpost.com/investigations/interactive/2022/bodybuilding-health-risks/.

Bernstein, Jacob. "The Bruce Jenner Story Goes from Gossip to News." *New York Times*, February 4, 2015. https://www.nytimes.com/2015/02/05/fashion/the-bruce-jenner-story-goes-from-gossip-to-news.html.

Blackistone, Kevin B. "NCAA Should Make a Stand against States with Strict Abortion Laws." *Washington Post*, June 11, 2019. https://www.washingtonpost.com/sports/colleges/almost-half-the-ncaas-athletes-are-women-it-needs-to-make-a-stand-for-them/2019/06/10/cd52be66-8b8a-11e9-adf3-f70f78c156e8_story.html.

———. "State Agencies Can Suspend Concussed Fighters. Why Not NFL Players?" *Washington Post*, October 9, 2022. https://www.washingtonpost.com/sports/2022/10/07/nfl-concussions-policy/.

Blanton, Kayla. "Simone Biles Says She Still Has the 'Twisties' and 'Literally Cannot Tell Up from Down in the Air." *Prevention*, July 30, 2021. https://www.prevention.com/health/a37179324/simone-biles-twisties-olympics-instagram/.

Blinder, Alan, Richard Fausset, and Marc Tracy. "U.N.C. Women's Basketball Coach Sylvia Hatchell Faces a Reckoning." *New York Times*, April 6, 2019. https://www.nytimes.com/2019/04/06/sports/sylvia-hatchell-unc-racially-insensitive-comments.html.

Bogage, Jacob. "A Football Recruit Uses Medical Cannabis for Epilepsy. He Says It Cost Him a Roster Spot." *Washington Post*, June 1, 2018. https://www.washingtonpost.com/news/early-lead/wp/2018/06/01/an-auburn-football-recruit-uses-medical-cannabis-for-epilepsy-he-claims-it-cost-him-his-roster-spot/.

———. "Caster Semenya Appeals Testosterone Ruling to Swiss Supreme Court." *Washington Post*, May 29, 2019. https://www.washingtonpost.com/sports/2019/05/29/caster-semenya-appeals-testosterone-ruling-swiss-supreme-court/.

Bonesteel, Matt. "U.S. Soccer Vows Improved Vetting, Training, Transparency after Yates Report." *Washington Post*, January 31, 2023. https://www.washingtonpost.com/sports/2023/01/30/ussf-yates-recommendations/.

Boogaard v. National Hockey League, 255 F. Supp 3rd 753 (N.D. Ill. 2017).

Booher, Christopher. "Antonio Brown Asked about Mental Health, CTE During Wild Podcast: 'I've Got Mental Wealth.'" *Sports Illustrated*, January 8, 2022. https://www.si.com/nfl/lions/news/antonio-brown-asked-about-mental-health-cte-podcast-interview.

Borden, Sam. "Abby Wambach, Retired U.S. Soccer Star, Reflects on Her Addiction." *New York Times*, October 10, 2016. https://www.nytimes.com/2016/10/11/sports/soccer/abby-wambach-addiction-alcohol-painkillers.html.

———. "Female Star Comes Out as Gay, and Sports World Shrugs." *New York Times*, April 18, 2013. https://www.nytimes.com/2013/04/19/sports/ncaabasketball/brittney-griner-comes-out-and-sports-world-shrugs.html.

———. "Freed of a Secret's Burden, a Soccer Player Looks Ahead." *New York Times*, March 29, 2013. https://www.nytimes.com/2013/03/29/sports/soccer/robbie-rogers-feels-free-after-revealing-he-is-gay.html.

Boren, Cindy. "Dolphins' Jones Says NFL Career Has Left Him Unable to Run or Jump." *Washington Post*, February 26, 2023. https://www.washingtonpost.com/sports/2023/02/26/dolphins-byron-jones/.

———. "ESPN Says It Regrets Michael Sam Shower Report That Drew Criticism." *Washington Post*, August 27, 2014. https://www.washingtonpost.com/news/early-lead/wp/2014/08/27/espn-says-it-regrets-michael-sam-shower-report-that-drew-criticism/.

———. "'Everything Was Spinning': Keven Love Opens Up about His In-Game Panic Attack." *Washington Post*, March 6, 2018. https://www.washingtonpost.com/news/early-lead/wp/2018/03/06/everything-was-spinning-kevin-love-opens-up-about-his-in-game-panic-attack/.

———. "A Pregnant Runner's Open Letter to the Boston Marathon Helped Spur Change." *Washington Post*, February 3, 2023. https://www.washingtonpost.com/sports/2023/02/02/pregnant-runner-boston-marathon/.

———. "USA Gymnastics Leaders Resign over Nassar Scandal." *Washington Post*, January 23, 2018. https://www.washingtonpost.com/news/early-lead/wp/2018/01/22/as-victims-continue-to-speak-out-three-of-usa-gymnastics-top-leaders-resign-over-larry-nassar-scandal/.

Boren, Cindy, Des Bieler, and Steven Goff. "San Diego Pro Soccer Team Walks Off after Opponent Allegedly Targets Openly Gay Player with Slur." *Washington Post*, October 2, 2020. https://www.washingtonpost.com/sports/2020/10/01/san-diego-loyal-gay-slur/.

Boston University CTE Research Center. "BU Researchers Find CTE in 345 of 376 Former NFL Players Studied." Boston University Chomanian & Avedisian School of Medicine, February 6, 2023. https://www.bumc.bu.edu/camed/2023/02/06/researchers-find-cte-in-345-of-376-former-nfl-players-studied/.

Bourmistrova, Nicole Wallbridge, Tomas Solomon, Philip Braude, Rebecca Strawbridge, and Ben Carter. "Long-Term Effects of COVID-19 on Mental Health: A Systematic Review." *Journal of Affective Disorders* 299 (2022): 118–25. https://doi.org/10.1016/j.jad.2021.11.031.

Branch, John. "Derek Boogaard: A Brain 'Going Bad.'" *New York Times*, May 12, 2013. https://www.nytimes.com/2011/12/06/sports/hockey/derek-boogaard-a-brain-going-bad.html.

———. ****"In Emails, N.H.L. Officials Conceded Concussion Risks of Fights." *New York Times*, March 29, 2016. https://www.nytimes.com/2016/03/29/sports/hockey/nhl-emails-link-concussions-fighting-bettman.html.

———. N.H.L. "N.H.L. Commissioner Gary Bettman Continues to Deny C.T.E. Link." *New York Times*, July 26, 2016. https://www.nytimes.com/2016/07/27/sports/nhl-commissioner-gary-bettman-denies-cte-link.html.

———. "N.F.L. Prospect Michael Sam Proudly Says What Teammates Knew: He's Gay." *New York Times*, February 10, 2014. https://www.nytimes.com/2014/02/10/sports/michael-sam-college-football-star-says-he-is-gay-ahead-of-nfl-draft.html.

———. "The Tragic Diagnosis They Already Knew: Their Brother Died with C.T.E." *New York Times*, May 3, 2018. https://www.nytimes.com/2018/05/03/sports/nhl-cte-jeff-parker.html.

Brassil, Gillian R., and Jere Longman. "Who Should Compete in Women's Sports? There Are 'Two Almost Irreconcilable Positions.'" *New York Times*, August 18, 2020. https://www.nytimes.com/2020/08/18/sports/transgender-athletes-womens-sports-idaho.html.

———. "World Rugby Bars Transgender Women, Baffling Players." *New York Times*, Oct. 26, 2020. https://www.nytimes.com/2020/10/26/sports/olympics/world-rugby-transgender-women.html.

Brewer, Jerry. "NFL Protocols Couldn't Protect Tua Tagovailoa from Careless Humans." *Washington Post*, Sept. 30, 2022, https://www.washingtonpost.com/sports/2022/09/30/tua-injury/

———. "The NFL's Protocols Didn't Save Miami QB." *Washington Post*, October 2, 2022.

Breiler, Christopher. "Horrific Details of Sexual Abuse at Michigan Largely Ignored amid Debates over Legacies." *Sports Illustrated*, July 12, 2021. https://www.si.com/college/michigan/football/university-of-michigan-football-doctor-robert-anderson-bo-schembechler.

Brown, Chip. "What the Hell Happened to David Duval?" *Men's Journal*, December 4, 2017. https://www.mensjournal.com/entertainment/what-the-hell-happened-to-david-duvall-19691231.

Brown, Larry. "Analysis: Naomi Osaka Suffering from Ronda Rousey Disease." *Larry Brown Sports* (blog), June 1, 2021. https://larrybrownsports.com/tennis/naomi-osaka-suffering-ronda-rousey-disease/579713.

Bruni, Frank. "Panic in the Locker Room!" *New York Times*, February 10, 2014. https://www.nytimes.com/2014/02/11/opinion/bruni-panic-in-the-locker-room.html.

Bryant, Howard. "More Than Words." *ESPN The Magazine*, June 24, 2013.

———. "Equal Forces from Serena Williams to the UConn Huskies, Female Athletes Have Set Their Own Marks for Greatness. So Stop Weighing Them against the Men's Game." *ESPN The Magazine*, May 23, 2016.

Bumbaca, Chris. "Concussion Nearly Derailed Her Career. Now Amanda Kessel Is Starring Again for US Women's Hockey Team." *USA Today*, February 11, 2022. https://www.usatoday.com/story/sports/olympics/beijing/2022/02/11/amanda-kessel-usa-hockey-concussions-womens-hockey/6748317001/.

Cacciola, Scott. "Charlotte Eligible to Host 2019 N.B.A. All-Star Game, Commissioner Says." *New York Times*, April 17, 2017. https://www.nytimes.com/2017/04/07/sports/basketball/charlotte-eligible-to-host-19-nba-all-star-game-commissioner-says.html.

Cacciola, Scott, and Alan Binder. "N.B.A. to Move All-Star Game from North Carolina." *New York Times*, July 21, 2016. https://www.nytimes.com/2016/07/22/sports/basketball/nba-all-star-game-moves-charlotte-transgender-bathroom-law.html.

Callaway, Ewen, Heidi Ledford, Giuliana Viglione, Traci Watson, and Alexandra Witze. "COVID and 2020: An Extraordinary Year for Science." *Nature*, December 2022. https://www.nature.com/immersive/d41586-020-03437-4/index.html.

Carlisle, Jeff. "Hope Solo's Painful Journey." ESPN, June 27, 2011. https://www.espn.com/sports/soccer/news/_/columnist/carlisle_jeff/id/6691703/hope-solo-overcoming-physical-emotional-issues-women-world-cup-soccer.

Cash, Meredith. "The Syracuse Women's Basketball Team Is in Disarray as Almost the Entire Team Transferred in an End-of-Season Mass Exodus." Yahoo Sports, April 26, 2021. https://sports.yahoo.com/syracuse-womens-basketball-team-disarray-184603123.html.

Cazaneuve, Brian. "Chris Pronger Has a Headache." *Sports Illustrated*, June 30, 2015. https://www.si.com/nhl/2015/06/30/si-vault-chris-pronger-has-headache-2013-feature-story-brian-cazeneuve.

Centers for Disease Control and Prevention. "Traumatic Brain Injury and Concussion." https://www.cdc.gov/traumaticbraininjury/index.html. Accessed July 17, 2023.

Chang, Cindy, Margot Putukian, Giselle Aerni, Alex Diamond, Gene Hong, Yvette Ingram, Claudia L. Reardon, and Andrew Wolanin. "Mental Health Issues and Psychological Factors in Athletes: Detection, Management, Effect on Performance and Prevention: American Medical Society for Sports Medicine Position Statement—Executive Summary." *British Journal of Sports Medicine* 54, no. 4. https://doi.org/10.1136/bjsports-2019-101583.

Chavez, Chris. "Inside the Toxic Culture of the Nike Oregon Project 'Cult.'" *Sports Illustrated*, November 13, 2019. https://www.si.com/track-and-field/2019/11/13/mary-cain-nike-oregon-project-toxic-culture-alberto-salazar-abuse-investigation.

Chiari, Mike. "Jonathan Martin–Richie Incognito Investigative Report Released." *Bleacher Report*, February 14, 2014. https://bleacherreport.com/articles/1960345-jonathan-martin-richie-incognito-investigation-report-released.

Cimini, Rich. "Ainge: 'I Had to Go Get Help Before I Died.'" ESPN, March 31, 2011. https://www.espn.com/new-york/columns/story?columnist=cimini_rich&id=6267822.

Clarke, Liz. "After Outcry over Serena's Rankings, WTA Alters Rules." *Washington Post*, December 18, 2018. https://www.washingtonpost.com/sports/2018/12/18/after-outcry-over-serena-williamss-rankings-wta-alters-rules-moms-returning-competition/.

———. "Larry Probst to Step Down as USOC Board Chair." *Washington Post*, September 10, 2018. https://www.washingtonpost.com/sports/olympics/larry-probst-to-step-down-as-usoc-board-chair/2018/09/10/a79fe0f8-b53a-11e8-a7b5-adaaa5b2a57f_story.html.

———. "Senate Panel: Negligence by Olympic, USA Gymnastics Officials Enabled Abuse by Ex-Team Doctor Nassar." *Washington Post*, July 30, 2019. https://www.washingtonpost.com/sports/olympics/panel-to-introduce-legislation-to-reform-us-olympic-and-paralympic-committee/2019/07/30/7472683e-b266-11e9-8f6c-7828e68cb15f_story.html.

———. "Like Novak Djokovic, Many Elite Athletes Go to Extremes to Gain an Edge." *Washington Post*, January 10, 2022. https://www.washingtonpost.com/sports/2022 /01/10/novak-djokovic-vaccine-health-diet/.

———. "U.S. Open Plans to Factor Pregnancy into Seeding." *Washington Post*, June 23, 2018. https://www.washingtonpost.com/news/sports/wp/2018/06/23/u-s-open-to -change-seeding-process-in-wake-of-serena-williamss-pregnancy-leave/.

Cohn, Jonathan. "ESPN's Report on Michael Sam's Shower Habits Was Delinquent Journalism." *New Republic*, August 27, 2014. https://newrepublic.com/article /119237/espn-report-michael-sam-shower-habits-was-delinquent-journalism.

Cole, Brendan. "Piers Morgan Criticizes Manuel in Latest Olympics Comments." *Newsweek*, August 7, 2021. https://www.newsweek.com/piers-morgan-simone-manuel -simone-biles-olympics-interview-mental-health-1617186.

Coleman, Ashley. "Troubled Soccer Star Hope Solo Reveals She Is Seeing a Therapist for 'Anger' Issues as She Rejoins Team USA Following 30-Day Suspension." *Daily Mail*, March 26, 2015. https://www.dailymail.co.uk/news/article-3013348 /Troubled-soccer-star-Hope-Solo-reveals-s-seeing-therapist-anger-issues-rejoins -Team-USA-following-30-day-suspension.html.

Copage, Eric V. "Male Survivor Conference Examines Sexual Abuse in Sports." *New York Times*, November 18, 2012. https://www.nytimes.com/2012/11/19/sports/ malesurvivor-conference-examines-sexual-abuse-in-sports.html.

Crasnick, Jerry. "Putting the Pieces Back Together." ESPN, November 24, 2009, https:// www.espn.com/mlb/columns/story?columnist=crasnick_jerry&id=4686519.

Crouse, Karen. "A Fun-Loving, Carefree Spirit Becomes the Face of Anxiety." *New York Times*, January 3, 2013. https://www.nytimes.com/2013/01/04/sports/golf/charlie -beljan-lives-a-life-of-high-anxiety-and-low-golf-scores.html.

———. "For Champion Swimmer, a Simpler Time." *New York Times*, July 31, 2010. https: //www.nytimes.com/2010/08/01/sports/01swimmer.html.

Crouse, Karen, and Bill Pennington. "Panic Attack Leads to Hospital on Way to Golfer's First Victory." *New York Times*, November 13, 2012. https://www.nytimes.com /2012/11/13/sports/golf/charlie-beljans-panic-leads-to-hospital-and-then-pga -title.html.

Culpepper, Chuck. "A Belarusian Tennis Star, a Ukrainian Reporter, a Tense Media Session." *Washington Post*, June 2, 2023. https://www.washingtonpost.com/sports/2023 /06/02/aryna-sabalenka-french-open-ukraine-war/.

Daneshvar, Daniel H., et al. "Leveraging Football Accelerometer Data to Quantify Associations Between Repetitive Head Impacts and Chronic Traumatic Encephalopathy in Males." *Nature Communications* 14 (2023). https://www.nature.com/articles /s41467-023-39183-0.

Daugherty, Paul. "Doc: Redemption for Bengals' Bad Boy, Chris Henry." *Cincinnati Enquirer*, December 14, 2014. https://www.cincinnati.com/story/sports/columnists /paul-daugherty/2014/12/13/former-bengal-chris-henry-remembered-5-years -after-death/20205991/.

Davis, Seth. "After Addiction and Arrest, Ex-UK Star Rex Chapman Trying to Rebuild His Life." *Sports Illustrated*, July 27, 2015. https://www.si.com/college/2015/07/28 /rex-chapman-kentucky-nba-painkillers-theft.

Deitsch, Richard. "Man behind the Mic: Fox NFL Analyst Troy Aikman on Broadcasting, More." *Sports Illustrated*, January 14, 2015. https://www.si.com/nfl/2015/01/14 /troy-aikman-fox-nfl-analyst-qa.

Dewey, Caitlan. "Her Biggest Save." *Washington Post*, November 2, 2013. https://www .washingtonpost.com/sf/national/2013/11/02/her-biggest-save/.

Dhote, Vipin V., Muthu Kumaradoss, Mohan Maruga Raja, Prem Samundre, Supriya Sharma, Shraddha Anwikar, and Aman B. Upaganlawar. "Sports-Related Brain Injury and Neurodegeneration in Athletes." *Current Molecular Pharmacology* 15, no. 1 (2022): 51–76. https://doi.org/10.2174/1874467214666210910114324.

Diamond, Dan. "Tua Tagovailoa's Head Injury Spurs Scrutiny of NFL Concussion Protocol." *Washington Post*, September 30, 2022. https://www.washingtonpost.com/ health/2022/09/30/tua-concussion-protocol-nfl.

Diaz, Jaime. "The Sad Story of Tiger Woods Grows Even Sadder." *Golf Digest*, May 29, 2017. https://www.golfdigest.com/story/the-sad-story-of-tiger-woods-grows-even -sadder.

Dickson, E. J. "Rep. Jim Jordan, Alleged Campus Sexual Abuse Ignorer, Attacks Michael Cohen's Character." *Rolling Stone*, February 27, 2019. https://www.rollingstone .com/culture/culture-news/jim-jordan-michael-cohen-congress-800948/.

Ding Productions. "NFL 'Brutal' Hits." Video. YouTube, January 28, 2021. https://www .youtube.com/watch?v=622zSYBbHmE.

———. "20 Biggest Hits in NFL History." Video. YouTube, March 11, 2022. https:// www.youtube.com/watch?v=6c4mtfRry0Y.

Dixon, Tris. *Damage: The Untold Story of Brain Trauma in Boxing*. London: Hamilcar Publications, 2021.

Doehler, Steph. "Role Model or Quitter? Social Media's Response to Simone Biles at Tokyo 2020." *International Journal of Sports Communication* 16, no. 1 (2022): 64– 79. https://doi.org/10.1123/ijsc.2022-0143.

Dorman, Larry, and Joseph Berger. "Woods Says Car Accident Is His Fault, but Private." *New York Times*, November 29, 2009. https://www.nytimes.com/2009/11/30/sports /golf/30woods.html.

Draper, Kevin, and Mathew Futterman. "Disgraced Running Coach Was Barred for Life for Alleged Sexual Assault." *New York Times*, January 31, 2022. https://www .nytimes.com/2022/01/31/sports/alberto-salazar-sexual-assault.html.

Dryden, Ken. "The National Hockey League Is Skating around Brain Injuries." *Washington Post*, June 24, 2018. https://www.washingtonpost.com/opinions/the -national-hockey-league-is-skating-around-the-brain-injury-problem/2018/06 /24/9d173d58-763c-11e8-b4b7-308400242c2e_story.html.

Economist. "What Caster Semenya's Case Means for Women's Sport." May 9, 2019. https: //www.economist.com/international/2019/05/09/what-caster-semenyas-case -means-for-womens-sport.

Edmondson, Catie. "Jim Jordan Claims Vindication, but Inquiry Says Talk of Abuse at Ohio State Rampant." *New York Times*, May 17, 2019. https://www.nytimes.com /2019/05/17/us/politics/jim-jordan-sexual-abuse-ohio-state.html.

———. "More Than 100 Former Ohio State Students Allege Sexual Misconduct." *New York Times*, July 20, 2018. https://www.nytimes.com/2018/07/20/us/politics/sexual -misconduct-ohio-state.html.

Ellis, Philips, "Dwyane Wade Just Made a Powerful Statement about Being a Father to an LGBTQ+ Child." *Men's Health*, December 20, 2019. https://www.menshealth .com/entertainment/a30296136/dwyane-wade-father-lgbtq-child/.

Empowering Olympic, Paralympic, and Amateur Athletes Act of 2020. S. 2330, 116th Cong. (2019–2020).

ESPN. "Drugs and Sports: Amphetamines." Special Section, September 6, 2021. https:// www.espn.com/special/s/drugsandsports/.

———. "Ben Simmons Timeline: All of the Major Happenings with the Philadelphia 76ers Star in 2021–2022." February 18, 2022. https://www.espn.com/nba/story/ _/id/32877959/ben-simmons-line-all-major-happenings-philadelphia-76ers-star -2021-2022.

ESPN News Services. "Adrian Peterson against Gay Marriage." ESPN, May 28, 2013. https://www.espn.com/nfl/story/_/id/9315572/adrian-peterson-minnesota -vikings-says-gay-marriage.

———. "Blackhawks Won't Wear Pride Warmups Over Security Concerns." ESPN, March 22, 2023. https://www.espn.com/nhl/story/_/id/35920976/chicago -blackhawks-wear-pride-themed-jerseys.

———. "Commish Welcomes Michael Sam." ESPN, February 12, 2014. https://www .espn.com/nfl/story/_/id/10447810/roger-goodell-welcomes-michael-sam-says -good-him.

———. "Fins GM Suggested 'Punch.'" ESPN, November 7, 2013. https://www.espn .com/nfl/story/_/id/9938868/jeff-ireland-miami-dolphins-suggested-jonathan -martin-physically-confront-richie-incognito.

———. "Justin Turner of Dodgers Pulled from World Series after Positive COVID-19 Test." ESPN, October 29, 2020. https://www.espn.com/mlb/story /_/id/30206824/justin-turner-los-angeles-dodgers-pulled-world-series-positive -covid-19-test.

———. "Ryan Freel Had CTE, Parents Say." ABC News, December 15, 2013. https:// abcnews.go.com/Sports/ryan-freel-cte-parents/story?id=21227773.

Fagan, Kate. "Waiting for the One," *ESPN The Magazine*, October 15, 2012. https://www .espn.com/espnw/news-commentary/story/_/id/8448590/kate-fagan-turning-tide -gay-rights-movement-sports-espn-magazine.

Fainaru-Wada, Mark. "Abby Wambach Plans to Exit Drug Company Linked to Brett Favre Welfare Fraud Case." ESPN, October 13, 2022. https://www.espn.com/nfl/ story/_/id/34695437/abby-wambach-plans-exit-drug-company-linked-brett-favre -welfare-fraud-case.

Fainaru-Wada, Mark, and Steve Fainaru. "League of Denial," *Sports Illustrated*, October 7, 2013, 64–68.

Farrar, Doug. "Aaron Rodgers Admits Lying about COVID Vaccination Status Last Year," *TouchdownWire*, August 28, 2022. https://touchdownwire.usatoday.com /2022/08/28/aaron-rodgers-joe-rogan-covid-vaccinated/.

Favale, Dan. "Daryl Morey Says Royce White 'Could' Be Worst 1st-Round Draft Pick Ever." *Bleacher Report*, January 26, 2014. https://bleacherreport.com/articles /1937127-daryl-morey-says-royce-white-could-be-worst-first-round-nba-draft -pick-ever.

Federal Baseball Club v. National League, 259 U.S. 200 (1922).

Feinberg, Doug. "Phoenix Mercury's Brittany Griner Opens up about Getting Counseling." AP News, February 4, 2021. https://apnews.com/article/health-brittney -griner-basketball-mental-health-9c2b379ca0ee3cf37d700cb0d847c0d0.

Felix, Allyson. "Allyson Felix: My Own Nike Pregnancy Story." *New York Times*, May 22, 2019. https://www.nytimes.com/2019/05/22/opinion/allyson-felix-pregnancy -nike.html.

Felt, Hunter. "NBA Is Right to Fine but Not Suspend Roy Hibbert for 'No Homo' Slur." *Guardian*, June 3, 2013. https://www.theguardian.com/sport/2013/jun/03/roy -hibbert-fined-gay-slur.

Fichera, Angelo. "Claims Baselessly Link COVID Vaccines to Athlete Deaths." AP News, January 9, 2023. https://apnews.com/article/fact-check-covid-vaccines -athlete-deaths-1500-989195878254.

Fitzsimmons, Emma G., and Sopan Deb. "'Kyrie Carve Out' in Vaccine Mandate Frees Irving to Play in New York." *New York Times*, March 23, 2022. https://www .nytimes.com/2022/03/23/sports/kyrie-irving-nyc-vaccine-mandate.html.

Florio, John, and Ouisie Shapiro. "Orlando Cruz Fights to Become Boxing's First Openly Gay Champion. *New Yorker*, November 25, 2016. https://www.newyorker .com/sports/sporting-scene/orlando-cruz-fights-to-become-boxings-first-openly -gay-champion.

Ford, Bonnie D. "Out of the Blue." ESPN, July 16, 2016. https://www.espn.com/espn /feature/story/_/id/17125857/us-olympic-swimmer-allison-schmitt-takes-aim -stigma-depression.

Forde, Pat. "Simone Manuel Had to Conquer More Than Her Competitors to Make the Tokyo Olympics." *Sports Illustrated*, July 13, 2021. https://www.si.com/olympics /2021/07/13/simone-manuel-tokyo-olympics-50-freestyle-overtraining.

Fortier, Sam. "Senior Bowl Restrictions Can Challenge Big Hitters." *Washington Post*, February 4, 2023. https://www.washingtonpost.com/sports/2023/02/03/senior -bowl-big-hits/.

Foss, Mike. "Aaron Rodgers Denies Rumors That He Is Gay." *USA Today*, December 31, 2013. https://ftw.usatoday.com/2013/12/aaron-rodgers-denies-rumors-that-he-is -gay.

Franklin, Kantele. "Suits against Ohio State over Sex Abuse by Doc Are Dismissed." AP News, September 22, 2021. https://apnews.com/article/sports-health-courts -education-ohio-9ed6895f0c35cd9b928f51a26638053f.

Freed, Benjamin. "ESPN Radio Hosts Suspended after Terrible Anti-Transgender Rant." DCist, December 11, 2012. https://dcist.com/story/12/12/11/espn-radio-hosts-suspended-after-te/.

French, David. "The Legal Foundation of Women's Sports Is Under Fire." *New York Times*, June 25, 2023. https://www.nytimes.com/2023/06/25/opinion/womens-sports-under-fire.html.

Friedell, Nick. "Brooklyn Nets' Kyrie Irving: Gave Up 4-Year, $100 Million-Plus Extension to Be Unvaccinated." ESPN, September 26, 2022. https://www.espn.com/nba/story/_/id/34672230/gave-4-year-100m-plus-extension-unvaccinated.

Frizell, Sam. "Oprah's Michael Sam Documentary Put on Hold." *Time*, May 17, 2014. https://time.com/103699/michael-sam-own-documentary-rams-oprah/.

Futterman, Mathew. "Olympic Bobsledder Who Killed Himself Likely Had C.T.E." *New York Times*, September 29, 2021. https://www.nytimes.com/2021/04/08/sports/olympics/bobsled-cte-concussions-sledhead.html.

Garber, Greg. "A Tormented Soul." ESPN, January 28, 2005. https://www.espn.com/nfl/news/story/_/id/1972285.

Gay, Timothy James. *Football Physics: The Science of the Game* (New York: Random House, 2017)

Gecker, Jocelyn, and Jerome Pugmire. "Rising above Reality: How Djokovic Bends His Mind to Succeed." AP News, January 15, 2022. https://apnews.com/article/coronavirus-pandemic-novak-djokovic-sports-health-australia-37993234c4814893c1abfedf5cdaf884.

Gelber, Jonathan. "How Len Bias's Death Helped Launch the U.S.'s Unjust War on Drugs." *Guardian*, June 29, 2021. https://www.theguardian.com/sport/2021/jun/29/len-bias-death-basketball-war-on-drugs.

Glier, Ray. "N.C.A.A. Leader Mark Emmert Says Discrimination Policy Is Clear." *New York Times*, March 17, 2017. https://www.nytimes.com/2017/03/17/sports/ncaabasketball/ncaa-discrimination-north-carolina-mark-emmert.html.

Goessling, Ben. "Vikings Respond to Kluwe Allegations." WABC News, July 19, 2014. https://abc7ny.com/sports/vikings-respond-to-kluwe-allegations/199345/.

Goff, Steven. "Bruce Murray Spent Years Heading the Ball. He Worries It Took a Toll." *Washington Post*, July 5, 2022. https://www.washingtonpost.com/sports/2022/07/05/bruce-murray-dementia-cte/.

Goldstein, Richard. "Jimmy Piersall, Whose Mental Illness Was Portrayed in 'Fear Strikes Out,' Dies at 87." *New York Times*, June 4, 2017. https://www.nytimes.com/2017/06/04/sports/baseball/jimmy-piersall-died-mental-illness.html.

Golen, Jimmy. "CTE Diagnosed in Ex-MLS Player Vermillion, a 1st for League." AP News, June 28, 2018. https://apnews.com/article/sports-health-soccer-major-league-high-school-ad6e8e9e10aca1f3533d8067a8463d77.

Gordon, Meryl. "Before 'Concussion': An Inside Glimpse of NFL Player Mike Webster's Utterly Tragic Final Days." The Healthy *@Reader's Digest*, September 4, 2019. https://www.thehealthy.com/neurological/mike-webster-brain-injury/.

Graham, Ruth. "Players Rely on an Unseen Teammate: Their Faith." *New York Times*, January 8, 2023. https://www.nytimes.com/2023/01/08/pageoneplus/quotation-of-the-day-players-rely-on-an-unseen-teammate-their-faith.html.

Granderson, L. Z. "To Ask or Not to Ask." *ESPN The Magazine*, May 30, 2013. https://www.espn.com/espn/story/_/id/9315552/reporters-need-address-athlete-sexuality-avoid-homophobia-media-espn-magazine.

Green, Laura. "What's Next for USA Gymnastics as the USOC Tries to Decertify It?" *Sports Illustrated*, November 6, 2018. https://www.si.com/olympics/2018/11/07/usa-gymnastics-larry-nassar-usoc-decertification.

Gregory, Sean. "U.S. Ranks Worst in Sports Homophobia Study." *Time*, May 9, 2015. https://time.com/3852611/sports-homophobia-study/.

Gross, Josh. "Ronda Rousey Finds Time, Energy for Charity." ESPN, March 12, 2013. https://www.espn.com/blog/mma/post/_/id/17068/ronda-rousey-finds-time-energy-for-charity.

Guardian Sport. "Michael Phelps Did Not Want to 'Be Alive Anymore' after DUI Arrest." *Guardian*, November 10, 2015. https://www.theguardian.com/sport/2015/nov/10/michael-phelps-did-not-want-to-be-alive-anymore-after-dui-arrest.

Haag, Matthew, and Marc Tracy. "Michigan State President Lou Anna Simon Resigns amid Nassar Fallout." *New York Times*, January 24, 2018. https://www.nytimes.com/2018/01/24/sports/olympics/michigan-state-president-resigns-lou-anna-simon.html.

Harmon, Amy, and Thomas Kaplan. "Sexual Abuse Accusations at Ohio State Could Tar Powerful Republican." *New York Times*, July 3, 2018. https://www.nytimes.com/2018/07/03/us/politics/jim-jordan-sexual-abuse-accusations.html.

Harriston, Keith, and Jenkins, Sally. "Maryland Basketball Star Len Bias Dead at 22." *Washington Post*, June 20, 1986. https://www.washingtonpost.com/wp-srv/sports/longterm/memories/bias/launch/bias1.htm.

Hasmar, Jessica. "Michael Sam Filming Oprah Reality TV Show: Report." *Washington Times*, May 15, 2014.

Hensley-Clancy, Molly. "With the NCAA Silent on Abortion Bans, College Sports Face Confusion." *Washington Post*, July 28, 2022. https://www.washingtonpost.com/sports/2022/07/27/college-sports-ncaa-abortion-bans/.

Herman, Martyn. "Andre Agassi Crystal Meth Revelations Shock Tennis World." Reuters, October 28, 2009. https://www.reuters.com/article/us-agassi-idUSTRE59R4NK20091028.

Hesse, Monica. "We Celebrated Michael Phelps's Genetic Differences. Why Punish Caster Semenya for Hers?" *Washington Post*, May 2, 2019. https://www.washingtonpost.com/lifestyle/style/we-celebrated-michael-phelpss-genetic-differences-why-punish-caster-semenya-for-hers/2019/05/02/93d08c8c-6c2b-11e9-be3a-33217240a539_story.html.

Himmelsbach, Adam. "Players' Support of Gay Marriage Alters N.F.L.'s Image." *New York Times*, September 9, 2012. https://www.nytimes.com/2012/09/09/sports/football/players-support-of-gay-marriage-alters-nfl-image.html.

Hobson, Will. "Doctor at Center of USA Gymnastics Scandal Left Warning Signs at Michigan State." *Washington Post*, April 25, 2017. https://www.washingtonpost .com/sports/olympics/doctor-at-center-of-usa-gymnastics-scandal-left-warning -signs-at-michigan-state/2017/04/25/eed48834-2530-11e7-a1b3-faff0034e2de _story.html.

————. "Following Sex Abuse Report, USA Gymnastics Pledges Stronger Oversight of Clubs." *Washington Post*, June 28, 2017. https://www.washingtonpost.com/sports/ olympics/following-sex-abuse-report-usa-gymnastics-pledges-stronger-oversight -of-clubs/2017/06/27/a7c799cc-5b4a-11e7-9fc6-c7ef4bc58d13_story.html.

————. "Former Head of USA Gymnastics Pleads the Fifth on Larry Nassar Questions from Congress." *Washington Post*, June 5, 2018. https://www.washingtonpost.com/ news/sports/wp/2018/06/05/former-head-of-usa-gymnastics-pleads-the-fifth-on -larry-nassar-questions-from-congress/.

————. "Former NFL Players Sue over Disability Claims, Accuse Plan of 'Disturbing' Denials." *Washington Post*, February 9, 2023. https://www.washingtonpost.com/ sports/2023/02/09/nfl-disability-plan-lawsuit/.

————. "How the NFL Avoids Paying Disabled Players—with the Union's Help." *Washington Post*, February 8, 2023. https://www.washingtonpost.com/sports/2023/02/08 /nfl-disability-players-union/.

————. "McKayla Maroney Sues USA Gymnastics, Saying it Tried to Buy Her Silence on Abuse," *Washington Post*, December 20, 2017, https://www.washingtonpost.com /sports/mckayla-maroney-sues-usa-gymnastics-saying-it-tried-to-buy-her-silence -on-abuse/2017/12/20/1e54b482-e5c8-11e7-a65d-1ac0fd7f097e_story.html.

————. "UNC Women's Hoops Coach Sylvia Hatchell Resigns amid Allegations of Berating Players, Racial Remarks." *Washington Post*, April 20, 2019. https://www .washingtonpost.com/sports/colleges/they-make-me-sick-unc-womens-hoops -coach-berated-injured-players-parents-say/2019/04/18/7259c7c0-6146-11e9 -9412-daf3d2e67c6d_story.html.

————. "USA Gymnastics CEO Steve Penny Resigns in Wake of Sex Abuse Scandal." *Washington Post*, March 16, 2017. https://www.washingtonpost.com/sports/ olympics/usa-gymnastics-ceo-steve-penny-resigns-in-wake-of-sex-abuse-scandal /2017/03/16/fe4f27de-0a77-11e7-93dc-00f9bdd74ed1_story.html.

Hobson, Will, and Steven Rich. "USOC Was Alerted to Sex Abuse Problems Long Before Taking Action." *Washington Post*, March 7, 2017. https://www.washingtonpost.com /sports/olympics/documents-usoc-alerted-to-sex-abuse-problems-long-before -taking-action/2017/03/06/8ca2a89e-0230-11e7-ad5b-d22680e18d10_story.html.

Hoffman, Benjamin. "Contrary to 49ers Stance, Culliver Says He Wouldn't Accept a Gay Teammate." *New York Times*, January 30, 2013. https://archive.nytimes.com /fifthdown.blogs.nytimes.com/2013/01/30/contrary-to-49ers-stance-culliver-says -he-wouldnt-accept-a-gay-teammate/.

————. "Sixers Guard Markelle Fultz out Indefinitely with Nerve Disorder." *New York Times,* December 4, 2018. https://www.nytimes.com/2018/12/04/sports/markelle -fultz-injury-76ers.html.

Hogshead-Maskar, Nancy, and Elizabeth A. Sorensen. *Pregnant and Parenting Student-Athletes: Resources and Model Policies.* NCAA Gender Equity, June 2018. https://www.uncp.edu/sites/default/files/2018-06/NCAA%20Pregnant %20and%20Parenting%20Students%20Resources%20and%20Model%20Policies .pdf.

Howe, P. David. *Sport, Professionalism, and Pain: Ethnographies of Injury and Risk.* New York: Routledge, 2004.

Hruby, Patrick. "Oscar Pistorius and the 'Roid Rage' Defense: It's No Get-Out-of-Jail-Free Card." *Washington Times,* February 18, 2013. https://www.washingtontimes.com/ news/2013/feb/19/oscar-pistorius-and-roid-rage-its-no-get-out-jail-/.

Hull, James. "The Road to Recovery for Athletes with Long Covid." Physiological Society, March 24, 2022. https://www.physoc.org/blog/the-road-to-recovery-for -athletes-with-long-covid/.

In re: NFL's Concussion Injury Litigation, No. 19–2085 (3d Cir. 2020).

Ingle, Sean. "Caster Semenya Out of World 5,000m as Coe Signals Tougher Female Sport Rules." *Guardian,* July 21, 2022. https://www.theguardian.com/sport/2022/ jul/21/caster-semenya-out-of-world-5000m-as-coe-signals-tougher-female-sport -rules.

———. "Caster Semenya to Run in Doha as Sebastian Coe Welcomes CAS Ruling." Guardian, May 2, 2019. https://www.theguardian.com/sport/2019/may/02/caster -semenya-doha-sebastian-coe-iaaf-cas-ruling-athletics.

———. "Semenya Loses Landmark Legal Case against IAAF over Testosterone Levels." *Guardian,* May 1, 2019. https://www.theguardian.com/sport/2019/may/01/caster -semenya-loses-landmark-legal-case-iaaf-athletics.

Inter, Laura, and Mara Cristina Toledo. "What Is Intersex?" Suffolk University: Our Bodies Ourselves, accessed July 21, 2023. https://www.ourbodiesourselves.org/ health-info/what-is-intersex/

International Olympic Committee. "IOC Framework on Fairness, Inclusion and Non-discrimination on the Basis of Gender Identity and Sex Variations." November 16, 2021. https://stillmed.olympics.com/media/Documents/Beyond-the-Games /Human-Rights/IOC-Framework-Fairness-Inclusion-Non-discrimination-2021 .pdf.

Irby, Mathew. "To Hell and Back: The Josh Hamilton Story." *Bleacher Report,* May 30, 2008. https://bleacherreport.com/articles/26169-to-hell-and-back-the-josh -hamilton-story.

Jabber Head, "Diagnoses: Delonte West Watched Desperado One Too Many Times." *Bleacher Report,* October 10, 2009. https://bleacherreport.com/articles/269465 -diagnoses-delonte-west-watched-desperado-one-too-many-times.

Jenkins, Sally. "Another 'Report' on Abuse in Women's Sports. When Is Enough Enough?" *Washington Post,* October 3, 2022, https://www.washingtonpost.com/ sports/2022/10/03/yates-report-womens-soccer-abuse/.

———. "The Breathtaking Violence of an Ordinary NFL Hit." *Washington Post,* January 13, 2023. https://www.washingtonpost.com/sports/2023/01/12/nfl-physics -violence/.

———. "Chemique Holsclaw Confronts Her 'Little Secret' of Depression." *Washington Post*, May 17, 2012. https://www.washingtonpost.com/sports/othersports/chamique-holdsclaw-confronts-her-little-secret-of-depression/2012/05/17/gIQAoUe7WU_story.html.

———. "Kyrie Irving Wants to Leave a Legacy. With His Stance on Vaccination, He Just Might," *Washington Post*, September 27, 2021. https://www.msn.com/en-us/news/us/kyrie-irving-wants-to-leave-a-legacy-with-his-stance-on-vaccination-he-just-might/ar-AAOSQdn.

———. "Novak Djokovic Is Driven by an Obsession, but That Always Has a Cost." *Washington Post*, January 17, 2022. https://www.washingtonpost.com/sports/2022/01/17/novak-djokovic-vaccination-philosophy/.

———. "What Happens to a Company That Dopes Its Workers? If It's an NFL Team, Not Much." *Washington Post*, May 9, 2017. https://www.washingtonpost.com/sports/redskins/what-happens-to-a-company-that-dopes-it-workers-if-its-an-nfl-team-not-much/2017/05/09/572672a4-34df-11e7-b412-62beef8121f7_story.html.

Jenkins, Sally, and Rick Maese. "Do No Harm: Who Should Bear the Costs of Retired NFL Players' Medical Bills?" *Washington Post*, May 9, 2013. https://www.washingtonpost.com/sports/redskins/do-no-harm-who-should-bear-the-costs-of-retired-nfl-players-medical-bills/2013/05/09/2dae88ba-b70e-11e2-b568-6917f6ac6d9d_story.html.

Jesse, David. "Study: MSU's Simon Raked in $855,000 in Total Compensation in 2017." *Detroit Free Press*, July 16, 2018. https://raejphillips.wordpress.com/2018/07/16/study-msus-simon-raked-in-855000-in-total-compensation-in-2017-3/.

Jones, Mike. "Opinion: With COVID-19 Cases on the Rise, NFL's Best Hope Is to Revert to Vigilance and Sacrifices of 2020." *USA Today*, December 15, 2021. https://www.usatoday.com/story/sports/nfl/columnist/mike-jones/2021/12/15/nfl-covid-cases-protocols-positive-tests-team-players/8911311002.

Jordan-Young, Rebecca, and Katrina Karkazis. "Sex Verification: You Say You're a Woman? That Should Be Enough." *New York Times*, June 17, 2012. https://www.nytimes.com/2012/06/18/sports/olympics/olympic-sex-verification-you-say-youre-a-woman-that-should-be-enough.html.

Just, Amie. "Briana Scurry Embraces New Role as Women's Brain Health Advocate." *Washington Post*, June 19, 2016. https://www.washingtonpost.com/sports/briana-scurry-embraces-new-role-as-womens-brain-health-advocate/2016/06/19/17aad636-33d4-11e6-8758-d58e76e11b12_story.htm.

Kaplan, Daniel. "NHL Paid $70.6 Million in Legal Fees for Concussion Settlement That Paid Players $18.49 Million." *Athletic*, April 29, 2021. https://theathletic.com/2549607/2021/04/29/nhl-paid-70-6-million-in-legal-fees-for-concussion-settlement-that-paid-players-18-49-million/.

Kaplan, Emily. "NHL Reaches Settlement in Concussion Lawsuit," ESPN, November 12, 2018. https://www.espn.com/nhl/story/_/id/25256208/nhl-reaches-settlement-concussion-lawsuit.

Karkazis, Katrina, and Rebecca Jordan-Young. "The Trouble with Too Much T." *New York Times*, April 10, 2014. https://www.nytimes.com/2014/04/11/opinion/the-trouble -with-too-much-t.html.

Kay, Emily. "Bubba Watson, Charlie Beljan Blame Panic Attacks on Poor Eating Habits." *SB Nation*, January 3, 2013. https://www.sbnation.com/golf/2013/1/3/3833464/ bubba-watson-charlie-beljan-blame-panic-attacks-on-poor-eating-habits.

Keh, Andrew. "A Diagnosis Brings C.T.E. into American Pro Soccer." *New York Times*, June 28, 2022. https://www.nytimes.com/2022/06/28/sports/soccer/cte-soccer .html.

Kennedy, Kostya. "Brotherly Love: Beset by Panic Attacks, Toronto's Shayne Corson Turned to Linemate and In-Law Darcy Tucker for Help," *Sports Illustrated*, October 22, 2001, https://vault.si.com/vault/2001/10/22/brotherly-love-beset-by-panic -attacks-torontos-shayne-corson-turned-to-linemate-and-in-law-darcy-tucker -for-help.

Kepner, Tyler. "Jose Altuve, the Yips, and Some Sympathy for the Astros." *New York Times*, October 14, 2020. https://www.nytimes.com/2020/10/14/sports/baseball/ astros-jose-altuve-rays.html.

Kilgore, Adam. "Washington Nationals Prospect Aaron Barrett Overcomes 'Yips' to Regain Control of Career," *Washington Post*, February 23 2014. https:// www.washingtonpost.com/sports/nationals/washington-nationals-prospect-aaron -barrett-overcomes-yips-to-regain-control-of-career/2014/02/23/96f034d4-9cde -11e3-975d-107dfef7b668_story.html.

Kilgore, Adam, and Scott Clement. "Poll: Nine in 10 Sports Fans Say NFL Brain Injuries Are a Problem, but 74 Percent Are Still Football Fans." *Washington Post*, September 6, 2017. https://www.washingtonpost.com/sports/poll-nfl-remains-as-popular -as-ever-despite-head-injuries-other-concerns/2017/09/06/238bef8a-9265-11e7 -8754-d478688d23b4_story.html

Klapper, Rebecca. "Novak Djokovic Says Athletes Must 'Start Learning How to Deal with the Pressure.'" *Newsweek*, July 28, 2021. https://www.newsweek.com/novak -djokovic-says-pro-athletes-must-start-learning-how-deal-pressure-1613959.

King, Peter. "Trump Calls on NFL Owners to Fire Players Who Protest, and Mocks Efforts to Make the Game Safer." *Sports Illustrated*, September 23, 2017. https:// www.si.com/nfl/2017/09/23/trump-nfl-fire-players-who-protest-during-anthem.

Kishen Neelam et al., "Pandemics and Pre-Existing Mental Illness: A Systematic Review and Meta-Analysis," *Brain, Behavior, and Immunity—Health* (2021) https://doi.org /10.1016/j.bbih.2020.100177.

Klein, Jeff Z., and Stu Hackel. "In the N.H.L., a Stricter Standard for Safety's Sake." *New York Times*, December 29, 2013. https://www.nytimes.com/2013/12/29/sports /hockey/in-the-nhl-a-stricter-standard-for-safetys-sake.html.

Kliegman, Julie. "Ben Simmons's Mental Health Is Not a Joke." *Sports Illustrated*, February 15, 2022. https://www.si.com/nba/2022/02/15/ben-simmons-mental-health -brooklyn-nets.

———. "Understanding the Different Rules and Policies for Transgender Athletes." *Sports Illustrated*, July 6, 2022. https://www.si.com/more-sports/2022/07/06/transgender-athletes-bans-policies-ioc-ncaa.

Kozowolski, Kim. "Court Vacates Conviction of Former MSU Gymnastics Coach Kathie Klages." *Detroit News*, December 21, 2021. https://www.detroitnews.com/story/news/local/michigan/2021/12/21/kathie-klages-larry-nassar-conviction-vacated-lying-to-police-michigan-state-university/8985174002/.

Kwayie, Mame M. "Chamique Holdsclaw Speaks on Her Depression." *Ebony*, August 14, 2014. https://www.ebony.com/chamique-holdsclaw-speaks-on-her-depression-354/.

Kwiatkowski, Marisa, Mark Alesia, and Tim Evans. "A Blind Eye to Sex Abuse: How USA Gymnastics Failed to Report Cases," *Indianapolis Star*, August 4, 2016; updated June 24, 2020. https://www.indystar.com/story/news/investigations/2016/08/04/usa-gymnastics-sex-abuse-protected-coaches/85829732/.

Laine, Jenna. "Vincent Jackson Died from Chronic Alcohol Use, Medical Examiner Says." ESPN, December 23, 2021. https://www.espn.com/nfl/story/_/id/32925482/vincent-jackson-died-chronic-alcohol-use-medical-examiner-says.

Langmann, Brady. "Terry Bradshaw Is Finally Becoming Himself." *Esquire*, January 27, 2022. https://www.esquire.com/entertainment/tv/a38900889/terry-bradshaw-interview-depression-legacy-going-deep/.

———. "What Happened to Delonte West Tells a Larger Story about How We Treat Athletes." *Esquire*, January 19, 2021. https://www.esquire.com/sports/a34209617/delonte-west-nba-homeless-now/.

Langmuir, Molly. "The Audacity of Hope Solo." *Elle*, July 2019. https://www.elle.com/culture/a27891036/hope-solo-soccer-fifa-womens-world-cup/.

Lavietes, Matt. "Tony Dungy's Anti-LGBTQ History Gets Renewed Attention after Controversial Tweet." NBC News, January 25, 2023. https://www.nbcnews.com/nbc-out/out-news/tony-dungy-tweet-nfl-homophobic-football-transphobic-rcna67322.

Lee, Michael. "How the NBA Got Serious about Mental Health." *Washington Post*, April 19, 2022. https://www.washingtonpost.com/sports/2022/04/19/nba-mental-health-demar-derozan/.

———. "Slowed and Sidelined, Some Athletes Struggle to Return from Long-Haul COVID." *Washington Post*, April 19, 2021. https://www.washingtonpost.com/sports/2021/04/19/athletes-long-haul-covid-justin-foster/.

———. "Wizards' Plans Not Affected by Jason Collins Announcement." *Washington Post*, April 30, 2013. https://www.washingtonpost.com/news/wizards-insider/wp/2013/04/30/wizards-never-planned-to-bring-back-jason-collins/.

Leitch, Will. "Antonio Brown and the Specter of CTE." *New York*, January 3, 2022. https://nymag.com/intelligencer/2022/01/antonio-brown-and-the-specter-of-cte.html.

Levenson, Michael. "Hope Solo, Former U.S. Soccer Star, Charge with Impaired Driving." *New York Times*, April 1, 2022. https://www.nytimes.com/2022/04/01/us/hope-solo-arrest.html.

Levenson, Michael, and Neil Vigdor. "Inclusion of Transgender Athletes Violates Title IX, Trump Administration Says." *New York Times*, May 20, 2020. https://www .nytimes.com/2020/05/29/us/connecticut-transgender-student-athletes.html.

Levin, Dan. "A Clash Across America over Transgender Rights." *New York Times*, March 12, 2020, updated June 15, 2020. https://www.nytimes.com/2020/03/12/us/ transgender-youth-legislation.html.

Levitz, Eric. "Eighth Former OSU Wrestler Says Jim Jordan Knew about the Sexual Abuse." *Intelligencer*, July 10, 2018. https://nymag.com/intelligencer/2018/07/ eighth-ex-osu-wrestler-says-jordan-knew-about-sexual-abuse.html.

Lewis, Brian. "Nets' Kyrie Irving on Being in Middle of Vaccine Debate: 'Life of a Martyr.'" *New York Post*, May 4, 2022. https://nypost.com/2022/05/04/nets-kyrie-irving -on-being-in-middle-of-vaccine-debate-life-of-a-martyr/.

Lewis, Tanya. "Sexist Science in Soccer Harms Women in an Epic Own Goal." *Scientific American*, November 18, 2022. https://www.scientificamerican.com/article/sexist -science-in-soccer-harms-women-in-an-epic-own-goal/.

Lindsay, Rosie K., Jason J. Wilson, Mike Trott, Olawale Olanrewaju, Mark A. Tully, Guillermo F. López-Sánchez, Jae Il Shin, Damiano Pizzol, Peter Allen, Laurie T. Butler, Yvonne Barnett, and Lee Smith. "What Are the Recommendations for Returning Athletes Who Have Experienced Long Term COVID-19 Symptoms?" *Annals of Medicine* 53, no. 1 (2021): 1935–44. https://doi.org/10.1080/07853890 .2021.1992496.

Local8Now. "Crimetracker: Former Vol QB Arrested for DUI." July 28, 2013.

Longman, Jere. "Scientists Correct Study That Limited Some Female Runners." *New York Times*, August 18, 2021. https://www.nytimes.com/2021/08/18/sports/ olympics/intersex-athletes-olympics.html.

———. "U.S. Olympics Chief Received $2.4 Million Severance amid Scandal." *New York Times*, July 3, 2019. https://www.nytimes.com/2019/07/03/sports/olympics-scott -blackmun.html.

Longman, Jere, and Juliet Macur. "Caster Semenya Loses Case to Compete as a Woman in All Races." *New York Times*, May 1, 2019. https://www.nytimes.com/2019/05/01 /sports/caster-semenya-loses.html.

Louis-Jacques, Marcel. "Tua Tagovailoa Ruled Out Again; Dolphins to Start Skylar Thompson." ESPN, October 12, 2022. https://www.espn.com/nfl/story/_/id /34782013/tua-tagovailoa-ruled-again-dolphins-start-skylar-thompson.

Lyons, Craig. "$75 Million NCAA Settlement to Fund Concussion Screening for 4 Million Former Athletes." *Lansing State Journal*, August 15, 2019. https:// www.lansingstatejournal.com/story/news/2019/08/15/ncaa-concussion-settlement -athlete-medical-testing/2012186001/.

Lypsyte, Robert. "Backtalk; Harnisch a Reluctant Role Model." *New York Times*, November 22, 1998. https://www.nytimes.com/1998/11/22/sports/backtalk-harnisch-a -reluctant-role-model.html.

Macur, Juliet. "Ex-Gymnastics Chief's Career: Swift Success Marred by Years of Scandal. "*New York Times*, March 17, 2017. https://www.nytimes.com/2017/03/17/sports/ olympics/macur-steve-penny-usa-gymnastics-scandal.html.

———. "Inaction and Inequality on Women's World Cup Turf Issues." *New York Times*, December 5, 2014. https://www.nytimes.com/2014/12/05/sports/soccer/inaction -and-inequality-on-womens-world-cup-turf-issue.html.

———. "Olympic Committee Moves to Revoke U.S.A. Gymnastics' Governing Body." *New York Times*, November 5, 2018. https://www.nytimes.com/2018/11/05/sports /usa-gymnastics-usoc.html.

———. "Suspension Reduced for Gymnastics Coach Accused of Emotional and Physical Abuse." *New York Times*, December 9, 2020. https://www.nytimes.com/2020/12 /09/sports/olympics/maggie-haney-gymnastics-abuse.html.

MacMullan, Jackie. "NBA and Players Aim to Erase Stigma Surrounding Mental Health." ESPN, March 19, 2018. https://www.espn.com/nba/story/_/id/22806905 /nba-players-aim-erase-stigma-surrounding-mental-health.

Macur, Juliet, and Danielle Allentuck. "Gymnasts Push for Lasting Change after Coach Is Suspended for Abuse." *New York Times*, May 20, 2020. https://www.nytimes.com /2020/05/20/sports/olympics/gymnastics-haney-abuse-safesport.html.

Maese, Rick. "Ohio State Team Doctor Sexually Abused 177 Students over Decades." *Washington Post*, May 17, 2019. https://www.washingtonpost.com/sports/2019/05 /17/ohio-state-team-doctor-sexually-abused-students-over-decades-report-finds/.

———. "Olympics Reform Bill Passes House, Promising Sweeping Change after Abuse Scandals Rocked Sports." *Washington Post*, October 1, 2020. https://www .washingtonpost.com/sports/2020/10/01/olympics-reform-bill-house-abuse/.

———. "Players Union Complains to NFL about Handling of Opioids and Other Drugs." *Washington Post*, May 9, 2017. https://www.washingtonpost.com/sports /redskins/players-union-complains-to-nfl-about-handling-of-opioids-and-other -drugs/2017/05/09/6f638c54-34b6-11e7-b4ee-434b6d506b37_story.html.

Mahdawi, Arwa. "Stalk of the Town: The Shaky Science behind the 'Global Celery Movement.'" *Guardian*, April 9, 2019. https://www.theguardian.com/food/2019/ apr/09/anthony-william-medical-medium-green-celery-juice.

Maske, Mark. "Midway Through Its Season, the NFL Knows Its Biggest Coronavirus Challenges Lie Ahead." *Washington Post*, November 7, 2020. https://www .washingtonpost.com/sports/2020/11/06/nfl-coronavirus-season-schedule/.

———. "Recent NFL Memo to Teams Reinforces Anti-discrimination Policies." *Washington Post*, February 17 2014. https://www.washingtonpost.com/news/ football-insider/wp/2014/02/17/recent-nfl-memo-to-teams-reinforces-anti -discrimination-policies/.

Masling, Sharon. "The Conversation Is Changing for Athletes' Mental Health." *Sports Business Journal*, May 31, 2022. https://www.sportsbusinessjournal.com/SB-Blogs/ COVID19-OpEds/2022/05/31-Masling.aspx.

Mather, Victor. "Antonio Brown's Tumultuous N.F.L. Career." *New York Times*, September 11, 2019; updated January 22, 2020. https://www.nytimes.com/2019/09/11/ sports/football/antonio-brown-career.html.

———. "U.S.A. Gymnastics Cuts Ties with Karolyi Ranch Training Center." *New York Times*, January 18, 2018. https://www.nytimes.com/2018/01/18/sports/usa -gymnastics-karolyi-ranch.html.

McCann, Michael A. "Aaron Hernandez Found Not Guilty of Boston Double Murder: Breaking Down Jury's Decision." *Sports Illustrated*, April 14, 2017. https://www
.si.com/nfl/2017/04/14/aaron-hernandez-not-guilty-boston-murder.
———. "Do You Believe He Can Fly? Royce White and Reasonable Accommodations under the Americans with Disabilities Act for NBA Players with Anxiety Disorder and Fear of Flying." *Pepperdine Law Review* 41, no. 2 (2014). https://
digitalcommons.pepperdine.edu/plr/vol41/iss2/7.
———. "Loaded Questions." *Sports Illustrated*, March 25, 2013.
McGroaty, Neil K., Symone M. Brown, and Mary K. Mulcahey. "Sport-Related Concussion in Female Athletes: A Systematic Review." *Orthopaedic Journal of Sports Medicine* 8, no. 7 (2020). https://doi.org/10.1177/2325967120932306.
McMahon, James. "Ranking the 10 Worst Cases of the Yips in Golf History." *Bleacher Report*, May 29, 2013. https://bleacherreport.com/articles/1654754-ranking-the
-10-worst-cases-of-the-yips-in-golf-history.
McRae, Donald. "'Boxing Is a Mess': The Darkness and Damage of Brain Trauma in the Ring." *Guardian*, May 27, 2021. https://www.theguardian.com/sport/2021/may/27
/time-to-find-out-who-cares-boxing-brain-damage-tris-dixon.
———. *A Man's World: The Double Life of Emile Griffith*. London: Simon and Schuster, 2015.
Medina, Jennifer. "Jason Collins Took Personal Steps before Coming Out Publicly," *New York Times*, April 30, 2013. https://www.nytimes.com/2013/05/01/sports/jason
-collins-took-personal-steps-before-coming-out-publicly.html.
Meister, Alyson, and Maude Lavanchy. "Athletes Are Shifting the Narrative around Mental Health at Work." *Harvard Business Review*, September 24, 2021. https:
//hbr.org/2021/09/athletes-are-shifting-the-narrative-around-mental-health-at
-work.
Mencarini, Matt. "MSU to Pay for Lou Anna Simon's Defense as Legal Bills for Larry Nassar Scandal Near $20M." *Lansing State Journal*, January 23, 2019. https://
www.lansingstatejournal.com/story/news/local/2019/01/23/larry-nassar-lou-anna
-simon-msu-michigan-state-bills/2645371002/.
Mendelsohn, Peter. "'You're Not Alone': How Shayne Corson Found Hope in His Battle with Mental Health." *Athletic*, September 10, 2019. https://theathletic.com
/1183302/2019/09/10/youre-not-alone-how-shayne-corson-found-hope-in-his
-battle-with-mental-health/.
Mihoces, Gary. "NFL Concussion Suit: Becher's Daughter Opted In." *USA Today*, October 13, 2014. https://www.usatoday.com/story/sports/nfl/2014/10/13/nfl
-concussion-suit-belchers-daughter-opted-in/17231511/.
Montaño, Alysia, with Lindsay Crouse. "Nike Told Me to Dream Crazy, Until I Wanted a Baby." *New York Times*, May 12, 2019. https://www.nytimes.com/2019/05/12/
opinion/nike-maternity-leave.html.
Monty602. "Naomi Osaka's Boundary Setting Invokes Memories of Rick Williams' Struggles with Insensitive Media." Canal Street Chronicles, June 7, 2021. https:
//www.canalstreetchronicles.com/2021/6/7/22517607/naomi-osakas-boundary
-setting-invokes-memories-ricky-williams-struggles-insensitive-media.

Murphy, Dan. "Michigan State: NCAA Finds No Rule Violations in Sexual Assault Cases." ESPN, August 30, 2018. https://www.espn.com/college-sports/story/_/id /24523562/michigan-state-says-cleared-violations-larry-nassar-scandal-ncaa.

Nagesh, Ashitha. "Simone Biles: What Are the 'Twisties' in Gymnastics?" BBC, July 29, 2021. https://www.bbc.com/news/world-us-canada-57986166.

National Institute of Aging. "What Happens to the Brain in Alzheimer's Disease?" https: //www.nia.nih.gov/health/what-happens-brain-alzheimers-disease.

National Women's Law Center. "Fulfilling Title IX Promise: Let Transgender and Intersex Students Play." June 14, 2022. https://nwlc.org/resource/fulfilling-title-ixs -promise-let-transgender-and-intersex-students-play/.

NCAA. *NCAA Student-Athlete Well-Being Survey.* May 2022. https://ncaaorg.s3 .amazonaws.com/research/other/2020/2022RES_NCAA-SA-Well-BeingSurvey .pdf.

Neelam, Kishen, Venu Duddu, Nnamdi Anyim, Jyothi Neelam, and Shôn Lewis. "Pandemics and Pre-Existing Mental Illness: A Systematic Review and Meta-Analysis." *Brain, Behavior, and Immunity—Health* (2021). https://doi.org/10.1016/j.bbih .2020.100177.

New York Times Editorial Board. "The Solution to America's Mental Health Crisis Already Exists." *New York Times,* October 4, 2022. https://www.nytimes.com/2022 /10/04/opinion/us-mental-health-community-centers.html.

NFL. "Guardian Cap Debuts at Training Camps League Wide." NFL Player Health and Safety, July 27, 2022. https://www.nfl.com/playerhealthandsafety/equipment -and-innovation/engineering-technology/guardian-cap-debuts-at-training-camps -league-wide.

NFL Communications. "Statement from NFL Commissioner Roger Goodell on Raiders DE Carl Nassib." 2021. https://nflcommunications.com/Pages/Statement-from -NFL-Commissioner-Roger-Goodell-on-Raiders-DE-Carl-Nassib.aspx.

NFL Concussion Settlement website. https://www.nflconcussionsettlement.com. Accessed November 27, 2022.

Nowinski, Chris. "Troubling Trend." *Sports Illustrated,* July 2, 2018. https://vault.si.com/ vault/2018/07/16/troubling-trend.

Ortiz, Erik. "Tiger Wood DUI Arrest: Golfer Had Five Drugs in His System, Toxicology Report Shows." NBC News, August 15, 2017. https://www.nbcnews.com/news/ sports/tiger-woods-dui-arrest-golfer-had-five-drugs-system-toxicology-n792856.

Panja, Tariq. "A #MeToo Wave Hits Global Soccer as the Women's World Cup Begins." *New York Times,* June 7, 2019. https://www.nytimes.com/2019/06/07/sports/metoo -soccer-sexual-harassment.html.

Park, Alice. "Can Anyone Save USA Gymnastics at this Point? New CEO Li Li Leung Is Determined to Try." *Time,* June 13, 2019; updated June 17, 2019. https://time .com/5606251/li-li-leung-usa-gymnastics-interview/.

Parry, John Weston. *The Athlete's Dilemma: Sacrificing Health for Wealth and Fame.* Lanham, MD: Rowman and Littlefield, 2017.

———. *Mental Disability, Violence, and Future Dangerousness: Myths behind the Presumption of Guilt.* Lanham, MD: Rowman and Littlefield, 2013.

Patel, Vimal. "San Jose State to Pay $1.6 Million to 13 Students in Sexual Harassment Case." *New York Times*, September 21, 2021. https://www.nytimes.com/2021/09/21/sports/san-jose-sexual-harassment-settlement.html.

Pells, Eddie. "Sex-Abuse Reports on Rise; SafeSport Center Seeks More Money." AP News, September 17, 2019. https://apnews.com/a154938aef9a4361a7fefbe78442 5fd3.

Pennington, Bill. "To Calm His Jittery Nerves, Keegan Bradley Embraces Them." *New York Times*, July 15, 2016. https://www.nytimes.com/2016/07/16/sports/golf/keegan-bradley-british-open.html.

Piacentino, Daria, Georgios D. Kotzaldis, Antonio Del Casale, Maria Roasaria Aromatario, Cristoforo Pomara, Paolo Girardi, and Gabriele Sani. "Anabolic-Androgenic Steroid Use and Psychopathology in Athletes, A Systematic Review." *Current Neuropharmacology* 13, no. 1 (2015): 101–21. https://doi.org/10.2174/1570159x13666141210222725.

Piastowski, Nick. "Why Brandel Chamblee Sensed Lexi Thompson Was Going to Struggle on Sunday." *GOLF*, June 6, 2021. https://golf.com/news/brandel-chamblee-lexi-thompson-putting/.

Pickman, Ben. "Alberto Salazar Placed on SafeSport's Temporarily Banned List After Alleged Verbal Abuse." *Sports Illustrated*, January 31, 2020. https://www.si.com/track-and-field/2020/02/01/alberto-salazar-safesport-suspension-mary-cain.

Pierce, Scott. "Michael Sam Should Forego Reality TV Show and Concentrate on Football." *Salt Lake Tribune*, May 14, 2014. https://archive.sltrib.com/article.php?id=57944506&itype=CMSID.

Pilon, Mary, and Ken Belson. "Seau Suffered from Brain Disease." *New York Times*, January 10, 2013. https://www.nytimes.com/2013/01/11/sports/football/junior-seau-suffered-from-brain-disease.html.

Pompey, Keith, "Something Obviously Bothers Sixers Rookie Markelle Fultz That Has Nothing to Do with His Shoulder." *Philadelphia Inquirer*, February 18, 2018. https://www.inquirer.com/philly/sports/sixers/sixers-markelle-fultz-shoulder-shot-hitch-mental-injury-bryan-colangelo-20180210.html.

Pope, Ben. "Jonathan Toews Rejoins Blackhawks as Training Camp Begins: 'It's a Good Feeling.'" *Chicago Sun-Times*, September 23, 2021. https://chicago.suntimes.com/blackhawks/2021/9/23/22690224/jonathan-toews-blackhawks-returns-training-camp-covid-cirs-nhl.

Pope, S. W. *Patriotic Games: Sporting Traditions in the American Imagination, 1876–1926*. New York: Oxford University Press, 1997.

Popke, Michael. "Can a Player's Posthumous Diagnosis of CTE Convince Soccer to Take Precautions?" Sports Destination Management, July 18, 2022. https://www.sportsdestinations.com/sports/soccer/can-players-posthumous-diagnosis-cte-convince-30560.

Price, S. L. "Moment of Truth." *Sports Illustrated*, February 17, 2014. https://vault.si.com/vault/2014/02/17/moment-of-truth.

Rafael, Dan. "Orlando Cruz a 'Proud Gay Man.'" ESPN, October 5, 2012. https://www
.espn.com/boxing/story/_/id/8460484/puerto-rican-featherweight-orlando-cruz
-comes-proud-gay-man.

Reardon, Claudia L, and Shane Creado. "Drug Abuse in Athletes" *Substance Abuse Rehabilitation* 5 (2014): 95–105. https://doi.org/10.2147%2FSAR.S53784.

Reardon, Claudia L., Abhinav Bindra, Cheri Blauwet, Richard Budgett, Niccolo Cam-
priani, Alan Currie, Vincent Gouttebarge, David McDuff, Margo Mountjoy,
Rosemary Purcell, Margot Putukian, Simon Rice, and Brian Hainline. "Mental
Health Management of Elite Athletes during COVID-19: A Narrative Review
and Recommendations." *British Journal of Sports Medicine* (2020). https://doi.org
/10.1136/bjsports-2020-102884.

Reid, Jason. "Is the NFL Ready for Michael Sam?" *Washington Post*, February 20, 2014,
https://www.washingtonpost.com/sports/redskins/is-the-nfl-ready-for-michael
-sam/2014/02/20/85858a0c-9a48-11e3-b931-0204122c514b_story.html.

Reid, Scott M. "Delays in Maggie Haney Case by USA Gymnastics Have Both Sides
Upset." *Orange County Register*, October 25, 2019. https://www.ocregister.com
/2020/04/23/usa-gymnastics-mistake-in-maggie-haney-abuse-case-leads-to-more
-frustration/.

———. "UC Berkeley Swimmers Allege Coach Teri McKeever Bullied and Verbally
Abused Them for Years." *Orange County Register*, May 24, 2022. https://www
.ocregister.com/2022/05/24/cal-swimmers-allege-coach-teri-mckeever-bullied
-and-verbally-abused-them-for-years/.

Reimer, Alex. "Collin Martin Says He Had Mixed Feelings When His Team Forfeited
a Game after He Was Called an Anti-Gay Slur." *OutSports*, June 30, 2022. https:
//www.outsports.com/2022/6/30/23189758/collin-martin-san-diego-loyal-soccer
-gay-slur.

———. "Delonte West's Mental Illness, Once Treated as a Joke, Was Never a Laughing
Matter." *Forbes*, January 21, 2020. https://www.forbes.com/sites/alexreimer/2020
/01/21/delonte-wests-mental-illness-used-to-elicit-laughs/.

Reuters Staff. "54 Days without a Positive Covid Test." October 23, 2020. https://www
.reuters.com/article/us-baseball-mlb-covid-19-testing-idUSKBN2782CT.

Revegno, Lindsay, "Athletes Often Forced into Heartbreaking Decisions," ESPN, May
13, 2007.

Rhoden, William C. "In Putting the Team First, Players Put Themselves at Risk." *New
York Times*, October 24, 2015. https://www.nytimes.com/2015/10/25/sports/
baseball/in-putting-the-team-first-players-put-themselves-at-risk.html.

———. "In Report on Bullying, the Vile and the Gripping." *New York Times*, February 15, 2014. https://www.nytimes.com/2014/02/16/sports/football/in-report-on
-bullying-the-vile-and-the-gripping.html.

———. "Michael Sam Has a Spot in History, If Not with the Rams." *New York Times*,
August 30, 2014. https://www.nytimes.com/2014/08/31/sports/football/michael
-sam-still-an-inspiration-after-his-release.html.

———. "On the Court, Finding an Outlet, and a Voice." *New York Times*, February 26, 2012, https://www.nytimes.com/2012/02/27/sports/basketball/chamique-holdsclaw-is-sharing-her-struggles-off-the-court.html.

Rich, Motoko, and Matthew Futterman. "Despite Uncertainly Olympics Promoted as Light at the End of the Pandemic Tunnel." *New York Times*, November 19, 2020. https://www.nytimes.com/2020/11/19/sports/olympics/tokyo-olympics-covid-postponed.html.

Ritter, Aaron, Guogen Shan, Arturo Montes, Rebekah Randall, and Charles Bernick. "Traumatic Encephalopathy Syndrome: Application of New Criteria to a Cohort Exposed to Repetitive Head Impacts." *British Journal of Sports Medicine* 57, no. 7 (2023): 389–94. https://doi.org/10.1136/bjsports-2022-105819.

Rogers, Katie. "Biden Plan for Transgender Title IX Rules Began on Inauguration Day." *New York Times*, April 7, 2023. https://www.nytimes.com/2023/04/07/us/politics/transgender-athletes-schools-title-ix.html.

Rohan, Tim. "For Football's Sake, Closely Guarding Sexual Orientation." *New York Times*, June 9, 2012. https://www.nytimes.com/2012/06/10/sports/football/for-footballs-sake-closely-guarding-sexual-orientation.html.

Rosenberg, Michael. "Sportswashing Is Everywhere, but It's Not New." *Sports Illustrated*, December 29, 2022. https://www.si.com/olympics/2022/12/29/sportswashing-olympics-world-cup-daily-cover.

Ruiz, Rebecca R., and Mathew Futterman. "Scott Blackmun Steps Down as Head of U.S.O.C. Under Pressure from Nassar Case." *New York Times*, February 28, 2018. https://www.nytimes.com/2018/02/28/sports/scott-blackmun-usoc-nassar.html.

Sandomir, Richard. "Curt Schilling, ESPN Analyst, Is Fired over Offensive Social Media Post." *New York Times*, April 20, 2016. https://www.nytimes.com/2016/04/21/sports/baseball/curt-schilling-is-fired-by-espn.html.

———. "O.J. Who? Rogues Vanish from Annals of Sport." *New York Times*, January 5, 2014. https://www.nytimes.com/2014/01/06/sports/ncaafootball/oj-who-rogues-vanish-from-annals-of-sport.html.

Santora, Marc, and Judy Battista. "Chiefs Player Kills Woman and, at Stadium, Himself." *New York Times*, December 2, 2012. https://www.nytimes.com/2012/12/02/sports/football/police-chiefs-player-shot.html.

Sarris, Eno. "How Does COVID Impact MLB Players' Performance? What Athletes, Trainers and the Stats Say" *Athletic*, August 26, 2022. https://theathletic.com/3488516/2022/08/26/mlb-players-covid-return-effects/.

Saul, Stephanie. "Calls Grow for Michigan State University President to Resign over Nassar Case." *New York Times*, January 19, 2018. https://www.nytimes.com/2018/01/19/us/michigan-state-nassar.html.

Schad, Chris. "Aaron Rodgers Explains Why He Chose to Say He Was 'Immunized' over Vaccinated." *Sports Illustrated*, August 28, 2022. https://www.si.com/fannation/bringmethesports/nfl-news-and-rumors/aaron-rodgers-explains-why-he-chose-to-say-he-was-immunized-over-unvaccinated.

Schiavenza, Matt. "The Tragic Legacy of Junior Seau." *Atlantic*, August 9, 2015. https://www.theatlantic.com/entertainment/archive/2015/08/the-tragic-legacy-of-junior-seau/400856/.

Schudel, Matt. "H. Wayne Huizinga, Florida Billionaire and Sports Franchise Owner, Dies at 80." *Washington Post*, March 23, 2018. https://www.washingtonpost.com/local/obituaries/h-wayne-huizenga-florida-billionaire-and-sports-franchise-owner-dies-at-80/2018/03/23/813dfafc-2eae-11e8-8ad6-fbc50284fce8_story.html.

Schwartz, Alan. "Duerson's Brain Trauma Diagnosed." *New York Times*, May 2, 2011. https://www.nytimes.com/2011/05/03/sports/football/03duerson.html.

———. "Hockey Brawler Paid Price, with Brain Trauma." *New York Times*, March 2, 2011. https://www.nytimes.com/2011/03/03/sports/hockey/03fighter.html.

Sears, Ted. "The Dreaded Subdural Hematoma." *The Sweet Science*, July 12, 2022. https://tss.ib.tv/boxing/featured-boxing-articles-boxing-news-videos-rankings-and-results/73338-the-dreaded-subdural-hematoma.

Seattle Times. "Coaches Who Prey." Special Section, December 14–17, 2003. https://special.seattletimes.com/o/news/local/coaches/index.html.

Seifert, Kevin. "NFL Says Regular Season Concussions Increased 18 Percent in 2022," ESPN, February 3, 2023. https://www.espn.com/nfl/story/_/id/35582897/nfl-says-regular-season-concussions-increased-18-2022.

Sheridan, Chris. "Amaechi Becomes First NBA Player to Come Out." ESPN, February 9, 2007. https://www.espn.com/nba/news/story/_/id/2757105.

Shore, Rebecca. "Flying with Ease." *Sports Illustrated*, July 9, 2012. https://vault.si.com/vault/2012/07/09/flying-with-ease.

Shutdown Corner. "Saints Linebacker Jonathan Vilma Clarifies Homophobic Views Prior to Michael Sam's Announcement." Yahoo News, February 11, 2014. https://news.yahoo.com/blogs/nfl-shutdown-corner/saints-linebacker-jonathan-vilma-clarifies-homophobic-views-prior-151112471--nfl.html.

SI Wire. "Hall of Fame Won't Allow Junior Seau's Family to Speak at His Induction." *Sports Illustrated*, July 24, 2015. https://www.si.com/nfl/2015/07/24/junior-seau-hall-of-fame-induction-family-speech.

Sissons, Claire. "How Much Blood Is in the Human Body?" *Medical News Today*, updated February 14, 2023. https://www.medicalnewstoday.com/articles/321122.

Siwak, Miranda. "Hope Solo Voluntarily Enters In-Patient Alcohol Treatment after Arrest." *Us Weekly*, April 30, 2022. https://www.usmagazine.com/celebrity-news/news/hope-solo-enters-in-patient-alcohol-treatment-after-dui-arrest/.

Smith, Doug. "Raptors' DeRozan Hopes Honest Talk on Depression Helps Others." *Toronto Star*, February 26, 2018. https://www.thestar.com/sports/raptors/2018/02/25/raptors-derozan-hopes-honest-talk-on-depression-helps-others.html.

Smith, Gary. "Stand Up and Speak Out." *Sports Illustrated*, December 17, 2012. https://vault.si.com/vault/2012/12/17/stand-up-speak-out.

Smith, Rory. "Does Soccer Still Need the Header?" *New York Times*, July 23, 2022. https://www.nytimes.com/2022/07/22/sports/soccer/soccer-headers.html.

Sneed, Brandon. "Rex Chapman Isn't Sure He Deserves Good Things." *New York Times*, April 4, 2015. https://www.nytimes.com/2022/04/04/sports/basketball/rex -chapman-cnn-basketball.html.

Snowbeck, Christopher. "Behind Bradshaw's Bravado Was Depression." *Pittsburgh Post-Gazette*, October 28, 2003. https://www.post-gazette.com/news/health/2003 /10/28/Behind-Bradshaw-s-bravado-was-depression/stories/200310280062.

Sobel, Jason, "Bradley Can Relate to Na's Slow Play Backlash." GOLF Channel, May 15, 2012. https://www.golfchannel.com/news/keegan-bradley-can-relate-kevin-nas -slow-play-backlash.

Solari, Chris. "Michigan State Athletic Director Mark Hollis Resigns in Wake of Larry Nassar Scandal." *Detroit Free Press*, January 26, 2018. https://www.freep.com/story /sports/college/michigan-state/spartans/2018/01/26/michigan-state-university -mark-hollis-resigns/1068989001/.

Sorensen, Elizabeth A. "Debunking the Myth of Pregnancy Doping." *Journal of Intercollegiate Sport* 2, no. 2 (2009): 269–85. https://doi.org/10.1123/jis.2.2.269.

Steinberg, Dan. "Dexter Manley Apologizes for Insulting Troy Aikman on WTOP (updated)." *Washington Post*, October 28, 2013. https://www.washingtonpost.com/ news/dc-sports-bog/wp/2013/10/28/dexter-manley-insults-troy-aikman-on-wtop /.

Stevens, Matt. "2 U.S.A. Swimming Officials Resign amid Accusations of Ignored Abuse." *New York Times*, Februuary 24, 2018. https://www.nytimes.com/2018/02 /24/sports/usa-swimming-resignations.html.

Streeter, Kurt. "Female Soccer Players Are Done Taking Abuse. Let's Stop Dishing It Out." *New York Times*, October 8, 2021. https://www.nytimes.com/2021/10/03/ sports/soccer/women-soccer-league-abuse.html.

———. "Markelle Fultz's Lonely Search for His Jump Shot." *New York Times*, March 9, 2018. https://www.nytimes.com/2018/03/09/sports/basketball/markelle-fultz -philadelphia-76ers.html.

———. "Tiger Woods and Another Terrible Turn of Fate." *New York Times*, April 9, 2021. https://www.nytimes.com/2021/02/25/sports/golf/tiger-woods-accident .html.

Strong, James. "Adrian Peterson, Christianity and Child Abuse." *Birmingham Times*, October 9, 2014. https://www.birminghamtimes.com/2014/10/adrian-peterson -christianity-and-child-abuse-2/.

Stubbs, Roman. "As Transgender Rights Debate Spills into Sports, One Runner Finds Herself at the Center of a Pivotal Case." *Washington Post*, July 27, 2020. https: //www.washingtonpost.com/sports/2020/07/27/idaho-transgender-sports-lawsuit -hecox-v-little-hb-500/.

Substance Abuse and Mental Health Services Administration. "Mental Health and Substance Use Disorders." https://www.samhsa.gov/find-help/disorders. Accessed January 18, 2023.

Sullivan, Matthew. "'I've Heard It All': Shaq Questions Simmons' Mental Health Battle in Brutal Swipe." Fox Sports, February 17, 2022. https://www.foxsports.com.au/

basketball/nba/ive-seen-real-mental-health-shaquille-oneal-blasts-ben-simmons/
news-story/fd0d783f423e274c0b090f592849ec23.

Svrluga, Barry. "In North Carolina, Sticking to Sports Means Confronting Controversial
Law." *Washington Post*, February 8, 2017. https://www.washingtonpost.com/sports
/colleges/in-north-carolina-sticking-to-sports-means-confronting-controversial
-law/2017/02/08/c39fb43c-ee34-11e6-b4ff-ac2cf509efe5_story.html.

Szekely, Peter. "Ex-Ohio State Wrestlers Sue School Claiming It Ignored Sexual Abuse."
Reuters, July 17, 2018. https://www.reuters.com/article/us-wrestling-ohio-lawsuit
-idUSKBN1K72F7.

Taylor, Phil. "Act of Intolerance." *Sports Illustrated*, January 13, 2014. https://vault.si.com
/vault/2014/01/13/act-of-intolerance.

———. "A Storm That May Not Come," *Sports Illustrated*, April 15, 2013. https://vault
.si.com/vault/2013/04/15/a-storm-that-may-not-come.

Teng, Elaine. "Figure Skater Vincent Zhou Worked His Whole Life for the Beijing
Olympics. COVID-19 Had Other Plans." ESPN, March 24, 2022. https://www
.espn.com/olympics/story/_/id/33216401/figure-skater-vincent-zhou-worked
-whole-life-beijing-olympics-covid-19-had-other-plans.

Thamel, Pete, and Greg Bedard. "A Murder in Massachusetts." *Sports Illustrated*, July 1,
2013. https://vault.si.com/vault/2013/07/01/a-murder-in-massachusetts.

Thomas, Louisa. "A Year That Changed How Athletes Think about Mental Health." *New
Yorker*, December 20, 2021. https://www.newyorker.com/culture/2021-in-review/a
-year-that-changed-how-athletes-think-about-mental-health.

Thomas, Summer-Solstice. "It Could Have Been Me: The NCAA Must Do More to
Protect Student-Athletes from Sexual Abuse." *Fortune*, November 3, 2021. https://
fortune.com/2021/11/03/ncaa-sexual-abuse-student-athletes/.

Thompson, Jaylon. "Chicago Blackhawks Captain Steps Away from Team Due to Long
COVID Symptoms." *USA Today*, February 20, 2023. https://www.usatoday.com
/story/sports/nhl/blackhawks/2023/02/20/jonathan-toews-steps-away-chicago
-blackhawks-due-long-covid/11303922002/.

Thompson, Phil. "Jonathan Toews Asks for 'Patience' as He Struggles with COVID
and CIRS Symptoms." *Chicago Tribune*, February 19, 2023. https://www
.chicagotribune.com/sports/blackhawks/ct-chicago-blackhawks-jonathan-toews
-illness-20230219-iujaul45gzfppgd3sarugfa3gq-story.html.

Thurston, Andrew, and Gina Digravio. "8 Major Findings and Headlines from BU CTE
Researchers in the Past Year." Boston University, May 24, 2022. https://www.bu
.edu/articles/2022/8-major-findings-from-bu-cte-researchers-last-year/.

Today. "Simone Biles: I'm Trying to Navigate My Own Unique Mental Health Journey." October 21, 2021. https://www.today.com/video/simone-biles-i-m-trying-to
-navigate-my-own-unique-mental-health-journey-124255813897.

Toronto Star Editorial Board. "How to Reduce Brain Injuries in Youth Hockey." *Toronto
Star*, October 9, 2022. https://www.thestar.com/opinion/editorials/2022/10/09/
how-to-reduce-brain-injuries-in-youth-hockey.html.

Tracy, Marc. "N.C.A.A. Ends Boycott of North Carolina after So-Called Bathroom Bill Is Repealed." *New York Times*, April 4, 2017. https://www.nytimes.com/2017/04/04/sports/ncaa-hb2-north-carolina-boycott-bathroom-bill.html.

Traina, Jimmy. "Star NFL Players' Lack of Public Support for Carl Nassib Was Disappointing." *Sports Illustrated*, June 22, 2021. https://www.si.com/extra-mustard/2021/06/22/nfl-star-players-silent-on-carl-nassib-coming-out-as-gay.

Triplett, Mike. "Vilma Clarifies His Opinion of a Gay Teammate," ESPN, February 10, 2014. https://www.espn.com/blog/new-orleans-saints/post/_/id/5057/vilma-clarifies-opinion-on-accepting-gay-teammate.

Tufekci, Zeynep. "If You're Suffering after Being Sick with COVID, It's Not Just in Your Head." *New York Times*, August 25, 2022. https://www.nytimes.com/2022/08/25/opinion/long-covid-pandemic.html.

Umeri, Sydney. "How Elite Athletes Have Struggled with the Long-Term Effects of COVID." SB Nation, March 3, 2021. https://www.sbnation.com/nba/2021/3/3/22292213/athletes-covid-recovery-stories-jayson-tatum-mo-bamba-asia-durr.

US Department of Education. "Fact Sheet: U.S. Department of Education's Proposed Change to Its Title IX Regulations on Students' Eligibility for Athletic Teams." April 6, 2023. https://www.ed.gov/news/press-releases/fact-sheet-us-department-educations-proposed-change-its-title-ix-regulations-students-eligibility-athletic-teams.

Vensel, Matt. "Depressed Duchscherer Is "a Soft Guy in a Profession of Hard Guys.'" *Baltimore Sun*, April 14, 2011. https://www.baltimoresun.com/sports/bal-sportsblitz-duchscherer-depression0414-story.html.

Viloria, Hida. "Stop Trying to Make Caster Semenya Fit a Narrow Idea of Womanhood. It's Unscientific and Unethical." *Washington Post*, May 3, 2019. https://www.washingtonpost.com/opinions/2019/05/03/stop-trying-make-caster-semenya-fit-narrow-idea-womanhood-its-unscientific-unethical/.

Wadman, Meredith. "COVID-19 Patients Face Higher Risks of Brain Fog and Depression, Even 1 Year after Infection." *Science*, February 16, 2022. https://www.science.org/content/article/covid-19-patients-face-higher-risk-brain-fog-and-depression-even-1-year-after-infection.

Wahl, Grant. "Out and About." *Sports Illustrated*, May 13, 2013. https://vault.si.com/vault/2013/05/13/out-and-about.

Walstein, David. "Hiding from Yips Will Only Make It Worse." *New York Times*, July 26, 2023. https://www.nytimes.com/2023/07/26/sports/baseball/yips-eileen-canney-linnehan.html.

Walters, Anne S. "Female Athletes and Mental Health: An Under-Resourced Relationship." *Brown University Child and Adolescent Letter*, September 6, 2021, https://doi.org/10.1002/cbl.30579.

Washington Post Editorial Board. "Abuse of Women's Soccer Players Is a Sadly Familiar Story." *Washington Post*, October 5, 2022. https://www.washingtonpost.com/opinions/2022/10/05/womens-soccer-abuse-report-sally-yates/.

———. "Opinion: Long COVID Continues to Haunt Millions of People." *Washington Post*, February 8, 2023. https://www.washingtonpost.com/opinions/2023/02/08/long-covid-challenges-economy-health-care/.

Watkins, Calvin. "John Lucas Disagrees with Steve Kerr's Thoughts on Marijuana Use for Pain." ESPN, December 5, 2016. https://www.espn.com/blog/houston-rockets/post/_/id/3201/john-lucas-disagrees-with-steve-kerrs-thoughts-on-marijuana-use-for-pain.

Weinreb, Michael. "The Day Innocence Died." ESPN. http://www.espn.com/espn/eticket/story?page=bias&redirected=true. Accessed January 23, 2023.

Weintraub, Robert "Play (Hard) Ball: Why the Sports Beat Must Evolve." *Columbia Journalism Review*, September/October 2017. https://archives.cjr.org/feature/play_hard_ball.php.

Wertheim, Jon. "Prisoners of Depression." *Sports Illustrated*, September 8, 2003, https://vault.si.com/vault/2003/09/08/prisoners-of-depression-mental-illness-still-carries-a-powerful-stigma-in-pro-sports-but-there-are-signs-that-teams-are-finally-facing-the-problem-and-trying-to-help-troubled-athletes.

Whitlock, Jason. "Dungy Wrong about Michael Sam." ESPN, July 25, 2014. https://www.espn.com/nfl/story/_/id/11252669/tony-dungy-michael-sam-nfl.

Wigdor, Douglas. "Statute of Limitations on Sexual Assault Eliminated for One Year in New York Following Passage of the Adult Survivors Act." *Forbes*, May 25, 2022. https://www.forbes.com/sites/douglaswigdor/2022/05/25/statute-of-limitations-on-sexual-assault-eliminated-for-one-year-in-new-york-following-passage-of-the-adult-survivors-act/?sh=45e988a546fd.

Williams, Anthony. "Cilantro—Life Changing Food." Medical Medium, February 11, 2021. https://www.medicalmedium.com/blog/cilantro-life-changing-food.

Wine, Steven. "Serena Williams Says Naomi Osaka Must Find Her Own Way to Handle Media Scrutiny," *Chicago Sun-Times*, June 1, 2021. https://chicago.suntimes.com/2021/6/1/22463063/serena-williams-naomi-osaka-must-find-her-own-way-to-handle-media-scrutiny.

Wise, Mike. "Critics Should Practice What They Preach." *Washington Post*, April 30, 2013.

———. "Dave Kopay Knows What Questions Should Be Asked by NFL." *Washington Post*, March 2, 2013. https://www.washingtonpost.com/sports/redskins/dave-kopay-knows-what-questions-should-be-asked-by-nfl/2013/03/02/2a12ebd2-82c1-11e2-b99e-6baf4ebe42df_story.html.

———. "Jason Collins's Religious Critics Need to Practice What They Preach." *Washington Post*, April 30, 2013. https://www.washingtonpost.com/sports/wizards/jason-collins-religious-critics-need-to-practice-what-they-preach/2013/04/30/3129e752-b1df-11e2-9a98-4be1688d7d84_story.html.

Withiam, Hannah. "Abby Wambach's New Life after Drug, Alcohol Rock Bottom." *New York Post*, March 21, 2018. https://nypost.com/2018/03/21/abby-wambachs-found-peace-purpose-in-drug-free-life-after-soccer/.

Witz, Billy "As Women's Basketball Grows, Equity Is Trying to Catch Up." *New York Times*, March 29, 2023. https://www.nytimes.com/2023/03/29/sports/ncaabasketball/womens-basketball-equity.html.

Wolke, Dan. "Bucks Assistant Vin Baker Lost Millions to Addiction, Found Salvation in a Starbucks." *Los Angeles Times*, July 10, 2021. https://www.latimes.com/sports/story/2021-07-10/bucks-vin-baker-redemption-story-addiction-lost-millions.

Xie, Xan, Evan Xu, and Ziyad Aly-Aly. "Risks of Mental Health Outcomes in People with Covid-19: Cohort Study." *BMJ*, February 16, 2022. https://doi.org/10.1136/bmj-2021-068993.

Yancey-Bragg, N'dea. "1 in 4 College Athletes Say They Experienced Sexual Abuse from an Authority Figure, Survey Finds." *USA Today*, August 26, 2021. https://www.usatoday.com/story/news/nation/2021/08/26/college-athlete-report-sexual-assault-common-survey/8253766002/.

Yates, Sally Q. *Report of the Independent Investigation of the U.S. Soccer Federation Concerning Allegations of Abusive Behavior and Sexual Misconduct in Women's Professional Soccer.* King and Spalding, October 3, 2022. https://assets.bwbx.io/documents/users/iqjWHBFdfxIU/rkHnb7fgThLU/v0.

Yahoo Sport Australia. "'I Cried for Days': Djokovic Reveals 'Guilt' of Elbow Surgery." November 9, 2018. https://au.sports.yahoo.com/cried-days-djokovic-reveals-guilt-elbow-surgery-110236103.html.

Young, Shalise Manza. "Florida Basketball Abuse Is Latest Example of How Women Athletes Are Constantly Betrayed by Those Expected to Protect." Yahoo Sports, September 27, 2021. https://uk.news.yahoo.com/florida-basketball-abuse-is-latest-example-of-how-women-athletes-are-constantly-betrayed-by-those-expected-to-protect-001553116.html.

Zagorski, Nick. "Misuse of Steroids, Other Performance Enhancers Slips under Radar." *Psychiatric News*, Feb. 24, 2022. https://doi.org/10.1176/appi.pn.2022.03.10.42.

Zakrzewski, Cat, and Lauren Weber. "COVID Misinformation Spikes in the Wake of Damar Hamlin's On-Field Collapse." *Washington Post*, January 4, 2023. https://www.washingtonpost.com/technology/2023/01/03/covid-misinfo-damar-hamlin-collapse/.

Zaldivar, Gabe. "Team USA Goalkeeper Hope Solo Admits to Being Drunk on 'Today' Show." *Bleacher Report*, July 13, 2012. https://bleacherreport.com/articles/1257664-team-usa-goalkeeper-hope-solo-admits-to-being-drunk-on-today-show.

Zirin, Dave. "Jovan Belcher's Murder-Suicide: Did the Kansas City Chiefs Pull the Trigger?" *Nation*, January 6, 2014. https://www.thenation.com/article/archive/jovan-belchers-murder-suicide-did-kansas-city-chiefs-pull-trigger/.

Index

Beljan, Charlie, 71–72
Bell, Travis, 144
Belson, Ken, 275, 286–89, 303–4
benefit packages, 3
Bettman, Gary, 131–33
Beyond Belief, 165
bias, 11
Bias, Len, 163–64
Biden administration, 242, 244, 255
Biles, Simone, 3, 64, 77, 80–82, 195, 239
"bingeing and purging," 56
bipolar disorder, 5, 35, 45, 50; diagnosis of, 46
Bird, Larry, 163
Bird, Sue, 225
Biscotti, Steve, 218
bisexual, 226. *See also* LGBTQ+ athletes
Blackistone, Kevin, 130, 295
Blackmun, Scott, 192, 194
blame, 4
Blatter, Sepp, 182
Bleacher Report, 50, 70
blood-brain barrier, 264
blood clots, 249
body: fat, 237; image, 64
bodybuilders, 161
body checking, in hockey, 130
Boitano, Brian, 230
Bolt, Usain, 246
Boogaard, Derek, 139, 158, 163
Borden, Sam, 226, 228, 294, 305

Boston Athletic Association (BAA), 184
Bountygate, 119, 220
"Bountygate," 12
boxing, brain damage in, 2
Bradley, Keegan, 64, 72–73
Bradshaw, Terry, 47–48
Brady, Tom, 146, 239
brain: COVID and, 97; damage, 2–3, 12–14, 23, 89, 98, 111–52, 156, 161, 264; development, 124; fog, 88, 101; impacts, 113; injury, 33, 111; surgery, 217; trauma, 32, 35, 114, 119
Brain, Behavior and Immunity—Health, 99
breath, shortness of, 88
Brinton, Sam, 255
British Journal of Sports Medicine, 99, 114
"Brotherly Love," 277
Broussard, Chris, 215
Brown, Antonio, 145–47
Brown, Jerry, 189
Brown, Larry, 56, 279
Brown, Ronnie, 167
Brown, Sacha, 52
Bruni, Frank, 214, 302
Bryant, Howard, 213, 295, 302
Bryant, Kobe, 215
Buck, Joe, 217
"Built & Broken," 161
bullying, 4, 40, 120; of LGBTQ+ athletes, 32
burnout, 20

misogyny and discrimination with, 180–82; pregnancy and abortion in, 182–86; sexual abuse of, 23, 32, 186–201
feminization, 268
Fetterman, John, 2
"Figure Skater Vincent Zhou Worked His Whole Life," 284
Fisher, Jeff, 223
flexibility, 237
football, 2; aggressive and violent tactics in, 117–21; Christianity in, 32; dangers, 121–28; as most dangerous sport, 118; safety, 123; tackle, 26, 121–25; violence in, 119. *See also* National Football League
Football Physics, 124
Fortier, Sam, 119, 286
Forward, 172
Foster, Justin, 10
Foxworth, Domonique, 14
Frazier, Leslie, 219
Freel, Ryan, 140
Frontline, 29
The Full Send Podcast, 147
Fultz, Markelle, 75

Gaines, Riley, 256
gambling, 18
Gay, Tim, 124
Gay Pride events, 212, 230, 271
gender: advantages, 239; binary, 236; discrimination, 177–80, 248, 258; identification, 235;

identity, 177–78, 244, 255; tokenism, 181
gender-affirming surgery, 247
genetics, 258
genital: mutilation, 252; surgery, 249
"getting high," 156–57
Gifford, Frank, 119
Goodell, Roger, 125, 129, 216, 218, 220, 224
Granderson, L. Z., 212
Griffin, Chad, 245
Griffith, Emile, 226
Grimsley, John, 136–37
Griner, Brittney, 42, 227–29
Gruden, John, 218
Gu, Eileen, 27
Guardian Cap, 124, 145–46; evidence of, 125; helmet shield, 117; methodology, 126; in NFL, 125–28; preliminary results for, 126–28
gun: possession, 50; violence, 59

hallucinations, 160
Hamilton, Josh, 164–65
Hamlin, Damar, 32–33, 96, 124
"Hamlin's Injury Highlights Precarious Position of Many Young NFL Players," 275
Haney, Maggie, 197, 202
harassment, 219; of LGBTQ+ athletes, 32
Hard Knocks, 222
Harnisch, Pete, 46–47, 51

Harris, C. J., 159
Harris, Kwame, 217
Harrison, James, 147
Hatchell, Sylvia, 202–3
head. *See* brain
headaches, 111, 143
"head case," 10–11, 41–42, 98
healthcare: for athletes, 10; for
    former athletes, 14; lifetime,
    14–15; mental, 31, 43
health incentives, 267
heart: condition, 33, 96–97;
    failure, 139
Hecox, Lindsay, 255
helmets: improved, 121; shield,
    117. *See also* Guardian Cap
Henry, Chris, 137
Hernandez, Aaron, 141–44
heroin, 170
Hesse, Monica, 251, 309
Heyward, Cameron, 125
Hibbert, Roy, 75, 213
Higgins, Tee, 96
higher education, 18
Hippocratic oath, 157
Hirshland, Sarah, 194–95
HIV positive, 229
Hobson, Will, 122, 197, 276, 287,
    291, 296–300
hockey, 2; aggressive and violent
    tactics in, 117–21; body
    checking in, 130; CTE in,
    130–33; dangers, 130–33;
    NHL, 130
Holdsclaw, Chamique, 49–50

Hollis, Mark, 199
"homers," 28
homicide, 141
homophobia, 6, 177, 178, 266,
    271; attitudes about, 234; in
    Christianity, 210, 219, 223,
    227; justification of, 26; in
    male wrestling, 230; overt, 215;
    sports, 209–34
hormone, 236; levels, 258;
    suppressants, 252; testing,
    255. *See also* testosterone
Howe, P. David, 10, 275
Huizinga, Wayne, 41
human rights violations, 26–30
Hunter, Tab, 46
hydrocodone, 155
hyperandrogenism, 246

IAAF. *See* International
    Association of Athletics
    Federations
ignorance, 3, 262
illegal drugs, 154
inclusion, 177, 239
Incognito, Richie, 54
incompetence, 262
injuries: catastrophic, 14; knee,
    237; management of, 5;
    psychological response to, 40;
    repeated, 10; risk of, 33; sports-
    related, 2; substance abuse and,
    154–60. *See also* brain; chronic
    traumatic encephalopathy;
    traumatic brain injury

injury prone, 10
institutions, 18, 45
International Association
of Athletics Federations
(IAAF), 167
International Olympic Committee
(IOC), 95, 240
intersex athletes, 6, 177, 178,
236–37, 247–52, 266; allowed
in competition, 257–59;
athlete narratives, 253–57;
definition, 235; female-
identifying, 241; LGBTQ+
discrimination law, 244–46;
unfair competitive advantage
and related restrictions, 238–44;
women, 257
*In the Water They Can't See You
Cry*, 53
IOC. *See* International Olympic
Committee
Irving, Kyrie, 3, 78, 90, 103–5, 270

Jackson, Vincent, 145
James, LeBron, 51, 239
Jansen, Kenley, 102
Jenkins, Sally, 49, 120, 157, 206,
277–78, 284–86, 291, 301
Jenner, Bruce, 253
Jenner, Caitlyn, 253
Johnson, Magic, 163
Jones, Byron, 157
Jordan, Jim, 231
Jordan, Michael, 163, 245
journalism, 29

Journal of Affective Disorders, 100
Journal of Intercollegiate Sport, 185
Jovanovic, Pavle, 144

Karolyi, Bela, 194
Karolyi, Martha, 194
Kerr, Steve, 160
Kessel, Amanda, 143–44
Kick, Charlie, 97
Kilgore, Adam, 67, 280, 286
King, Billie Jean, 230
Klages, Kathie, 190, 192, 199
Kluwe, Chris, 218–20
Kopay, Dave, 212
Kornheiser, Tony, 53
Krzyzewski, Mike, 245

labor relations, 18
Ladies Professional Golf
Association (LPGA), 73
laissez-faire approach, 18
language deficits, 112
La Russa, Tony, 66
law enforcement, 18
Lawrence, DeMarcus, 222
Lawrence, Trevor, 92
lawsuits, 115–16; class action, 264
Lee, Michael, 103, 279, 283, 302
legal fictions, 17–18
legal privileges, 263
legal status, of sports
organizations, 268–69
legal system: American, 8; colleges
and, 23–24; favored treatment
from, 17; favors spectator

Robinson, Jackie, 214, 225, 271
Rodgers, Aaron, 90, 96, 104, 217
Roe v. Wade, 185
Rogers, Aaron, 103
Rogers, Robbie, 226–27
roid rage, 161–62
Rolling Stone, 231
Rose, Pete, 140
Rousey, Ronda, 56–57, 63
"Rousey Disease," 56
Russia, 229–30
Ryan, Greg, 168
Rypien, Rick, 139

Sabalenka, Aryna, 61
safety, threat to, 64
salaries, 264
Salazar, Alberto, 201
Salt Lake Tribune, 222
Sam, Michael, 212–24
Sandomir, Richard, 129, 287, 301
Sandusky, Jerry, 190
Sauerbrunn, Becky, 206
scandals, 28, 30, 118
Schembechler, Bo, 233
Schilling, Curt, 211
Schmitt, Allison, 57–58
scholarships, 13, 18
Schwarzenegger, Arnold, 161
Science, 100
Scientific American, 182
Scurry, Briana, 137–38
Seattle Times, 187
Seau, Junior, 128, 140–41, 144
secrecy, 2, 4, 18, 266

self-care, 61
self-injury, 52
self-medication, 11, 42, 153
Semenya, Caster, 250–51
sex-related eligibility criteria, 242
sexual abuse, 5, 10, 80, 179;
complaints, 232; cover up,
187; of female athletes, 32,
186–201; of female gymnasts,
23; of female students, 23; of
male athletes, 178; of male
wrestlers, 230–33; at MSU,
197–200; NCAA and, 200–
201; prevention, 192; scandal,
233–34; in US Olympic sports,
187–97
sexual assault, 188
sexual crimes, 191
sexual orientation, 213, 244
sex verification, 238; protocols,
240; testing, 241
Shanahan, Brendan, 159
Sheppard, Mathew, 215
Sherman Antitrust Act, 17
Silver, Adam, 245–46
Simmons, Ben, 76–78
Simon, Lou Anna, 198
sleep: disorders, 40;
disturbances, 88
Smith, Naomi, 97
Smith, Rory, 134, 288
Snyder, Dan, 218
soccer, 2; aggressive and violent
tactics in, 117–21; brain
injuries, 133–34; CTE in,

stereotypes, 2, 41, 61, 98, 262, 266; homophobic, 228; with mental illness, 19; negative, 11; stigma and, 18
Stern, David, 50, 215
Stern, Robert, 148
steroids, 160–62, 221
stigma, 11, 46–47, 61, 98, 262, 266; athletic career and, 40–44; culture and, 18; mental health, 43; with mental illness, 19; result of, 2; stereotypes and, 18
stimulants, 155, 160
Strauss, Richard, 231–32
Streeter, Kurt, 76, 174, 281, 294, 300
stress: of competition, 2; competitive, 35; COVID, 100; extreme, 3; heightened levels of, 9; relief, 5; sports-related, 63; "yips," anxiety, depression and, 63–86
subconcussive impacts, 12, 111; repeated, 35, 123, 264. See also chronic traumatic encephalopathy; concussion; traumatic brain injury
substance abuse, 1–5, 52, 98, 147; addiction and, 163–75; athletes and, 163; COVID and, 154; dependency, 35, 153–75; disorders, 265; health and behavioral effects of, 35; injuries and, 154–60; mental health concerns in, 153–75; for pain

and injuries, 154–60; PEDs and, 160–62; protocols, 164
Substance Abuse and Mental Health Services Administration, 153
suicide, 40, 128, 136–38, 140–44, 161, 231; thoughts of, 112
Super Bowl, 30, 47
Svrluga, Barry, 244, 308
Sweeney, Tommy, 102
Swinney, Dabo, 103
Swoopes, Sheryl, 228

tackle football: CTE in, 121–28; dangers of, 121–28; starting ages for, 122. See also football
Tagliabue, Paul, 216
Tagovailoa, Tua, 117, 148–50
Tator, Charles, 131
Tatum, Jack, 119
Tatum, Jayson, 91, 102
Taylor, Phil, 213, 220, 301, 303
TBI. See traumatic brain injury
Teng, Elaine, 108, 284
Te'o, Manti, 213, 224
"Terry Bradshaw Is Finally Becoming Himself," 277
testosterone: in female athletes, 246–53; focus on, 239; injections, 253–54; levels, 236, 246–53, 258; naturally high levels of, 250–51; production, 246; suppressing treatment, 256; testing, 248, 258, 272
Theodore, Nicholas, 122

About the Author

John Weston Parry, JD, is a lawyer, writer, and former substantive legal editor with many years of experience covering issues related to sports, mental health law, and disability rights. He has been the host and primary content provider for the website and blog Sportpathogies.com since 2012. He is also the author of *The Athlete's Dilemma: Sacrificing Health of Wealth and Fame* (2017).

For many years, John Parry was the director of the American Bar Association's Commission on Disability Rights (formerly the Commission on Mental and Physical Disability Law) and editor/editor-in-chief of the *Mental and Physical Disability Law Reporter*. He has written numerous books and articles on mental health law and the rights of persons with mental disabilities, including *Mental Disability, Violence, Future Dangerousness: Myths Behind the Presumption of Guilt* (2013). In addition, he is a past recipient of the Manfred Guttmacher Award from the American Psychiatric Association and the American Academy of Psychiatry and Law. His primary residence is Silver Spring, Maryland.